INSTITUTIONS OF LITERATURE, 1700–1900

This collection provides students and researchers with a new and lively understanding of the role of institutions in the production, reception, and meaning of literature in the period 1700–1900. The period saw a fundamental transition from a patronage system to a marketplace in which institutions played an important mediating role between writers and readers, a shift with consequences that continue to resonate today. Often producers themselves, institutions processed and claimed authority over a variety of cultural domains that never simply tessellated into any unified system. The collection's primary concerns are British and imperial environments, with a comparative German case study, but it offers encouragement for its approaches to be taken up in a variety of other cultural contexts. From post offices to museums, from bricks and mortar to less tangible institutions like authorship and genre, this collection opens up a new field for literary studies.

JON MEE is Professor of Eighteenth-Century Studies at the University of York. His books include *Conversable Worlds: Literature, Contention, and Community 1762–1830* (2011), and *Print, Publicity, and Popular Radicalism in the 1790s* (2016). He is currently completing a book on cultural networks in the Industrial Revolution, for which he held a British Academy-Leverhulme Senior Research Fellowship, 2020–21.

MATTHEW SANGSTER is Senior Lecturer in Romantic Studies, Fantasy and Cultural History at the University of Glasgow, and the author of *Living as an Author in the Romantic Period* (2021). He is co-investigator on two AHRC projects on historical library borrowings and has served on the Executive of the British Association for Romantic Studies for twelve years.

INSTITUTIONS OF LITERATURE, 1700–1900

The Development of Literary Culture and Production

EDITED BY

JON MEE
University of York

MATTHEW SANGSTER
University of Glasgow

Shaftesbury Road, Cambridge CB2 8EA, United Kingdom

One Liberty Plaza, 20th Floor, New York, NY 10006, USA

477 Williamstown Road, Port Melbourne, VIC 3207, Australia

314–321, 3rd Floor, Plot 3, Splendor Forum, Jasola District Centre, New Delhi – 110025, India

103 Penang Road, #05–06/07, Visioncrest Commercial, Singapore 238467

Cambridge University Press is part of Cambridge University Press & Assessment, a department of the University of Cambridge.

We share the University's mission to contribute to society through the pursuit of education, learning and research at the highest international levels of excellence.

www.cambridge.org
Information on this title: www.cambridge.org/9781108822015

DOI: 10.1017/9781108909501

© Cambridge University Press & Assessment 2022

This publication is in copyright. Subject to statutory exception and to the provisions of relevant collective licensing agreements, no reproduction of any part may take place without the written permission of Cambridge University Press & Assessment.

First published 2022
First paperback edition 2025

A catalogue record for this publication is available from the British Library

ISBN 978-1-108-83020-1 Hardback
ISBN 978-1-108-82201-5 Paperback

Cambridge University Press & Assessment has no responsibility for the persistence or accuracy of URLs for external or third-party internet websites referred to in this publication and does not guarantee that any content on such websites is, or will remain, accurate or appropriate.

Contents

List of Figures	*page* vii
List of Contributors	ix
Acknowledgements	xiv

    Introduction: Literature and Institutions   1
    Jon Mee and Matthew Sangster

1 Knowledge Exchange in the Seventeenth Century: From the Third University to the Royal Society   24
   Willy Maley

2 'Supporting Mutual Benevolence': Libraries, Civic Benefaction, and the Spalding Gentlemen's Society, 1709–1755   44
   Dustin M. Frazier Wood

3 Institutions without Addresses   65
   David A. Brewer

4 Eighteenth-Century *Musenhof* Courts as Bridges and Brokers for Cultural Networks and Social Reform   83
   Nicole Pohl

5 Becoming Institutional: The Case of the Anacreontic Society   101
   Ian Newman

6 Circulating Libraries as Institutional Creators of Genres   120
   Anne H. Stevens

7 Lecturing Networks and Cultural Institutions, 1740–1830   135
   Jon Klancher

8 Catalogues as Instituting Genres of the Nineteenth-Century Museum: The Two Hunterians   157
   Dahlia Porter

9	Charles Lamb and the British Museum as an Institution of Literature *Gillian Russell*	178
10	A Disruptive and Dangerous Education and the Wealth of the Nation: The Early Mechanics' Institutes *John Gardner*	196
11	'The Ladies' Contribution': Women and the Mechanics' Institute on the Goldfields of Victoria *Sarah Comyn*	215
12	'[L]etters Must Increase': Reading and Writing the Post Office as a Literary Institution *Karin Koehler*	234
13	Networks, Nodes, and Beacons: Cultural Institutions in Nineteenth-Century Southeast Asia *Porscha Fermanis*	255
14	The Book as Medium *Sarah Crofton*	275
Index		292

Figures

1.1	Watercolour image by Robert Dennis Chantrell of the proposed design for the Leeds Philosophical Hall	page 17
2.1	Title page of Maurice Johnson's manuscript *Catalogus Librorum Bibliotheca Spaldingensis*	49
2.2	Photograph of the original Spalding Gentlemen's Society collection cabinet in the upper lecture room	53
3.1	Jonathan Richardson the Elder, *The Artist and His Son, Jonathan, in the Presence of Milton*, undated, oil on canvas, 64 × 77 cm. Private collection	79
3.2	Jonathan Richardson the Elder, frontispiece and title page of *Explanatory Notes and Remarks on Milton's Paradise Lost. By J. Richardson, Father and Son. With the Life of the Author, and a Discourse on the Poem* (London, 1734)	80
5.1	'The Newly Dubb'd Jew Written and Sung by Mr Hewerdine at the Beef Steak Club and the Anacreontic Society'	113
7.1	Three network types from Paul Baran's 1962 paper *On Distributed Communications Networks*	138
7.2	Map showing often-traveled itinerant lecturing routes of Adam Walker, Thomas Garnett and others to the north; Benjamin Martin, James Ferguson and others to the south	139
8.1	Intestines, from *Catalogue of the Museum 1800: Gallery*, Hunterian Museum and Library, MS 0007/1/1/1/7	168
8.2	Intestines, from the *Original Fascicules of Hunterian Museum Catalogues, Bound in One Quarto Volume*, Hunterian Museum and Library, MS 0189/2/16	169
10.1	Mechanics' class ticket from the Andersonian Institution, 1812	197

11.1 Alfred May and Alfred Martin Ebsworth, 'Reading-Room, Ballarat Mechanics' Institute', 1881 — 225

11.2 John Leech, 'Alarming Prospect The Single Ladies off to the Diggings', 1853 — 228

Contributors

DAVID A. BREWER teaches at The Ohio State University. His books include *The Afterlife of Character, 1726–1825* (2005), an edition of Richard Brinsley Sheridan's *The Rivals* and George Colman the Elder's *Polly Honeycombe* (2012), the collaboratively written *Interacting with Print: Elements of Reading in the Era of Print Saturation* (2018), and the co-authored *The Book in Britain: A Historical Introduction* (2019). He is currently completing a study of the uses to which authorial names and images were put in the eighteenth-century Anglophone world titled *The Fate of Authors* and an edition of Penelope Aubin's *The Life of Charlotta Du Pont* and *The Life of Madam de Beaumount*.

SARAH COMYN is an assistant professor and Ad Astra Fellow at University College Dublin. Her publications include *Political Economy and the Novel: A Literary History of 'Homo Economicus'* (Palgrave, 2018), *Early Public Libraries and Colonial Citizenship in the British Southern Hemisphere* (with Lara Atkin et al., Palgrave, 2019), and *Worlding the South: Nineteenth-Century Literary Culture and the Southern Settler Colonies* (edited with Porscha Fermanis, Manchester University Press, 2021). She is currently working on a monograph titled *A New Reading Public: The Mechanics' Institute on the Goldfields of Victoria, 1851–1901*.

SARAH CROFTON is a specialist in the literature of nineteenth-century occultism and has taught classes on the supernatural in Victorian culture at King's College London and the University of Birmingham. Her publications include work on W. T. Stead's spirit writing and on the cross-pollinations of psychical research and detective fiction. Her current research examines the critical reading practices promoted as magical by Helena Blavatsky. She also has a background in digital humanities and was a postdoctoral researcher and technical lead on

The Letters of Hannah More, digitising the writer's correspondence. She currently works as a learning technologist at the London School of Economics.

PORSCHA FERMANIS is a professor of Romantic literature at University College Dublin. Her most recent books are *Worlding the South: Nineteenth-Century Literary Culture and the Southern Settler Colonies* (edited with Sarah Comyn, Manchester University Press, 2021) and *Romantic Pasts: History, Fiction and Feeling in Britain, 1790–1850* (Edinburgh University Press, 2022). She is currently the principal investigator of the European Research Council-funded project 'SouthHem' and is completing a monograph titled *Southern Settler Fiction and the Transcolonial Imaginary, 1820–1890*.

DUSTIN M. FRAZIER WOOD is a senior lecturer in the School of Humanities at the University of Roehampton, specialising in reception studies, antiquarianism, cultural heritage, and book history. Dustin is also Librarian of the Spalding Gentlemen's Society. Dustin's publications include *Anglo-Saxonism and the Idea of Englishness in Eighteenth-Century Britain* (2020) and a number of articles on medievalism, antiquarianism, and print culture. Dustin's current research concerns the production of manuscript facsimiles in the medieval and early modern periods.

JOHN GARDNER is a professor of English literature at Anglia Ruskin University, Leverhulme Trust Research Fellow on the project Engineering Romanticism, and editor of the Charles and Mary Lamb journal, *The Charles Lamb Bulletin*. John is currently working on an edition of Pierce Egan's *Life in London*, a Cambridge University Press collection of essays on the 1830s, and the monograph *Engineering Romanticism*.

JON KLANCHER is a professor of literary and cultural studies at Carnegie Mellon University, where he teaches Romantic and Victorian literature, print history, and the sociology of culture. His most recent book, *Transfiguring the Arts and Sciences: Knowledge and Cultural Institutions in the Romantic Age*, won the Jean-Pierre Barricelli Prize in 2016. He is currently working on two projects: a study of writing and the mechanical arts in the long eighteenth century and a book on print-media networks and social formations ca. 1750–1950.

KARIN KOEHLER is a lecturer in nineteenth-century British literature at Bangor University. She researches nineteenth-century literary engagements with media and technologies of communication and infrastructural development more broadly, drawing on both

Anglophone and Welsh-language materials. Her first monograph *Thomas Hardy and Victorian Communication* appeared in 2016 with Palgrave, and she has published several articles and chapters on epistolary elements in Victorian fiction. She is currently co-editing a sourcebook on nineteenth-century communications for Routledge and working on a book project that studies how popular poetry responded to developments such as the penny post and the telegraph networks.

WILLY MALEY is a professor of Renaissance studies at the University of Glasgow. He is the author of *A Spenser Chronology* (1994), *Salvaging Spenser* (1997), and *Nation, State and Empire in English Renaissance Literature: Shakespeare to Milton* (2003). Edited essay collections include, with Brendan Bradshaw and Andrew Hadfield, *Representing Ireland: Literature and the Origins of Conflict, 1534–1660* (1993); with David J. Baker, *British Identities and English Renaissance Literature* (2002); with Andrew Murphy, *Shakespeare and Scotland* (2004); with Philip Schwyzer, *Shakespeare and Wales* (2010); with Margaret Tudeau-Clayton, *This England, That Shakespeare* (2010); and with Rory Loughnane, *Celtic Shakespeare: The Bard and the Borderers* (2013).

JON MEE is a professor of eighteenth-century studies at the University of York. He has held major research fellowships and visiting professorships with the British Academy, the Henry E. Huntington Library (where he was the R. Stanton Avery Distinguished Visiting Professor), the Leverhulme Trust, and the University of Chicago. He is the author of many articles and essays on the period 1780–1840; his most recent monographs are *Conversable Worlds: Literature, Contention, and Community 1762–1832* (Oxford University Press, 2011) and *Print, Publicity, and Popular Radicalism in the 1790s* (Cambridge University Press, 2016). He is currently completing a book on cultural networks in the industrial revolution.

IAN NEWMAN is an associate professor of English at the University of Notre Dame and a fellow of the Keough-Naughton Institute for Irish Studies. He specialises in eighteenth- and nineteenth-century British and Irish literature. He is the author of *The Romantic Tavern: Literature and Conviviality in the Age of Revolution* (Cambridge University Press, 2019). He is co-editor with Oskar Cox Jensen and David Kennerley of *Charles Dibdin and Late Georgian Culture* (Oxford University Press, 2018) and with David O'Shaughnessy of

Charles Macklin and the Theatres of London (Liverpool University Press, 2022).

NICOLE POHL is a professor of English at Oxford Brookes University. She has published and edited books on women's utopian writing in the seventeenth and eighteenth centuries, European salons and epistolarity, and the bluestockings. She is the editor-in-chief of the Elizabeth Montagu Correspondence Online project: www.elizabethmontagunetwork.co.uk/. She is currently working on a book on transnational salon sociability and patriotism in eighteenth-century Northern and Central Europe.

DAHLIA PORTER is a senior lecturer in English literature and material culture at the University of Glasgow. Her research – including *Science, Form, and the Problem of Induction in British Romanticism* (Cambridge University Press, 2018) – sits at the intersection of the history of science and medicine, book history, and literary studies. A devotee of collaboration, she joined the Multigraph Collective to publish *Interacting with Print: Elements of Reading in the Era of Print Saturation* (University of Chicago Press, 2018) and recently co-edited an issue of *Nuncias* on 'Unruly Objects: Material Entanglements in the Arts and Sciences'. She is currently writing a book on inventories and catalogues and co-editing *The Collected Letters of Thomas Beddoes*.

GILLIAN RUSSELL is a professor of eighteenth-century literature and director of the Centre for Eighteenth Century Studies at the University of York. She is the author of, most recently, *The Ephemeral Eighteenth Century: Print, Sociability, and the Cultures of Collecting* (Cambridge University Press, 2020; awarded the Rose Mary Crawshay Prize by the British Academy), as well as *The Theatres of War: Performance, Politics, and Society, 1793–1815* (Oxford, 1995) and *Women, Sociability and Theatre in Georgian London* (Cambridge University Press, 2007). With Clara Tuite, she edited *Romantic Sociability: Literary and Social Networks in Britain 1740–1840* (Cambridge University Press, 2002), and she was the co-editor, with Neil Ramsey, of *Tracing War in British Enlightenment and Romantic Culture* (Palgrave, 2015).

MATTHEW SANGSTER is a senior lecturer in Romantic studies, Fantasy and cultural history at the University of Glasgow. He is the author of *Living as an Author in the Romantic Period* (2021) and has published widely on literary institutions, the affordances of genre, and Romantic-period London. He is currently working on two Arts and Humanities

Research Council-funded projects exploring reading history using historical borrowing records, as well as explorations of the histories of Fantasy, the sociality of poetry, the 1820s, and David Bowie.

ANNE H. STEVENS is Dean of the College of Letters and Science at the University of Wisconsin Oshkosh. She is the author of *British Historical Fiction Before Scott* (2010) and *Literary Theory and Criticism: An Introduction* (2015; rev. 2nd ed. 2021) and the co-editor, with Molly C. O'Donnell, of *The Microgenre: A Quick Look at Small Culture* (2020).

Acknowledgements

The editors would like to thank the Arts and Humanities Research Council for the award of the 'Institutions of Literature, 1700–1900' network grant, which underpinned the research that led to this book. The network grant provided support for a series of workshops held in 2017; these were generously hosted by the Hunterian Museum, the Society of Antiquaries, and York Medical Society, as well as the University of York and the University of Glasgow. We would like to thank these institutions, and, especially, Jola Zdunek, for their help. The contributors to our three workshops were co-creators of this volume whose input we would like gratefully to acknowledge: Ruth Abbott, Lara Atkin, Bill Bell, Susan Bennett, Giles Bergel, Robert Betteridge, Alexandrina Buchanan, Mungo Campbell, Carmen Casaliggi, Suchitra Choudhury, Sophie Coulombeau, Richard De Ritter, Jill Dye, Sibylle Erle, Anna Fleming, Katherine Ford, Laura Forsberg, Nathan Garvey, Gabor Gelleri, Oindrila Ghosh, Katie Halsey, Jessica Hamal-Akré, Noah Heringman, Felicity James, Catherine Jones, Crystal B. Lake, Kristin Lindfield-Ott, Lucy Linforth, Tom Lockwood, Annemarie McAllister, Ralph McLean, Gena McNutt, Giles Mandelbrote, Melanie Manwaring-McKay, Carolyn Oulton, Emma Peacock, Julian Pooley, Neil Ramsey, Sharon Ruston, Richard Salmon, Susanne Schmid, Roey Sweet, Judith Thompson, Mark Towsey, Sandra Tuppen, Cassie Ulph, Nicola Watson, John West, and David Worrall. Jennifer Buckley participated in all three workshops and worked tirelessly as the administrator for the network, greatly helping to shape its intellectual ambitions in the process.

The research offices and administrative staff at the University of Birmingham, the University of Glasgow, and the University of York provided the best kind of institutional help and assistance. Bethany Thomas, George Paul Laver, and the rest of the team at Cambridge University Press have been unfailingly supportive and helpful as we have worked to complete this volume. Our thanks are also due to Cambridge

University Press's two anonymous readers for their constructive suggestions and to the participants in a Romanticism in the Meantime meeting organised by Jonathan Mulrooney and Emily Rohrbach, who kindly discussed a draft of the introduction with us.

Jon Mee would like to thank the British Academy for the award of a Senior Research Fellowship that allowed him time to work on drawing together the collection; Jennifer Douglas of the Philosophical and Literary Society of Leeds; Kay Easson, librarian of the Literary and Philosophical Society of Newcastle upon Tyne; and Peter D. McDonald, whose conversation helped shape the earliest version of this project for him. Matthew Sangster would like to thank the Royal Literary Fund for supporting a 2014 symposium at which the seeds of this book were sown and the University of Glasgow for research leave that assisted greatly with the latter stages of this project.

Finally, we would both like to thank our contributors, who have stuck with us with unfailing good cheer through a long process of pitching, composition, refinement, and editing, the latter parts of which have been conducted during the unique and stressful circumstances of the coronavirus pandemic. We decided against a collective bibliography for this volume largely because of the huge diversity of topics and points of reference across the essays, something that we think constitutes this book's main strength. The ultimate point of networks and of institutions is to achieve things collectively that would be impossible to do as well individually. Everyone acknowledged here has played a crucial part in the work that has made this volume possible. Responsibility for any errors remains our own.

Introduction
Literature and Institutions
Jon Mee and Matthew Sangster

Why Study Institutions of Literature?

In most common conceptions of how literature functions, the author and the reader are dominant: one seen as the originator of the literary work, the other as its recipient and (perhaps) arbiter. The shift towards the idea of an author-function oriented to sensitively receptive individual readers is often identified with a late-eighteenth-century transition to market relations. As reading publics expanded, older practices of elite composition and coterie circulation were slowly decentred through gradual processes of 'liberal' reform (with all the complexity and ambiguities of that adjective for this period acknowledged). However, even as the degrees of separation between individuals engaged in literary production and reception increased, mandating increasingly complex layers of mediation, the idea also developed that literature involved a privileged, almost telepathic communion between writer and reader.[1] The quintessential stereotypes of literary engagement that arose during this period – and which remain in many respects current – focus on rapt, solitary figures: the writer labouring at their desk; the poet wandering among the mountains; the leisured author in their study; the reader ensconced in a comfortable armchair, who for Friedrich Kittler epitomises the condition of literature around 1800.[2]

However, individuals were far from the only stakeholders in the creation and reception of literary texts in this period. Since at least the early eighteenth century, distinctively literary institutions have developed and endured, coming to play integral roles in culture and society. These

---

[1] For discussions of ideas of communication that transcend mediation, see John Durham Peters, *Speaking into the Air: A History of the Idea of Communication* (Chicago: University of Chicago Press, 1999) and Tilottama Rajan, *The Supplement of Reading: Figures of Understanding in Romantic Theory and Practice* (Ithaca: Cornell University Press, 1990).

[2] Friedrich A. Kittler, *Discourse Networks, 1800/1900*, trans. by Michael Metteer with Chris Cullens (Stanford: Stanford University Press, 1990).

institutions provide sites for discussion and networks for circulation; serve as archival repositories; raise and disburse money; disseminate praise and criticism; author works and conduct readings; and teach people how to define and value culture. The development of such institutions was caught up in the process of sorting the disciplines of knowledge into something like their modern forms. As a result of this process, literature took its place as a distinctive domain, but one often defined as resisting specialism in the name of more purely 'human' sets of relations, as elaborated in works like Wordsworth's 'Preface' (1802) to the *Lyrical Ballads*:

> If the time should ever come when what is now called Science, thus familiarized to men, shall be ready to put on, as it were, a form of flesh and blood, the Poet will lend his divine spirit to aid the transfiguration, and will welcome the Being thus produced, as a dear and genuine inmate of the household of man.[3]

In passages such as this one, as Maureen N. McLane points out, poetry appears as 'an enemy both of professionalization and of specialization': both qualities intimately bound up with the increasingly influential domains of institutions.[4]

This book considers the hitherto-neglected roles that institutions played in shaping literary culture during the eighteenth and nineteenth centuries, extending to either side of the period when Wordsworth was writing. One of the most significant characteristics of this period was the progressive transfer of kinds of authority previously invested in a small number of privileged individuals to organisations and bureaucracies. The more familiar narrative of these changes as part of an extended shift from patronage to the marketplace has often blinded observers to the fact that the latter – with its appearance of a form of liberal freedom – did not bring an end to the institutional life of literature, but rather reinstituted it on different grounds and in new forms.[5] The profound impact of these developments has not yet been granted due attention, in no small measure because of the persistence of Romantic notions of reading as a form of direct communion, an ideal somewhat perversely disseminated by literary institutions themselves. Sites of literary tourism have often found the idea of the numinous genius very

---

[3] *The Prose Works of William Wordsworth*, ed. by W. J. B. Owen and Jane Worthington Smyser, 3 vols (Oxford: Oxford University Press, 1974), I, 141.
[4] Maureen N. McLane, *Romanticism and the Human Sciences: Poetry, Population, and the Discourse of the Species* (Cambridge: Cambridge University Press, 2000), p. 6.
[5] The shift away from patronage was also slower than traditional Whiggish accounts have implied, as Dustin Griffin shows in *Literary Patronage in England 1650–1800* (Cambridge: Cambridge University Press, 1996).

convenient.[6] It was during our period that John Keats made his pilgrimage to Scotland to pay homage with many others to Robert Burns at his place of birth. By the time Keats visited in 1818, the cottage had become an alehouse – 'The Burns Head Inn' – presided over by 'a great Bore with his Anecdotes ... a mahogany faced old Jackass who knew Burns'.[7] By 1838 there was a visitor's album; 1847 saw a museum appended to the cottage; and souvenirs and Burns-related paraphernalia were on sale by 1876.[8]

While Keats reacted negatively to 'great Bore' who greeted him, our discomfort with institutional authority means that both individuals and institutions are often more comfortable when powerful organising influences are masked behind human faces. This is perhaps especially true where the humanities are concerned. It is no coincidence that this book appears at a time when academics are feeling increasingly alienated by institutional forms as a management revolution in universities creates an unsettling sense that the free exchange of ideas is being marketised or, at least, subjected to increasingly intensive forms of bureaucratic mediation.

Perceiving and discussing the effects of institutions is often made difficult by their sheer scale, but also by the strange intangibility if not of their presences, then of their influence. Delineating the life of an author (or a founder) is relatively straightforward when compared with accounting for a literary institution that may have hundreds or thousands of stakeholders, might serve or educate tens of thousands, and that could have persisted for centuries, accumulating huge collections and voluminous records that will still only give a partial account of its activities. The large scales that successful institutions operate on have strongly determined how they have been approached by scholars. When institutional histories have been written, they have often comprised the history of a single particular institution, in a tradition stretching from Thomas Sprat's early history of the Royal Society to modern works like Nigel Cross's accounts of the Royal Literary Fund.[9] This approach can be extremely fruitful, but does not necessarily

---

[6] See Nicola J. Watson, *The Literary Tourist: Readers and Places in Romantic and Victorian Britain* (Basingstoke: Palgrave Macmillan, 2006), especially Chapter 2, and *The Author's Effects: On Writer's House Museums* (Oxford: Oxford University Press, 2020).
[7] 'To J. H. Reynolds', 11, 13 July 1818, in *The Letters of John Keats 1814–1821*, ed. by Hyder Edward Rollins, 2 vols (Cambridge, MA: Harvard University Press, 1958), I, 324.
[8] Watson, p. 69.
[9] Thomas Sprat, *The History of the Royal-Society of London for the Improving of Natural Knowledge* (London: T. R. for J. Martyn, 1667); Nigel Cross, *The Royal Literary Fund, 1790–1918: An Introduction to the Fund's History and Archives, with an Index of Applicants* (London: World Microfilms, 1984) and *The Common Writer: Life in Nineteenth-Century Grub Street* (Cambridge: Cambridge University Press, 1985).

provide a good platform for considering wider social drivers, or for apprehending the ways in which institutions interconnect to promote common practices and assumptions. Important accounts have sought to describe the development of particular types of literary institution, including subscription libraries, universities, and writer's house museums. But what of the larger aggregate institutional infrastructure that has come to underpin how modern culture has been produced, circulated, and valued? Complicating that question further is the fact that the institutional scene's involvedness is not just a matter of a mixed landscape of bricks and mortar, but also of less tangible sets of assumptions precipitating themselves into what Mary Poovey calls 'protocols for knowing and representing institutions', a process that she defines in relation to modern 'domains' of knowledge. Although it is easy to exaggerate the extent to which the order of things was consolidated in any given age, it is certainly true that the early nineteenth century saw the disciplines arranged into something like their modern forms. 'Material' and 'symbolic' institutions were formed, in Poovey's terms – 'territory ... appropriated; boundaries ... drawn; rules governing usage ... established; unequal privileges ... codified by law and then naturalised by repetition'.[10] 'Territory' in this understanding is both literal and metaphorical: often a grand building, but also a 'field' of forces in the sense familiar from Pierre Bourdieu's sociology of culture.[11] Chapter 3 by David A. Brewer and Chapter 6 by Anne H. Stevens treat 'authorship' and 'genre', respectively, as symbolic institutions in something like Poovey's sense, but in practice even the most material institutions manage complex sets of symbolic relations, as many of the other contributions here acknowledge and explore.[12]

Examining the increasingly prominent roles played by institutions and institutional practices in producing, circulating, and defining literature over the course of two centuries is obviously an enormous topic that a collection of this scale can only broach, rather than cover comprehensively. The institutional landscape never achieved the completeness of the 'panopticism' often ascribed to Michel Foucault's early thinking on governmentality and regulation.[13]

---

[10] Mary Poovey, *Making a Social Body: British Cultural Formation, 1830–1864* (Chicago: Chicago University Press, 1995), p. 5.
[11] Pierre Bourdieu, *The Field of Cultural Production: Essays on Art and Literature*, ed. by Randal Johnson (Cambridge: Polity Press, 1993).
[12] Further examples of less tangible forms of institution are discussed in *The Institution of English Literature: Formation and Mediation*, ed. by Barbara Schaff, Johannes Schlegel, and Carolina Surkamp (Göttingen: V&R unipress, 2017).
[13] The editors adopt the term 'panopticism' from Lauren M. E. Goodlad's *Victorian Literature and the Victorian State: Character and Governance in a Liberal Society* (Baltimore: Johns Hopkins University Press, 2011), especially pp. 11–12.

However interlocked various institutions became, however much they served established and emergent authorities and class interests – not to mention the formations of colonial and imperial power – they functioned in and helped shape a system in which domains never tessellated exactly. The field of literary production has never been closed and determinate, but is rather constituted by interactive forces rendered especially unstable when it comes to defining the literary in relation to other aspects of the cultural scene. In this 'detotalized' picture, as Anthony J. Cascardi puts it, 'the modern subject is defined by its insertion into a series of separate value-spheres, each one of which tends to exclude or attempts to assert its priority over the rest'.[14]

However, when it comes to accounting for such complexities, a collection of this kind has the advantage of being able to incorporate different perspectives under one roof, allowing the diverse expertise of a variety of scholars to present a toolbox of different approaches for studying institutions, thereby suggesting by juxtaposition and contextualisation how ideas and circumstances changed over the period in question while never fitting together into a totality. Our focus is primarily on the distinctively decentred nature of the British institutional scene in the period 1700 to 1900, but Chapter 1 by Willy Maley, Chapter 11 by Sarah Comyn, and Chapter by 13 Porscha Fermanis track the way this distinctive governmentality translated into different arenas of the imperial situation, while Chapter 4 by Nicole Pohl allows for a comparison with the courtly institutions of the late eighteenth-century German states as they developed towards their own forms of liberal modernity.

The defining institutional form in Britain was the voluntary association. Centralised authority was treated with suspicion, even as bureaucracy and governmentality intensified over the course of the nineteenth century.[15] Max Weber famously observed that Britain was the first state to develop industrial capitalism, but also 'the slowest of all countries to succumb to bureaucratization'.[16] Especially with the rolling back of the fiscal-military state after the Napoleonic Wars, there was a strong rearticulation of the long-standing idea of self-governance as intrinsic to the British character.[17] 'Subscriber democracy', as R. J. Morris has described it, with its formal

---

[14] Anthony J. Cascardi, *The Subject of Modernity* (Cambridge: Cambridge University Press, 1992), p. 3.
[15] See Peter Clark, *British Clubs and Societies 1580–1800: The Origins of an Associational World* (Oxford: Oxford University Press, 2000) and R. J. Morris, 'Voluntary Societies and British Urban Elites, 1780–1850: An Analysis', *The Historical Journal*, 26 (1983), 95–118.
[16] Max Weber, 'Bureaucracy', in *From Max Weber: Essays in Sociology*, ed. by H. H. Gerth and C. Wright Mills (New York: Oxford University Press, 1946), pp. 196–244 (p. 214).
[17] Philip Harling and Peter Mandler, 'From "Fiscal-Military" State to Laissez-Faire State, 1760–1850', *Journal of British Studies*, 32.1 (1993), 44–70. On the idea of 'self-governance' in nineteenth-century liberal thinking, see Goodlad, p. 2.

observation of norms of free exchange – in practice contained within strict boundaries – became the distinctive form of the voluntary association.[18] Literature was increasingly defended in the nineteenth century as the haven of an intangible national character that was resistant to institutionalisation even as its institutional locations proliferated. By drawing attention to the place of institutions in the literary landscape, this book seeks more clearly to articulate their immense significance and continuing relevance to modern society within this distinctive 'liberal' tradition. Despite the fact that many of the institutions it studies still exist, our study stops in 1900, partly for practical reasons of space, but also as this date suffices as an endpoint for considering the maturation of many of the key forms of institutionality. Institutions of Modernism have been studied in depth by Lawrence Rainey in terms of a retreat to deluxe editions, small magazines, and private patronage, but it is also true that in the twentieth century much of the institutional infrastructure explored in this volume was supplemented and even challenged by increasing state intervention, followed by the development of interstate agencies and organisations like UNESCO and PEN, with their developing sense of the 'literary' as a domain worthy of legal and other forms of sponsorship and protection on a worldwide scale.[19]

What Is an Institution?

Before proceeding further in discussing institutions, it seems appropriate to say more about what the editors understand an institution to be, an understanding that developed from a series of workshops in which all the contributors to the volume were involved at one stage or another.[20] The chapters included in this book are by no means governed by the attempt at definition that follows, but they have all played an important part in its evolution.

The word 'institution' is most commonly understood in line with the seventh definition offered in the *Oxford English Dictionary*:

> An establishment, organization, or association, instituted for the promotion of some object, esp. one of public or general utility, religious, charitable,

---

[18] Morris, 'Voluntary Societies', p. 152. Morris points out that this formally democratic principle made institutions vulnerable to complaints about access and diversity.
[19] Lawrence Rainey, *Institutions of Modernism: Literary Elites and Public Culture* (New Haven: Yale University Press, 1999). Peter D. McDonald's *Artefacts of Writing: Ideas of the State and Communities of Letters from Matthew Arnold to Xu Bing* (Oxford: Oxford University Press, 2017) is particularly illuminating on international institutions of culture.
[20] These workshops were facilitated by the institutional support of an Arts and Humanities Research Council research networking grant, and venues were made available by the Society of Antiquaries, York Medical Society, and the universities of Glasgow and York.

educational, etc., e.g. a church, school, college, hospital, asylum, reformatory, mission, or the like; as a literary and philosophical institution, a deaf and dumb institution, the Royal National Life-boat Institution, the Royal Masonic Benevolent Institution (instituted 1798), the Railway Benevolent Institution, etc. The name is often popularly applied to the building appropriated to the work of a benevolent or educational institution.[21]

Tellingly for the chronology of this book, the earliest example the *OED* provides of this usage is from 1707, when the word appeared in a sermon given by Francis Atterbury on benevolent organisations: "'Tis not necessary to plead very earnestly in behalf of these Charities.... These, of which you have had an account, are such Wise, such Rational, such Beneficial Institutions."[22] While the sermon describes the activities of organisations with long-standing remits – charities associated with the church and with the City of London – it suggests such organisations were beginning to be seen in new ways around this time, proliferating and operating in manners that were increasingly independent from the state, the church, and civic corporations.

In his *Keywords*, originally published in 1976, Raymond Williams identified a shift in the eighteenth century from an earlier sense of 'institute' and 'institution' as verbs or nouns of performative action, 'part of a general sense of practices established in certain ways', to 'a general and abstract noun describing something apparently objective and systematic'.[23] This last sense Williams saw as coinciding with the appearance of 'institution' and 'institute' in the titles of specific organisations or certain types of organisation, although this phenomenon really took off in the first two decades of the nineteenth century with the birth of the Royal Institution and its cognates and rivals the Surrey and British Institutions (not to mention provincial upstarts like the Royal Liverpool Institution, of which the London original seems to have heartily disapproved).[24] The chronology that Williams presented is in many ways convenient for our purposes, but also somewhat misleading in the sharpness of its contrast. The idea of an act of institution as founding or decreeing into being, as Jon

---

[21] 'institution, n.', *Oxford English Dictionary*, 3rd edn (Oxford: Oxford University Press, 2000-) <www.oed.com/view/Entry/97110>.
[22] Francis Atterbury, *A Sermon Preach'd before [...] the Ld Mayor [...] of the City of London in St. Bridget's Church on Easter Tuesday, April 17, 1707* (London: Jonah Bowyer, 1707), p. 14.
[23] Raymond Williams, *Keywords: A Vocabulary of Culture and Society* (New York: Oxford University Press, 1985), p. 168.
[24] On this early nineteenth-century phenomenon, see Jon Klancher, *Transfiguring the Arts and Sciences: Knowledge and Cultural Institutions in the Romantic Age* (Cambridge: Cambridge University Press, 2013). On the Royal Institution's response to Liverpool, see pp. 209–13.

Klancher has pointed out, remained part of a 'far more mixed picture where the nouns of *structure* intermingle with those of *action* (or agency)'.[25] Part of this mixed picture is the strong and self-conscious sense of a whole cultural landscape being repopulated with new – and new kinds of – foundations. The *OED* definition quoted earlier provides a helpful summary of the types of organisations that came to be seen as being institutions and its point about the ways that institutional identities can inhere in buildings is one that deserves further consideration, particularly when discussing how institutions endure. However, it is less helpful for describing what an institution does. Consequently, the research network from which this book arose developed a working definition of an institution as 'an assemblage that organises, transmits, and validates, and that self-consciously represents itself as doing so'. This is more prescriptive than the definitions the *OED* provides, but a closer examination will hopefully serve to demonstrate both what it seeks to encompass and its utility.

The mixed and open nature of the idea of 'assemblage' allows for the relatively easy inclusion of both things and processes within an institution's identity. These are factors that become increasingly important as institutions age and human participants disaffiliate or pass on. Many institutions continue due to their legacy properties and holdings, with the process of instituting their authority remaining always necessarily incomplete.[26] That is not to say, of course, that institutions do not pretend to the authority of completeness. Histories emerging from institutions themselves have often sought to promote and sustain their identities, as evidenced by memorial practices like collecting portraits and naming rooms and buildings. For this reason, the definition of institution pursued here would also give emphasis to practices that depend upon self-conscious claims to represent authority or a sphere of action, an aspect of institutions that might distinguish them from the less formal networks from which they often spring (and which they commonly play roles in sustaining). An institution's authority, to develop this point further, depends on the social recognition of the value of its work, which is often demonstrated through affiliations advertised in forms such as the membership list or the annual report. Even when in practice the vast majority of an institution's work is carried out by a particular individual or a small group, this work is legitimised as being institutional through the tacit consent of larger groups of stakeholders.

---

[25] Klancher, pp. 39–40.
[26] As Manuel DeLanda contends, 'unlike organic totalities, the parts of an assemblage do not form a seamless whole': *A New Philosophy of Society* (London: Continuum, 2006), p. 4.

The third definition the *OED* provides for 'institution' discusses an early usage that saw 'institution' as connoting 'The giving of form or order to a thing', a sense clearly related to the idea of institution as an act of bringing into being. This ordering aspect of institutional practice has remained important for modern institutions and occasions the inclusion of 'organises' in our definition. What an institution organises can vary widely. Many institutions organise forms of knowledge in some manner (often with a disciplinary focus), many curate physical collections – like the Hunterian museums discussed by Dahlia Porter in Chapter 8 – and many manage social processes and practices. Regardless of precise forms, the chapters gathered in this book show that all institutions aspire to be organisers (even if, in practice, they are not always successful ones). This organising propensity is demonstrated by many of the key genres of institutional interaction, including the minute, the constitution, the catalogue genre discussed by Porter, and the official report. These genres of institutionality seek to impose structures characterised by performances of authority and accountability. More loaded (Foucauldian) terms might be employed to describe institutional actions ('regulate'; 'control'), but 'organise', in the first instance at least, is both broadly applicable and helpful in terms of figuring how institutions seek (and potentially fail) to create meaning.

Part of the historical process of institutional development has been a mission to transmit through circulating (although this implies a reciprocity that is not always present in their operations) or publishing (a more heavily determined possibility). Whichever word is preferred, within our definition of institution, the concept of transmission serves as a token of the crucial role that communication plays in institutional work. The nature of what institutions transmit varies widely – from knowledge or expertise to capital to access to physical objects – and any given institution usually transmits in a range of different manners. A literary museum, like the Wordsworth Trust's Dove Cottage, for example, could be figured as transmitting knowledge over quite small distances to its visitors or to attendees at conferences or events, but the Trust also transmits on a larger spatial scale through publications, loan arrangements, reproductions, and training. In the nineteenth century, the Literary Fund confidentially transmitted the funds it collected to impoverished authors its committee deemed worthy, but it also promoted literature through its reports and its lavish, self-consciously well-documented Anniversary Dinners, at which literary genius was lauded by the great and the good, often in execrable poetry memorialised by Byron as 'creaking couplets' bawled 'in a tavern hall'.[27] In addition, the Fund communicated with a wide-ranging networks beyond its membership and collaborated with other institutional actors, including the Civil List, the Royal Bounty Fund, the Society of Authors, and the Professional Classes Aid Council.[28] These sorts of interactions were and remain crucial for effective institutional operations, serving both to advance an institution's objectives directly and to raise awareness of its activities in ways that buttress its disciplinary and organisational authority. In the Literary Fund's case, successful circulations and communications were recognised through the award of its royal charter in 1818 and the right to add 'Royal' to its name in 1842.

Our definition also acknowledges the importance of institutions' roles as propagators of discourses of validation. Institutions commonly seek to define fields of knowledge or practice. Through doing so, they implicitly or explicitly reserve for themselves the right to police boundaries and determine value within them. The giving of prizes or charitable aid to worthy objects is one obvious mediating mechanism, but this aspect of institutionality is evident in a diverse range of practices, including the admission of members, the accessioning or deaccessioning of collection items, and the construction of syllabi and curricula. The sixth *OED* definition describes an institution as an 'established law, custom, usage, practice, organization, or other element in the political or social life of a people; a regulative principle or convention subservient to the needs of an organised community or the general ends of civilization'. Successful institutions, both material and discursive, will often seek to represent their activities along these lines, claiming recognition for their judgements and assent for their regulative ideals.

Of course, success, on these terms, requires social and cultural acceptance. While institutions may sometimes organise, transmit, and validate in clandestine manners as part of their core activities, it is crucial for their long-term success that they be perceived to be acting effectively in the interests of their domain.[29] Institutional self-advertisement can take many forms, from actual advertisements to grand buildings, published transactions, and commemorations of achievements. Such forms do not necessarily exclusively serve the function of representing an institution as conducting valuable work. However, they are often crucial for ensuring

---

[27] *English Bards and Scotch Reviewers*, lines 1–2, in *Byron: The Complete Poetical Works*, ed. by Jerome J. McGann, 7 vols (Oxford: Oxford University Press, 1980–93), I, 229.

[28] These correspondences are documented in the Archive of the Royal Literary Fund, British Library Loan 96 RLF.

[29] We are grateful to Katie Halsey for suggesting this refinement of the definition we initially proposed.

that an institution is seen as worthwhile and legitimate, forming a feedback loop that empowers it to intervene more effectively in its chosen field, further increasing its perceived legitimacy: a set of requirements explored in relation to competing spiritualist societies in Sarah Crofton's concluding contribution to this volume. In the case of spiritualist organisations, as with Anacreontic Society – explored here by Ian Newman – meeting the social requirements for recognition as an effective institution proved difficult, ultimately undermining their authority.

The Emergence of Literary Institutions

One historical issue with our definition in relation to the literary is the shifting meaning of the word 'literature' over the course of the eighteenth and nineteenth centuries. During this period, 'literature' moved from denoting learning in general to knowledge – understood as narrower but deeper – represented in books to a subset associated with the creative imagination, and within that set a qualitative distinction about value. However, the older senses of 'literature' remained active in many institutional contexts, so a literary institution might be defined accurately as 'an assemblage that organises, transmits, and validates knowledge'. Certainly, the mutual development of the 'arts and sciences' in the early-nineteenth-century Institutions discussed by Jon Klancher seems to have echoed a more general sense – at least among the progressive middle classes – that these activities were not mutually exclusive.[30] Nevertheless, the same period sees some powerful statements along the lines of Thomas De Quincey's distinction between 'a literature of power' and 'a literature of knowledge' that impose a categorical difference between the arts and sciences, appealing to Romantic ideas of individual genius and artistry against institutional values associated with emergent scientification and the operations of political economy.[31] This is something like Pierre Bourdieu's idea of authentic artists inhabiting 'a relation to time embodied in the pure poetic disposition as a pure openness to the world', a relation actually based on distance from 'the ordinary existence of ordinary people'. From this perspective, institutions, even literary institutions, play their roles in Bourdieu's 'signposted universe, full of injunctions and prohibitions,

---

[30] Philip Connell suggests that middle-class opinion continued to find spaces for poetry alongside science in configuring notions of improvement. See *Romanticism, Economics, and the Question of 'Culture'* (Oxford: Oxford University Press, 2001), p. 106.

[31] *Collected Writings of Thomas de Quincey*, ed. by David Masson, 14 vols (Edinburgh: A. and C. Black, 1889–90), XI, 56–58.

signs of approbation and exclusion, obligatory routes or impassable barriers'.[32] However, this book demonstrates the extent to which the consolidation of this idea of 'poetic disposition' coincided with the proliferation of formal and material institutions of literature. Literature and its institutions have always been – and remain – mutually implicated and cannot simply be defined against each other. The institution of literature as imaginative creativity, as it were, increasingly relied on the mediation of literary institutions whose influence it denied. Part of the aim of this book is to restore to literary history – so often in collusion with the idea of a non-institutional literature of power – a fuller sense of the historical complexity of this phenomenon.

The period 1700–1900 has been chosen as our date range partly because it pivots around the Romantic disavowal of literature as an institution. Institutions in the service of literature as such were not a new phenomenon in the eighteenth century, but they were starting an uneven process of change in their forms and roles of the kind indicated by Raymond Williams. As Willy Maley discusses in Chapter 1, institutional ferment was a key characteristic of culture and society in the seventeenth century. It is not difficult to find older institutions that have had a considerable influence on the forms of literature and that have remained – to use the parlance of Williams – residual, and not passively so, in the strange institutional birth of modern liberalism. Churches and aristocratic courts are obvious examples, and in a British context, we might also mention the state censorship of the theatre or the Stationers' Company's long-standing authority over print publication. However, there were considerable step changes in how institutions functioned during the eighteenth and nineteenth centuries that served both to modify the forms of their influence and to make them more integral to the mediation of literary culture. The characteristic liberal form of British institutions emerged in the context of the state's notionally hands-off approach to regulation in most fields, the inexorable growth of a cultured public, and the emergence of an idea of culture as the expression of a national character. Institutions and their forms and genres were means of mediating culture when relying on networks of personal connections was no longer practical. In a bewildering literary marketplace, institutions could serve as beacons of value, although they were necessarily less agile in this regard than

---

[32] Pierre Bourdieu, *Pascalian Meditations*, trans. by Richard Nice (Cambridge: Polity Press, 2000), p. 181.

Introduction: Literature and Institutions

proliferating magazines and periodicals and were frequently open to accusations of being always already behind the times. Thus, the campaigns by professional authors like Charles Dickens to reform and update the Royal Literary Fund, although in this case what was perceived to be institutional inertia proved to be too difficult to overcome.[33]

While in some European states, most notably France, institutional development was driven in large part from the centre through the formation of national institutions wielding state-derived authority, British institutional development was typically driven by groups of bourgeois individuals. Authors regularly presented arguments that the state should intervene more forcibly in institutionalising literary matters, but during the eighteenth and nineteenth centuries, such calls went largely unheeded. In 1712, Jonathan Swift proposed to Robert Harley, Earl of Oxford, the Lord High Treasurer, that a group of experts should be sought to stabilise the English language. These men would 'assemble at some appointed Time and Place, and fix on Rules by which they design to proceed'. After setting out some parameters of his own, he purported to leave the fine details to 'that Society, which I hope will owe its Institution and Patronage to Your LORDSHIP'.[34] However, Harley did not act on Swift's suggestion, and a century later, in 1812, Robert Southey continued to bemoan the lack of such a centralised institution, writing that if the government were to establish an academy, it 'would confer greater benefit upon literature than it have ever received from the most boasted benefactors'.[35] Fifty years further on, in 1862, Matthew Arnold had positive things to say about the French and Italian Academies, but saw Britain as having taken a definitively different line: 'When a literature has produced Shakespeare and Milton, when it has even produced Barrow and Burke, it cannot well abandon its traditions; it can hardly begin, at this late time of day, with an institution like the French Academy.'[36] The British Academy was eventually established in 1902, just as our period ends, but it began as and remains a very different organisation to the Académie Française.

Discussing the metropolitan institutions that arose in the late eighteenth and early nineteenth centuries, Jon Klancher writes that

---

[33] Cross, *Common Writer*, pp. 30–37.
[34] [Jonathan Swift], *A Proposal for Correcting, Improving and Ascertaining the English Tongue* (London: Benjamin Tooke, 1712), pp. 29, 36.
[35] [Robert Southey], 'D'Israeli's *Calamities of Authors*', *Quarterly Review*, 8 (September 1812), 93–114 (p. 113).
[36] Matthew Arnold, 'The Literary Influence of Academies', *Cornhill Magazine*, 10.56 (August 1864), 154–72 (p. 172).

the new collective formations were not specifically *in* the market, but instead forged a kind of parallel presence, formations which had sprung up between the traditional order and the aggressive, unbounded commercial markets of the past century. Hence, they defined themselves as both economic agents – directing and at the same time protecting themselves from market energy and anarchy – and political agents outside and beyond the traditional apparatus of the state.[37]

This characterisation does a good job of capturing the positions institutions in Britain tended to occupy. They had political goals and could exert forms of soft power, but they were not straightforwardly agents of the state. Independence from government authority was a key element of the British mythology of self-governance that became a powerful part of nineteenth-century institutional liberalism. Literary institutions, like most others across the two centuries of this study, were underpinned by commercial wealth, but were not in themselves designed as engines of direct profit. They could even operate a species of high-minded money laundering, disguising the reliance of commercial wealth on violence, slavery, and expropriation. This was glaringly the case in Liverpool, where civic pride smoothed the way for the collaboration in the city's new Royal Institution between the veteran abolitionist William Roscoe and his old opponent John Gladstone, father of the future prime minister, plantation owner, and defender of slavery.[38] Institutions like the Liverpool Royal Institution often presented themselves as fulfilling social and cultural functions by regulating flows, defining excellence, and building a knowledge infrastructure that fundamentally shaped the perceptions and realities of a wide range of epistemological fields, including literature. The fact that they were at arm's length from the government was often taken to be a guarantee of disinterestedness.

While literature had been regulated in institutions previously, it was during the eighteenth century that self-consciously literary institutions were founded in increasing numbers and began to persist for longer terms. A College of Antiquaries first met in London between around 1586 and 1607 but fell into abeyance after signs of royal disapproval. The modern Society of Antiquaries was founded in 1707 and received its royal charter in 1751. Over

---

[37] Klancher, p. 49.
[38] See Guy Kitteringham, 'Science in Provincial Society: The Case of Liverpool in the Early Nineteenth Century', *Annals of Science*, 39.4 (1982), 329–48 on the way the Institution brought together important members of differing groups in the town (p. 340). The Institution did not end the antagonism between Gladstone and Roscoe on slavery. By 1830, after his old adversary had accepted the presidency of the new Liverpool Anti-Slavery Society, Gladstone was complaining that Roscoe had managed to 'infect with radicalism a new generation of young men'. See S. G. Checkland, *The Gladstones: A Family Biography, 1764–1851* (Cambridge: Cambridge University Press, 1971), p. 224.

the course of the eighteenth century, it accrued collections and found dedicated quarters in Somerset House, in rooms opposite those assigned to the fledgeling Royal Academy. The pattern of foundations preceding foundation stones was a common one, partly reflecting the decentralised nature of British institutional life. The Society of Antiquaries' role as an organising force was articulated most strongly through its collaborative publications: first its long-running plate series *Vetusta Monumenta* (commenced in 1718) and then its periodical of record *Archaeologia* (commenced in 1770). Other institutions followed similar patterns. One of the earliest public libraries – Innerpeffray – can trace its foundations to 1680, but its books were initially kept in St Mary's Chapel and only moved into a dedicated building in the middle decades of the eighteenth century. It was during the 1710s and 1720s, as Dustin Frazier Wood shows in his contribution, that the Spalding Gentlemen's Society took control of collections from older foundations and established itself through association, collection-building, and local regulation. Many institutions were formed through an initial sociable phase as extensions of the informal clubs Peter Clark has described as comprising an increasingly 'vital component of the social life of the educated English-speaking classes, whether at home or abroad' from the seventeenth century onwards, although not all such groups settled comfortably into institutional formations, as Ian Newman shows here when discussing the consequences of rude Anacreontic sociability.[39] At this stage, literary sociability was defined in various broad ways in relation to 'learning' or a broader ideal of the republic of letters, both usually taken to have affiliations beyond any nation state. Many authors from this period boasted of their membership of societies and academies from across Europe and beyond on the colophons of their books. The Aberdonian poet and philosopher James Beattie, for instance, declared himself 'Professor of Moral Philosophy in Marischal College, Aberdeen, and Member of the Zealand Society of Arts and Sciences, and of the Literary and Philosophical Society of Manchester' on the title page of his *Evidences of the Christian Religion*.[40]

The ever-expanding world of print spawned numerous other kinds of institution that played roles in regulating its flow, not all of which were viewed as equally legitimate in their claims to authority. Subscription libraries might be regarded as sound 'literary' institutions in terms of their respectability, for instance, but circulating libraries of the kind that

---

[39] Clark, p. 3.
[40] James Beattie, *Evidences of the Christian Religion Briefly and Plainly Stated*, 2 vols (London: Strahan and Cadell, 1786).

disseminated the early genre fiction discussed by Anne H. Stevens here might not be. Literary and philosophical societies like those founded in Manchester in 1781 and Newcastle upon Tyne in 1793 aspired to a civic role in the circulation and regulation of knowledge in the arts and sciences. This visibly civic aspiration distinguishes them from something like the Lunar Society, with which they otherwise overlapped in terms of intellectual orientation and even membership. Early on, at least, founders from the community of Dissenters in both places were closely watched by the local Tory hierarchy lest they presume too much in terms of their public roles. Neither of these two institutions had their own bricks and mortar at first, with buildings arriving in 1799 in Manchester and in 1823 at Newcastle, partly to provide space for a library (where novels and similar publications were not encouraged).

Grand buildings might attest to the success of an institution's claim to authority, or at least their aspirations in that regard, but funding such edifices could mean reaching beyond 'subscriber democracy' to draw on funds from local aristocrats and gentry. In Newcastle, this ruffled the feathers of those members who saw the institution as a bastion of democratic form, at least within its emergent middle-class base.[41] In Leeds, the 'Philosophical Hall' (completed in 1821) followed fairly quickly from the foundation of the Philosophical and Literary Society (1819), principally because the local textile magnates were willing to pay to have their new-minted ascendancy confirmed in stone (Figure I.1). The middle-class membership seems to have found this patronage from within less objectionable.[42] By the 1820s, though, such societies could presume on their rising social power to act as the founders and patrons of mechanics' institutes meant to attract the urban working classes to a particular kind of education but within which, as John Gardner in Chapter 10 and Sarah Comyn in Chapter 11 show, both reading and conduct were formally and informally regulated in the interest of middle-class notions of good order.[43] Across these various institutions, there was a remarkable similarity of rules and regulations, the most obvious being the ban on topical politics and religious opinions (which remained explosive elements in any

---

[41] See the discussion of early developments in both places in Jon Mee and Jennifer Wilkes, 'Transpennine Enlightenment: The Literary and Philosophical Societies and Knowledge Networks in the North, 1781–1830', *Journal for Eighteenth Century Studies*, 38.4 (2015), 599–612.

[42] For an excellent account of institutional developments in Leeds in the 1820s, see R. J. Morris, *Class, Sect and Party: The Making of the British Middle Class: Leeds 1820–1850* (Manchester: Manchester University Press, 1990), especially Chapters 9 to 11.

[43] The influence of Newcastle's literary institutions reached as far as the Cape Colony and New South Wales. See Jon Mee, '"A Reading People?" Global Knowledge Networks and Two Australian Societies of the 1820s', *Australian Literary Studies*, 29.3 (2014), 79–91 (pp. 80, 84).

Figure I.1 Watercolour image by Robert Dennis Chantrell of the proposed design for the Leeds Philosophical Hall. © Leeds City Council / Bridgeman Images.

institution and a threat to the attempt to create a consensus around middle-class hegemony). The buildings that followed as monuments to nineteenth-century liberal improvement are often now struggling for survival, one of many aspects of neo-liberal neglect that make that political neologism somewhat misplaced.

While these institutions flourished in a variety of provincial and imperial settings as the nineteenth century proceeded, London frequently hosted institutions that self-consciously presumed to a national or, increasingly, imperial authority, including the British Museum, discussed by Gillian Russell in Chapter 9, and the Royal Institution, discussed by Jon Klancher in Chapter 7. The aftermath of the Napoleonic Wars, especially, witnessed a distinct scaling up of institutional activity and with it an attempt to reach new audiences, like those in the mechanics' institutes. Institutional forms spread rapidly across the empire, but always in ways that had to adapt to local circumstances, never functioning straightforwardly as a rollout of imperial power. By the middle of the nineteenth century, the machinery of government had increased in Britain itself, often taking over libraries and museums formed by literary and philosophical societies and their ilk in provincial towns, for instance, under the provisions of the Museums Act of 1845 and the Public Libraries Act of 1850. However, such legislation rarely brought institutions under direct central control, instead allowing local councils to raise money on the rates. When the Education Act of 1870 finally brought in a national system of education, it did so only after years of struggle between special interest groups, not least those non-conformist voluntarists who feared it would give too much power to the Church of England. Nevertheless, this cumulative process served to create a larger-scale institutional infrastructure out of an array of interlocking organisations, with this still-uneven system playing a paramount role in mediating the transmission and validation of knowledge and culture. Such processes of development also produced the templates governing the constitutions and practices that granted authority to literary institutions. These templates and conventions could not be transposed universally, as Sarah Crofton shows when discussing the failure of Spiritualism to achieve institutional authority, but they did prove to be durable and operationally effective across a wide range of developing specialisms within the broader literary landscape.

However, perhaps tellingly, one field in which the advent of strong institutions was relatively belated was professional writing. As Penelope Corfield has put it, during the early nineteenth century, it 'proved insuperably difficult to translate literary freedom into the trappings of formal professionalism'.[44] The Literary Fund hoped to be an organisation that would raise the respectability and profitability of authorship, but social preconceptions and circumstances forced it to scale back its ambition.[45] The Royal Society of Literature, founded in 1820, was initially well supported by state grants, but used these mainly to maintain a few famous names, and after the withdrawal of funding in the 1830s, it became a relatively minor player until its revivification in the late nineteenth century.[46] It was only in 1884 that the Society of Authors was established, and even at this late stage, one of its founders, Walter Besant, recorded that the 'innocent ... general propositions' that underpinned the nascent organisation gave 'dire offence in certain quarters'.[47] He ascribed this to

---

[44] Penelope J. Corfield, *Power and the Professions in Britain 1700–1850* (London: Routledge, 1995), p. 185.
[45] See Matthew Sangster, *Living as an Author in the Romantic Period* (Cham: Palgrave Macmillan, 2021), pp. 179–94.
[46] See Edward W. Brabrook, *The Royal Society of Literature of the United Kingdom: A Brief Account of its Origin and Progress* (London: Harrison, 1891).
[47] Walter Besant, *The Society of Authors: A Record of its Action from its Foundation* (London: Society of Authors, 1893), p. 4.

a feeling that had 'existed for a hundred and fifty years at least . . . that it is unworthy [of] the dignity of letters to take any account at all of the commercial or pecuniary side'.[48] Once it was established, the Society of Authors achieved some notable successes in stopping scams and improving the lots of its members through collective action and expert negotiation, but the fact that it took so long for an idea mooted by the Literary Fund's founder David Williams in the 1770s to be put into practice speaks to the peculiar cultural space that sharpening notions of the literary came to occupy.

Literature against Institutions

The scepticism or even downright hostility that modern literary writing often shows towards literary institutions would have seemed perverse in earlier periods when 'learning' was largely unthinkable outside the framework of the church, the court, or aristocratic patronage, but as the 'literary' came to be understood as a particular kind of writing, it was increasingly figured as operating most authentically beyond the boundaries of institutionality. In his revised version of 'Fears in Solitude' (1817), Samuel Taylor Coleridge inserted verses that responded negatively to what he perceived to be the new vogue:

> Meanwhile, at home,
> All individual dignity and power
> Engulfed in Courts, Committees, Institutions,
> Associations and Societies,
> A vain, speach-mouthing, speech-reporting Guild,
> One Benefit-Club for mutual flattery.[49]

The irony was that Coleridge – along with others like William Hazlitt and Thomas Campbell – forged a successful career as a star lecturer at these same new institutions throughout the 1810s.[50] He was also bankrolled in part by the Royal Society of Literature during the 1820s, a relationship that certainly involved elements of 'mutual flattery'. While their works posited the value of individual freedoms, Romantic authors often flirted ambivalently with the nascent potential of institutionality, as Gillian Russell explores in Chapter 9 with regard to Charles Lamb's complex and changing

---

[48] Besant, p. 14.
[49] Samuel Taylor Coleridge, 'Fears in Solitude' (1817), quoted in Klancher, p. 28.
[50] See Sarah Zimmerman, *The Romantic Literary Lecture in Britain* (Oxford: Oxford University Press, 2019).

relationship with the British Museum. However, as the network of institutions thickened, it became increasingly common to figure it as strangling imagination and creativity in a deadening undergrowth of bureaucracy, as satirised by Charles Dickens in *Hard Times* (1854) and *Little Dorrit* (1857). Earlier, in *The Pickwick Papers* (1837), Dickens had indulged in amiable mockery of an amateur literary association, but he was to become deeply implicated in the nineteenth century's institutions of literature. Like the literary lecturers of the previous generation, he cemented his reputation at venues like mechanics' institutes from the 1840s onwards.[51] The strong claims for the autonomy of the literary imagination in *Hard Times* have a complicated relationship to his defence of 'Literature' as 'a dignified profession'.[52] Very much engaged with the practical aspects of writing careers, Dickens worked sporadically but industriously for the Guild of Literature and Art and the Royal Literary Fund, served on the London Shakespeare Committee, and campaigned with vigour for the reform of the copyright laws. His involvement in campaigns for the reform of the postal system – discussed by Karin Koehler in Chapter 12 – was at least partly to do with his sense of its importance as a literary institution. Activities of this kind tainted his claim to be a properly 'literary' author for some observers at the time, but they were part of his larger commitment to literary endeavour: 'Whoever is devoted to an Art must be content to deliver himself wholly up to it', he wrote, 'and to find his recompense in it'.[53] Dickens is an interesting example of authorship as an institution, a concept discussed in this volume by David A. Brewer. While 'Miltonic' – Brewer's example – only appeared as an adjective in the century after Milton's death, 'Dickensian' as a signature that could be adopted by others – in all its diverse implications – appeared as early as the 1850s according to the *OED*.

Following in the footsteps of the sceptical rhetorics developed by many nineteenth-century authors, literary scholarship has evolved in ways that work to occlude both the institutionality of its objects of study and its own institutionality. School and university literature teaching tends to present institutions as only the frame, at best, of the picture that should really be the focus of attention. However, you are probably reading this book in

---

[51] A simple search for 'mechanics' institutes' in the online Pilgrim-British Academy edition of the letters comes up with multiple hits from the 1840s onwards, including many more invitations than Dickens was able to accept. See also the list of the venues at which he performed in Malcolm Andrews, *Charles Dickens and His Performing Selves* (Oxford: Oxford University Press, 2006), Appendix 1.
[52] *The Speeches of Charles Dickens*, ed. by K. J. Fielding (Oxford: Clarendon Press, 1960), p. 389.
[53] *The Letters of Charles Dickens*, ed. by Madeline House and others, Pilgrim/British Academy Edition, 12 vols (Oxford: Clarendon Press, 1965–2002), VII, 584.

a university or a library, or in the form of a chapter downloaded from such an institution. You may be so immersed in its contents that this institutional framework melts into air around you, or it may be that an institutional framework is being experienced directly as a constraint. You can't take the book out of the library. You need it to finish an essay or an article or a review for which some other institution has prescribed a deadline. Why then add to your misery by asking you to think about literary institutions? The aim here is certainly not to suggest that the possibilities of literature are exhausted by its institutional forms. No institution has ever been able fully to define or encompass the idea of the literary, but the idea of literature as transcending institutions has a history of its own as an institution of literature, as shown in the reactions of authors like Coleridge. This idea fed into the development of English departments and the study of English Literature in Coleridge's own lifetime, not least via the Wordsworthian sense of poetry as 'the breath and finer spirit of all knowledge'.[54]

There have been several excellent institutional studies of the development of English Literature as an academic subject.[55] Some give emphasis to the conflict between the concepts of civil improvement and taste in the teaching of rhetoric and belles lettres in the Dissenting Academies and at the Scottish universities in the late eighteenth century. John Guillory notes the institutional influence of the Warrington Academy curriculum, especially via the textbooks and anthologies its teachers produced, in creating the idea of a 'vernacular canon'.[56] Thomas P. Miller identifies Hugh Blair and his compatriots with a trend away from the teaching of the civic function of rhetoric at Warrington towards stylistic criticism. The question of taste became paramount, but never really lost the idea of aesthetics as a vital ground of ethics.[57] These earlier developments fed into the emergence of English studies at the University of London in 1828. Wordsworth was much alarmed by the secular nature of the new institution at University College London and lent his support to King's College London as a counterweight.[58]

---

[54] Wordsworth, 'Preface' (1802), *Prose Works*, I, 141.
[55] See especially Gerald Graff, *Professing Literature: An Institutional History* (Chicago: University of Chicago Press, 1987) and Franklin E. Court, *Institutionalizing English Literature: The Culture and Politics of Literary Study, 1750–1900* (Stanford: Stanford University Press, 1992).
[56] John Guillory, *Cultural Capital: The Problem of Literary Canon Formation* (Chicago: University of Chicago Press, 1993), p. 101.
[57] See Thomas P. Miller, *The Formation of College English: Rhetoric and Belles Lettres in the British Cultural Provinces* (Pittsburgh: University of Pittsburgh Press, 1997), p. 9.
[58] See D. J. Palmer, *The Rise of English Studies: An Account of the Study of English Language and Literature from its Origins to the Making of the Oxford English School* (London: Oxford University Press, 1965). Palmer sees University College London, where composition was taught, as the more

Rapidly becoming an authorial institution in his own right, operating through disciples like F. D. Maurice, Wordsworth would provide an influential foundation to nineteenth-century English studies as a discipline that linked an intangible national spirit with the fulfilment of personality.[59] Gauri Viswanathan, in an argument developed by Porscha Fermanis in Chapter 13, has shown how the academic study of English Literature was used to justify British rule in India precisely on the basis of the spirit of English literary culture.[60] Karin Koehler similarly notes how the Wordsworthian 'human heart' was used to justify the reform of the Post Office as a medium for connecting up the national consciousness.

To think about literary institutions in these and other contexts is obviously not straightforwardly to celebrate or embrace them, nor to cede them forms of authority they do not possess. However, it is important to acknowledge that institutions have often provided refuge and succour to creative endeavour in unpropitious times, and to recognise the importance of their role as actors in framing relations between writers, readers, and texts, including relations of power. The conflicted roles of institutions are evident throughout this book, but so too is their positive potential, intentional or otherwise. The Spalding Gentlemen's Society, as Dustin Frazier Wood shows, sought to improve the lots of its members and its local community, including the less privileged among both. The female-led *Musenhof* sociability discussed by Nicole Pohl facilitated a flourishing of literary writing and positive reforms. The institutionalisation of authorship discussed by David A. Brewer and the developments in genres and subgenres facilitated by the circulating libraries Anne H. Stevens examines both made literary culture more legible and tangible to new entrants. The Literary Fund sometimes preened and postured, but it also provided very real material aid to many hundreds of writers facing illness and impoverishment. New lecturing institutions brought cutting-edge knowledge – in science and in poetry – before audiences of thousands. While the mechanics' institutes considered by John Gardner and Sarah Comyn aimed at a particularly regulated form of popular enlightenment, they reached out

---

obvious heir to the tradition at Warrington Academy (p. 16). Literature was taught at King's College London on the basis of moral principles associated with Wordsworth.

[59] Ian Reid, 'Fathering the Man: Journalism, Masculinity and the Wordsworthian Formation of Academic Literary Studies in Victorian England', *Journal of Victorian Culture*, 6 (2001), 201–30, developed further in his subsequent book, *Wordsworth and the Formation of English Studies* (Aldershot: Ashgate, 2004). For a discussion of the shape these debates took during the development of the English Faculty at Oxford in the 1870s, see McDonald, Chapter 1.

[60] Gauri Viswanathan, *Masks of Conquest: Literary Study and British Rule in India* (New York: Columbia University Press, 1989).

to substantial new audiences who proved more than capable of challenging or subverting the preconceptions of their founders and officials. Institutions are far from neutral, but their visibility – their claim to stand for something – makes them available for renegotiation or resistance in ways that more dispersed networks may not be, a point Jon Klancher makes forcefully in Chapter 7. Institutions are not machine-tooled hegemons laser-focused on single goals. In practice, they operate as arenas within which, and between which, competing social and cultural discourses can be made available and can play out. As Porscha Fermanis and Karin Koehler point out, they can even unintentionally foster networks of counter-institutions that undermine the stability of their own claims to power.

In 'Passions', Jacques Derrida wrote:

> Literature is a modern invention, it inscribes itself in conventions and institutions which, to hold on to just this trait, secure in principle its right to say everything. Literature thus ties its destiny to a certain non-censure, to the space of democratic freedom (freedom of the press, freedom of speech, etc.). No democracy without literature; no literature without democracy.[61]

Mark Robson has pointed out how the chiastic form of Derrida's final sentence 'guards against any sense of final determination or overdetermination of one term by the other'. The 'shared relation to freedom' Robson sees in Derrida's declaration 'pertains only if this freedom is understood as itself a matter of invention, convention and institution, and if it is also thought in terms of a *destin* – a fate or destiny – that projects literature towards or onto a future'.[62] In light of Robson's gloss, perhaps it might not be too presumptuous to mimic Derrida's chiastic form by saying: 'No literature without institutions; no institutions without literature.'

---

[61] Jacques Derrida, 'Passions: An Oblique Offering', trans. by David Wood, in *On the Name*, ed. by Thomas Dutoit (Stanford: Stanford University Press, 1995), p. 28.
[62] Mark Robson, '"A Literary Animal": Rancière, Derrida, and the Literature of Democracy', *Parallax*, 15.3 (2009), 88–101 (p. 88).

CHAPTER I

Knowledge Exchange in the Seventeenth Century
From the Third University to the Royal Society

Willy Maley

In his proposal for a new library on the south side of St James's Park at the end of the seventeenth century, Richard Bentley declared that it 'may be so contriv'd for Capaciousness and Convenience, that every one that comes there, may have 200,000 Volumes, ready for his use and service. And Societies may be formed, that shall meet, and have Conferences there about matters of Learning'.[1] Bentley's innovation was in part a restitution of the Royal Library established under James I, 'stored with all sorts of good Books of That and the preceding Age, from the beginning of Printing', but now in a state of disarray:

> There has been no supply of Books from abroad for the space of Sixty years last: nor any allowance for Binding; so that many valuable Manuscripts are spoil'd for want of Covers: and above a Thousand Books printed in England, and brought in Quires to the Library, as due by the Act for Printing, are all unbound and useless.[2]

Bentley advocated 'a radical transformation of the Royal Library into a great public institution of learning on the continental model'.[3] For the new building, he envisaged a structure of lasting value, drawing on domestic and foreign resources: 'The Wall that shall encompass the Library, may be cased on the inside with Marbles of ancient Inscriptions... either found in our own Kingdom, or easily and cheaply to be had from the *African* Coast, and *Greece*, and *Asia* the Less.'[4] Bentley's intention was for the new institution to become a magnet for international students: 'since the

---

[1] [Richard Bentley], *A Proposal for Building a Royal Library, and Establishing It by Act of Parliament* (London: [n. pub.], 1697), p. 2.
[2] [Bentley], p. 1.
[3] Paul A. Nelles, 'Libraries, Books and Learning, from Bacon to the Enlightenment', in *The Cambridge History of Libraries in Britain and Ireland, vol. 2: 1640–1850* ed. by Giles Mandelbrote and K. A. Manley (Cambridge: Cambridge University Press, 2006), pp. 23–35 (p. 32).
[4] [Bentley], p. 2.

Writings of the *English* Nation have at present that great Reputation abroad ... many Persons of all Countries learn our Language, and several travel hither for the advantage of Conversation'.⁵ Consequently, he anticipated the building swiftly paying for itself: "Tis our Publick Interest and Profit, to have the Gentry of Foreign Nations acquainted with *England* ... more Money will be annually imported and spent here by such Students from abroad, than the whole Charge and Revenue of this Library will amount to.'⁶

This late-seventeenth-century proposal for a Royal Library in a Republic of Letters that would form a cornerstone of a restored Imperial Monarchy exemplifies the heady mix of nationalism, colonialism and commerce that characterised the emerging British state. Periodisation affords us essential frameworks and starting points but obscures the roots of those things we take to begin with our own period of study, whether they be bodies, nations, selves or, in the case of this book, institutions. Often we are surprised by precedents for objects of study we take to be of later provenance. Our idea of modernity can be challenged in this way. For example, according to one source, the earliest periodical on record is the Roman *Acta Diurna*, dating from 623 BC.⁷ In this chapter, the aim is to push back our sense of the emergence of institutions of literature by pointing to some seventeenth-century precedents. The rediscovery and recovery of classical science had its freest rein in this period, intensified mid-century by a social and political revolution.⁸ According to Steven Shapin, 'Seventeenth-century England witnessed the rise and institutionalization of a program devoted to systematic experimentation, accompanied by a literature explicitly describing and defending practical aspects of that program.'⁹

John Milton refers to institutions twice in *Of Education* (1644), first with reference to a specific 'discipline', 'the institution of Physick', and then in an allusion to the kind of practical schooling he envisages will 'supply a defect as great as that which Plato noted in the common-wealth of Sparta; whereas that City train'd up their youth most for warre, and these in their Academies and Lycaeum, all for the gown, this institution of breeding which I here delineate, shall be equally good both for Peace and warre'.¹⁰

---

⁵ [Bentley], p. 2.   ⁶ [Bentley], p. 2.
⁷ F. Bayford Harrison, 'First Numbers', *Time*, 1.51 (1889), 66–82 (p. 66).
⁸ See J. J. O'Brien, 'Commonwealth Schemes for the Advancement of Learning', *British Journal of Educational Studies*, 16.1 (1968), 30–42.
⁹ Steven Shapin, 'The House of Experiment in Seventeenth-Century England', *Isis*, 79.3 (1988), 373–404 (p. 373).
¹⁰ John Milton, *Of Education: To Master Samuel Hartlib* ([London: for Thomas Underhill? for Thomas Johnson? 1644]), pp. 4, 6.

Milton's hybrid academy has prompted puzzlement: 'just what kind of an institution might include the study of biblical Aramaic alongside instruction in music, fortification, and wrestling?'[11] However, like their modern successors, seventeenth-century institutions depended on engagement and impact; on industry and empire; on internationalisation; on innovation, collaboration and interdisciplinarity; and on building the kind of external partnerships we take for granted today. Milton's *Of Education* exemplified the spirit of the age.

In this overview of the century, leading up to this volume's official start date, I am interested in how exactly the innovations of early modern research communities depended on, drew on and were driven by colonial design. This is a vast subject, entailing collective biography, depth bibliography, microhistory, interdisciplinary engagement and transdisciplinary collaboration. Here I can only sketch the outlines of an argument. Taking as my starting point a little-known text by George Buck titled *The Third Universitie* (1615) and as my end point the early years of the Royal Society, I explore how what began as a challenge to the universities of Oxford and Cambridge and an appeal to worldly engagement ended in an outward-facing trans-institutional sphere that drew its inspiration, founding figures and key personnel from the archipelagic and colonial contexts within which its pioneering interests developed. The seventeenth century marks a decisive shift from intellectual circles to learned societies, from armchair innovators to research hubs and from sequestered centres of knowledge to agencies of state power. The origins of the first Royal Society lie in a range of institutions identified by Buck, including Gresham College; in later developments such as the Invisible College; and in Samuel Hartlib's Circle's pursuit of useful knowledge through an 'Office of Address'.[12] The relatively late establishment of the Dublin Philosophical Society by William Molyneux in 1683 conceals the extent of the Royal Society's Irish roots.[13] 'Avant-gardeners', agricultural

---

[11] Timothy Raylor, 'Milton, the Hartlib Circle, and the Education of the Aristocracy', in *The Oxford Handbook of Milton*, ed. by Nicholas McDowell and Nigel Smith (Oxford: Oxford University Press, 2009), pp. 382–406 (p. 382).

[12] Lauren Kassell, 'Invisible College (act. 1646–1647)', *Oxford Dictionary of National Biography* (Oxford: Oxford University Press, 2004), <www.oxforddnb.com> (*ODNB*); Charles Webster, 'New Light on the Invisible College: The Social Relations of English Science in the Mid-Seventeenth Century', *Transactions of the Royal Historical Society*, 24 (1974), 19–42.

[13] See K. Theodore Hoppen, 'The Dublin Philosophical Society and the New Learning in Ireland', *Irish Historical Studies*, 14.54 (1964), 99–118; T. C. Barnard, 'The Hartlib Circle and the Origins of the Dublin Philosophical Society', *Irish Historical Studies*, 19.73 (1974), 56–71; W. R. Wilde, 'Memoir of the Dublin Philosophical Society of 1683', *Proceedings of the Royal Irish Academy (1836–1869)*, 3 (1844), 160–76.

materialists and bog-drainers active in Ireland and America from the 1580s to the 1660s were hard-wired into emerging networks of experts working across collaborative communities of scholar-practitioners.[14] There was no new medicine without frontiers, no advance in husbandry without fresh fields to plant and, crucially, no knowledge exchange without satiric responses that parodied the pamphlet literature of projectors.

The Third University

The University of London was officially established in 1836, with its two founding colleges, University College London and King's College London, dating from 1826 and 1829 respectively, but arguments for the de facto existence of a university in the city predated the Royal Charter by over two centuries. Buck's dedication to Edward Coke, dated 24 August 1612, offers a vision of a civic university promoting the liberal arts:

> I present here to your Lordship a view of the Academicall State, and of the Universality of the Studies, and of the liberall Arts, and Learnings taught, and professed in this Cittie of London . . . bestowed in the description of the Colledges, and collegiate houses founded in this Cittie for the professours of the Municipall, or common Law of this Land.[15]

Buck then lays out 'A CATALOGUE, OR TABLE OF ALL THE ARTS AND SCIENCES READ, and taught in this Universitie of LONDON'.[16] The list of thirty-six subjects includes brachygraphy, 'A system of writing using abbreviations or special characters; shorthand', and steganography, 'the practice of concealing messages or information within other non-secret text or data'. It also embraces the 'Art of Reuels' because Buck, as Master of the Revels, believed his role

---

[14] For a fascinating discussion of institutional development and a nascent 'expertise' in service to the state – although the word itself is of nineteenth-century provenance – see Eric H. Ash, 'Expertise and the Early Modern State', *Osiris*, 25.1 (2010), 1–24.

[15] George Buck, *The Third Universitie of England. Or a Treatise of the Foundations of All the Colledges, Aunciend Schooles of Priviledge, and of Houses of Learning, and Liberall Arts, within and Above the Most Famous Cittie of London*, in John Stow,*The Annales*, ed. by Edmund Howes (London: Thomas Adams, 1615), pp. 958–88 (p. 961). I am grateful to my colleague Bob MacLean for unravelling a complicated publication history. *The Third Universitie* was first published as an annex to the 1615 edition of John Stow's *Annals*, edited by antiquarian Edmund Howes, Stow having died in 1605. Earlier editions of Stow's *Annals* conclude with an account of the two main universities. Howes perhaps came across Buck's account (circulating in manuscript) and decided to augment Stow with this celebration of London.

[16] Buck, p. 963.

'required ... expertise in grammar, rhetoric, logic, philosophy, history, music, mathematics, and other arts'.[17]

Buck begins his discourse proper with a preface that sets up the question of a third university:

> Having observed in divers Writers, as well forraigne as English, the Citie of London to be stiled an Universitie, and doubting of it, I tooke occasion thereby to examine uppon what grounds and causes they had so stiled it, and after some search and consideration thereof, I found sufficient cause and reasons to satisfie me.[18]

Buck deals briskly with the objection that this third university has no papal bull to found it: 'this is frivolous, for then had *Athens* beene no Universitie, for there the Pope had nothing to doe'. He takes issue with the perceived need for such papal authority to grant university status, arguing that 'where the reformed Religion is professed, and established ... the Popes power and authoritie is excluded', adding that even if this were not the case, English monarchs had the right to establish 'Universities, and Publique Schooles within their owne Kingdomes and Dominions'.[19]

Buck escorts the reader around London and picks out the constituent parts of this third university work in progress, consisting of a remarkable array of existing institutions and activities, including 'Schools of Theologie, and of the Arts in Westminster', 'the fower Innes of Court', 'the Innes of Chauncery', 'Gresham Colledge', 'the Colledge of Herauldes', 'the Art of Revels' and 'divers Professors of many other Arts, and Faculties residing in this University, and of Art memorative'.[20] Summarising each of these institutions, Buck makes exalted claims for their combined efficacy:

> But not to be long in particularizing every art and every Science professed and taught in this Cittie ... who can then deny that London is not onely the third Universitie of England, but also to be preferred before many other Universities in Europe, or in any other parte of the world knowne.[21]

---

[17] Arthur Kincaid, 'Buck [Buc], Sir George (bap. 1560, d. 1622), Master of the Revels and Historian', *ODNB*.

[18] Buck, p. 965.   [19] Buck, pp. 965–66.

[20] Buck, pp. 967–88. On the Inns of Court, see John H. Baker, *The Third University of England: The Inns of Court and the Common-Law Tradition* (London: Selden Society, 1990); 'Roman Law at the Third University of England', *Current Legal Problems*, 55.1 (2002), 123–50 and 'The Third University 1450–1550: Law School or Finishing School', in *The Intellectual and Cultural World of the Early Modern Inns of Court*, ed. Jayne Elisabeth Archer, Elizabeth Goldring, and Sarah Knight (Manchester: Manchester University Press, 2011), pp. 8–27.

[21] Buck, p. 988.

Gresham College, which came into being in 1596–7, is a focal point of this distributed collegiate campus. Thomas Gresham, a younger son who served an apprenticeship in the Mercers' Company and had business interests in Paris and Brussels, founded the Royal Exchange and left as his other legacy the College that bore his name. A fluent French speaker who also spoke Flemish – as well as being versed in Latin and Greek – Cambridge-educated Gresham was committed to practical knowledge of the kind only a new institution could freely encourage.[22] Gresham College quickly became 'a meeting place of scientists and a clearing-house for scientific information'.[23]

Thomas Heywood's panegyric to London University in 1632 pressed the city's claim as the site of a third university further.[24] Heywood's dedication 'TO THE RIGHT Worshipfull *Hugh Perry,* and *Henry Andrewes:* the two Sheriffes of the *Honourable City* London, *last* Elected' makes clear the colonial origins of London's newfound wealth:

> your Trafficke and Commerce, (being free Merchant-aduenturers) testifis to the World your Noble Profession; as Trading in the *East-Indies, Turkey, Italy, Spayne,* and *France,* &c. to the Honour of our Nation abroad, and singular Profits redounding to the *Realme* at home. Your more private Imployments heretofore, aswell in furthering Arts, as incoureging Armes, adding no common Luster to these Offices, unto which Time and your owne Demerits have at this present called you.[25]

Having summarised the schools and activities around the city, Heywood pauses – 'So much for the Studies of the Braine' – and gets down to the business of trade, for it is as 'an open Mart' for 'forraigne Nations' that London excels.[26] For Heywood, London's knowledge economy is rightly a free market rather than a closed college.

Francis Kynaston's Covent Garden College was the next claimant to the throne of London learning. Kynaston signalled his intentions in an elaborate masque performed in 1635.[27] The following year *The Constitutions of the Musæum Minervæ* echoed some of Buck's arguments for a London university, opining that it would serve the purpose of 'bringing of vertue into

---

[22] Ian Blanchard, 'Gresham, Sir Thomas (c.1518–1579)', *ODNB*.
[23] Francis R. Johnson, 'Gresham College: Precursor of the Royal Society', *Journal of the History of Ideas*, 1.4 (1940), 413–38 (p. 427).
[24] Thomas Heywood, *Londini Artium & Scientiarum Scaturigo: Or, Londons Fountaine of Arts and Sciences* (London: Nicholas Okes, 1632). See also J. Caitlin Finlayson, 'Thomas Heywood's Panegyric to London's "University" in *Londini Artium & Scientiarum Scaturigo: Or, Londons Fountaine of Arts and Sciences* (1632)', *The London Journal*, 39.2 (2014), 102–19.
[25] Heywood, *Londini Artium*, A3r. [26] Heywood, *Londini Artium*, A4v.
[27] Francis Kynaston, *Corona Minervae* (London: William Sheares, 1635).

action, and the Theorie of liberall Arts into more frequent practise', but Kynaston also contended that such an institutional arrangement was desirable so 'that *England* may be as well furnished for the vertuous education, and discipline of her own Natives, as any other Nation of *Europe*'.²⁸ Here education is figured as a means of advancing native knowledge rather than creating an open market for foreigners. Arguing for Gresham College as a forerunner of the Royal Society, Francis Johnson dismissed Kynaston's royalist venture and his 'six professorships of Medicine, Languages, Astronomy, Geometry, Music, and Fencing' rather too readily as an irrelevance, the outbreak of civil war having scuppered Kynaston's plans.²⁹ But if we look at what Kynaston intended for his Covent Garden College for the Education of the Nobility, it looks fairly substantial and not so far removed from Milton's fusion of commerce and conceptual knowledge.³⁰ Kynaston's knightly museum never saw the light of day, but light was dawning elsewhere.

Filthy Lucre: From Royal Exchange to Royal Society

In his famous treatise on knowledge, Francis Bacon placed learning before lucre:

> For many have entred into a desire of Learning and Knowledge, some upon an imbred and restlesse *Curiosity;* ... others for *Lucre* and living; few to improve the gift of reason given them from God, to the benefite and use of men.³¹

However, the Bacon-inspired Hartlib Circle – 'not a tight-knit group but an affiliation of like-minded participants in overlapping correspondence and patronage networks' – embarked on its own adventures in etymology and 'lucriferous' learning.³² Following the fortunes of this pun, as Kevin

---

[28] Francis Kynaston, *The Constitutions of the Musæum Minervæ* (London: Thomas Spencer, 1636), Sig. 3. On Kynaston's contribution to courtly education, see Richard Cust, 'Charles I's Noble Academy', *The Seventeenth Century*, 29.4 (2014), 337–57.

[29] Johnson, p. 424.

[30] Kynaston, *Constitutions*, pp. 4–6. Kynaston's was one of a series of aristocratic initiatives. Earlier, under James I, Edmund Bolton had tried to establish an 'Academ Roial'. F. H. Thompson, 'The Society of Antiquaries of London: Its History and Activities', *Proceedings of the Massachusetts Historical Society*, 93 (1981), 1–16 (p. 4).

[31] Francis Bacon, *Of the Advancement and Proficience of Learning; or, the Partitions of Sciences* (Oxford: Leon Lichfield for Robert Young and Edward Forrest, 1640), p. 39.

[32] Ted McCormick, 'Food, Population, and Empire in the Hartlib Circle, 1639–1660', *Osiris*, 35.1 (2020), 60–83 (p. 61).

Dunn observes, reveals just how invested the new science was in making money:

> The Latin original of 'Lucriferous' – *lucriferum*, or 'lucre bearing' – is so uncommon that Hartlib's word seems likely to have been formed on a punning analogy to 'luciferous', 'light bearing', a Baconian key word. Criticizing those who would turn prematurely to profit taking ... Bacon writes in the Preface to the *Instauratio magna*, 'fructifera (inquam) experimenta, non lucifera, quaesivit'. The *Oxford English Dictionary* first records 'lucriferous' in 1648, in William Petty's *Advice ... to Mr. Samuel Hartlib*, and the brief life of this semantic unit coincides entirely with the efforts of Petty, Hartlib, Dury and others to identify more fully the Baconian project of scientific collaboration in the public interest with economic theories that private enrichment could serve the public good.[33]

'Lucriferous' – 'Bringing gain; lucrative, profitable' (*OED*) – captures beautifully that distinctive fusion of enlightenment and entrepreneurialism that characterised what Daniel Defoe called 'The Projecting Age'.[34] This neologism, fresh-minted as Dunn says when Sir William Petty deployed it in advice addressed to Hartlib, quickly took hold within the emerging scientific community: 'Schollers now disesteemed for their Poverty ... and unable even for want of lively-hood, to perfect any thing even in their own way, would quickly help themselves, by opening Treasures, with the Key of Lucriferous Inventions'.[35] Petty believed in making use of people and things, as he elaborates in his advice:

> The Compilers first scope in Inventions shall bee, how to apply all Materials that grow in Abundance in this Kingdome, and whereof but in considerable use and Profits are as yet made to more advantage to the Common-wealth. And also how all Impotents, whether onely blind, or onely lame, and all Children of above seven yeares old might earne their bread, and not be so long burdensome to their Parents and others.

---

[33] Kevin Dunn, 'Milton Among the Monopolists: *Areopagitica*, Intellectual Property and the Hartlib Circle', in *Samuel Hartlib and Universal Reformation: Studies in Intellectual Communication*, ed. by Mark Greengrass, Michael Leslie, and Timothy Raylor (Cambridge: Cambridge University Press, 1994), pp. 177–92 (pp. 180–81). On Hartlib's legacy, see Mark Greengrass, 'Interfacing Samuel Hartlib', *History Today*, 43 (1993), 45–49 and Leigh T. I. Penman, 'Omnium Exposita Rapinæ: The Afterlives of the Papers of Samuel Hartlib', *Book History*, 19.1 (2016), 1–65. On Dury's 1650 vision of the ideal library, see Catherine J. Minter, 'John Dury's *Reformed Librarie-Keeper*: Information and its Intellectual Contexts in Seventeenth-Century England', *Library & Information History*, 31.1 (2015), 18–34.

[34] Daniel Defoe, *An Essay upon Projects* (London: R. R. for Thomas Cockerill, 1697), p. 1.

[35] William Petty, *The Advice of W. P. to Mr. Samuel Hartlib for the Advancement of Some Particular Parts of Learning* (London: [n. pub.], 1647 [i.e. 1648]), p. 23. Text mispaginated; numbers given as they appear.

> There should be made a Preface to the Worke to teach men how to make the most of experiments and to record the successes of them whatsoever, whether according to hopes or no, all being equally Luciferous, although not equally Lucriferous.[36]

One can see where Swift got the idea for *A Modest Proposal*, and, as we shall discover, satires of the projecting age appeared at an early stage, almost in step with the projectors themselves.[37]

The word subsequently appeared in the title of a text attributed to Hartlib, where a link was made between colonial ventures and an Office of Address:

> Whosoever shall have relation to *Virginia*, the *Barbadoes*, New *England*, or any other Countrie inhabited with English, or shall have cause to send into any of those places, or would inhabit, or transplant himself into those parts, he may have all intelligence and expedients, with as much conveniency as may be.[38]

In an idolatrous passage vindicating the importance of lodestones, Robert Boyle exalts 'Lucriferousness' as a way of selling science to the state:

> if we impartially consider the Lucriferousness (if I may speak in my Lord of *St Albans* Stile) of the properties of Things, and their Medical Virtues, we shall finde, That we trample upon many things, for which we should have cause to kneel, and offer God Praises, if we knew all their Qualities and Uses.[39]

On 18 May 1669, Isaac Newton wrote offering advice to Francis Aston before the latter travelled abroad:

> Observe the products of nature in severall places especially in mines wth ye circumstances of mining & of extracting metalls and mineralls out of their

---

[36] Petty, p. 20. On Petty's proposal for institutions as 'literary work-houses', see Walter E. Houghton, 'The History of Trades: Its Relation to Seventeenth-Century Thought: As Seen in Bacon, Petty, Evelyn, and Boyle', *Journal of the History of Ideas*, 2.1 (1941), 33–60 (p. 43).

[37] On Swift, see David Alff, 'Swift's Solar Gourds and the Rhetoric of Projection', *Eighteenth-Century Studies*, 47.3 (2014), 245–60 and J. M. Treadwell, 'Jonathan Swift: The Satirist as Projector', *Texas Studies in Literature and Language*, 17.2 (1975), 439–60. For a nuanced treatment of projecting as indebted both to public good and private greed, see Mordechai Feingold, 'Projectors and Learned Projects in Early Modern England', *The Seventeenth Century*, 32.1 (2017), 63–79.

[38] Samuel Hartlib, *Cornu Copia, a Miscellanium of Lucriferous and Most Fructiferous Experiments, Observations and Discoveries* (London: [n. pub.], 1652), p. 16. See Thomas Leng, '"A Potent Plantation Well Armed and Policeed": Huguenots, the Hartlib Circle, and British Colonization in the 1640s', *The William and Mary Quarterly*, 66.1 (2009), 173–94 and Patrick McCabe, 'Samuel Hartlib: A Polish Promoter of Colonial Settlement in Ireland', *Seanchas Ardmhacha: Journal of the Armagh Diocesan Historical Society*, 19.2 (2003), 74–76.

[39] Robert Boyle, *Some Considerations Touching the Usefulnesse of Experimental Naturall Philosophy* (Oxford: Henry Hall for Richard Davis, 1663), p. 45.

oare... being ye most luciferous & many times lucriferous experiments... in Philosophy.[40]

Finally, Sir Hans Sloane, Irish physician, naturalist and collector, whose unique archive formed a cornerstone of the British Museum and who, being from Ulster-Scottish settler stock, knew a thing or two about plantations, used the coinage in *A Voyage to the Islands* (1707):

> The Blacks from the *East-Indies* are fed on Flesh and Fish at Home... and those from *Angola* run away from their Masters, and fancy on their deaths they are going Home again, which is no lucriferous Experiment, for on hard usage they kill themselves.[41]

These were the economic and imperialist underpinnings of the new learning, and the Royal Society drew on the rich veins of knowledge laid out by Hartlib and others.

Gresham College, part of the older distributed framework, provided the Royal Society with its first meeting place on 28 November 1660. By playing host, Gresham College 'helped the Royal Society through its crisis years' but suffered itself as a result as the new body shed the skin of the old.[42]

Christopher Hill cites Thomas Sprat's remark in his 1667 *History of the Royal-Society* that if Gresham College 'were beyond sea, it might well pass for a university' while also stressing that 'The Royal Society, the title of Sprat's book reminds us, was the Royal Society *of London*'.[43] But what does '*of London*' mean when the makeup of the original membership of the Royal Society covered the archipelago and when its interests lay, as Sprat insists in the same passage, 'in things forein, & Native'?[44] What Michael Hunter in his *ODNB* entry on the 'Founder members of the Royal Society' calls 'the foundational twelve' included two who were Irish by birth – Robert Boyle and William Brouncker. Another, William Petty, had considerable experience in Ireland. Both Boyle and Petty were key players in

---

[40] *The Correspondence of Isaac Newton*, vol. 1, 1661–1675, ed. by H. W. Turnbull (Cambridge: Cambridge University Press, 1959), p. 10.

[41] Hans Sloane, *A Voyage to the Islands*, vol. 1 (London: B. M., 1707), p. liii. See Kay Dian Kriz, 'Curiosities, Commodities, and Transplanted Bodies in Hans Sloane's *Natural History of Jamaica*', *The William and Mary Quarterly*, 57.1 (2000), 35–78 and David Buisseret, 'Studying the Natural Sciences in Seventeenth-Century Jamaica', *Caribbean Quarterly*, 55.3 (2009), 71–86.

[42] Ian Adamson, 'The Royal Society and Gresham College 1660–1711', *Notes and Records of the Royal Society of London*, 33.1 (1978), 1–21 (p. 15).

[43] Christopher Hill, *Intellectual Origins of the English Revolution* (Oxford: Clarendon Press, 1965; repr. 1980), p. 63; emphasis in original.

[44] Thomas Sprat, *The History of the Royal-Society of London for the Improving of Natural Knowledge* (London: T. R. for J. Martyn, 1667), p. 89.

the Irish wing of the Hartlib Circle. There were two Scottish members of the Royal Society: Alexander Bruce, the St Andrews-educated 2nd Earl of Kincardine, who had previously collaborated in Hamburg 'in attempts to devise a pendulum clock that could be used at sea to determine longitude', and Sir Robert Moray of Craigie in Perthshire, another well-travelled Scot with interests in maths, science and engineering. Jonathan Goddard was asked by Cromwell to serve as physician-in-chief to the army in Ireland and later served as physician to Cromwell in Scotland, 'where he helped him get through a serious illness'.[45] The Royal Society's founders thus aimed at 'the creation of a social basis for the institutionalized pursuit of natural philosophy', using the British peripheries as testing grounds for both theories and infrastructures.[46]

The archipelagic and Atlantic origins of the Royal Society reveal the extent to which it developed out of an internationalisation agenda established in Gresham College, the Invisible College and the Hartlib Circle, whose Irish branch was especially active, and in Hartlib's idea for an Office of Address, floated in the 1640s, based on the *bureau d'adresse* operated in Paris by Théophraste Renaudot.[47] Hartlib envisaged the Office of Address as 'a kind of central intelligence agency'.[48] Continental counterparts like Johannes Amos Comenius were initially sceptical about Hartlib's Office of Address, seeing it as less an international community of scholars than an attempt to install an English controlling interest in knowledge exchange.[49] The Office in its first unveiling looks like a small ads section writ large: 'a

---

[45] Michael Hunter, 'Founder Members of the Royal Society (act. 1660–1663)', *ODNB*. See also by the same author 'The Social Basis and Changing Fortunes of an Early Scientific Institution: An Analysis of the Membership of the Royal Society, 1660–1685', *Notes and Records of the Royal Society of London*, 31.1 (1976), 9–114.

[46] P. B. Wood, 'Methodology and Apologetics: Thomas Sprat's *History of the Royal Society*', *The British Journal for the History of Science*, 13.1 (1980), 1–26 (p. 1).

[47] See Raymond Phineas Stearns, 'Colonial Fellows of the Royal Society of London, 1661–1788', *The William and Mary Quarterly*, 3.2 (1946), 208–68. For the later colonial history, see R. W. Home, 'The Royal Society and the Empire: The Colonial and Commonwealth Fellowship Part 1. 1731–1847', *Notes and Records of the Royal Society of London*, 56.3 (2002), 307–32 and 'The Royal Society and the Empire: The Colonial and Commonwealth Fellowship Part 2. After 1847', *Notes and Records of the Royal Society of London*, 57.1 (2003), 47–84.

[48] John James O'Brien, 'The International Educational Interests of Robert Boyle', *Comparative Education Review*, 9.2 (1965), 195–200 (p. 196). O'Brien notes that there were two Offices of Address: 'The Office of Address for Accommodations was to be set up in London to look after the welfare of the poor, whereas the Office of Address for Communications was to be set up at Oxford and would deal with religious matters, the advancement of learning, and new inventions' (p. 196).

[49] Vladimír Urbánek, 'J. A. Comenius and the Practice of Correspondence Networking: Between the Office of Address and the Collegium Lucis', in *Gewalt sei ferne den Dingen! Contemporary Perspectives on the Works of John Amos Comenius*, ed. by Wouter Goris, Meinert A. Meyer, and Vladimír Urbánek (Fachmedien Wiesbaden: Springer, 2016), pp. 291–308 (pp. 305–06). For

Certaine Place should be designed by the Authority of the State, whereunto all Men might freely come to give Information of the Commodities which they have to be imparted unto others'.[50] This directory or registry of expertise, as an employment and information exchange, connected people and things, and periphery with centre, making readily available 'the kinds of information now found in a range of yearbooks and directories (including *Who's Whos*) that are the staple of ready reference sections of every modern public library'.[51] As Hartlib elaborated elsewhere, the Office enabled remote access to research:

> if any man living remote, shall be able to discover any material thing ... advantageous to the publick, or to himself, not being able to repair to *London*, to advance his designe ... he may have all prevalent advantages effectually pursued to promote the execution thereof, without putting himselfe to the charge of a great journy at adventure.[52]

The Royal Society in this sense was less metropolitan than it appears, with regional hubs, international correspondence and distance learning integral to its formation.[53]

The Office of Address was soon the subject of satire. In one coffee house comedy, a customer reads out the news:

> Here's an Advertisement of a Citizens Daughter of 17 handfull High, and 18 years of Age, who went without the Walls to drink Red-Cowes milk: 'tis fear'd she has stray'd among some of the neighbouring Parks. If any Male or Female Keepers of the said Chases will bring Notice of her to the Office of Address, they shall be honestly rewarded.[54]

The misogyny of contemporaries notwithstanding, the collaborative knowledge networks of Hartlib and others opened up a world where engagement mattered more than entitlement. The Hartlib Circle included

---

Hartlib's role in promoting Comenius in London, see Dorothy Stimson, 'Comenius and the Invisible College', *Isis*, 23.2 (1935), 373–88 (pp. 374–76).

[50] [Samuel Hartlib], *Considerations Tending to the Happy Accomplishment of Englands Reformation in Church and State* ([London: n. pub.], 1647), p. 37.

[51] W. Boyd Rayward, 'Some Schemes for Restructuring and Mobilising Information in Documents: A Historical Perspective', *Information Processing & Management*, 30.2 (1994), 163–75 (p. 166).

[52] Hartlib, *Cornu Copia*, p. 15.

[53] For later developments aimed at challenging a perceived metropolitan monopoly on knowledge, see Jon Mee and Jennifer Wilkes, 'Transpennine Enlightenment: The Literary and Philosophical Societies and Knowledge Networks in the North, 1781–1830', *Journal for Eighteenth-Century Studies*, 38.4 (2015), 599–612.

[54] Thomas St Serfe, *Tarugo's Wiles, or, the Coffee-House a Comedy* (London: Henry Herringman, 1668), p. 25. For an excellent discussion, see Jessica Reid, 'L'Écosse à l'envers: Scotland's Restoration Pamphleteer Thomas St Serfe', *Scottish Literary Review*, 12.1 (2020), 109–22 (pp. 112–14).

influential women such as Katherine Jones (Lady Ranelagh) and Dorothy Moore Dury, both part of the Irish scene, as well as pioneering Dutch thinkers like Anna Maria van Schurman.[55] Jones, sister of Robert Boyle, had her own hub connected to Hartlib's scriptorium.[56] Defending women's right to study, van Schurman, the first female student on the continent, answered the objection that 'The studies of Learning are not convenient for those that are destitute of means necessary to their studies', and thus women are excluded, by pointing out that while 'there be no Academies and Colledges, wherein they may exercise themselves ... they may exercise themselves at home'.[57] Emerging distributed networks thus held out the promise of kinds of access previously denied by spatial distance and older forms of institutional gatekeeping.

London to Leiden: The Fourth University?

Schurman attended lectures at Utrecht from its founding in 1636 – behind a screen so as not to distract her fellow students – but it was another Dutch university that impacted on developments across the North Sea. The Irish branch of the Hartlib circle, those Baconian protestant improvers whose various members included Arnold and Gerard Boate, Robert Boyle, Robert Child, John Durie, Myles Symner, William Petty, Robert Wood and Benjamin Worsley, had connections to Leiden University, a seedbed for the application of innovations in natural history to the Dutch colonies.[58]

---

[55] See Evan Bourke, 'Female Involvement, Membership, and Centrality: A Social Network Analysis of the Hartlib Circle', *Literature Compass*, 14.4 (2017), 1–17; Ruth Connolly, 'Viscountess Ranelagh and the Authorisation of Women's Knowledge in the Hartlib Circle', in *The Intellectual Culture of Puritan Women, 1558–1680*, ed. by Johanna Harris and Elizabeth Scott-Baumann (London: Palgrave Macmillan, 2010), pp. 150–61; David Norbrook, 'Autonomy and the Republic of Letters: Michèle Le Dœuff, Anna Maria van Schurman, and the History of Women Intellectuals', *Australian Journal of French Studies*, 40.3 (2003), 275–87 and Carol Pal, 'Accidental Archive: Samuel Hartlib and the Afterlife of Female Scholars', in *Archival Afterlives: Life, Death, and Knowledge-Making in Early Modern British Scientific and Medical Archives*, ed. by Vera Keller, Anna Marie Roos, and Elizabeth Yale (Leiden: Brill, 2019), pp. 120–49.

[56] Lynette Hunter, 'Sisters of the Royal Society: The Circle of Katherine Jones, Lady Ranelagh', in *Women, Science and Medicine 1500–1700: Mothers and Sisters of the Royal Society*, ed. by Lynette Hunter and Sarah Hutton (Stroud: Sutton, 1997), pp. 178–97 (p. 179).

[57] Anna Maria van Schurman, *The Learned Maid; or, Whether a Maid May Be a Scholar? A Logick Exercise* (London: John Redmayne, 1659), pp. 28–29.

[58] For a robust discussion of Bacon's ingenious secularising of nature, see Mordechai Feingold, '"And Knowledge Shall Be Increased": Millenarianism and the Advancement of Learning Revisited', *The Seventeenth Century*, 28.4 (2013), 363–93. Arnold Boate published *An Interrogatory Relating More Particularly to the Husbandry and Naturall History of Ireland* as an appendix to the second edition of *Samuel Hartlib His Legacie* (London: Richard Wodenothe, 1652), making him a pioneer in posting the first 'English' research questionnaire. See Adam Fox, 'Printed Questionnaires, Research

Founded in 1575 by William of Orange as a reward for withstanding the Spanish siege in 1573–4, Leiden proved a major locus of learning, almost a challenger for England's 'third university', certainly a prototype for those arguing for a university of London.[59] Well into the eighteenth century, Leiden University was where enterprising British students went for medical and scientific learning. Stan Mendyk says of Leiden:

> It is significant that this university, and the Dutch in general, were now beginning to attempt the systematic natural history of their equatorial colonies. Fieldwork was carried out notably in Brazil (from 1637 to 1644) and the results were published. Such early research into natural phenomena had its effect on [Gerard] Boate and his work on Ireland was of a similar type.[60]

Influential figures in the new learning studied medicine at Leiden: Edmund Borlase, Robert Child, Nathaniel Henshaw, William Petty and John Durie (who wrote the dedication to Boate's *Naturall History* under Hartlib's name). The Boate brothers' Leiden connections offer insights into the workings of colonialism, the limits of archipelagic history and the impact of Dutch intellectual culture on English colonial theory and practice. Innovation, interdisciplinarity and internationalisation characterise the brothers' shared activities. Building on important work by Keith Hoppen, Charles Webster and Toby Barnard, Nicholas Canny and Patricia Coughlan have emphasised the colonial context of the Boates' work.[61] Canny opens up an Atlantic dimension that embraces figures such as Robert Child and Balthazar Gerbier, while Coughlan sheds light on the colonialist assumptions of English scientists based in Ireland. Canny, recognising *Ireland's Naturall History* as 'a work of propaganda', pushes back the origins of the interest in colonial husbandry as far as agriculturalist and entrepreneur Robert Payne and Phane Beecher in the 1580s, but we could go back further still to Barnabe Googe in the 1570s and a work on farming and planting that was later applied to Massachusetts in the seventeenth century.[62] If Ireland –

Networks, and the Discovery of the British Isles, 1650–1800', *The Historical Journal*, 53.3 (2010), 593–621 (pp. 595–96).

[59] See Daniela Prögler, *English Students at Leiden University, 1575–1650* (London: Routledge, 2016).
[60] S. Mendyk, 'Gerard Boate and *Irelands Naturall History*', *The Journal of the Royal Society of Antiquaries of Ireland*, 115 (1985), 5–12 (p. 5).
[61] Nicholas Canny, 'Migration and Opportunity: Britain, Ireland and the New World', *Irish Economic and Social History*, 12 (1985), 7–32; Patricia Coughlan, 'Natural History and Historical Nature: The Project for a Natural History of Ireland', in *Samuel Hartlib and Universal Reformation*, ed. by Greengrass, Leslie, and Raylor, pp. 298–317.
[62] Canny, pp. 15, 25; Barnabe Googe, *Foure Bookes of Husbandrie* (London: Richard Watkins, 1577). Googe's pioneering work on agriculture impacted directly on Ireland and America, where experimental approaches to cultivation were more easily introduced. See William S. Powell, 'Books in the Virginia Colony before 1624', *The William and Mary Quarterly*, 5.2 (1948), 177–84 (pp. 179–80).

and New England – furnishes evidence of experimentation undertaken by improvers and projectors, then the advancement of knowledge in colonial contexts was intimately intertwined with political intelligence and economic exploitation. Knowledge exchange is not only implicated in empire, it is also advanced there.[63] Indeed, 'the problems and challenges faced by Europeans in the process of exploring and understanding the New World ... created a new context for the emergence of empirical and collaborative procedures to solve technical problems'.[64] Agricultural, medical and scientific advances were trialled in the field, and the colonies provided the ideal testing ground for new approaches and methods. As Brant Vogel notes, 'The English "cult of improvement" had already made climate changeability a commonplace notion in lands close to home.'[65] Colonialism played a triple role: as site of experimentation, source of income and birthplace of some of the most radical innovators and projectors – Robert Boyle being a notable example.

Parodying Projectors and Patentees

According to Koji Yamamoto, 'The terms "project" and "projector" came into circulation in response to a wave of technology transfer and economic improvements schemes that emerged in the later sixteenth century.'[66] This wave soon broke on the shore of satire: 'The projector or projectress as a popular character ... emerged between 1600 and 1630, along with the genre of character study itself.'[67] Parodying projectors became a pastime for playwrights and pamphleteers, which is why the Hartlib Circle, despite its own lucriferous leanings, presented its activities as part of a reforming impulse rather than being harnessed to the profit motive. In this light, John Milton's treatment of the projector is paradoxical. Having borrowed the language of 'card and compass' used by the new geographers in an extended metaphor of

---

[63] For the applicability of the 'truism that science was handmaid to empire' to an earlier period than is traditionally acknowledged, see Joyce Chaplin, 'The Natural History of British Imperialism', *Journal of British Studies*, 42.1 (2003), 127–31 (p. 127).

[64] Antonio Barrera-Osorio, 'Experts, Nature, and the Making of Atlantic Empiricism', *Osiris*, 25.1 (2010), 129–48 (p. 130).

[65] Brant Vogel, 'The Letter from Dublin: Climate Change, Colonialism, and the Royal Society in the Seventeenth Century', *Osiris*, 26.1 (2011), 111–28 (pp. 127–28).

[66] Koji Yamamoto, 'Reformation and the Distrust of the Projector in the Hartlib Circle', *The Historical Journal*, 55.2 (2012), 375–97 (p. 379).

[67] Jessica Ratcliff, 'Art to Cheat the Common-Weale: Inventors, Projectors, and Patentees in English Satire, ca. 1630–70', *Technology and Culture*, 53.2 (2012), 337–65 (p. 343).

surveying in his depiction of Paradise in the opening gambit of *The Reason of Church-Governement*, Milton goes on to decry clerical innovators: 'So far is it from the kenne of these wretched projectors of ours that bescraull their Pamflets every day with new formes of government for our Church.'[68] Milton could not have had in mind Hartlib's *Considerations Tending to the Happy Accomplishment of England's Reformation in Church and State*, which would not be published for another five years, but his point proves how thin the line between innovation and obfuscation was. What Hartlib and his collaborators objected to was monopoly in all its forms, like projectors stifling innovation by securing patents. What Milton abhorred was 'the outrageous desire of filthy lucre' in the church.[69] The separation of church and state that Milton argued for was slow to materialise – as he acknowledged in two pamphlets published in 1659, *Considerations Touching the Likeliest Means to Remove Hirelings out of the Church* and *A Treatise of Civil Power in Ecclesiastical Causes* – and the problem of patents persisted through to the bursting of the South Sea Bubble in 1720, when the Bubble Act called a halt to their luciferous lure.[70]

Between Ben Jonson's *The Devil Is an Ass* (1616) and Swift's *Modest Proposal* (1729), there was a century of satire on projectors. In one such lampoon, Thomas Heywood caricatures the projector as

> one whose Arse makes buttons by the Bushell at the noyse of a Parliament, more than the *Scots* do at the noyse of *English* Drummes, and hath wrought under hand with Seminaries and Jesuites like a Mole, to set dissention beteweene the two Kingdomes, on purpose that hee avoyd a Parliament, and hath gotten a Patent or Grant of all the Blew Bonnets that are taken in the first battell; but meanes not to be there himselfe, but stay behind, and engrosse all the Carrots and Parsnips that comes to *London*, to make Dildoes for the Citizens wives, old maidens, and poore whores that staid behind the Progresse.[71]

Slight though it seems, there is an edge to these observations. In *Machiavel's Ghost*, Heywood runs through all the commodities seized upon by patentees. The list includes '*The Tobacco Projectors*', who

---

[68] John Milton, *The Reason of Church-Governement* (London: John Rothwell, 1641 [i.e. 1642]), p. 4.
[69] Milton, *Reason of Church-Governement*, p. 63.
[70] Christine MacLeod, 'The 1690s Patents Boom: Invention or Stock-Jobbing?', *The Economic History Review*, 39.4 (1986), 549–71 (p. 571).
[71] Thomas Heywood, *Machiavel's Ghost: As He Lately Appeared to His Deare Sons, the Modern Projectors* (London: J. O. for Francis Constable, 1641), C3r.

[a]re great foes to Plantations: ... Most gentlemen tooke them in snuffe: nay, some had a project upon their bodies, viz. to beate them to sneezing powder, and transport them into *Ireland*. The Countrie Ale-wives curses has seased them, for 'tis thought, their Roll is rotten, and their pricke Tobacco even in the pipe putrified: so that they will bee smoaked themselves.[72]

Richard Brome's *Covent Garden Weeded* and *The New Academy* are further examples of the genre.[73] John Taylor's woodcut speech-bubble exchange between Tenter-Hooke and Dodger illustrates the kind of broadsheet circulating at the time:

> I have brought money to fill your Chest,
> For which I am curst by most and least.
>
> Ov'r many yeares scraping is left at a clap,
> All thou hast gotten by others mishap.[74]

John Wilson's comedy drama *The Projectors* (1665) has a revealing exchange about the fraudulent uses of scholarship:

> *Jocose.* I know thou hast been bred a Schollar, and thy invention not ill: – But canst thou Cant?
> *Driver.* How think you Sir, – Suppose I should tell him I had studied the *Emporeuticks, Lemnicks, Camnicks*, and *Plegnicks*, could demonstrate the *Minimum quod sit*, of *Homocrecious*, and *Heterocrasious*; and stripping *Materia Prima* to her smock, discover the most private recesses, and occult qualities, of *Ignicadrillica, Metallorgonica, Euricatactica*, and *Hydropanta pressoria*, Do you believe (I say) he would be able to understand more of it, than I do my self, which is just nothing? If you call this Canting, let me alone with him.
> *Jocose.* Excellent! – Then to subdivide 'um into as undemonstrable (yet seemingly probable) Projects, – We shall make such sport![75]

However, there was a serious side to this sport, a side to which writers such as Defoe and Swift were attuned: war and the pursuit of empire.

Studying War

The link between knowledge, war and empire cannot be overestimated, and in the early modern period, scholars applied themselves to military

---

[72] Heywood, *Machiavel's Ghost*, D1r.
[73] Richard Brome, *Five New Playes* (London: A. Crook and H. Brome, 1659).
[74] John Taylor, *The Complaint of M. Tenter-Hooke the Proiector, and Sir Thomas Dodger the Patentee* (London: Elizabeth Purslowe for Francis Coles, 1641).
[75] John Wilson, *The Projectors: A Comedy* (London: John Playfere and William Crook, 1665), p. 6.

strategy as a source of funding and employment.[76] Josias Bodley, son of merchant-turned-publisher John Bodley, after studying in Geneva and Oxford, served in Ireland as a surveyor from 1598.[77] Expert in mapmaking and military fortification, on a trip home to England in 1602 he 'donated a quadrant, an astronomical sphere, and other brass instruments, all signs of his mathematical and engineering skills, to the Bodleian Library in Oxford', newly founded by his older brother Thomas, a fitting gift from one enterprising son to another.

Daniel Defoe's *An Essay Upon Projects* (1697) takes aim at innovators with an eye to a quick profit and identifies the influence of the nascent military-industrial complex in knowledge exchange. Defoe declares his to be the age of projects: 'Necessity, which is allow'd to be the Mother of Invention, has so violently agitated the Wits of men at this time, that it seems not at all improper, by way of distinction, to call it, The Projecting Age.'[78] Defoe spells out exactly what the mother of invention gives birth to:

> The Art of War, which I take to be the highest Perfection of Human Knowledge, is a sufficient Proof of what I say, especially in conducting Armies, and in offensive Engines; *witness* the new ways of Mines, Fougades, Entrenchments, Attacks, Elodgments, and a long *Et Cetera* of New Inventions which want Names, practised in Sieges and Encampments; *witness* the new sorts of Bombs and unheard-of Mortars, of Seven to Ten Ton Weight, with which our Fleets standing two or three Miles off at Sea, can imitate God Almighty himself, and rain *Fire and Brimstone* out of Heaven, as it were, upon Towns built on the firm Land; *witness also* our new-invented *Child of Hell*, the Machine, which carries Thunder, Lightning, and Earthquakes in its Bowels, and tears up the most impregnable Fortifications.[79]

Defoe adds another layer of irony: the money-grubbing merchants now supporting the arms industry are those whose mistakes led to so much loss in the late war with France, so that the mother of invention gives birth not just to the child of hell but to 'Abortions of the Brain'.[80] Defoe links innovation with poverty and inequality, as well as with military conflict:

> an incredible number of the best Merchants in the Kingdom sunk under the Load. ... These, prompted by Necessity, rack their Wits for New

---

[76] Lisa Jardine and Anthony Grafton, '"Studied for Action": How Gabriel Harvey Read His Livy', *Past and Present*, 129 (1990), 30–78.
[77] J. J. N. McGurk, 'Bodley, Sir Josias (c.1550–1617)', *ODNB*.   [78] Defoe, p. 1.
[79] Defoe, pp. 3–4.
[80] Defoe, p. 4. On the 'morally ambivalent figure of the "projector"', see Vera Keller and Ted McCormick, 'Towards a History of Projects', *Early Science and Medicine*, 21.5 (2016), 423–44.

Contrivances, New Inventions, New Trades, Stocks, Projects, and any thing to retrieve the desperate Credit of their Fortunes.[81]

Knowledge is not only implicated in empire; it is advanced there.[82] There are two chapters on bogs in Gerard Boate's *Naturall History*, including one on the 'Originall of the Bogs in Ireland; and the manner of Draining them practiced there by the English inhabitants'.[83] Ireland's wetness was an issue for colonists, especially those interested in how cultivation and deforestation could affect the weather.

There is no bog without flies. Mathematician John Wallis, writing to Robert Boyle in 1669, one Fellow of the Royal Society to another, quoted from 'a long oration of satirical invectives against Cromwell, fanaticks and the new philosophy' by Robert South, Prebendary of Westminster, canon of Christ Church and Public Orator of the University of Oxford, including the choice line 'They can admire nothing except fleas, flies and themselves.'[84] Elsewhere, South remarked: 'The Church is a Royal Society for settling old things, and not for finding out new.'[85] What can we make of fleas and flies? Margaret Cavendish, the first woman to attend a meeting of the Royal Society – on 30 May 1667 – saw several experiments conducted there.[86] In her pioneering prose fantasy, *The Blazing World* (1666), Cavendish has her Bear-Men seek to impress the empress with their microscopes, magnifying fleas and lice:

> But after the Empress had seen the shapes of these monstrous Creatures, she desir'd to know whether their Microscopes could hinder their biting, or at least shew some means how to avoid them? To which they answered, That such Arts were mechanical and below the noble study of Microscopical observations.[87]

So much for science, at least as practiced by Bear-Men. Coincidentally, while researching the Boates in Cambridge in the summer of 2016, I came across

---

[81] Defoe, pp. 5–6.
[82] On the Royal Society and empire, see John Gascoigne, 'The Royal Society, Natural History and the Peoples of the "New World(s)", 1660–1800', *The British Journal for the History of Science*, 42.4 (2009), 539–62 and Stearns, pp. 208–68.
[83] Gerard Boate, *Irelands Naturall History* (London: John Wright, 1652), pp. 112–17.
[84] Gerald Weissmann, 'Academic Boycotts and the Invisible College', *The FASEB Journal*, 21 (2007), 3017–20 (p. 3017); R. H. Syfret, 'Some Early Reactions to the Royal Society', *Notes and Records of the Royal Society of London*, 7.2 (1950), 207–58 (pp. 240–41).
[85] Syfret, p. 242.
[86] Samuel I. Mintz, 'The Duchess of Newcastle's Visit to the Royal Society', *The Journal of English and Germanic Philology*, 51.2 (1952), 168–76.
[87] Margaret Cavendish, Duchess of Newcastle, *The Description of a New World, called the Blazing World* (London: A. Maxwell, 1666), pp. 31–32.

a copy of that university's *Research Horizons*. It contained a fascinating article titled 'Think Small', about research into 'the hunting behaviours of various flying insects [primarily dragonflies and killer flies] to determine how their visual systems influence their attack strategy, and what sorts of trade-offs they have to make in order to be successful'.[88] This research was funded by the US Air Force. It seems a long way from drains to drones, or from bogs to bombs, but the targeted removal of native populations is common to both. It's all about empire, empiricism and impact.[89] It is indeed 'lucriferous' – the word may have died but the drive lives on, fuelled as ever by filthy lucre.[90] Institutions are less independent than they might imagine, with the state – domestic and foreign – exerting its influence. We remain suspended between Buck and Defoe, between a broad vision of a civic university and a profitable enterprise in the service of war and empire.

---

[88] Paloma Gonzalez-Bellido, Guillaume Hennequin, and Simon Laughlin, 'Think Small', *Research Horizons: Pioneering Research from the University of Cambridge*, 29 (2016), 24–25 (p. 25).

[89] For an intriguing sidelight on institutional input into a notorious seventeenth-century colonial venture, see C. P. Finlayson, 'Edinburgh University and the Darien Scheme', *The Scottish Historical Review*, 34.118 (1955), 97–102.

[90] See Marion Hersh, 'Ethics, Scientists, Engineers and the Military', in *Ethical Engineering for International Development and Environmental Sustainability*, ed. by Marion Hersh (London: Springer, 2015), pp. 325–60.

CHAPTER 2

'Supporting Mutual Benevolence'
Libraries, Civic Benefaction, and the Spalding Gentlemen's Society, 1709–1755

Dustin M. Frazier Wood

Introduction

The Spalding Gentlemen's Society (SGS), founded by the lawyer and antiquary Maurice Johnson II (1688–1755) in Spalding, Lincolnshire in 1710, has come to renewed and long overdue attention in recent years. The range and variety of its membership, its role in fostering antiquarian and scientific research, its institutional connections with the Royal Society and Society of Antiquaries of London and its exemplarity as a provincial instance of Enlightenment polite sociability have all come under examination.[1] The traditional narrative of the SGS's history was published by John Nichols in the late eighteenth century. It presents the SGS as a model of intellectual sociability and an important node in the antiquarian and natural philosophical knowledge networks of the first half of the eighteenth century. This narrative has also come under scrutiny, leading to fresh assessments of the SGS's relationship with contemporary institutions and new lines of inquiry into its activities in Spalding and the surrounding region. Among the most important of these is the composition and use of the SGS's library, archive and museum collections, originally referred to along with the physical space that housed them, as the Society's 'Musæum'. These collections have received scant attention relative to accounts of the Society's more illustrious members, despite the crucial role played by the books, specimens, instruments and other objects gathered, housed, organised and used by SGS members in their fashioning

---

[1] Michael Honeybone, 'The Spalding Gentlemen's Society: The Communication of Science in the East Midlands of England, 1710–1760' (unpublished doctoral thesis, Open University, 2001), pp. 359–76; Rosemary Sweet, *Antiquaries: The Discovery of the Past in Eighteenth-Century Britain* (London: Hambleden and London, 2004), pp. 114–16; Valerie Rumbold, 'Reading *The Tatler* in 1710: Polite Print and the Spalding Gentlemen's Society', *Eighteenth-Century Life*, 40 (2016), 1–35.

of an institutional identity. The ways in which the SGS drew on well-established institutional practices familiar to clergy, lawyers and members of the universities while simultaneously combining and modifying those practices to meet the needs of its locality and region, and of its far-flung and diverse membership, can be seen as important precedents for a variety of cultural organisations and institutions of the later eighteenth century and the nineteenth century.

Prior to the late twentieth century, Richard Gough's 'An Account of the Gentlemen's Society at Spalding', published twice by John Nichols, remained the most comprehensive account of the SGS's history available beyond the Society itself.[2] Dorothy Owen's study of the Society's minute books began to highlight the importance of the library to the Society's history, but a succession of reorganisations continued to obscure its history and composition.[3] And while scholars such as Nigel Ramsay recognise the social importance of the SGS library as a resource for Spalding and the surrounding area and as a model for the Peterborough Gentlemen's Society, most notices of the SGS remain brief and reliant on Nichols and Owen.[4] Following Michael Honeybone's investigation of scientific studies at the early SGS, however, further work by Diana and Michael Honeybone has emphasised the centrality of the libraries to the SGS's intellectual agenda.[5] Library and archive conservation and cataloguing projects since 2013 have revealed an abundance of manuscripts and printed ephemera related to the library that went unrecognised by or remained undiscoverable to earlier scholars.

The survival of the library books with their ample inscriptions, lending records, catalogues and classification schemes, and the extensive contextual

---

[2] [Richard Gough], 'An Account of the Gentlemen's Society at Spalding' (London, 1784), in *Antiquities in Lincolnshire; Being the Third Volume of the Bibliotheca Topographica Britannica*, ed. by John Nichols (London: J. Nichols, 1790), pp. i–xxiv, followed by substantial documentation and correspondence; John Nichols, *Literary Anecdotes of the Eighteenth Century*, vol. 6 (London: J. Nichols, 1812), pp. 1–135. The brief historical introduction to William Moore's *The Gentlemen's Society at Spalding: Its Origin and Progress* (London: William Pickering, 1851) adds little to Gough's account.

[3] Dorothy Owen, *The Minute Books of the Spalding Gentlemen's Society 1712–1755* (Lincoln: Lincoln Record Society, 1981), p. xii.

[4] Nigel Ramsay, 'Libraries for Antiquaries and Heralds', in *The Cambridge History of Libraries in Great Britain and Ireland, vol. 2: 1640–1850*, ed. by Giles Mandelbrote and K. A. Manley (Cambridge: Cambridge University Press, 2006), pp. 134–57 (p. 155).

[5] *The Spalding Gentlemen's Society; the Correspondence of the Spalding Gentlemen's Society 1710–1761*, ed. by Diana Honeybone and Michael Honeybone (Lincoln: Lincoln Record Society, 2010), pp. xii, xxi–ii [hereafter *Corr. SGS*]; *The Correspondence of William Stukeley and Maurice Johnson 1714–1754*, ed. by Diana Honeybone and Michael Honeybone (Lincoln: Lincoln Record Society, 2014), pp. xxviii, xxxi [hereafter *Corr. Stukeley-Johnson*].

information about them in contemporary correspondence, subscription notices and minutes, presents an array of potential avenues of investigation. This chapter draws on this material to resituate the SGS's early and enduring commitment to library provision as a form of civic benefaction. As the focus of the Society's first and longest lasting corporate project, and as the collections that it developed most assiduously, the libraries offer an insight into the Society's founding ideals as well as its wider intellectual and social agenda. Examining the local development and use of libraries by SGS members during the period 1710–56 – commonly seen as the SGS's heyday – allows us to situate the SGS's library activities within the wider context of eighteenth-century library and institutional history.

Charity and Libraries in Eighteenth-Century Spalding

Eighteenth-century commentators and modern scholars alike have identified charity – including the charitable foundation of libraries – as a characteristic feature of the public and private lives of middle-class eighteenth-century Britons.[6] The Parochial Libraries Act 1708 formalised the proper regulation and preservation of parish libraries that 'several charitable and well-disposed Persons have by charitable Contributions erected'. Intended to provide libraries particularly for clergy without the means of buying books for themselves, the Act required that parish libraries be catalogued and kept clean and safe, and that registers of donors be kept; donors and clergy were to decide together the rules for their library's use and maintenance.[7] Spalding's parish library, founded in the sixteenth century, contained 'Valuable Editions of the best authors in no very good Condition' and must have presented a particularly poignant example of a library in need of preservation to Maurice Johnson, a bibliophile with highly developed interests in manuscript studies and the history of printing.[8] Spalding's grammar school library, also housed in a side chapel in the parish church, contained a single volume: Joseph Lang's edition of *Polyanthea Nova* (most likely in the printing of 1607 or 1617). It is telling that after only a few months of informal meetings in a newly established

---

[6] David Owen, *English Philanthropy 1660–1960* (Cambridge, MA: Harvard University Press, 1965), pp. 11–84; Donna T. Andrew, *Philanthropy and Police: London Charity in the Eighteenth Century* (Princeton: Princeton University Press, 1989); Mordechai Feingold, 'Philanthropy, Pomp, and Patronage: Historical Reflections upon the Endowment of Culture', *Daedalus*, 116 (1987), 155–78; James Raven, 'The Representation of Philanthropy and Reading in the Eighteenth-Century Library', *Libraries & Culture*, 31 (1996), 492–510.
[7] Parochial Libraries Act 1708 (7 Ann c.14). [8] SGS Minute Book I, fol. 16r.

Spalding coffee house in 1709–10, members of the embryonic SGS committed themselves to re-founding both the parish and grammar school libraries. It would be another two years before they founded the Society itself, on 3 November 1712.[9] Civic philanthropy in the form of library preservation and development might fairly be seen as a key explanation for the SGS's very existence. While Maurice Johnson's desire to recreate London's intellectual culture in microcosm might well have seemed innovative to his Spaldonian contemporaries, their assumption of responsibility for local library (and therefore educational) provision anchored the nascent Society and its members in a centuries-long tradition of local philanthropy.

In 'An Essay towards an Historical Account of the State of Learning in Spalding', first written in 1720, Johnson framed the history of the SGS in explicitly charitable terms. He asserts that 'Ingenuous Science & Letters have for many Ages indeed been cultivated in this Village' and locates the origin of Spalding's library tradition in the foundation of Spalding Priory in 1051 by monks from 'Croyland, then the most Learned Convent in Britain'.[10] After five centuries of intellectual distinction, the Priory found itself the victim of 'what Wee have since stiled the Reformation'. Although elsewhere Johnson indulged in the kind of anti-Catholic rhetoric all too common in the early eighteenth century, his disgust at the manner in which the English Reformation was carried out is palpable. Henry VIII permitted 'cruel Spoile' to be made of religious houses and their contents, 'of which their noble & well-furnished Libraries, the Supellex Literaria Clericorum may Justly be accounted the chiefest'.[11] Johnson mourns the loss of the Priory not in religious terms but in civic ones. It was there that 'the Hopefuller Youth had a liberal Education given 'Em'; and where the poor had 'allways been Plentifully fedd' at its 'charitable gate'. The dissolution of the Priory was not a religious loss to Spalding, but a loss of its library, its educational provision, its intellectual culture and the primary source of local charity.

Johnson's 'Essay' moves quickly through a roll call of notable benefactors who filled the void left by the dissolution of the Priory, such as John

---

[9] SGS Minute Book I, fols 16r–19r.
[10] The text quoted here and throughout is the final version of this essay, composed c.1740 following a series of revisions by Johnson over the course of nearly two decades. It survives in a bound volume labelled *Tracts*, now in the SGS Archive. Maurice Johnson, 'Essay', p. 1. A new edition of the 'Essay' with an extensive introduction by Diana and Michael Honeybone is forthcoming in *Occasional Papers of the Spalding Gentlemen's Society, New Series*, vol. 1.
[11] Johnson, 'Essay', p. 8.

Gamlyn, who obtained a charter for the grammar school in 1588; the families who in 1591 established the Town Husbands to provide relief to the poor; Robert Ram, the minister of Spalding who in 1637 established a parish library; and Thomas Willesby, who in 1683–4 bequeathed land to establish a 'Petit Schole for the benefitt of poor mens children'. The final entry in a register of headmasters of the grammar school (which includes the brief tenure of the future Cambridge classicist and Royal Librarian Richard Bentley in 1682–3) is John Waring, Johnson's own headmaster and one of the SGS's founding members. The narrative of post-Reformation Spalding's benefactors, charitable institutions and learned denizens is much briefer than the history of Spalding Priory. Part of the explanation for such brevity lies in Johnson himself. As an antiquary and lawyer, he naturally emphasised that part of his town's history on which he had expended considerable time and energy, and which aligned most closely with his own interests and professional expertise. There is also a rhetorical motive. The SGS members to whom Johnson addressed the 'Essay' constituted the intellectual, professional and social elites of Spalding and the surrounding area. They served as governors of the grammar school, as Town Husbands, as masters of the grammar and petit schools, as clergy of Spalding and neighbouring parishes. Even before the foundation of the SGS, they were providing, in their various if overlapping civic roles, for the charitable and educational provision interrupted – but *only* interrupted – by the Dissolution. When those same men gathered to read *The Tatler* and *The Spectator* in a building that had formerly been part of the Priory, the nascent SGS was born on 'that Ground which had, as I have made appeare, been for so many Ages Sacred to the Muses'. Johnson's insistent collocation of his own Society and Spalding Priory geographically, physically and conceptually constitutes not only the foundation of a provincial learned society but also the re-foundation of an 800-year-old tradition in which libraries, education and public charity are necessarily and inextricably intertwined.

A heavily abbreviated form of the 'Essay' appears on the first pages of the grand *Catalogus Librorum Bibliotheca Spaldingensis* (Figure 2.1), Johnson's personal 'Catalogue of Books in the Library of Spalding'. Here Johnson once again draws a direct line of descent from the prior and monks who founded Spalding Priory to himself and the founding members of the Spalding Gentlemen's Society in the form of a list of priors, sub-priors and librarians. Like the monks of the Priory for whom 'a library [was] a necessary furnishing', the SGS members to whom Johnson addressed the 'Essay' were 'Lovers of Literature' who 'insist on the Usefullness of

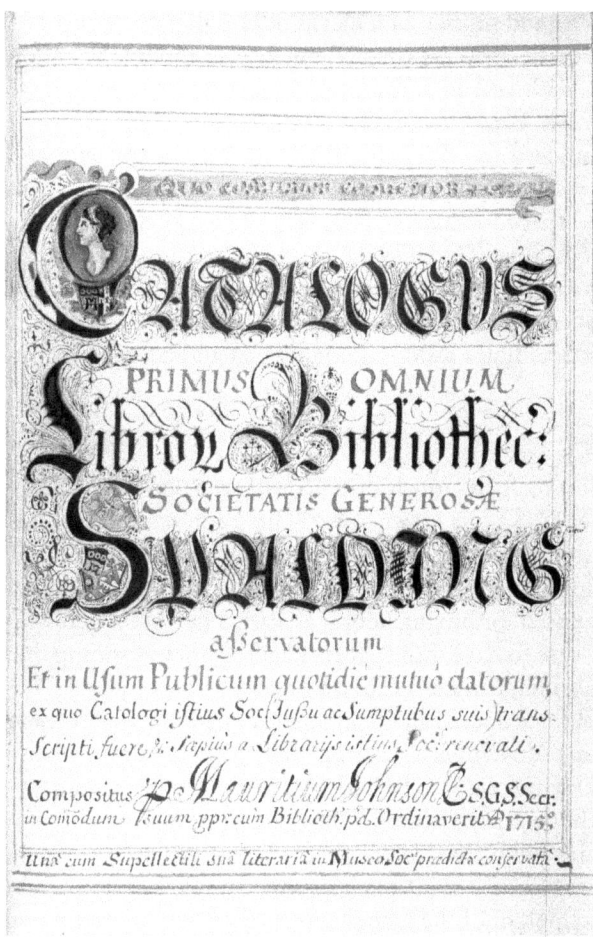

Figure 2.1 Title page of Maurice Johnson's manuscript *Catalogus Librorum Bibliotheca Spaldingensis*. By kind permission of the Spalding Gentlemen's Society.

Books in general' for developing knowledge and judgment, 'which is the greatest Benefit of Conversation, & what renders a Man best able to serve his Country, & himself'.[12] Quoting his friend William Nicolson, who praised earlier authors, editors, donors and collectors of books to public collections as the 'Generous Heroes, that have afforded us noble Advantages of Education', Johnson advocated the establishment of libraries

[12] Johnson, 'Essay', p. 1.

not only as a good in itself or a means of bringing the 'Benefits' of previous generations to bear on the present, but also as a means of endowing future generations with resources for creating new knowledge.[13] His inclusion of versions of the 'Essay' in the SGS's first minute book and both its library catalogues underscores this point. It also clarifies the concept for the 'Library of Spalding' as a triune of three bibliographical collections (parish, school and Society) that functioned collectively as a resource for the town – a truly 'Publick' collection. The SGS thus becomes not just evidence of or a locus for polite sociability of the sort that many scholars have identified in library discourse of the early and middle decades of the eighteenth century, but an assertion of Spalding's historical, intellectual and cultural identity.[14]

Methods of Acquisition

The decision to focus much of its corporate energy on library provision shaped the SGS's very structure. The earliest coffee-house meetings revolved around collectively funded subscriptions to periodicals, and on poems, letters and essays brought by members. Although no explicit provision existed for buying books, an early interest in archiving is evident from their 'care to have those papers kept together', forming the nucleus of what would emerge in 1717–18 as the Society's own library.[15] The 'Proposals for Establishing a Society of Gentlemen at Spalding' that formally founded the SGS on 3 November 1712 stipulated a fine of 2d. for members absent from a weekly meeting, to be added to a book fund. From 1713–14 all new members, both regular (those who lived in or near Spalding) and extra-regular (those who lived more than three miles away), were obliged to donate a book or books 'of the Value of One Pound' to the library of the grammar school, or of the school and parish.[16] This donation requirement was strenuously enforced: numerous annual lists of 'Members Deficient in their Donations' survive in the SGS archive, and in 1723, a new rule made

---

[13] William Nicolson, *English Historical Library*, 2nd edn (London: Timothy Childe and Robert Knaplock, 1714), p. 154.
[14] See, e.g. James Raven, *The Business of Books: Booksellers and the English Book Trade 1450–1850* (New Haven: Yale University Press, 2007), p. 113; James Raven, 'From Promotion to Proscription: Arrangements for Reading and Eighteenth-Century Libraries', in *The Practice and Representation of Reading in England*, ed. by James Raven, Helen Small, and Naomi Tadmor (Cambridge: Cambridge University Press, 1996), pp. 175–201; Michael Powell, 'Endowed Libraries for Towns', in *History of Libraries*, ed. by Mandelbrote and Manley, pp. 83–101; Barbara M. Benedict, 'Reading Collections: The Literary Discourse of Eighteenth-Century Libraries', in *Bookish Histories: Books, Literature, and Commercial Modernity*, ed. by Ina Ferris and Paul Keen (Basingstoke: Palgrave Macmillan, 2009), pp. 169–95.
[15] SGS Minute Book I, fol. 16r.   [16] SGS Minute Book I, fol. 18r.

proposers liable for a one-pound cash payment in the event a new member they had proposed failed to make his donation within a year of admission.[17] Regular members paid a shilling per week to cover the Society's operating costs, the surplus from which was added to the book fund (the penalty for absence being abandoned). On 18 January 1721 regular members began paying an additional shilling per month, earmarked for acquisitions of books, and later also for specimens and scientific instruments. A comparison can be drawn with the town library at nearby Wisbech, where a group of clergy and gentlemen contributed 20 shillings annually for acquisitions. In 1718, the physician, antiquary and bibliophile Richard Middleton Massey presented Maurice Johnson with a copy of his recently published catalogue of the Wisbech library, and three years later joined the SGS as an honorary member. Johnson's cousin, the lawyer, antiquary and bibliophile Beaupré Bell, was also a subscriber to the Wisbech library and a major donor to the Spalding libraries, as well as an SGS member and frequent correspondent. Given Johnson's close relationships with Massey and Bell, their shared passion for library building and cataloguing, and Johnson's familiarity with the Wisbech library's operations, the similarity of the Wisbech and Spalding library arrangements could be a result of formal and informal sharing of institutional practices.[18]

Unlike many parish, town, school and club libraries, which were established with an initial gift but without the provision for additional buying, or which relied exclusively on members' donations or subscriptions, Spalding's library benefited from a mixed system established by the SGS.[19] The mandatory joining donation allowed individual members to become donors, choosing books they themselves deemed appropriate or necessary for the parish or school, in what Graham Best refers to as the 'eleemosynary method'.[20] From 1717–18 onward donations could also be directed to the Society itself, a shift in practice that led to the development of a more specialist collection of antiquarian, scientific, literary and artistic works that would later be housed in the Society's museum. Weekly and monthly fees, on the other hand, provided a means whereby SGS members – gentry, clergy, lawyers, doctors, merchants, engineers, artists and

---

[17] Lists of 'Members Deficient' can be found among the miscellaneous papers in the 'ABC of Arts and Sciences'. SGS Account Book I, 20 December 1722, p. 53.
[18] Richard Middleton Massey, *A Catalogue of Books in the Library at Wisbech* (Wisbech: Wisbech Parochial Library, 1718); Graham Best, 'Books and Readers in Certain Eighteenth-Century Parish Libraries' (unpublished doctoral thesis, Loughborough University, 1985), pp. 36–37, 97–99.
[19] Powell, pp. 83–101; Paul Kaufman, *Libraries and Their Users: Collected Papers in Library History* (London: Library Association, 1969), p. 58.
[20] Best, p. 34.

others – could purchase books deemed desirable or necessary for enhancing the collections. A large collection of proposals and subscription receipts testifies to SGS members' awareness of new publications and their willingness to engage in a kind of patronage by subscribing corporately and individually to works. In some cases, these subscriptions consumed a large proportion of a year's book fund, for instance the £1.11s.6d. paid to subscribe to member Roger Gale's *Registrum Honoris de Richmond* in 1722. In some instances, subscription was mixed with donation. Also in 1722, for instance, members paid a guinea to subscribe to Joseph Sparke's *Historiæ Anglicanæ Scriptores varii*, the second volume of which Sparke presented as his joining donation.[21]

A preliminary survey of books donated to or purchased for the three collections suggests at least half were acquired on the second-hand market. As Christopher Edwards has noted, and as studies of contemporary auction catalogues attest, early eighteenth-century Britain's book market must have relied heavily on the second-hand trade, in which book values (of considerable importance given the SGS's admission requirements) were determined by a book's size as much as its rarity.[22] Thus, while the Society could afford to pay a pound or more to subscribe to a new publication, it paid just 10s.6d. for an unspecified number of seventeenth- and early eighteenth-century octavo, quarto and folio volumes from the library of recently deceased member and deputy librarian Henry Howard in 1729.[23] In the case of former Spalding Grammar School headmaster John Waring's books, purchased in 1716 for an unspecified amount and 'distributed ... between the Library of the Church & Schoole & Society', the explicit reference to payment made to Waring's widow hints at a charitable motivation as well as an affiliative or intellectual one. By 1718, SGS member Dr Edward Green referred to 'poor Widdow Wareing' in a letter discussing his attempts to find a scholarship to Christ's Hospital for one of her children.[24] The fact that the Society paid for the funeral and burial of an impoverished local language teacher in 1719 to 'shew their regard for Letters' suggests that charity played a role in the purchase of Waring's

---

[21] SGS Account Book I, 27 September 1722, p. 50.
[22] Christopher Edwards, 'Antiquarian Bookselling in Britain in 1725: The Nature of the Evidence', in *A Genius for Letters: Booksellers and Bookselling from the 16th to the 20th Century*, ed. by Robin Myers and Michael Harris (Winchester: St. Paul's Bibliographies, 1995), pp. 85–102. See also, e.g. A. N. L. Munby and Lenore Coral, *British Book Sale Catalogues 1676–1800: A Union List* (London: Mansell, 1977) and Raven, *Business of Books*, pp. 107–09.
[23] SGS Account Book I, 24 April 1729, p. 144. As of February 2020, six volumes bearing inscriptions relating to this purchase have been identified in the SGS library.
[24] SGS Minute Book I, fol. 19r; Edward Green to Mrs [Elizabeth] Johnson, 10 July 1718, SGS Archive.

and later of Howard's books, and perhaps others of the many second-hand books from the collections of early SGS members added to one of the libraries after their owners' deaths.

The amount spent on the library in a given year could be considerable. In 1723, the SGS spent £4.7s.3d. on a fourth class (a lockable cabinet for books; Figure 2.2) to hold the parish library and an additional 17s. on books, and in 1724 a total of £9.4s.6d. on books alone. Although it is not yet possible to determine the specific titles or volumes acquired in these years, by early 1721 the Society had added 206 volumes to the parish and grammar school libraries, an average of about 20 per year.[25] By 1747 Johnson noted that the entire collection had grown to approximately 1,000; the *Catalogus*, continued at least to 1754, contains 1,093 titles in

Figure 2.2 Photograph of the original collection cabinet in the upper lecture room. By kind permission of the Spalding Gentlemen's Society.

---

[25] SGS Minute Book I, fols 56r, 66r.

addition to the manuscripts, prints, drawings, maps, loose essays, pamphlets, correspondence and herbaria also housed in the Society's museum.[26] Although Johnson's 'Alphabetical List of Benefactors to Spalding Publick Libraries' includes a number of seventeenth-century donors, it is clear that between 1710 and 1754 the SGS was responsible for a tenfold increase in the stock of books available in Spalding's libraries.[27]

Aside from newspapers, some prints and a small number of apparently accidental exceptions, each new volume was inscribed with the donor's name and the year of donation, and often with further identifying information such as the donor's title, profession and affiliations, and occasionally more lengthy comments. In most cases, a note including the donor's name and the title of the work was also entered in the Society's minutes or accounts. Books subscribed for by the Society were inscribed and recorded in the same way as those given by individual donors; although the SGS does not appear in Johnson's 'List of Benefactors', individual SGS members living and dead are marked with asterisks and circled asterisks, respectively. As Charles Benson notes, library benefaction registers like this one recorded generosity with the 'hidden purpose of attracting further gifts by example'.[28] Because the list of benefactors appears alongside Johnson's 'Essay' in the 'Catalogue', and thus is at least in part contextualised by it, the register and the inscriptions in the books to which it relates also function as encouragements to civic philanthropy. While Paul Kaufman's assertion that the various motivations for donations to libraries share 'a common denominator of some kind of individual pride' remains correct, the SGS added a further incentive.[29] In Spalding, book donation promised the donor memorialisation in the 'List of Benefactors' in the 'Catalogue' and the inscription in a title intended for a public audience. Discovering and reading an inscribed text brought each new reader into the social, intellectual and cultural community of the SGS as well as the history and intellectual life of Spalding. If the inscriptions also encouraged membership in the SGS, that membership carried with it an additional requirement and constant encouragement to engage in further civic benefaction through regular cash payments and donations of additional titles to the libraries of church, school and Society.

---

[26] Johnson to Stukeley, 6 February 1747, in *Corr. Stukeley-Johnson*, pp. 111–13 (p. 111); Maurice Johnson, *Catalogus Librorum Bibliotheca Spaldingensis*, SGS Archive.

[27] Johnson, 'Catalogue', fols 2r–3v, SGS Archive.

[28] Charles Benson, 'Libraries in University Towns', in *History of Libraries*, ed. by Mandelbrote and Manley, pp. 102–21 (p. 113).

[29] Kaufman, p. 98.

Library Management, Circulation and Access

Despite an abundance of evidence for the contents and intended organisation of the three library collections under the SGS's care, the physical arrangement and location of the books themselves – and thus their accessibility and use – have proven difficult to discern. This is due in large part to the repeated changes to the SGS's physical spaces and financial fortunes since 1755, when the Society undertook the first of a series of moves to different premises. The SGS's reorganisation of its bibliographic holdings as a lending library in 1814 further complicated matters, as did the continued circulation of books from all three collections until relatively recently. The relocation of the grammar school and the parish libraries to the SGS's current museum over the course of the first half of the twentieth century, and their subsequent rearrangement, confused matters further. Although dedicatory inscriptions provide some indication as to whether a given title was bound for the parish, school or Society collection, many volumes remain interspersed among later additions to the Society's library, awaiting identification.

According to the slender manuscript catalogue originally kept in the vestry, the books were originally housed together in four classes of the Church of St Mary and St Nicolas. The first class contained 'Bibles, the Fathers, & Antient Commentators'; the second 'Modern Divinity, Sermons'; the third 'Canon Law, History Ecclesiastical and Civil, Councels and Antiquities'; and the fourth 'Glossaries, Physick, Moral Philosophy, Anatomy, Botany, Chymistry, Pharmacy'. A smaller, fifth class over the door held duplicates.[30] This arrangement persisted until 1727, when books on philology and classics were moved to a side chapel that housed the grammar school, and 'the Books Chiefly Voyages' were taken to the Society's newly established museum. Johnson's much grander *Catalogus* reflects the tripartite arrangement: theological materials remained in the vestry; law, history, antiquities, geography, chronicles, cosmography, biographies, itineraries, annals and ethics were divided between the vestry, school and museum; and philosophy, philology, poetry, mathematics and miscellaneous subjects were housed primarily in the school but with some 'reliqui', including manuscripts, maps, prints, drawings and ephemera in the Society's museum. A final group, including lexicography, etymology, vocabularies and glossaries, occupied an

---

[30] Johnson, 'Catalogue', fol. 1r.

uncategorised fourth division and were presumably located alongside the works in other categories to which they related, or kept in the museum for reference.[31] The two arrangements mirror the evolution of the collection and the Society itself. A smaller composite library in an easily managed, single location suited the needs of a relatively small number of members focused on providing resources for the parish and grammar school libraries. As the Society's membership and museum collections expanded and its resources allowed it to lease larger premises with more elaborate furnishings for socialising, experimentation, exhibition and discussion, new arrangements became necessary.

Among the earliest of these was a reconfiguration of the role of librarians. Stephen Lyon, minister of Spalding and SGS President from 1712 until his death in 1747, also acted ex officio as librarian, a natural fit given his daily presence in the church. In September 1723, however, Lyon appointed Timothy Neve and Henry Howard 'as his Deputy Liberarians' and provided them with keys to the classes. As headmaster of the grammar school, Neve was present in the church every day and one of the primary users and beneficiaries of the books in the collection. Howard, Lyon's lecturer, was also 'constantly attending to performe Divine Service Twice each day', and probably carried out some of Lyon's more mundane duties. Unlike Neve and Lyon, however, Howard may have been appointed for more than simply practical reasons. In January 1724, SGS members agreed by ballot to exempt Howard from 'all payments whatsoever to the Treasurer of this Society' in exchange for maintaining a lending book in the vestry, recording loans and returns and replacing books in their proper classes.[32] This arrangement has been interpreted as evidence of a parsimonious approach to librarianship in which the SGS 'merely excused Henry Howard his subscription in return for supervising its library'.[33] But with two librarians already in place, and with Johnson taking responsibility for the Society's papers in his role as Secretary, there was little need for another librarian to look after a collection of what was then only a few hundred volumes.

Howard, who had been elected a member of the SGS at the end of August, was almost certainly the lowest-paid member of the Spalding clerical establishment with a salary less than £30 per year.[34] Waiving not

---

[31] Johnson, *Catalogus*, fol. 2r.   [32] SGS Minute Book I, fols 21r–22r.
[33] P. S. Moorish, 'Baroque Librarianship', in *History of Libraries*, ed. by Mandelbrote and Manley, pp. 212–37 (p. 216).
[34] For clerical incomes in the early eighteenth century, see Francis Godwin James, *Historical Magazine of the Protestant Episcopal Church*, vol. 18 (1949), 311–25.

only the requirement of a joining donation but also the monthly and weekly shilling gave Howard an effective 'salary' of £4.3s.0d. in the first year and £3.3s.0d. each year thereafter. This amount is significantly higher than that paid to fellow SGS member Richard Middleton Massey, who in 1714 was appointed 'Keeper of the Publick Library' at Wisbech at a salary of 40s., and comparable to the £3 paid to the town librarian at Leicester at about this time.[35] For the twenty-two regular members of the Society, of whom an average of seven to ten attended each week, an affirmative vote to waive Howard's financial obligation amounted to a vote to lower the Society's income by the same £3.3s.0d. at a time when total annual additions to the book fund amounted to just over £13 per year.[36] Equally important was the fact that waiving Howard's fees allowed him to remain a member, participating fully in the life of the Society and benefiting from access to its sociability, hospitality and collections. By contrast, Maurice Johnson's legal clerk William Stagg received cash payments for his work for the SGS and was not invited to become a member.[37] Howard's appointment might therefore be interpreted both as evidence of SGS's aspiration to ensure the books in their care were managed by a semi-professional librarian, and as an instance of the members engaging in a form of corporate charity to ensure their learned friend's continued intellectual and social contributions to their meetings.

Despite the requirement that Howard record loans of books from the vestry and repeated references to lending registers kept there, the only surviving records of loans are those found in the final leaves of the three volumes of SGS accounts covering the period 1723–56. Although the list in the first volume of accounts must bear some relationship to the composite library kept in the vestry and could be a – or the – register kept by Howard, the list in the second volume, begun in mid-1731, refers explicitly to 'Books lent out of the Society's museum'. The appearance of this heading reflects the gradual physical separation of the three collections after 1727. Unfortunately, the first list contains no evidence of Howard's involvement in its creation or maintenance.[38] Where initials do appear against cancelled entries on any of the lists, they are those of Neve and Maurice Johnson, or

---

[35] Best, p. 37; Moorish, pp. 214–16.   [36] SGS Account Book I, pp. 55–78.
[37] For payments to Stagg, see SGS Accounts 1 and 2, *passim*. Similar arrangements were made for the SGS's operators, who received accommodation in exchange for their services while also remaining members.
[38] The earliest identifiable entries date from 1725 and bear the initials 'T. N.', or Timothy Neve, the SGS's second treasurer. Entries after 1729, when Neve moved to Peterborough, are initialled 'MJ', or Maurice Johnson.

in rare cases of Johnson's brothers Walter and John. The absence of Howard's name or initials could perhaps indicate the existence of a second, now lost register maintained by him in the vestry. The order that Howard maintain a register in the vestry from January 1724 also suggests a book separate from the accounts. If such a register did exist, it is likely that the primary borrowers were the clergy themselves, who had access to the library on a daily basis and whose professional duties required access to the kinds of theological texts that would remain in the church even after the division of the library in 1727. The keeping of a second register also suggests a larger number of loans from – and therefore a higher level of engagement with – the Spalding libraries in the early eighteenth century than can be constructed from the SGS account books alone. Such evidence as does survive, however, provides an uncommonly detailed picture of borrowing and reading habits amongst SGS members over three decades.

Each entry in these registers includes the name of the borrower, a shorthand version of the title(s) of book(s) borrowed, the date of borrowing and, in some cases, the date the book was passed from one member to another.[39] Returns are indicated either by cancellation with a line or cross or the date the book was returned. Although a detailed discussion of borrowing patterns is beyond the scope of this chapter, it is worth noting that the most frequently borrowed titles – John Harris's *Navigantium Atque Itinerantium Bibliotheca: or, A Compleat Collection of Voyages* (1705), borrowed twenty times, and the English edition of Joseph Pitton de Tournefort's *A Voyage into the Levant* (1718), borrowed sixteen times – are travels and voyages, the first category of books recorded as being moved out of the vestry and into the Society's museum. The next most frequently borrowed titles include various volumes of the *Philosophical Transactions of the Royal Society* and Michel de La Roche's *Memoirs of Literature*, popular throughout the period covered by the loans register, the former title a donation to the Society's museum by successive Royal Society secretaries and the latter purchased by the Society for its own use. The fifth most frequently borrowed title is *Gulliver's Travels*, which the SGS purchased in 1727, and which occupied a place alongside other popular contemporary works by Alexander Pope and John Gay, both members. Also in this class is Samuel Butler's *Hudibras*, the SGS's copy of which contains on its flyleaf the instruction that it is 'To be ready in the Soc Room for such as come before the Company'. The admixture of

[39] SGS Accounts Vols. 1 (1710–31), 2 (1732–49), and 3 (1749–1813).

popular literature, travel narratives, scientific accounts and book reviews in the SGS's museum library reflect the more or less standard gentlemanly interests of its members and the breadth of its remit: politics was the only topic forbidden in meetings. Questions necessarily remain as to the completeness of these registers, their accuracy and their relationship to others that may or may not have been kept with the parish or grammar school libraries. Yet considered alongside fragmentary lists recently discovered in the SGS archive, they reveal much about the arrangement and accessibility of books in Spalding during the first half of the eighteenth century.

Johnson's description of the library as 'Publick' and 'of Spalding' might be identified as something of a contradiction in terms, particularly if 'publick' is read in its familiar eighteenth-century institutional sense as referring to members of a particular university, society or other body.[40] On the other hand, Johnson's introduction to the first SGS minute book defines the SGS as one among many contemporary Societies that existed 'for the same publick Benefitt & good of Mankind', a formula that yokes the limited public of the institution to the wider public of the community, the nation and all of humanity. Indeed, of Johnson's four uses of the term in his two-page introduction none can be identified definitively as referring exclusively to SGS members; the instance quoted earlier comes closest.[41] In physical terms, the understanding that the library existed for a broader public might be construed from the fact that only a small fraction of the overall number of titles included in the three collections were housed in the Society's museum. By 1746 there were six classes in the vestry 'for the more immediate use of our Clergy the Minister as Librarian & his Curate & the School Master', one in the grammar school for the use of the master and students, and five in the museum to hold not only books but also scientific instruments, specimens and the music and musical instruments of the town's music consort (which used the museum gratis – another instance of civic benefaction) alongside four cabinets for manuscripts, prints, drawings and plans.[42] A fragmentary list probably created between 1758 and 1760 suggests that there were only 127 'Books in the Museum', including the SGS minutes and print portfolios, or about 10 per cent of the total number in the *Catalogus*.[43] If the primary

---

[40] See esp. Powell, p. 83. Johnson's usage reflected the range of overlapping definitions being catalogued by his contemporary Samuel Johnson, and which appear in the second volume of *A Dictionary of the English Language*, 2 vols (London: J. and P. Knapton et al., 1755).
[41] SGS Minute Book I, fol. 2r–v.
[42] Johnson to Stukeley, 15 March 1746, in *Corr. Stukeley-Johnson*, pp. 95–100 (p. 96).
[43] 'A Catalogue of the Books in the Museum of the Gentlemens Society of Spalding', c.1758x60, SGS Archive.

beneficiaries of the remaining 90 per cent were clergy, teachers and students, then the public for which these books were intended necessarily extended beyond the Society's membership.

While we might expect volumes kept in the museum to be the most restricted in terms of access, it must be remembered that throughout this period one member of the Society served as its 'operator' – a role that combined caring for the collections in the museum, preparing materials and experiments for and during meetings, and providing access for members and other visitors. Not all the loans recorded in the account book registers coincide with meeting dates, indicating that members had access to the museum and SGS library outside formal Society hours. Indeed, there are hints that not even the books kept in the museum were restricted to use by SGS members. On 12 February 1756, George Ballard's *Memoirs of Several Ladies of Great Britain* (1752) was loaned to Mrs Thompson, who returned it to an SGS meeting a week later. Even if this was the wife of Major Thompson, who attended the first (but not the second) meeting, it is significant that the loan was issued in his wife's name rather than his own.[44] Although singular, the record suggests that in at least some cases the public served by the Society's library also included members' families, including women. Such a position may well reflect – if it does not anticipate – the emergence of increasing numbers of circulating and subscription libraries that appeared throughout the later eighteenth century just as it anticipates the SGS's decision to admit women as non-voting members when new rules for the library were set out in 1814.[45]

Loans of theological and grammatical works are largely absent from the account book registers despite the fact that by 1728 Maurice Johnson assured William Stukeley that 'Our publick Library is very much encreased, and frequented; Our Free Schole well accommodated with good Editions of the Classicks &c'.[46] One possible explanation for the absence of these types of books from the lending record may lie in the fact that the library was 'frequented'; books could have been consulted in situ after the Society's decision to remove the parish library from a cramped, cold room over the north porch accessible via a narrow winding staircase and into the warmer, dryer, more comfortable vestry. It may also be the case that the Society's books were frequently consulted but the parish

---

[44] SGS Account Book 3, p. 32.
[45] For contemporary comparisons of women as borrowers at Reigate, Doncaster and Wisbech, see W. M. Jacob, 'Parochial Libraries and Their Users', *Library & Information History*, 27 (2011), 211–16 (pp. 214–15).
[46] Johnson to Stukeley, 16 April 1728, in *Corr. Stukeley-Johnson*, pp. 52–55 (p. 53).

library was not, or that neither was frequently used despite Johnson's claim, but rather that the library's size and relative accessibility were as important symbolically as practically.[47] At the same time, the economic and cultural context in which the SGS operated made the library a valuable resource for local users, particularly members of the clergy.

Spalding's library was one of few parish libraries in the region, the nearest being those at Boston, Grantham, Stamford and Wisbech, though with the exception of Wisbech most were relatively static collections during the early eighteenth century.[48] This paucity of parish libraries must have been keenly felt in the Deanery of Holland where clerical livings were poorly remunerated. According to John Ecton's 1742 survey, Spalding (valued at £70 per year) was the most valuable in the region, with the majority of the livings worth £20 to £40 and some curacies considerably less.[49] Given the predominance of small formats and second-, third- and even fourth-hand provenance among books donated by or purchased from clerical members and an apparent willingness to value less expensive books at £1 when they were offered as admission donations, it is probably safe to say that few clergy in the area could have afforded to purchase new or specialist publications for themselves. For these members of the clergy, many of whom were regular or extra-regular members of the SGS, the library at Spalding represented the largest and most up-to-date lending library available. The Spalding library benefited from the SGS's reputation as a learned society, its solicitation of books from its wide network of members, the cultivation of local clergy as potential members, and from Howard and a succession of subsequent sub- and deputy librarians. Although it is ultimately impossible to prove how many and what types of books were used or borrowed in the absence of additional documentary evidence, it is almost certain that the parish library was used by contemporary SGS members and other inhabitants of Spalding and the surrounding area.

Tracing the use of books from the grammar school library is, if anything, more difficult still. The early removal of grammar and classics to a class in the side chapel that housed the grammar school effectively separated those

---

[47] Powell, pp. 97–98.
[48] For overviews of these libraries, see Michael Perkin, *A Directory of the Parochial Libraries of the Church of England and the Church in Wales*, rev. edn (London: Bibliographical Society, 2004), pp. 144–46, 217–19, 353–54, 395–96; Spalding appears at pp. 351–52.
[49] John Ecton, *Thesaurus Rerum Ecclesiasticarum: Being an Account of the Valuations of all the Ecclesiastical Benefices in the Several Dioceses in England and Wales* (London: D. Browne et al., 1742), pp. 256–58.

volumes from the parish and Society libraries. The development of this collection for the headmaster to have 'at hand' suggests an intention for personal and instructional use by the headmaster, and perhaps for use by more advanced students in attendance.[50] For regular members of the SGS and their peers, almost all of whom had received education in and beyond grammar schools, basic grammars and editions of the classics probably occupied spaces on their private library shelves for their own and their children's use. Only particularly technical, rare or expensive works are likely to have been of interest to this educated adult readership.

Just as important, however, are the loans of books from the Society's library that, according to the *Catalogus*, ought to have been kept elsewhere. In 1741, for example, Revd Samuel Whiting borrowed a series of 'Ecclesiastical Addresses', probably three volumes of seventeenth-century sermons that seem an unlikely fit for the museum. Joseph Spence's *Polymetis* (1747) appears seven times in the list of books loaned from the museum, despite the explicit instruction in its inscription by Maurice Johnson that it was 'to be kept in the Class of Books in the Royal & Free Grammar School'. These volumes, like John Pine's edition of the works of Horace donated by the Duke of Buccleuch in 1738, or Bernard Picart's *Cérémonies et Coutumes Religieuses de tous les Peuples du Monde* donated by Sir Richard Ellys, belonged to categories whose contents were divided between two or all three collections.[51] Their presence in the museum suggests that especially rare, valuable or high-status works of literature, theology and classics were more likely to be kept in the museum than in the vestry or school despite the fact that their contents were more appropriate to those collections. Scientific books, on the other hand, a wide variety of which predominate in the later registers, were kept in the museum regardless of format or rarity, a natural arrangement given the absence of scientific instruction from the grammar school curriculum, the theological focus of the parish library and the fact that most gentlemen's libraries in the period contained relatively few scientific books.[52]

On the whole, the titles included in the account book registers thus suggest quite distinct intended primary and extended user groups for the three Spalding libraries despite their intermingling in the vestry, school and

---

[50] Johnson to Stukeley, 15 March 1746, in *Corr. Stukeley-Johnson*, pp. 95–100 (p. 96).
[51] Francis Scott to Maurice Johnson, 29 August 1738, plus draft reply dated 9 September 1738, SGS Archive. SGS Account Book 2 records a loan of both volumes to Johnson in November 1748.
[52] For ownership of scientific books in this period, see Giles Mandelbrote, 'Scientific Books and their Owners', in *Thornton and Tully's Scientific Books, Libraries and Collectors*, ed. by Andrew Hunter, 4th edn (London: Routledge, 2016), pp. 333–66.

museum classes. Those titles in the museum served the relatively small group of local SGS members, whose borrowing was recorded in the account books as one element of meetings during which conversations ranged from literature, history and art to science and mathematics to current events. The absence from the later 1720s of titles of books kept in the parish library suggests that it, at least, operated and enjoyed accessibility beyond the Society's formal structures, reaching at least as far as local clergy and probably clergy throughout the region. It is entirely possible that the parish and grammar school libraries were also more generally accessible under the supervision of those clergy who lived near and worked in the parish church, to whom the Parochial Libraries Act of 1708 gave considerable power to allow use of the books as they saw fit. Whether a more restricted or a more open policy applied, however, the Spalding libraries were indeed 'publick' to an extent that reached beyond the Society's membership.

Conclusion: Libraries, History and Posterity

Already by 1728 Maurice Johnson had begun to consider Spalding's libraries as an integral part of his legacy. Writing to William Stukeley, Johnson expressed his hope that 'I may hereafter be thought to have been a Friend to the whole Neighbourhood & a Sort of Father to this place, if by this Meanes the Arts & Sciences are advanced in It, & the People betterd by It.'[53] Over the course of another two decades during which SGS members more than doubled the number of books in 'The Library of Spalding' and assembled a collection of their own manuscripts carefully ordered, arranged, edited and indexed for the benefit of their successors, Johnson devised a method of ensuring that the civic philanthropy led by the SGS would outlive him, while at the same time ensuring his own legacy. In contrast to a contemporary trend away from posthumous benefactions, Johnson bequeathed the income from the living at Wykeham, then in his family's gift, to the governors of Spalding grammar school.[54] In exchange the governors agreed that the master, under school master or usher would

> Conscientiously constantly and Honestly take charge and care of the Museum Books papers and Supellex Literaria of and belonging to Spalding Gentlemens Society ... which I had the Happiness to be the Institutor of and for many years after secretary and whereof I now have

---

[53] Maurice Johnson to William Stukeley, 16 April 1728, in *Corr. Stukeley-Johnson*, pp. 52–55 (p. 54).
[54] Raven, 'Philanthropy and Reading', pp. 492–93; Andrew, pp. 46–49.

the Honour to be president being the best services I could to my native place and ffamily.

In this passage, Johnson's will becomes an extension of the narrative of civic benefaction begun in his 'Essay Towards an Historical Account of the State of Learning in Spalding'. His personal act of charity consolidated that of the SGS as a community of charity, each supporting the other in acts of 'mutual benevolence' that the Society was founded to support.

Just as importantly, Johnson's will established the kind of legal protections that already existed for the parish and grammar school libraries to the Society's library, museum and archive, by creating a contractual obligation for the grammar school governors to maintain it regardless of the Society's fortunes. While the SGS remained without a charter or any other legal status of its own, the bibliographic resources for the parish and school that it had developed with remarkable success over the course of half a century experienced a subtle identity shift, becoming legally a civic resource linked to local public education. The early SGS reflected the more informal associations that predominated in the early eighteenth century; its members engaged in the kinds of communal reading and book-lending practices that establish it as a precursor of the book clubs and subscription libraries that proliferated from mid-century onward. At the same time, those members' adoption of the parish library and development of the grammar school library led to their informal society becoming inextricably intertwined with the legally constituted charitable institutions that had served the wider public of Spalding – just as their counterparts throughout the country had served their own local publics – for centuries, and that would continue to do so. It is within in this web of interconnected individual and institutional forms of civic benefaction, formal and informal, consciously historic and forward-looking, that the SGS's libraries took shape and that they must be understood. More broadly, the SGS members' self-identification as the custodians of history and education, and as patrons and arbiters of local civic culture, provides insights into the developing patterns of thought and behaviour that would characterise later eighteenth-century institutions and institutionality. The SGS prefigured and shared with many of those institutions a commitment to enlightenment ideals of sociability, improvement and intellectual exchange with a practical focus on pragmatic arrangements for assembling, maintaining and managing access to the tools that supported those ideals in ways that were attuned to the changing circumstances of their local communities.

CHAPTER 3

Institutions without Addresses

David A. Brewer

In the introduction to this volume, the editors offer a new and exceedingly useful definition of institutions. An institution, they propose, is 'an assemblage that organises, transmits, and validates' something, 'and that self-consciously represents itself as doing so'. Nothing in this definition obviously requires a physical plant, staff, collections, scheduled meetings, minutes that record such meetings, and so on. And yet, as most of the other contributions to this volume suggest, those kinds of brick-and-mortar institutions (subscription libraries, learned societies, commercial lecture halls, and the like) are what most readily come to mind when we think of institutions of literature. Presumably the solidity and heft of the surviving buildings and archives from which we're reconstructing the workings of these particular institutions make it easier to imagine institutions more generally as firmly place-bound, positioned in a specific time and location and so not amorphous, diffuse, or free-floating in the way that concepts like 'discourse' or 'ideology' (or indeed 'literature') can often seem. Institutions, to this way of thinking, have addresses. One can plot them on a map: the Society of Antiquaries isn't some nebulous social construct; rather, one can walk up to it and enter at Burlington House in Piccadilly. Institutions may even have names, such as the Spalding Gentlemen's Society, that will tell you where to go to find them (in this case, Lincolnshire).

Yet this highly concrete and localized understanding of institutions of literature is hardly the only way to think about them. Scholarship from earlier decades and other disciplines routinely refers to things like 'the institution of the Law' or 'the institution of the Church' that cannot be wholly pinpointed on a map or enumerated in an inventory. Obviously, institutions of this sort have some physical locations. The Law presumably includes all the court rooms, judges' chambers, jury rooms, Inns of Court, sponging houses, jails, prisons, pillories, and gallows in the realm. But surely these do not exhaust the list of all the places in which the Law might be found. What about ships carrying felons sentenced to transportation? What about saddlebags in which royal proclamations or new statutes were carried into the provinces? What about all the books containing case law or offering legal advice to readers hoping to take care of routine transactions without having to hire a professional? And as these examples should suggest, at least some of the places in which the Law shows up are mobile and temporary and so don't lend themselves particularly well to mapping. Nor do many of the other elements we would probably want to count as part of the Law: say, the unwritten Constitution or the ideologies of property underlying the 1720s expansion of capital crimes or the wigs worn by judges and barristers as signs of their office. And we haven't even touched upon the folk wisdom operating at the peripheries of the Law: say, the 'moral economy' underlying bread riots, or the socioeconomic factors widely held to promote crime, such as the artificially low price of gin.[1] And even if we were to pin down and account for all of these things, there are countless others that probably also need to be included. The point is, something like the Law does not lend itself to what seems to be the currently dominant way of thinking about institutions.[2] Yet the Law certainly has the impersonal, self-perpetuating, and agential qualities that have long been regarded as characteristic of institutions.

This is why Mee and Sangster's definition is so useful. By asking us to think about institutions as assemblages, they open up an intellectual space in which we can consider both the Spalding Gentlemen's Society *and* the Law as institutions, just ones that are differently configured and operating on potentially incommensurate scales. Of course, the large, diffuse institutions I've mentioned so far (the Law; the Church; we could throw in the State) are not explicitly literary and so may not seem a fair comparison, although we could certainly point out some of the ways in which those institutions shape literary life through prosecutions and threats of prosecutions and various sorts of patronage. Perhaps literary institutions work on a more place-bound and localizable level than those in other areas of cultural life. Perhaps, but I think not.

---

[1] For 'the moral economy', see E. P. Thompson, *Customs in Common* (New York: New Press, 1991), pp. 185–351.

[2] For a good example of this approach, see Jon Klancher, *Transfiguring the Arts and Sciences: Knowledge and Cultural Institutions in the Romantic Age* (Cambridge: Cambridge University Press, 2013), which focuses on brick-and-mortar operations like the Royal Institution, the London Institution, and the Surrey Institution in order to make its argument regarding the 'immense', 'complex[,]' and lasting' impact of institutions on 'public knowledge', 'forms of communication', 'discipline formation', and 'what we may call learning-publics' (pp. 2–3).

In what follows, I would like to rehabilitate a phrase fairly frequently employed in scholarship from the 1980s, 1990s, and 2000s, but that seems to have more recently fallen out of favor: the 'institution of Authorship'. In most of its uses several decades ago, 'institution' seems to have been synonymous with something like 'ideology' or 'disciplinary power'. The institution of Authorship, for Peggy Kamuf, whose *Signature Pieces: On the Institution of Authorship* appears partially responsible for popularizing the phrase, is that which 'masks or recuperates the disruptive implications of literary signature'.[3] As the Derridean language of 'signature' should suggest, Kamuf is interested in the ways in which, by attaching texts to authors by means of their names, scholars and critics attempt to limit the signification of those texts in order to preserve some sort of 'psychological, historical, formal, [or] ideological' consistency.[4] Not surprisingly, these attempts inevitably fail: the signature – the very thing that is supposed to demonstrate that an authorial subject is present to himself and that the text uniquely represents his particular intended thoughts and no one else's – is fatally flawed as a concept because it needs to be both distinct from anyone else's mark (including the author's at any other point in time) and yet repeatable across time, without which it could not be recognizable.[5] There are obvious problems with this account, not least the way in which 'signature' in the precise sense of a name handwritten by the being to whom that name refers (e.g., the thing that would authenticate a financial transaction) slips into a more general sense of semiotic constraint akin to Michel Foucault's notion of the 'author function' as 'the principle of thrift in the proliferation of meaning'.[6] But for now, let it suffice to note that Kamuf's sense of 'institution' is largely immaterial. She disparagingly refers to 'the modern study of literature', and so implicitly indicts all the secondary schools, universities, book reviews, scholarly journals, talk shows (at least in France), and so on that help sustain that study.[7] But they also hardly figure in her account, and so it's difficult to see how they matter, except in the most pedestrian way (someone has to pay, feed, and house all those pernicious teachers and critics conspiring against the free

---

[3] Peggy Kamuf, *Signature Pieces: On the Institution of Authorship* (Ithaca: Cornell University Press, 1988), p. x.
[4] Kamuf, p. x.
[5] For an overview of the ways in which traditional notions of the signature tie themselves in knots, see Jonathan Culler, *On Deconstruction: Theory and Criticism after Structuralism* (Ithaca: Cornell University Press, 1982), pp. 125–28, 192–94.
[6] Michel Foucault, 'What is an Author?', in *Textual Strategies: Perspectives in Post-Structuralist Criticism*, ed. by Josué V. Harari (Ithaca: Cornell University Press, 1979), pp. 141–60 (p. 159).
[7] Kamuf, p. ix.

play of the signifier). My point here is not to beat up on a more than thirty-year-old book, but rather to point out that there's remarkably little that seems institutional about Kamuf's 'institution of Authorship'. Rather, as in so much of the literary thinking of the past two-and-a-half centuries, institutions are here merely a convenient foil epitomizing all the things that literature supposedly is not: conventional, stultifying, complicit, and irredeemably middlebrow.[8] Perhaps that's a sign that institutions are not a very useful way to think about authorship or literature more generally, that 'institutions of literature' are at best misguided constraints on the gloriously radical potential of what authorship or literature could be. Or perhaps, and I find this far more likely, we just need a more sophisticated sense of what institutions are and what they actually do.

Let's return to Mee and Sangster's definition of an institution as 'an assemblage that organises, transmits, and validates' something, 'and that self-consciously represents itself as doing so'. Much of this seems spot on. Authorship, as I understand its operations in the period I know best (roughly 1650–1780), was fundamentally about reputation, not literary property or the decline of patronage or any of the other issues that tend to dominate our usual accounts of the eighteenth century as 'the Age of Authors'.[9] Reputation was what determined 'the Fate of Authors' (a phrase that crops up repeatedly; indeed, I have adopted it as the title for my book-in-progress on the centrality of reputation to authorship in the eighteenth-century Anglophone world). And as even a moment's consideration should suggest, authorial reputations, both individually and collectively, are nothing if not an assemblage: a shifting, dynamic set of relations between texts, qualities, anecdotes, evaluations, persons, objects, and emotions held together by a proper name or set of proper names. In an assemblage, what has agency and what is central at any given moment depends more on its particular location within the larger assemblage and its relations with the other components than on its supposed ontological status (there are

---

[8] Mee and Sangster discuss this tendency to minimize the importance of literary institutions in the final section of the introduction.

[9] Samuel Johnson proclaimed that 'the present age ... may be stiled with great propriety THE AGE OF AUTHORS; for ... there never was a time, in which men of all degrees of ability, of every kind of education, of every profession and employment, were posting with ardour so general to the press' (*The Adventurer*, 115 [11 December 1753]). For the usual accounts of eighteenth-century authorship, see, for example, Brean S. Hammond, *Professional Imaginative Writing in England, 1670–1740: 'Hackney for Bread'* (Oxford: Clarendon Press, 1997); Mark Rose, *Authors and Owners: The Invention of Copyright* (Cambridge, MA: Harvard University Press, 1993); and Betty A. Schellenberg, *The Professionalization of Women Writers in Eighteenth-Century Britain* (Cambridge: Cambridge University Press, 2005). These are all good, deservedly influential books. But the explanations they offer are limited by their not engaging with some very important categories of evidence.

situations in which shop signs have agency and epic poets do not).[10] Hence, 'Authorship is an assemblage.' So far, so good.

'Authorship is an assemblage that organizes.' Again, this seems uncontestably right. Eighteenth-century talk about authors is full of taxonomies and rankings and positionings of various writers vis-à-vis one another. Often, these are explicitly hierarchical. For example, a 1691 survey of the literary scene proposes to range from 'Great *Mr.* Bays *down to* little Mr. D----y.'[11] Similarly, James Bramston professes that 'tho'' no great Connoisseur, I make a shift / Just to find out a *Durfey* from a *Swift*; / I can discern with half an eye, I hope, / *Mist* from *Jo Addison*, from *Eusden Pope*: / I know a Farce from one of *Congreve*'s Plays, / And *Cibber*'s Opera from *Johnny Gay*'s.'[12] These names are clearly not all on an equal footing. Rather, the second in each pairing is presented as if it were self-evidently superior, just a part of 'what everyone knows'. But even when explicit hierarchies are not being erected (and then treated as uncontroversial fact), categorization still abounds. Remember only Martinus Scriblerus's description of the games in Book Two of *The Dunciad Variorum*:

> Each ... relateth to some or other vile class of writers. The first concerneth the Plagiary, to whom [our author] giveth the name of *More* [James Moore Smyth]; the second the libellous Novellist, whom he styleth *Eliza* [i.e., Haywood]; the third the flattering Dedicator; the fourth the bawling Critick or noisy Poet; the fifth the dark and dirty Party-writer; and so of the rest, assigning to each some *proper name* or other, such as he cou'd find.[13]

To this way of thinking, there is a place (not necessarily an exalted place, but a place nonetheless) for almost all writers, and on the few occasions when there isn't (say, when *The Critical Review* tells the 'Farmer's Daughter in Gloucestershire', who has supposedly written *Virtue in Distress; or, the History of Miss Sally Pruen, and Miss Laura Spencer* [1772], that she 'has totally mistaken the use of her hands' and 'may turn them to a better account by making *butter*, than by making *books*'), the exclusion is

---

[10] For more on the structure and logic of assemblages, see Thomas Nail, 'What is an Assemblage?', *SubStance*, 46.1 (2017), 21–37.

[11] *A Search after Wit; or, a Visitation of the Authors* (London: E. Hawkins, 1691), Sig. A2r. 'Bayes' is John Dryden (so called because of his long service as the laureate and because of his supposed resemblance to the over-the-top heroic poet of that name in *The Rehearsal*). Given the rhyme in the previous line ('scurvy'), 'D----y' would be Thomas D'Urfey.

[12] [James Bramston], *The Art of Politicks, in Imitation of Horace's Art of Poetry* (London: Lawton Gilliver, 1729), p. 28.

[13] Alexander Pope, *The Dunciad (1728) and the Dunciad Variorum (1729)*, ed. by Valerie Rumbold (Harlow: Pearson Longman, 2007), p. 166.

itself telling and a form of organization: one needs a Pale in order for someone to be beyond it.[14]

'Authorship is an assemblage that organizes [and] transmits.' Yet again, this seems correct. Authorship transmits by reproducing, altering, and perpetuating reputation. Indeed, one of the most striking things about eighteenth-century authorship, once one starts to think about it in terms of reputation, is how 'sticky' reputations were and how long they lingered. The verse of John Wilmot, Earl of Rochester, was still being held up more than eighty years after his death as *the* standard of obscenity against which to measure *Tristram Shandy* and the craze surrounding it.[15] Similarly, Sir Richard Blackmore was still functioning as what Samuel Johnson termed a 'bye-word of contempt' decades after his work ceased to be published.[16] This persistence of reputation is a form of transmission. Those reputations lingered because they were being continually reiterated, reinforced, and transmitted as self-evident (and self-evidently useful) truths about the literary world.

'Authorship is an assemblage that organizes, transmits, and validates.' And since we need a grammatical object at this point (e.g., banks are assemblages that organize, transmit, and validate capital), let's say 'Authorship is an assemblage that organizes, transmits, and validates authors.' Pretty much every conceivable use to which I've discovered authors being put is employing them (or, more often, their names and/or images as proxies for all that makes them authors) as a shorthand for value.

---

[14] *The Critical Review*, 33 (1772), p. 327.

[15] *The Monthly Review* suggests that what Jenny whispered to Tristram in Book Seven of *Tristram Shandy* (consoling words regarding his impotence?) 'will be the ruin' of him: 'Why you might as well write *broad Rochester* as set down all these obscene asterisms!' (32 [1765], p. 125). Similarly, 'a prude' ventriloquized by a contributor to *The Gentleman's Magazine* insists that 'The woman of pleasure / And *Rochester*'s treasure / Are brother and sister to *Shandy*' (30 [1760], p. 243). And 'An Account of the Rev. Mr. ST**** and his Writings' wonders at how the author of *Tristram Shandy* has 'almost out-rochestered Rochester himself' (*The Grand Magazine*, 3 [1760], p. 309).

[16] Samuel Johnson, *The Lives of the Most Eminent English Poets; with Critical Observations on their Works*, ed. by Roger Lonsdale, 4 vols (Oxford: Clarendon Press, 2006), III, 84. The life of Blackmore was written in 1780 and published the following year. Blackmore's most commercially successful poem, *Prince Arthur*, had last been reprinted in 1714. Yet close to forty years later, Francis Coventry could still ask rhetorically, 'What is contained in the mighty and voluminous Epic Poems of Sir Richard Blackmore, Knight?', and expect the answer to be 'absolute Nothing' ([Francis Coventry], *The History of Pompey the Little* [London: M. Cooper, 1751], p. 128). Similarly, Robert Lloyd could inquire, in the early 1760s, 'who can bear to read or hear, / Tho' not offensive to the ear, / The mighty BLACKMORE gravely sing / Of ARTHUR PRINCE, and ARTHUR KING, / Heroic poems without number, / Long, lifeless, leaden, lulling lumber; / Nor pity such laborious toil, / And loss of midnight time and oil? / Yet glibly runs each jingling line, / Smoother, perhaps, than yours or mine, / But still, (tho' peace be to the dead,) / The dull, dull poems weigh down lead' ('On Rhyme: A Familiar Epistle to a Friend', in *Poetical Works*, 2 vols [London: T. Evans, 1774], II, 114).

When Johnson envisioned 'distant Times', in which 'new *Behns*, new *Durfeys*, yet remain in Store', he wasn't being merely descriptive. Those names are an implicit set of instructions regarding what to do with the texts and persons in the vicinity of those names: in this case, presumably lament that the audience's taste in the far future is still as debased as it supposedly was in the present.[17] As such, 'Behn' and 'Durfey' are instruments of evaluation and so of validation (or a pointed refusal to provide such).

The only potential difficulty with Mee and Sangster's definition lies with its ending. Is it really correct to say that 'Authorship is an assemblage that organizes, transmits, and validates authors, *and that self-consciously represents itself as doing so*'? The place where it's easy to get tripped up is the 'self-consciously represents', which, both grammatically and logically, requires that there be an entity that's doing the representing and that this entity is somehow self-conscious. This formulation seems perfectly fine for thinking about institutions that have a specific, finite location and corporate identity. The Society of Antiquaries can undertake publicity campaigns that highlight all the ways in which they're organizing, transmitting, and validating the past. But what about more abstract, diffuse entities? It seems harder to talk about their capacity for agency and self-consciousness, and when we do, it's often in ways that we quickly assure ourselves are merely metaphorical: say, the invisible hand of the market, in which no one is seriously insisting that there's an actual hand, much less an arm, a shoulder, a torso, a spleen, and so on. But yet we can all point to ways in which the market seems to make things happen in the world that are not reducible to the actions, individual or even in any straightforward sense collective, of the persons and objects involved in the market. That is, the market is often 'perceived to be capable of performing actions' quite apart from those undertaken by any or all of its constituent parts.[18] Indeed, that is one of the characteristic marks of an assemblage: the whole is more than (and different than) the sum of its parts and has its own sort of agency.[19] I submit that authorship works in much the same way. Its power to organize, transmit, and validate authors seems both to precede and to outlast the efforts of any or all of its individual components to do the same

---

[17] Samuel Johnson, 'Prologue *Spoken by* Mr. GARRICK, at the Opening of the Theatre in *Drury-Lane* 1747', in *The Poems of Samuel Johnson*, ed. by David Nichol Smith and Edward L. McAdam, 2nd edn (Oxford: Clarendon Press, 1974), p. 109.

[18] The phrase quoted comes from the initial call for papers for the conference at which an earlier version of this chapter was presented: <http://institutionsofliterature.net/call-for-participants/>.

[19] See Jane Bennett, 'The Agency of Assemblages and the North American Blackout', *Public Culture*, 17.3 (2005), 445–65.

thing. The latter are operating within constraints and ways of thinking that have already been set, but not set by charismatic prior participants (e.g., Dryden or Pope) so much as by someone or something else, something I propose we call the institution of Authorship itself.

Key both to traditional sociological methods for thinking about institutions and to Mee and Sangster's new definition is a notion of self-perpetuation. Whatever else they do, institutions reproduce themselves and so keep the institution going, often with at least the illusion of unchanging continuity and solidity.[20] This is where a lot of their apparent agency appears and so where an institution can most easily seem to be self-consciously representing its own activities. At least in the case of Authorship, this self-conscious representation tends to cluster in seemingly 'minor' microgenres, like the sessions poem or the stylistic imitation.[21] Such microgenres do the kind of organizing, transmitting, and validating of authors that we've been considering, but they do so in a way that highlights the supposedly playful artifice of those operations, the ways in which they're all just part of the ongoing game of sociable wit. Of course, as with most games, there are rules and significant stakes (not all financial), and 'winning' or 'losing' can affect the future prospects of the various participants. But the serious, often disciplinary consequences of playing the game (which is to say, of engaging with the institution and at least tentatively acquiescing to its authority) are accorded a sort of plausible deniability by virtue of these microgenres' cleverness and apparently minor status in the traditional hierarchies of genre.[22] In other words, the ways in which the institution of Authorship self-consciously represents itself organizing, transmitting, and validating authors have been hiding in plain sight because of the seemingly unserious, minor forms that representation has taken, forms which, because of their tone and lack of monumentality, may come off as the very antithesis of the institutional. And yet . . .

---

[20] For a brief account of some of the ways in which Authorship both seemed and was an *ancien régime* for much of the eighteenth century and so is best considered over the *longue durée*, see my 'The Even Longer Restoration', *Restoration: Studies in English Literary Culture, 1660–1700*, 40.2 (2016), 96–104.

[21] For an intriguing discussion of microgenres, see *The Microgenre: A Quick Look at Small Culture*, ed. by Molly C. O'Donnell and Anne H. Stevens (New York: Bloomsbury Academic, 2020), especially pp. 1–7. 'Sessions poems' are brief, satiric surveys of the literary scene organized by the conceit that Apollo has called a quasi-juridical meeting (akin to the 'session' of a court) to decide who should be the next laureate. Various candidates put themselves forward and are almost all sent away with a dismissive jab that supposedly encapsulates who they are as authors and why they're unworthy of elevation.

[22] For example, Johnson describes the sessions poem as 'a mode of satire, by which, since it was first introduced by Suckling; perhaps every generation of poets has been teazed' (*Lives of the Most Eminent English Poets*, I, 197–98). Teasing the new generation is a rather less exalted function for poetry than what tends to be claimed for, say, epic or panegyric.

To better understand both how these self-conscious representations of the institution of Authorship's activities work and why they've been so difficult for us to notice and take seriously, despite the ways in which they organize, transmit, and validate authors who remain incredibly important to us, let's consider the microgenre of stylistic imitation. Poets imitating the style of other poets is a phenomenon that dates back to antiquity (indeed, it may lie at the heart of the oldest kinds of genre formation). But the early eighteenth century saw a significant and significantly new development in such imitations: the separation of manner from matter that we get in poems like John Philips's *The Splendid Shilling*.[23] Like Philips's other, apparently more serious ventures into Miltonic imitation, *Blenheim* (1705) and *Cyder* (1708), *The Splendid Shilling* employs a putatively Miltonic style to write about topics that John Milton never touched: in this case, poverty, debt, cold, and thirst. Similar ventures followed in the ensuing decades, offering still further imitations of Milton, plus most other English writers of any prominence, including Joseph Addison, Richard Blackmore, Samuel Butler, Geoffrey Chaucer, Colley Cibber, Thomas Gray, Aaron Hill, Samuel Johnson, William Mason, Ambrose Philips, Alexander Pope, Matthew Prior, William Shakespeare, Edmund Spenser, Laurence Sterne, Jonathan Swift, James Thomson, John Tutchin, and Edward Young.[24]

What unites all these imitations, despite their different tones and publication circumstances, is the way in which they detach an author's style from both his biographical self and his known subject matter, thereby redefining it as a set of formal devices and techniques: effectively a checklist of conventions to follow and so, at least in a reductive sense, a microgenre.[25] That is, stylistic imitations, especially when they bring that style to bear on a new and seemingly incongruous topic, take what we tend to regard as the individuating, perhaps even ineffable or inimitable mark of an author – his style – and make it detachable. In so doing, they invite us to consider style as simultaneously stemming from a writer, standing in for that writer, and yet being separable from him. That is, they invite us to consider something like 'Milton's style' as a sort of distributed person (in the anthropological

---

[23] *The Splendid Shilling* was first published as 'An Imitation of Milton' in *A Collection of Poems* (London: Daniel Brown and Benjamin Tooke, 1701), pp. 393–400. An authorized version followed four years later as *The Splendid Shilling. An Imitation of Milton. Now First Correctly Publish'd* (London: Tho. Bennet, 1705).

[24] For a useful bibliography of many of these, see Richmond P. Bond, *English Burlesque Poetry, 1700–1750* (Cambridge, MA: Harvard University Press, 1932).

[25] I am using masculine pronouns because this kind of imitation was, so far as I've been able to discern, something done exclusively with male writers.

sense of 'person': 'a man clad in a condition'), a way in which 'Milton' is spread across literary culture and continues to act long after the biographical Milton was dead.[26] Yet such actions (what the imitated 'Milton' does in, say, *The Splendid Shilling*) are not merely delayed or spatially extended versions of what the biographical Milton did or wanted to do. But neither are they just delayed or spatially extended versions of what the biographical John Philips (or any other imitator of Milton) wanted to do. Rather, 'Milton's style' (and the 'Milton' for which it stands) is a nexus where all sorts of agencies come together, some directly and some through being imputed (however improbably) to Milton himself.[27] In this way of thinking, there's a distinction between an author *qua* author ('Milton' and the style that supposedly characterizes and defines him) and the individual who shares that name (John Milton) and the former both can and does exist apart from the latter. One need not be Milton or be blind or hold his political beliefs or write about the Fall in order to write in a Miltonic style. One need only to use certain kinds of enjambment and lofty diction, match the sound to the sense, and employ mimetic, Latinate syntax.[28] One need only apprehend the ways in which those devices 'could be extended to other instances or occasions' and still bear a family resemblance to their supposed original.[29] One need only try on the style as one might try on a new coat.[30] And in taking up the Miltonic style, one could

---

[26] Marcel Mauss, 'A Category of the Human Mind: The Notion of Person; the Notion of Self', trans. by W. D. Halls, in *The Category of the Person: Anthropology, Philosophy, History*, ed. by Michael Carrithers, Steven Collins, and Steven Lukes (Cambridge: Cambridge University Press, 1985), pp. 1–25 (p. 19).

[27] My thinking is here obviously indebted to Alfred Gell's *Art and Agency: An Anthropological Theory* (Oxford: Clarendon Press, 1998).

[28] For a survey of Restoration and eighteenth-century commentary on Milton's style, see John Leonard, *Faithful Labourers: A Reception History of Paradise Lost, 1667–1970*, 2 vols (Oxford: Oxford University Press, 2013), I, 3–80.

[29] Jeff Dolven, 'Reading Wyatt for the Style', *Modern Philology*, 105.1 (2008), 65–86 (p. 72).

[30] I take the sartorial analogy from Dolven's account of the circulation of verse 'among a courtly audience with little apparent interest in the project of exegesis. Let us say, for the sake of argument, that a poem there might not be so much read as worn, like a new coat. What difference should that make to the project of reading Wyatt's poems for the style?' ('Reading Wyatt for the Style', p. 71). But the analogy was at least as available in the eighteenth century. See, for example, *An Essay on Criticism*. Pope proposes that style can be too highly prized: 'Others for *Language* all their Care express, / And value *Books*, as Women *Men*, for *Dress*: / Their praise is still—*The Stile is excellent*. / The *Sense*, they humbly take upon Content.' And too obtrusive or archaic a style might be vulgar and outlandish: 'In *Words*, as *Fashions*, the same Rule will hold; / Alike Fantastick, if *too New*, or *Old*; / Be not the *first* by whom the *New* are try'd, / Nor yet the *last* to lay the *Old* aside.' But the fundamental parallel between style and clothing is presented as self-evident and commonsensical. After all, '*True Wit* is *Nature* to Advantage drest, / What oft was *Thought*, but ne'er so well *Exprest*' (Alexander Pope, *Pastoral Poetry and an Essay on Criticism*, ed. by E. Aubra and Aubrey Williams [London: Methuen, 1961], pp. 272, 274, 276).

perhaps demonstrate one's own possession of style (*The Splendid Shilling* made Philips's reputation), but it would be a style that's come from outside of the self, one that asks and perhaps requires the writer to accommodate himself to preexisting notions of 'Milton' and the Miltonic. What can be expressed easily or well in that style becomes dominant; what is difficult or impossible to express in that style may well go unsaid (and perhaps even unthought). Miltonic style, far from giving voice to Milton's own private ambition, anguish, or experience of defeat, here becomes that which can mark other writers as stylish, precisely because they are adapting a style that is not their own to subjects that are not Milton's. At the same time, though, it further reinforces the collective sense of 'Milton' as an author who can somehow be epitomized by his style (and thereby separated from the biographical details that many eighteenth-century readers found distasteful, such as his antimonarchical politics or his treatment of his daughters).

Thinking about style in this manner might seem to take us away from institutions and into the realm of individual careers: into, say, what Mark Akenside gains from using 'Miltonic verse' in *The Voice of Liberty: or, A British Philippic: A Poem, in Miltonic Verse. Occasion'd by the Insults of the Spaniards, and the Preparations for War* (1738). But, as the idea of 'Milton' as a distributed person and the nexus of an indefinite number of agencies should suggest, style is not individual (despite the best efforts of would-be tastemakers), but rather a matter of collective judgment dispersed throughout a social group and rarely able to be given an exact origin. And it is in that lack of a clear origin (one cannot point to a single source that authoritatively defined what 'Miltonic verse' meant in the 1730s) that we can begin to understand how these stylistic imitations work as self-conscious representations of the institution of Authorship organizing, transmitting, and validating authors (in this case, 'Milton'). Consider only a baker's dozen of poems that explicitly flag themselves on their title pages as imitations of Milton:

- *Cerealia: An Imitation of Milton* (1706)
- *Ramillies. A Poem, Humbly Inscrib'd to His Grace the Duke of Marlborough. Written in Imitation of Milton* (1706)
- *The Mohocks: A Poem, in Miltonic Verse: Address'd to the Spectator* (1712)
- *Prae-Existence. A Poem, in Imitation of Milton* (1714)
- *Geneva: A Poem. In Miltonic Verse* (1729)
- *The Blanket. A Poem, in Imitation of Milton* (1733)
- *Money. A Poem in Imitation of Milton. Humbly inscrib'd to The Right Honourable, The Earl of Chesterfield* (1740)

- *The Fire-Works. A Poem. In Miltonic Verse* (1749)
- *The Empty Purse. A Poem in Miltonics. Dedicated to the Thrice Worthy Person that Fills It* (1750)
- *Stigand: or, The Antigallican. A Poem, in Miltonic Verse* (1750)
- *Clackshugh, A Poem. In Miltonic Verse* (1755)
- *Quebec: A Poetical Essay, In Imitation of the Miltonic Stile: Being a Regular Narrative of the Proceedings and Capital Transactions Performed by the British Forces under the Command of Vice-Admiral Saunders and Major-General Wolfe, in the Glorious Expedition against Canada, in the Year 1759* (1760)
- *Liberty. A Poem. In Imitation of Milton* (1763)

What these and the hundreds of other Miltonic imitations of the period, not to mention the various announced imitations of *The Splendid Shilling* (effectively Miltonic imitations once removed), all have in common is not a biographical origin, nor a political stance, nor a commitment to justifying the ways of God to men, but rather the 'Miltonic' style in which they all claim to be working.[31] But given the sheer variety of tones, topics, and hoped-for patrons, the 'Miltonic' here is almost wholly divorced from the specifics of Milton's own work. It is just style. Yet in their repetition of the terms 'Milton' and 'Miltonic', these poems suggest, both individually and collectively, that somehow the essence of Milton is to be found in this shared style. As such, they are (again, both individually and collectively) organizing, transmitting, and validating 'Milton'. But if they're all doing it (and this list is but a small fraction of the total amount of 'Miltonic' verse produced in the eighteenth century) and yet they vary so much from one another and aren't obviously following a specific predecessor – even the announced imitations of *The Splendid Shilling* are simply using Miltonic style to describe 'low' subjects and so are operating more in parallel to Philips than owing a debt to him – then the shared sense of 'Milton' at work here is not one that's attributable to any particular individual.[32] Nor is it simply what all those

---

[31] For a still helpful bibliography of 'Poems Influenced by' various works of Milton, see Raymond Dexter Havens, *The Influence of Milton on English Poetry* (Cambridge, MA: Harvard University Press, 1922), pp. 637–84. Avowed imitations of *The Splendid Shilling* include 'The Oyster Woman, in Imitation of Philips's Splendid Shilling', in *Sedition. A Poem* (London: J. Roberts, 1733), pp. 14–21; *Geneva. A Poem in Blank Verse. Occasioned by the Late Act of Parliament for Allowing Liquors Compound of English Spirits. Written in Imitation of Philips's Splendid Shilling* (London: T. Cooper, 1734); *The Dunoscope. In Imitation of the Splendid Shilling* (Dublin: E. Rider, 1736); ' The Poet: or, a Muse in Distress. In Imitation of the Splendid Shilling', in *A Collection of Miscellany Poems, Never before Publish'd* (London: H. Woodfall, 1737), pp. 1–7; ' Armour, An Imitation of the Splendid Shilling', in *The Potent Ally: Or, Succours from Merryland* (Paris [i.e. London]: [E. Curll], 1741), pp. 1–8; and 'Poverty. In Imitation of Mr. Philips's Splendid Shilling', *The Gentleman's Magazine*, 18 (1748), 88.
[32] It seems telling that *Bartholomew Fair: or, a Ramble to Smithfield. A Poem in Imitation of Milton* (London: J. Roberts and A. Dodd, 1729) also claims in a letter to the publisher to be '*the only Imitation of Mr. Philips's* Splendid Shilling, *which is so great a Master-piece in its kind*' (sig. A2r).

individual senses of 'Milton' have in common in some simplistic Venn diagram. Rather, 'Milton' here seems to have something of the status of folk wisdom; it's just what 'we all know' is characteristic and important about 'him'. It is, I submit, the voice of the assemblage, one of the ways in which the institution of Authorship gets to pronounce on what 'Milton' is and means and to what uses 'he' can be put. And as such, it's part of how the institution of Authorship gets to demonstrate its title to make such pronouncements.[33]

Of course, stylistic imitations aren't the only means through which the institution of Authorship organized, transmitted, and validated 'Milton', much less other authors. And it's in their connections with other modes of organization, transmission, and validation that the true power of the institution emerges. Those modes are potentially countless, so for now let it suffice to briefly touch on two. The first would be the use of Milton's head (i.e., a portrait of him from the shoulders on up) as a shop sign in an age before street numbering. At least eight booksellers and printers operated at the sign of Milton's Head over the course of the eighteenth century, some for decades at a time: George Hawkins in Fleet Street, London, from 1737 to 1760; Oliver Nelson 'in Skinner-Row' [now Christchurch Place], Dublin, from 1739 to 1769; Ebenezer Gardner in Gracechurch Street, London, from 1740 to 1743 (moving to 'within Aldgate' in 1746); J. Robinson in Maiden Lane, Covent Garden, London, in 1750; John Wood at the 'West End of the New Exchange' in Edinburgh from 1761 to 1765; first Robert Smith, Jr and then Archbald M'Lean at the 'Salt-Mercat' in Glasgow from 1762 to 1766; and R. Carr 'near the Grand Magazine' in Portsmouth in 1777. In each case, Milton's head, like other authorial heads used as shop signs, signified something like 'literary quality', rather than anything more specific to the Commonwealth's Secretary for Foreign Tongues (indeed, Wood was the only one ever to publish anything written by Milton). If only one or two booksellers had employed this sign, we might be able to see it as revealing something specific about them (say, republican political sympathies). But once Milton's Head

---

[33] Such pronouncements are what Pierre Bourdieu would call a 'rite of institution': the 'imposition of a name, i.e., of a social essence. To institute, to assign an essence ... is to impose a right to be that is an obligation of being so (or to be so)'; 'social essence is the set of those social attributes and attributions, produced by the act of institution as a solemn act of categorization which tends to produce what it designates'; 'it signifies to someone what his identity is, but in a way that both expresses it to him and imposes it on him by expressing it in front of everyone ... thus informing him in an authoritative manner of what he is and what he must be' ('Rites of Institution', in *Language and Symbolic Power*, ed. by John B. Thompson, trans. by Gino Raymond and Matthew Adamson [Cambridge: Polity Press, 1991], pp. 117–26 (pp. 120–21)). Bourdieu is describing rites involving the living, but his account works equally well to describe the 'social essence' assigned to the celebrated dead.

became a visual fixture of the principal cities of the realm (with two at a time in London for a decent chunk of the 1740s), the 'Milton' of the signs became detached not only from Milton's own work, but also from the specific publishing programs of these booksellers. A case might be able to be made that there's something appropriate about Hawkins publishing Gilbert West's *A Canto of the Faerie Queen. Written by Spenser. Never before Published* (1739) at the sign of Milton's Head, but the argument would quickly grow strained with, say, his edition of *The City Farce* two years earlier or Nelson's edition of *Pamela* three years later. Instead, Milton's Head joined the heads of Addison, Cowley, Dryden, Gay, Otway, Pope, Prior, Rowe, Shakespeare, and Swift (plus fictitious authors such as Yorick) in serving as painted wooden guarantors of the worth of the wares to be had within. But what is serving as the foundation for that guarantee is not anything specific about Milton's own work, but rather his status as part of an emerging national canon. Milton's Head could work as a sign hanging over the entrance to a bookseller's shop because 'Milton' (as a reputation, which is to say as a name) had been organized, transmitted, and validated enough that 'he' was self-evidently a sign of literary value. And as we've seen, that organization, transmission, and validation is the result of not only many thousands of individual acts along those lines, but also of the additional acts that arise out of the assemblage itself, additional acts that we could describe as the workings of the institution of Authorship.

Together, the stylistic imitations and the shop signs and a number of other seemingly minor microgenres, such as scenes of Milton's ghost engaging with other writers, interacted in complex and not always predictable ways with the more familiar materials of reception history (editions, controversies over editions, commentaries, essays in periodicals like *The Spectator*, etc.) to sever 'Milton' the great poet from Milton the apologist for regicide, divorce, and other unsavory things. In Jonathan Richardson's painting of himself and his son with the specter of Milton, for example, Milton's status as an entirely literary figure (rather than an ordinary being of flesh and blood and disagreeable ideas) is driven home by the heavenly light streaming down on him, the wreath of laurels around his head, the way his body disappears within its velvet drapery, and the fact that his face is taken from the frontispiece to Richardson's *Explanatory Remarks and Notes on Milton's Paradise Lost* (see Figures 3.1 and 3.2). This is a creature of pure reputation, what Johnson would call, in a different context, a 'Being of another Species'.[34] The result was that

---

[34] In *Rambler* 4, Johnson describes the heroes and villains of romance as 'Beings of another Species' (*The Rambler*, 4 [31 March 1750]). For a different version of the spectral Milton, see 'The Apotheosis

Figure 3.1 Jonathan Richardson the Elder, *The Artist and His Son, Jonathan, in the Presence of Milton*, undated, oil on canvas, 64 × 77 cm. Private collection. Photo courtesy of the Courtauld Institute of Art.

'Milton' could become an exemplary author, despite all of the biographical Milton's heterodox positions and other baggage. This is not to say the latter were entirely forgotten (they certainly weren't), but they could be explained away as evidence of his personal integrity and love of liberty or bracketed as primarily of interest to Milton's biographers and would-be political heirs, which meant they could therefore be safely ignored by those with more 'literary' interests – a far larger and more sociable

---

of Milton: A Vision', *The Gentleman's Magazine*, 8 (1738), 232–35, 469, 521–22 and 9 (1739), 20–21, 73–75, in which the Genius of Westminster Abbey escorts a (possibly dreaming) visitor to a secret room '*sacred to the Spirits of the Bards*' who are buried in or have monuments in the abbey (8, 233). There he invisibly observes '*the Admission of the Great Milton into their Society*' (8, 233), a club comprised of the ghosts of Chaucer, Drayton, Spenser, Jonson, Beaumont, Dryden, Shadwell, Otway, Cowley, Prior, Davenant, Butler, John Philips, Sheffield, Rowe, Lee, Congreve, Addison, Gay, Betterton, Garth, and Stepney.

Figure 3.2 Jonathan Richardson the Elder, frontispiece and title page of *Explanatory Notes and Remarks on Milton's Paradise Lost. By J. Richardson, Father and Son. With the Life of the Author, and a Discourse on the Poem* (London, 1734).

group.[35] And it's in Milton's becoming an exemplary author ('Milton'), a shorthand for value, an easily grasped and no longer toxic – or even particularly partisan – reputation that we can see the institution of Authorship at work. 'Milton' emerges out of the assemblage organized, transmitted, and validated, and his status as a writer who has been subject to such treatment is marked by the sheer ubiquity of these minor, playful, highly self-conscious microgenres that call attention to (and so represent) 'him' as just a given,

---

[35] For the reframing of Milton's politics as misguided, but 'sincere', see Dustin Griffin, *Regaining Paradise: Milton and the Eighteenth Century* (Cambridge: Cambridge University Press, 1986), pp. 11–21. Cf. Griffin's claim that 'those who disapproved of the man or his politics found it convenient to remember only the poet' (p. 33). On the relative size of the camps of his literary and political admirers, see [Francis Blackburne], *Memoirs of Thomas Hollis, Esq* (London: J. Nichols, 1780): 'Milton the poet and Milton the politician were two different men. The latter is known to few in comparison with the numerous acquaintance of the other' (p. 509).

a fixture of literary culture so self-evidently important that his very name – a proper noun – can be turned into both an adjective ('Miltonic') and a common noun (the 'Miltonics' in which *The Empty Purse* is composed).[36] Without the distributed person of 'Milton' and the assemblage that it both helps hold together and is, 'he' could not have become a type and so there would be no 'mute inglorious *Milton*[s]' to mourn.[37] Nor would it be as easy to eventually imagine literature as separable from politics (something that both Milton and the two generations after him would have found both ridiculous and jaw-droppingly naïve).[38] Nor would it have been necessary for Johnson to point out the absurdity of expecting the work of exemplary authors to manifest a uniformly high level of quality: 'Such is the power of reputation justly acquired, that its blaze drives away the eye from nice examination. Surely no man could have fancied that he read *Lycidas* with pleasure, had he not known its author.'[39] Indeed, the winnowing down of the genres that actually count as 'literary' that's such a huge part of the modern idea of Literature (the institution that denies its status as such) is in many ways a product of the workings of the assemblage that I've been describing here. The 'Milton' produced by all the microgenres that are key to the functioning of the institution of Authorship would never have designed to write in such genres. Their self-evidently minor status (which has allowed them to hide in plain sight for three centuries) is the pyrrhic result of their success. We can, I propose, best grasp the power of the institution of Authorship as it worked in the eighteenth century by taking seriously all the seemingly trivial ephemera the descendants of that institution have taught us to forget.

Large, diffuse institutions, like Authorship, may work differently than their more localizable counterparts with addresses. But they are every bit as

---

[36] Cf. the conversion of 'Rochester' into a verb in the piece from *The Grand Magazine* cited in note 15.
[37] [Thomas Gray], *An Elegy Wrote in a Country Church Yard* (London: R. Dodsley, 1751), p. 8.
[38] Carol Kay describes how the mid-eighteenth-century 'national settlement' seemed 'to allow ... what Hobbes denied; a stable, nonpolitical realm, not a private world of the self, but a leisure space for reading and writing which could never be troubled by questions of power' and so 'made differences of opinion fun.' Readers could assure themselves that 'someone else somewhere else ... is taking reasonably good care of things, looking after the state', while they indulged themselves in the literary (*Political Constructions: Defoe, Richardson, and Sterne in Relation to Hobbes, Hume, and Burke* [Ithaca: Cornell University Press, 1988], pp. 11, 203, 222).
[39] Johnson, *Lives of the Most Eminent English Poets*, I, 279. Cf. his comments on *Samson Agonistes*: 'it is only by a blind confidence in the reputation of Milton, that a drama can be praised in which the intermediate parts have neither cause nor consequence, neither hasten nor retard the catastrophe' (I, 292).

much institutions of literature and so both deserve and need to be thought about within the same frame and using at least most of the same categories. Mee and Sangster's definition offers a good start, one that the eighteenth century would have easily recognized. We would do well to follow their lead.

CHAPTER 4

Eighteenth-Century Musenhof *Courts as Bridges and Brokers for Cultural Networks and Social Reform*

Nicole Pohl

In the German-speaking territories of eighteenth-century Europe, *Musenhof* courts were sites where rulers surrounded themselves with artists and intellectuals, writers and musicians. They were a conspicuous feature of geopolitical environments where smaller courts and principalities were being fashioned into the larger cultural units of the Holy Roman Empire and Brandenburg-Prussia (later the Kingdom of Prussia). Though aristocratic in inception and genesis, *Musenhof* courts functioned as bridges and brokers for diverse artistic, social and literary networks across the German-speaking world. They provided a permeable environment where overlapping social networks straddled the court and the public sphere.

This chapter juxtaposes three contrasting *Musenhof* courts in order to highlight their contribution as sites for cultural brokering in their regions and on a national level. Through the juxtaposition of the different models of the *Musenhof*, I will chart a paradigm shift in the history of the *Musenhof* from an aristocratic space of (cosmopolitan) sociability and patronage to *exempla* for sociopolitical and economic reforms.

My first case study will be the most prominent: Anna Amalia (1739–1807) and her provincial *Musenhof* court at Weimar. I will explore how her investment in her provincial coteries fed into a wider attempt to forge a cultural nation out of the political, cultural and administrative patchwork of small states and principalities of the Holy Roman Empire. My second case study contrasts provincial Weimar with the East Prussian *Musenhof* of Charlotte Caroline Amalia von Keyserling(k) (1727–91) in Königsberg – a regional hub of Enlightenment sociability and cultural production in a cosmopolitan environment. My third case study turns to the Baltic noblewoman Dorothea von Kurland (1761–1821) and her provincial *Musenhof* court in Löbichau, Saxony-Gotha-Altenburg. Her sociability in the region brought the Dukedom to greater cultural prominence, but her investment in agricultural and social schemes in the region introduced lasting changes. The changes the once aristocratic *Musenhof* culture saw were an embourgeoisement – a 'neuständische Vergesellschaftung' – but one that occurred without the courts losing their significant roles as cultural brokers and mediators.¹

Ilm-Athen

Quite a number of small courts in the Holy Roman Empire and Prussia in the eighteenth century were fashioned into *Musenhof* courts by regents who attracted and patronised artists and writers.² *Musenhof* court sociability was defined by the extensive patronage of the arts and sciences with the aim to elevate the standing of the courts beyond the provincial to national recognition.² These courts were essentially outward looking, well connected between different European courts through dynastic marriage and patronage alliances. Though aristocratic in inception and genesis, their function as bridges and brokers for artistic and literary networks made them permeable, with overlapping social networks that straddled the court and what Habermas termed the public sphere.³ *Musenhof* courts were founded by both men and women who – in different degrees – presided over their activities.

The literature on *Musenhof* courts currently is dominated by the most prominent of all, the court of Anna Amalia (1739–1807), hailed as the birthplace of German Classicism and indeed the rebirth of middle Germany with the intellectual centres of Weimar, Jena and Wittenberg – Ilm Athen.⁴ Anna Amalia was the duchess of Saxe-Weimar-Eisenach, by marriage, and was also regent of the states of Saxe-Weimar and Saxe-Eisenach between 1758 and 1775 after her husband, Ernst August II Konstantin, Duke of Saxe-Weimar-Eisenach, suddenly died. Anna Amalia ruled the principalities on behalf of her oldest son Karl August

---

¹ Reinhard Blänkner, '"Neuständische Gesellschaft" – Europäische Gesellschaft im globalen Kontext (1750–1830/40)', *Ungleichheiten*, 47 (2009), 218–22.
² Volker Bauer, *Die Höfische Gesellschaft in Deutschland von der Mitte des 17. bis zum Ausgang des 18. Jahrhunderts: Versuch einer Typologie* (Tübingen: Niemeyer, 1993).
³ Michael Michie, *Working Cross-Culturally: Identity Learning, Border Crossing and Culture Brokering* (Rotterdam: Sense, 2014), pp. 83–106.
⁴ Athens on the Ilm. See Justus H. Ulbricht, 'Der "Weimarer Musenhof" – vom Fürstenideal zur Finalchiffre: Eine erinnerungskulturelle Spurensuche', in *Anna Amalia, Carl August und das Ereignis Weimar*, ed. by Hellmut Th Seemann (Köln: Wallstein Verlag, 2007), pp. 191–208; Joachim Berger, 'Anna Amalia und das Ereignis Weimar-Jena', in *Anna Amalia*, ed. by Seemann, pp. 13–30.

until 1775, when her role significantly shifted from ruler to the Dowager duchess.

The historian Joachim Berger has explored perhaps most critically the myth of the *Musenhof* that was projected onto Anna Amalia's court in Weimar and queried the central role Anna Amalia had in the creation of Weimar as the seat of the classicist muses.[5] Berger argues that it was mainly Anna Amalia's son and heir to the Duchy who attracted literary giants such as Goethe who in turn drew other prominent writers and philosophers to Weimar. Justus Ulbricht shifts the focus of the discussion to the point that Anna Amalia's *Musenhof* court served a role in the emerging debates about national identity and cultural nationhood to which guests of Weimar, in particular Goethe and Christoph Martin Wieland (1733–1813), contributed. In the following, I will argue that Anna Amalia indeed hosted a successful *Musenhof*. However, I will show that her *Musenhof* adapted to the sociopolitical and geopolitical changes of the Holy Roman Empire, and provided a model for later incarnations.

In 1807, Goethe wrote his necrologue on Anna Amalia, *Zum feyerlichen Andenken der Durchlauchtigsten Fürstin und Frau Anna Amalia, verwittweten Herzogin zu Sachsen-Weimar und Eisenach, gebornen Herzogin von Braunschweig und Lüneburg*.[6] Here he extols Anna Amalia's regency as one determined by justice, economic prudence and good policies ('Polizen'). He praised Anna Amalia's attracting a mixed society of learned men, artists and high-ranking visitors to Weimar and sponsoring a library and a theatre that provided for the education of coming generations. In a letter to Johann Heinrich Merck of 3 January 1784, Wieland compared

---

[5] See Joachim Berger, *Anna Amalia von Sachsen-Weimar-Eisenach (1739–1807): Denk- und Handlungsräume einer ‚aufgeklärten' Herzogin* (Heidelberg: Winter, 2003) and Joachim Berger, 'Geselligkeit, Mäzenatentum und Kunstliebhaberei am "Musenhof" Anna Amalias – neue Ergebnisse, neue Fragen' (pp. 1–17) and '"Tieffurth" oder "Tibur"? Herzogin Anna Amalias Rückzug in ihren "Musensitz"' (pp. 125–64), in *Der 'Musenhof' Anna Amalias: Geselligkeit, Mäzenatentum und Kunstliebhaberei im klassischen Weimar*, ed. by Joachim Berger (Köln: Böhlau, 2001). See also Angela Borchert, 'Die Entstehung der Musenhofvorstellung aus den Angedenken an Anna Amalia von Sachsen-Weimar-Eisenach', in *Der 'Musenhof' Anna Amalias*, ed. by Berger, pp. 165–87. Other biographies and scholars maintain that Anna Amalia was indeed instrumental in moulding Weimar into, if not the birthplace, the pivot of German Classicism: see Ursula Salentin, *Anna Amalia: Wegbereiterin der Weimarer Klassik* (Köln: Böhlau, 1996) and Annette Seemann, *Anna Amalia: Herzogin von Weimar* (Frankfurt: Insel Verlag, 2007).

[6] Johann Wolfgang Goethe, *Zum feyerlichen Andenken der Durchlauchtigsten Fürstin und Frau Anna Amalia, verwittweten Herzogin zu Sachsen-Weimar und Eisenach, gebornen Herzogin von Braunschweig und Lüneburg* (Weimar: [n. pub.], 1807) <https://haab-digital.klassik-stiftung.de/viewer/!metadata/765125390/1/-/>. Six hundred copies were initially printed, and the text was also published in a variety of periodicals and newspapers.

Anna Amalia to *Athena Poliás* and appreciated her as protector of Weimar and the goddess of art, providing for writers and artists.[7]

One can identify different phases of Anna Amalia's cultural brokerage. Anna Amalia supported the arts during her actual reign over the court of Weimar, motivated by her personal interest in the arts. What is often overlooked is that Anna Amalia shrewdly managed the education of her sons with their roles as future rulers in mind. Thus, Anna Amalia invited Wieland to tutor her son and future regent and encouraged him, after 1775, to continue living in Weimar on a pension and the patronage of the court. Wieland joined Johann Karl August Musäus (1735–87), who had come to Weimar in 1763 as governor of the pages. The poet and translator Karl Ludwig von Knebel (1744–1834) became tutor for Anna Amalia's son Constantin in 1774, and introduced Karl August to Goethe. Karl August quickly invited Goethe to Weimar and included him in the governing ranks of the court. In 1776, Goethe became a member of the Privy Council, in 1779 he took on the War Commission and the Mines and Highways Commissions and in 1782 he rose to the post of interim chancellor of the Exchequers.

Under the patronage of Anna Amalia, these men became active in literature and the arts. Musäus worked with the publisher Nicolai on the periodical *Allgemeinen deutschen Bibliothek* (1765–1806) and was consequently promoted to Professor of Classics and History at a grammar school in Weimar. Wieland edited *Der Teutsche Merkur* between 1773 and 1789, a journal based on the *Mercure de France* but with the aim to unite the disparate German-speaking territories under a common idea of cultural identity and history. A particular lover of music, a musician and a composer herself, Anna Amalia brought touring theatre and opera companies to Weimar, including the prominent Seyler company.[8] Anna Amalia supported the musical ambitions of Ernst Wilhelm Wolf (1735–92) by first inviting him as music teacher to her sons, then elevating him to court 'Konzertmeister' (1761), organist (1763) and finally 'Kapellmeister' (1772).

Before 1775, Weimar's court life was characterised by elaborate masque balls ('Redouten'), concerts and theatre performances and a newly founded freemason lodge. After 1775, Anna Amalia continued her activities, though

---

[7] Johann Heinrich Merck, *Briefe an und von Johann Heinrich Merck. Eine selbständige Folge der im Jahr 1835 erschienenen Briefe an J. H. Merck: Aus den Handschriften herausgegeben von Dr. Karl Wagner. Mit Facsimilien der Handschrift von Göthe, Herder, Wieland, Karl August und Amalia v. Weimar, W. Tischbein, Claudius und Merck* (Darmstadt: Verlag von Johann Philipp Diehl, 1838), pp. 230–31.

[8] Gisela Sichardt, *Das Weimarer Liebhabertheater unter Goethes Leitung* (Weimar: Arion Verlag, 1957).

with fewer financial means as she had to finance her cultural ventures herself. Until about 1780, she tried to include her own cultural programmes in the now somewhat separate court of her son and his wife, Luise Auguste, daughter of Louis IX, Landgrave of Hesse-Darmstadt.[9] Thus, the exclusive court assemblies continued after 1775, where Anna Amalia welcomed mainly aristocratic women of Weimar in the Wittumspalais whilst the separate princely table was solely attended by the military, civil servants and court officials. Anna Amalia also introduced a different and mixed sociability in smaller circles. She welcomed artists, courtiers and middling classes to her 'Tafelrunde' (1775–1807) at the Wittumspalais (in the winter) or in Tiefurt (during the summer months), where new works of literature or art and new scientific ideas were presented to the guests informally. Goethe, Herder and Wieland participated frequently at these events, as well as Friedrich Schiller, Charlotte von Stein, Anna Amalia's son Karl August, von Knebel, Johann Heinrich Meyer, Georg Melchior Kraus, Wieland and Luise von Göchhausen. Karl Wilhelm Heinrich Lyncker described a mixed sociability at these events:

> Zur Mittwochstafel der Herzogin wurden nur einer oder zwei von Adel, jederzeit aber mehrere schöne Geister eingeladen. Goethe, Wieland und Herder gerieten regelmäßig in lebhaften Streit; von Knebel und Einsiedel nahmen dann Partei. So entstand ein zwar an sich interessantes, aber oft solch lautes Gespräch, dass die Herzogin, Mäßigung gebietend, zuweilen die Tafel früher aufheben musste.[10]

After 1780, Anna Amalia relocated to her Palais in Tiefurt and scaled down her court to a small household of a few servants, publishing her manuscript periodical the *Journal von Tiefurt* and continuing an increasingly separate existence from the main court.

Anna Amalia's dynastic rule was motivated by courtly values, 'Tugend und Rechtschaffenheit', but also by an understanding of dynastic patriotism to further, through the establishment of a *Musenhof* court, a cultural unity in a region where tensions between the Austrian Habsburg monarchy and the Kingdom of Prussia dominated. If historically the 'republic of

---

[9] Berger, 'Anna Amalia und das Ereignis Weimar-Jena', p. 17.
[10] 'Only one or two members of the aristocracy but always several men of culture were invited to the Duchess' "Mittwochstafel". Goethe, Wieland and Herder got into lively fights on a regular basis; von Knebel and Einsiedel then took sides. This is how such interesting but always noisy conversations developed so much so that the Duchess, exercising moderation, had to rise from the table early' (my translation), Karl Wilhelm Heinrich Lyncker, *Am Weimarischen Hofe unter Amalien und Karl August: Erinnerungen von Karl Frhr. von Lyncker*, ed. by Marie Scheller and Wilhelm Bode (Berlin: E. S. Mittler und Sohn, 1912), p. 75.

letters', so desired by Goethe, was part of a cross-cutting social network, including the court, the *nobilitas literaria*, emerging public institutions and a political sphere independent from, or even counter to, the court, the *Musenhof* court under Anna Amalia was part of its paradigmatic development.

The genesis and evolution of the Weimar *Musenhof* court under Anna Amalia indicates historical changes that also affected the French salons of the *ancien régime*. The eventual decline of Anna Amalia's *Musenhof* court was partially effected by a predominantly masculinist literary and political culture, the end of a feminocentric *ancien régime* patronage and sociability, and the *embourgeoisement* of the public sphere. Nevertheless, as Marcus Ventzke suggested, Anna Amalia's Weimar remained a 'cultural export model' which provided the prototype for subsequent *Musenhof* courts hosted by women as far away as East Prussia.[11]

. . . A Learned Siberia

Königsberg, the most eastern city of the Prussian Empire, was prominent in the eighteenth century for diverse reasons. Its position as a Hanseatic League port, accessible also during the winter from the Baltic Sea, had attracted significant trade and wealth since the early modern period. Königsberg's original multi-ethnic population, consisting of Latvians, Lithuanians/Livonians, Polish, Old Prussians (Prußen) and Jews, was joined by Scottish Presbyterians, Dutch Remonstrants and Huguenots in the seventeenth century, as well as merchants and tradesmen. The plague of 1709–10 in East Prussia reduced the population significantly. However, Friedrich Wilhelm's repopulation programme attracted further Swiss, Dutch, French and Bohemian immigrants, as well as settlers from the Palatinate, the Rhineland, Franconia, Swabia and Nassau, making the city ethnically even more diverse. Königsberg was strategically placed between Berlin, St Petersburg, Riga, Reval and the Duchy of Courland. The home of a prominent Protestant university, the *Albertina*, founded in 1544, attracted scholars, students and, in the eighteenth century, a vibrant publishing industry publishing Kant, Herder, Hamann and Hippel.

However, the relations between the different ethnic groups were complex. Ludwig von Baczko claimed that the different communities lived and traded in separate neighbourhoods of the city, with only the Swedish,

---

[11] Marcus Ventzke, 'Der Weimarer Musenhof und seine ungeratenen Kinder: Zur Entwicklung eines kulturellen Exportmodell', *Goethe-Jahrbuch*, 119 (2002), 132–47.

Dutch, English and Danish living in one area together, the Licent.[12] The Jewish population was partially integrated into the cultural and social life of Königsberg. This was less the case for the Baltic ethnic groups. The East Prussians dominated Königsberg with their publishing enterprises, German-speaking societies, assemblies and salons. It was particularly Immanuel Kant who attracted students and philosophers. The *Albertina* recorded only a small number of students from Lithuania and Poland who belonged to the philosophical and medical faculties.[13]

Königsberg offered a vibrant sociability with salons hosted by the aristocratic Sophie Charlotte Albertine (zu Dohna-Lauck) von Auerswald (1760–1831); Friederike Amelie von Dohna-Schlobitten-Leistenau (Schlieben), Herzogin zu Schleswig-Holstein-Sonderburg-Beck (1757–1827); Johanna Elisabeth von Stägemann (1761–1835); and Charlotte Caroline Amalie Gräfin von Keyserling (1727–91), as well as the middling sorts Henriette Elisabeth Barckley (or Barclay, née Dittrich) and Johanna Motherby (1783–1842), the wife of the Scottish merchant and friend of Kant, Robert Motherby.[14] Other prominent circles were Kant's *Tischgesellschaft* (Table Society) and the exclusive *Blumenkranz des baltischen Meeres* (Floral Wreath of the Baltic Sea). The line-up indicates the cross-cutting nature of these social circles, where the hostesses acted as cultural brokers and patrons for the aristocratic and middling classes. They were not only interconnected but also connected to other circles in Berlin and Leipzig.

Charlotte Caroline Amalie Gräfin von Keyserling(k), daughter of Karl Ludwig Truchseß von Waldburg and Countess Sophie Charlotte of Wylich and Lottum, married into East Prussian and Courland aristocracy. In Königsberg, she gathered a *Musenhof*, prominent particularly because of her patronage of Immanuel Kant.[15] Given the courtly architecture and interior design of the *Schliebensche Palais* in Königsberg, the immense library, and von Keyserling(k)'s extensive patronage and connectedness

---

[12] Ludwig von Baczko, *Versuch einer Geschichte und Beschreibung Königsberg* (Königsberg: Goebbels & Unzer, 1804), pp. 96–97.
[13] Stanislaw Salmonowicz, 'Königsberg, Thorn und Danzig: Zur Geschichte Königsbergs als Zentrum der Aufklärung', in *Königsberg und Riga*, ed. by Heinz Ischreyt (Tübingen: Max Niemeyer Verlag, 1995), pp. 9–28 (p. 19).
[14] Klaus Garber, *Das Alte Königsberg: Erinnerungsbuch einer untergegangenen Stadt* (Köln: Böhlau, 2008), pp. 98–99.
[15] A note on the spelling of Keyserling(k). Caroline married Graf Grafen Gebhardt Johann von Keyserlingk (1699–1761) in 1744. After his death in 1761, she married his nephew Heinrich Christian von Keyserling and thus changed the spelling of her name. I will continue spelling her name Keyserling(k).

to prominent Enlightenment figures across Eastern Europe, the term seems appropriate. Furthermore, von Keyserling(k) was not only a cultural broker and patron, but she also produced literary criticism and scientific work herself as translator and author. Her *Musenhof* reflected the European make-up of Königsberg appropriately, welcoming aristocracy, middling classes, and, during the occupation, Russian soldiers, alike, thus involving a social diversity that the classical Weimar under Anna Amalia did not offer:

> Der Unterschied des Standes vermochte niemals die heitere Geselligkeit zu stören, den einem jeden der Gäste wurden die ihnen gebührenden Aufmerksamkeiten mit gleicher Achtung erwiesen und so mit zarter Sorgfalt innere und äussere Harmonie geschaffen und erhalten.[16]

There are two phases of von Keyserling(k)'s sociability. With her first husband, Gebhardt Johann von Keyserlingk, who acquired the *Palais* in 1755, Caroline von Keyserling(k) welcomed a range of prominent guests, including Immanuel Kant. He had been her sons' tutor between 1753 and 1754 at the rural estate Schloss Waldburg-Capustigalla and remained a close friend of the family.[17] Capustigalla was one of Truchseß' family estates and became the centre of Königsberg's polite society during the Seven Years' War (1756–63).

Caroline von Keyserling(k)'s second husband, Count Heinrich Christian von Keyserling, of Blieden (Pilsblidene), Courland, extended the Palais to a true *Musenhof*. He refurbished the *Palais* 'mit kostbaren Möbeln, Bildern, Büchern und Chinoiserien im französischen Geschmack'.[18] Von Keyserling also built a small theatre ('Comoedienhaus') in the park. There were different forms of gatherings: evening balls, *Tischgesellschaften* (lunch and dinner parties), garden parties and musical entertainments. The *Palais*'s sociability flourished particularly in the 1770s with visitors such as Karoline Henriette Christine Philippine Luise von Pfalz-Zweibrücken, the future Friedrich Wilhelm II, Kant, Johann Georg Hamann, Stanislaw August I, Theodor Gottlieb von

---

[16] 'The differences in rank never hindered the lively sociability, each guest was met with the attention and respect they deserved, and thus, with gentle care inner and outer harmony was created' (my translation), Benno Bobrik, *Immanuel Kant's Ansichten über das weibliche Geschlecht: Tischrede an Kant's Geburtstage in der Königsberger Kant-Gesellschaft* (Königsberg: Albert Rosbach'schen Buchdruckerei, 1877), p. 20.

[17] Rudolf Malter, 'Kant im Keyserlingschen Haus', *Kant-Studien*, 72 (1981), 88–95.

[18] 'With precious furniture, paintings, books and chinoiseries in the French taste' (my translation), Johann Ludwig Schwarz, *Denkwürdigkeiten aus dem Leben eines Geschäftsmannes, Staatsmannes, Dichters und Humoristen* (Leipzig: Rollmann, 1828), p. 179.

Hippel, and others. Herbert Meinhard Mühlpfordt lists further notable personalities who von Keyserling(k) painted and therefore we can assume that she welcomed them to her *Palais*, too. These include Johann Friedrich Domhardt, provost Friedrich Alexander Freiherr von Korff, Sophie Charlotte Albertine (zu Dohna-Lauck) von Auerswald and this chapter's other principal subjects, Anna Amalia of Weimar and Dorothea von Kurland.[19]

The gatherings were very successful. In a letter to Jacobi, Hamann raved, 'Dies Haus ist die Krone unseres ganzen Adels, unterscheidet sich von allen übrigen durch Gastfreiheit, Wohltätigkeit, Geschmack.'[20] Caroline von Keyserling(k) was clearly well connected. She also was francophile. She subscribed to all important French periodicals, and her library housed between 4,000 and 5,000 books, as well as mathematical and scientific instruments. She also contributed to periodicals with her own articles.[21] In his *Kurzen Reisebeschreibungen*, Bernoulli enthused:

> Es ist von dieser Dame bekannt, daß Sie eine vertraute Freundin der Musen und eine einsichtsvolle Liebhaberin der Wissenschaften ist. Sie ist Verfasserin verschiedener Schriften und Aufsätze, die aber ohne Ihren Namen herausgekommen sind. Sie zeichnet und malt nach dem Urtheil der Kenner vortrefflich sowohl in Pastel als mit Oel- und Wasserfarben; sticht auch in Kupfer.[22]

A rare document of this sociability and von Keyserling(k)'s creativity is the *Almanach domestique de Cléon et de Javotte avec des tableaux qui représentent*

---

[19] She also painted Kant, as Malter discusses. On the other portraits found in Rautenburg, see Herbert Meinhard Mühlpfordt, *Königsberger Leben im Rokoko: Bedeutende Zeitgenossen Kants*, vol. 7 (Siegen: Schriften der J. G. Herder-Bibliothek Siegerland, 1981), pp. 20–22. Von Korff and Dohna-Lauck were related by marriage to the Finckensteins who originated in East Prussia and then also settled in the Markgraviate of Brandenburg.

[20] 'This house is the pinnacle of our aristocracy, differs from all others in hospitality, benevolence, taste' (my translation), Letter to F. H. Jacobi, 7 January 1785, cited in Karl Vorländer, *Immanuel Kant: Der Mann und das Werk*, 2 vols (Leipzig: Felix Meiner, 1924) <www.textlog.de/35661.html>.

[21] It is not clear what she wrote exactly. The papers in the family's Rautenburg Sammmlung, near Tilsit, were destroyed in 1926 and the estate Rautenburg was also destroyed after WWII when the remaining family Keyserling became displaced. See Andrea Reichenberger, 'Die Rolle der Familie Keyserlingk und des Gottsched-Kreises für Kants Du Châtelet-Rezeption', in *Emilie Du Châtelet und die deutsche Aufklärung*, ed. by Ruth Hagengruber and Hartmut Hecht (Wiesbaden: Springer, 2019), pp. 245–71 (p. 258, fn. 40). I thank Andrea Reichenberger for making her chapter available to me during the COVID-19 lockdown.

[22] 'This Lady is known for being a trusted friend of the muses and a tolerant lover of sciences. She is the author of a variety of writings and essays, which were published without her name. According to specialists, she draws and paints perfectly in pastel as well as in oil and watercolours, she also engraves' (my translation), Johann Bernoulli, *Sammlung Kurzer Reisebeschreibungen und anderer zur Erweiterung der Länder und Menschenkenntniß dienender Nachrichten*, 18 vols (Berlin: Johann Bernoulli, 1781–87), IX, 78.

leur vie privée of 1782, with architectural plans of the *Palais*, a brief biographical note (written in Gothic script and added in 1869), the actual handwritten almanach and twelve hand-painted opaque watercolour miniatures, as well as a short piece, 'De la société acromatique'.[23] The *Almanach* gives insight into the daily lives of the Keyserling(k)s, thinly veiled as the pastoral shepherds Cléon and Javotte – the idyll of the domestic lives of the couple, their friends and visitors. It is here, as the signature to the ground plan of the *Palais* suggests, where the sage retires with his friends for pleasure and conversation.[24] The *Almanach* creates a tension between the idyllic courtly paradise inhabited by nobles who excel in the courtly *bienfaisance* (that is patronage), *honnêté*, the Horatian trope of retirement to a simpler way of existence – here frugal domesticity – and the actual luxurious *Musenhof* sociability in Königsberg.

These sociable evenings took place possibly only during the winter months on Tuesdays; summer evenings were spent with picnics to local country houses such as the Fuchshöfen (Slawjanskoje).[25] The conversation, as we know from contemporary guests, dedicated itself to politics, science and literature. The 'société acromatique' was the manifesto of Heinrich Christian von Keyserling and his wife's understanding of hospitality and sociability. The aims of the evenings were, as the short pamphlet indicates, conversation and enlightenment that transcended rank and nationality:

> J'appelle société acromatique, toute société qui s'assemble pour s'instruire par la lecture et par le discours. Le but en est d'entendre les connaissance humaines, de s'instruire mutuellement, et de contribuer par la a la felicité des hommes.[26]

---

[23] On the provenance of the *Almanach*, see Malter, p. 88; on the images, see also Sigrid von Moisy, 'Der "Almanch domestique" der Gräfin Caroline Amalie v. Keyserling', in *Einladung ins 18. Jahrhundert. Ein Almanach aus dem Verlag C.H.Beck im 225. Jahr seines Bestehens*, ed. by Ernst-Peter Wieckenberg (München: Beck, 1988), pp. 504–06. Zandt proposes that the latter was written by Heinrich Christian von Keyserling (Cleon) as a gift and memento of the Keyserling(k)'s time in Königsberg. Stephan Zandt, *Die Kultivierung des Geschmacks: Eine Transformationsgeschichte der Kulinarischen Sinnlichkeit* (Berlin: De Gruyter, 2019), pp. 267–68.

[24] 'C'est avec ses amis qu'en ces aimables lieux,/Le Sage se respose et jouit d'un fort tranquille:/Il remet son destin entre les mains de Dieux/ Le bonheur est pour luis aux champs comme a la ville.' ['It is with his friends that in these amiable places, / The Sage rests and enjoys a peaceful place: / He puts his destiny in the hands of Gods / Happiness is for him in the fields as in the city' (my translation)]. Caroline von Keyserling, *Almanach domestique de Cléon et de Javotte avec des tableaux qui représentent leur vie privée* (1782), Bayrische Staatsbibliothek, München, Cod.gall. 908, fol. 1.

[25] Helmut von Osterroht, 'Das fräuliche Fideikommiß Fuchshöfen', *Ostdeutsche Familienkunde*, 5.2 (April–June 1968), 39–41.

[26] 'I call acromatic society any society that assembles in order to learn through reading and conversation. Its goal is to understand human knowledge, to educate each other, and to contribute to the happiness of men' (my translation), fol. 17r–v. In his 'On the Manner of Teaching', Immanuel Kant

Immanuel Kant echoed this understanding of the civilising process of society through cosmopolitan hospitality and sociability, particularly when hosted by women. Zandt argues that Kant's experiences at the *Schliebensche Palais* shaped his reflections in his lectures at the Albertus University which were published in 1798 as *Anthropologie in pragmatischer Hinsicht,* and vice versa, von Keyserling's piece mirrored some of Kant's reflection. Kant praised the *Tischgesellschaften*, the small dining circles, as they happened at the Keyserling(k)s as 'die Vereinigung der geselligen Wohllebens mit der Tugend'.[27] His experience here is set against the luxurious, indeed wasteful, banquets of contemporary European courts – frugality and conversation amongst mixed society is the foundation of the ideal *société acromatique*. Indeed, as both Heinrich Christian von Keyserling and Kant seem to agree, this should be a universal model for all societies, 'Toutes les sociétés, à mon avis, devraient être acromatique.'[28] Kant highlights frugality in food and hospitality – set against aristocratic conspicuous consumption – and the illustrations in the *Almanach* complement this with a depiction of quite stripped downed interiors of the *Palais* and relatively simple clothing.[29] In the *Almanach,* the *Musenhof* of the *Schliebensche Palais* becomes a universal omphalos for humanising society and mankind.

In reality, the society at the *Palais* was less pastoral and more excessive, with elegant horses and carriages, attended by cossacks, moors and haiduks – a luxuriousness that matched the court of St Petersburg.[30] In this vein, the chosen language of conversation was French – spoken at the Russian court, the favoured language of Friedrich Wilhelm II, and indeed, as Kant himself identified, 'the *universal* language of conversation, especially in the feminine world'.[31] In 1786, von Keyserling(k) was elected an Honorary Member of the *Königlich-Preußische Akademie der Künste und*

---

distinguishes 'acromatic' as a lesser learning method, where 'someone only teaches', and the 'erotematic' method, where the teacher 'asks questions', so ergo, when teaching happens in dialogue. See Robert B. Louden, *Kant's Impure Ethics* (Oxford: Oxford University Press, 2014), p. 60. The concept of the *société acromatique* seems to echo the classical understanding of acroamatic learning through conversation and discourse in a closed social circle.

[27] 'The marriage of the social good living with virtue'. Immanuel Kant, *Anthropology from a Pragmatic Point of View*, ed. by Robert B. Louden and Manfred Kuehn (Cambridge: Cambridge University Press, 2015), p. 179.

[28] *Almanach*, fol. 17r–v.

[29] Kant distinguishes between luxury as a luxurious lifestyle with taste, which nevertheless does not serve the public good, and excess which is debauchery without taste (*Anthropology*, p. 147).

[30] Urte von Berg, *Theodor Gottlieb von Hippel: Stadtpräsident und Schriftsteller in Königsberg. 1741-1796*, Kleine Schriften zur Aufklärung Bd. 13 (Göttingen: Wallstein Verlag, 2004), p. 59.

[31] Kant, p. 214. Interestingly, Kant excludes mentioning the Germans in the list of 'civilized peoples on earth, England and France', as, coming from Kant, this would be self-praise.

Mechanischen Wissenschaften. This membership was in some ways an acknowledgement of von Keyserling(k)'s *Musenhof* activities, elevating it into an academy of sciences. The absence of personal documents makes it difficult to be certain, but the *Musenhof* at Königsberg and the witness statements of friends and guests indicates that von Keyserling(k)'s aristocratic *Musenhof* was essentially cosmopolitan – in the sense of Kant's moral cosmopolitanism.[32] It transcended patriotic and nationalistic limitations to create a cosmopolitan world of learned citizens.

Kurländische Wohltäterin

Dorothea von Kurland's *Musenhof* courts at Löbichau and Tannenfeld in Saxony-Gotha-Altenburg were modelled on Anna Amalia's Weimar. In that vein, they functioned as cosmopolitan cultural centres for the provincial duchy, with guests from Dresden, St Petersburg and Berlin. However, von Kurland's *Musenhöfe* in Saxony-Gotha indicates a paradigm shift in *Musenhof* culture. Holger Böning has suggested that the role of the aristocratic estate owners in the eighteenth-century debate on enlightened estate management has been somewhat ignored, despite their active involvement as authors and readers.[33] Von Kurland's reforms at her *Musenhöfe* fed into this significant strand within eighteenth-century Enlightenment thinking, transforming the original objective of *Musenhöfe* towards practical social and economic improvement. Whilst *Musenhof* courts were originally embedded in dynastic sociability, patronage and chivalric values, their eighteenth-century counterparts were influenced by sociopolitical changes in the ownership of land, estate management, cultural production and social mobility.[34] With these social changes, which Reinhard Blänker calls the emergence of the 'neuständige Geselligkeit', land ownership shifted from old feudal proprietorship to the land tenure of a 'new' nobility, entrepreneurs and – relevant particularly for Prussia – public servants and the military.[35]

---

[32] See Pauline Kleingeld, 'Kant's Cosmopolitan Patriotism', *Kant-Studien*, 94 (2003), 299–316.

[33] Holger Böning, 'Das "Volk" im Patriotismus der deutschen Aufklärung', *Goethezeitportal* <www.goethezeitportal.de/db/wiss/epoche/boening_volk.pdf>, p. 8 (fn. 26).

[34] I am following the work of Günter de Bruyn and Reinhard Blänker here in the evaluation of the evolution of the *Musenhof* court at the end of the eighteenth century. See Reinhard Blänker, 'Salons und Musenhöfe': Neuständige Geselligkeit in Berlin und in der Mark Brandenburg um 1800: Ein Forschungsumriss', in *Salons und Musenhöfe. Neuständische Geselligkeit in Berlin und in der Mark Brandenburg um 1800*, ed. by Reinhard Blänker and Wolfgang de Bruyn (Hannover: Wehrhahn, 2009), pp. 9–34.

[35] In England, Daniel Defoe recorded these socio-economic changes in his *A tour thro' the whole island of Great Britain, divided into circuits or journeys* (1724–1727).

Musenhof courts thus developed into provincial coteries, or, as the nineteenth-century novelist Theodor Fontane would call them, 'Dichterhöfe', where the noble and genteel patrons either played an active part in the literary/cultural production (literary coteries) and/or acted as cultural brokers beyond their roles as responsible landowners and estate managers. Dorothea von Kurland embodied the latter.

A distant relative of von Keyserling(k), Dorothea von Kurland led a precarious life between the states of Russia and Poland in the Dukedom of Courland.[36] Courland was nominally a vassal state of Poland but under threat from Russia. As Poland itself suffered internal conflicts (the new Polish Constitution in 1792, the Second Polish Partition in 1793), any settlement or alliance between Courland and Poland remained inconsequential. On the Third Polish Partition in 1795, the Duchy of Courland fell to Russia. During these difficult times, Dorothea and her husband Peter Biron became increasingly estranged.[37] After Duke Peter signed his abdication in 1795, he left for the Duchy of Sagan (Żagań) in Silesia. Johann Friedrich von Medem (1763–1838), Dorothea von Kurland's brother, bought the estates of Löbichau and Tannenfeld in the Duchy of Saxony-Gotha-Altenburg for his sister and transferred the property of Löbichau to her in 1796.[38] As the manor house was partially destroyed by fire in 1766, von Kurland used the opportunity to rebuild and extend the house between 1798 and 1800 under the direction of the classicist master builder and professor of architecture of Leipzig, Carl August Siegel (1757–1832). The gardens were designed in the contemporary fashion of English gardens with a small 'Comödienhaus' amidst them.

Löbichau was a small estate in the Duchy of Saxony-Gotha-Altenburg which had an established tradition of enlightened rule and reform absolutism, and patronage of the arts and sciences.[39] Before von Kurland's time, Luise Dorothea, Duchess of Saxony-Gotha-Altenburg (1710–67), had succeeded in raising the small provincial town of Gotha into the age of

---

[36] A note on spelling: I retain Dorothea von Kurland's German spelling while translating the Duchy into Courland.
[37] See Sabine Hofmann, 'Von Kurland nach Löbichau', in *Die Herzogin von Kurland im Spiegel ihrer Zeitgenossen: Europäische Salonkultur um 1800. Zum 250. Geburtstag der Herzogin von Kurland*, ed. by Klaus Hofmann (Posterstein: Museum Burg Posterstein, 2011), pp. 78–103 (pp. 80–81). On Courland, see Anne Sommerlat, *La Courlande et les Lumières* (Paris: Belin, 2009).
[38] Sabine Hofmann and Klaus Hofmann, *Zwischen Metternich und Talleyrand: Der Musenhof der Herzogin von Kurland im Schloss zu Löbichau* (Posterstein: Museum Burg Posterstein, 2004), p. 25.
[39] See Anneliese Klingenberg, *Sächsische Aufklärung* (Leipzig: Leipziger Universitätsverlag, 2001); *Ernst II. Von Sachsen-Gotha-Altenburg: Ein Herrscher im Zeitalter der Aufklärung*, ed. by Werner Greiling, Andreas Klinger, and Christoph Köhler (Köln: Böhlau, 2005).

Enlightenment by establishing her own small *Musenhof* court. She corresponded most famously with Voltaire and Frederick II, kept informed about the Parisian salon world by subscribing to Grimm's *La Correspondance littéraire, philosophique et critique* (1747–93) and established an impressive private library, maintained by the librarian, author and translator, Christian Gottfried von Freiesleben (1716–74).[40] Her son, Ernst II of Saxony-Gotha-Altenburg (1745 –1804), praised as the 'Vertraute der Gelehrsamkeit' ('confidant of scholarliness'), continued the work with the patronage of the arts and sciences, particularly astronomy. He founded his own private library and established the first ensemble theatre under the directorship of Conrad Ekhof in Gotha. His prominent charity school, the *Salzmannsches Philanthropin*, was visited and lauded by Goethe, Klopstock and Wieland, and became a popular destination for travellers and educational reformers.[41]

Dorothea von Kurland moved thus to a Duchy that had its own *Musenhof* tradition and was geographically and culturally close to Anna Amalia's Weimar. However, we have seen earlier that the *Musenhof* of Weimar had many different incarnations during Anna Amalia's time and ranged from the more formal assemblies and patronage model to the 'Theegesellschaften', 'Freundschaftsfrühstücke' and the more intimate pastoral meetings at Tiefurt. Dorothea von Kurland's circle at Löbichau emulated the latter and produced, akin to the *Journal of Tiefurt*, the Löbichauer 'Theeblätter', which were initially in manuscript, then printed.[42] Guests who recorded the meetings at Löbichau confirmed that Löbichau was a distinctly informal social venue with a mixed guest list.[43] Von Kurland acted more as a cultural broker and regional benefactor than an aristocratic patron. As a prominent and well-connected figure in European circles, she attracted new and old friends to the provinces, hosting cross-cutting cosmopolitan social circles from Berlin, Courland, Warsaw and Dresden. She also paid brief but regular visits to the court of Emil Leopold August, Duke of Saxony-Gotha-Altenburg.

[40] Günter Berger and Bärbel Raschke, *Luise Dorothea von Sachsen-Gotha-Altenburg: Ernestinerin und Europäerin im Zeitalter der Aufklärung* (Regensburg: Verlag Friedrich Pustet, 2017).
[41] Julia Burbulla, *Allumfassende Ordnung: Gartenkunst und Wissenschaft in Gotha Unter Ernst II. Von Sachsen-Gotha-Altenburg (1772–1804)* (Bern: P. Lang, 2010); Heinrich August Ottokar Reichard, *Handbuch für Reisende aus allen Ständen: Nebst zwey Postkarten, zur großen Reise durch Europa, von Frankreich nach England; und einer Karte von der Schweiz und den Gletschern von Faucigny* (Leipzig: Weygand, 1784), p. 444.
[42] They are now lost. See Clemens Brühl, *Die Sagan, das Leben der Herzogin von Sagan, Prinzessin von Kurland* (Berlin: Steuben/Esser, 1941).
[43] Emilie von Binzer, *Drei Sommer in Löbichau* (Stuttgart: W. Spemann, 1877); Paul Johann Anselm Feuerbach, *Ein Juristenleben* (Vienna: Springer, 1934), pp. 146–49. Tiedge recorded their experiences at the Musenhof after 1808.

The *Musenhof* blossomed particularly after 1808. Visitors included Czar Alexander I; the Körner family; the poet Christoph August Tiedge (1752–1841); the poet Jean Paul (1763–1825) and the legal scholar, Paul Johann Anselm Feuerbach (1775–1833); Abbé Scipione Piatolli (1749–1809), tutor to von Kurland's youngest daughter and advisor to King Stanislaw Augustus Poniatowski and to the Russian foreign minister, Czatoryski; the publisher Friedrich Arnold Brockhaus; the merchant David Friedländer (1750–1834); Johann Wolfgang von Goethe; and Karl August Böttiger, who brought a flair of the Weimar to Löbichau. Rare local visitors were Emil Leopold August, the Duke of Saxony-Gotha-Altenburg, and the Princes Heinrich LXIV of Reuss-Köstritz (1787–1856) and Heinrich XIX of Reuss-Greitz (1790–1836).[44] Regular guests during the early years at Löbichau were von Kurland's sister and writer Elisa von der Recke, the artist Dora Stock (1760–1832), her sister Minna Körner, who with her husband Christian Gottfried Körner (1756–1831) hosted herself a prominent literary and musical salon in Dresden, and Daniel Friedrich Parthey (1745–1822), who had been the tutor for the Medem family in Mitau and later became a prominent bookseller.[45] In short, Europe assembled in Löbichau's salon.

The assemblies were conducted leisurely and generously, without great adherence to rank and etiquette.[46] Breakfast was served at noon, with conversation and walks in the afternoon. After dinner at 5 pm, the guests assembled to converse, philosophise, read, write poetry or make music. Plays were performed in the park or on a small stage in the nearby Tannenfeld, which was part of the estate, and 'poets of the day' were celebrated in small (*Minne*) courtly ceremonies. The poet Jean Paul was a particularly detailed chronicler of the later meetings and praised the rule of freedom of speech ('die seelige Herrschaft der Sprechfreiheit') in Löbichau.[47]

Von Kurland was not merely a patron of the arts, a socialite or an adroit matriarch who supervised her daughters' prominent marriages carefully. Her reform policies in Courland, her political negotiations with Russia and

---

[44] Sabine Hofmann and Klaus Hofmann, '*Wo ich einst residierte, wo ich Fürstin des Landes war . . .*': *Lebensstationen der Herzogin von Kurland* (Posterstein: Museum Burg Posterstein, 2007), p. 36.

[45] Linda Siegel, *Dora Stock: Portrait Painter of the Körner Circle in Dresden (1785–1815)* (Lewiston: E. Mellen Press, 1993); Adolf Mirus, *Das Körner-Museum im Körner-Hause zu Dresden sowie Schloß Löbichau (Sachsen-Altenburg) mit seinen Erinnerungen an Theodor Körner und dessen Pathe Dorothee Herzogin von Curland* (Weimar: Thelemann, 1898). Dora Stock was later asked to paint not only von Kurland's daughter but also some of the other illustrious guests.

[46] Ventzke, p. 138; Hofmann and Hofmann, *Zwischen Metternich und Talleyrand*, pp. 69–87.

[47] Jean Paul, 'Briefblättchen an die Leserin des Damen-Taschenkalenders bei gegenwärtiger Übergabe meiner abgerissenen Gedanken vor dem Frühstück und dem Nachtstück in Löbichau', quoted in Hofmann and Hofmann, *Zwischen Metternich und Talleyrand*, p. 78.

Poland and later, though outside of the framework of this study, her skilled involvement in the Congress of Vienna highlight her political and diplomatic expertise. True change and (estatist) reform was, according to von Kurland, to come from education and learning, particularly during war and political conflict, and from a commitment to the common good:

> Auf diesem Boden wird schwerlich das wahre Heil der Menschheit hervorgehen und gedeihen. Von Innen heraus werden die Menschen dem Besseren zugeführt muessen; in den Erziehungs-und Bildungsanstalten muss der Zeitgeist seine Richtung nehmen.[48]

Von Kurland clearly appreciated her new home in Altenburg. Her love for the region was expressed in her commitment to public welfare on the estates of Löbichau and Tannenfeld as a responsible estate owner and reformer. Indeed, nomadic and stateless, the estates gave her a sense of ownership: 'bin ich wieder in mein liebes Löbichau, woselbst ich bequemer wohne, u. wo mich das Gefühl des Eigentumes . . . fesseln'.[49] Embedded in the neoclassical architecture and iconography of her estates were the Horatian and Virgilian ideals of simplicity, responsible use of wealth and property, good housekeeping and hospitality.

Certainly, von Kurland's injection of money into estates and regional agriculture, her establishment of schools and the investments in schools with books and materials elevated her to be known as the 'Kurländische Wohltäterin' and brought peace to the management of her estates.[50] Similarly to her endeavours in Courland, she planned to abolish serfdom on her Altenburg estates and worried about the legality of her arrangements after her death. She raised the minimum day wages for workers and introduced monthly donations to the impoverished of the region.[51] These improvements were celebrated by one the few close contacts that Dorothea von Kurland had with the Duchy of Altenburg: Hans Wilhelm Freiherr von

---

[48] 'Under these conditions, the true fate of humanity will hardly grow and prosper. Men have to be led towards Enlightenment from within; the *Zeitgeist* has to take lead in reform and education institutions' (my translation), Christoph August Tiedge, *Anna Charlotte Dorothea: Letzte Herzogin von Kurland* (Leipzig: F. A. Brockhaus, 1823), p. 348.

[49] '[H]ere I am back again in my beloved Löbichau where I live comfortably and where a sense of belonging, . . . captures me' (my translation), TB I, 16 November 1804, cited in Hofmann and Hofmann, *Zwischen Metternich und Talleyrand*, p. 68.

[50] 'Courlandian benefactrice' (my translation), Günther Elbin, *Macht in zarten Händen* (München: Ehrenwirth, 1968), p. 155.

[51] Tiedge, p. 180. The abolishment of serfdom on private estates follows a model across the German regions where estate owners pre-empted later estatist reforms. See Wolfgang Neugebauer, 'Aufgeklärter Absolutismus, Reformabsolutismus und struktureller Wandel im Deutschland des 18. Jahrhunderts', in *Ernst II. von Sachsen-Gotha-Altenburg*, ed. by Greiling, Klinger, and Köhler, pp. 23–40 (p. 37).

Thümmel (1744–1824), minister and privy counsel to the Duchy, and an early visitor to von Kurland's *Musenhof*.⁵² In return, von Kurland was a frequent guest at von Thümmel's 'Theegesellschaften' at his residence in the nearby Nöbdenitz. In his *Historische, Statistische und Topographische Beiträge zur Kenntniß des Herzogthums Altenburg*, Thümmel added a biographical appendix on Dorothea von Kurland which sketched out her life very briefly. With his closing remarks he underscored the reason why he had added Dorothea von Kurland to his treatise:

> Sollte man sich wundern, dass ich ihren Lebenslauf, der mehr Curland, als Altenbug betrifft, gegen meinem Plan in die Geschichte des merkwuerdigsten aus dem hohen Adel des Landes aufgekommen habe, so gestehe ich offenherzig, dass es aus Vaterlandsliebe geschehen ist. Denn wer sollte nicht auf so eine liebliche, wenn auch nur vielleicht ephemere Erscheinung stolz senn? – Und sollte es nicht von entschiedenem Nutzen für das Heil des Volkes seyn, wenn Frauen von solcher Klugheit, Umsicht und Lebenserfahrung eine Stimme bei den landschaftlichen Berathungen vergönnt wäre?⁵³

Thümmel elevates von Kurland to a patriotic emblem for the region of Altenburg. He, as much as von Kurland, was committed to social reforms. Since 1783 Thümmel had a significant role in the government of Altenburg, which, though part of the Duchy, functioned somewhat independently under Ernst II.⁵⁴ He served on special commissions on orphans and the labouring poor, workhouses and public welfare and, in 1796, became the director of the poor houses in the region, founded the first hospital in Altenburg and supported new road networks.⁵⁵ Thümmel actively targeted abuses of serfdom and the welfare of the labouring poor and destitute and his interests dovetailed with von Kurland's and with Ernst II, whom he styled in his biography as the 'milde-gerechte'.⁵⁶ His call to include women

---

⁵² *Im Dienste der Ernestiner: Hans Wilhelm von Thümmels Aufstieg vom Pagen zum Minister*, ed. by Klaus Hoffmann (Posterstein: Museum Burg Posterstein, 2016).
⁵³ 'In case one is surprised that I added her biography to the history of the most remarkable high aristocracy of the country against my initial plan as it references Courland more than Altenburg, then I admit freely that this was motivated by patriotism. And indeed who should not be proud of such a lovely if ephemeral presence? – And is it not to the distinct advantage for the welfare of the people if women of such distinguished intelligence, benevolence and experience have a voice in the regional counsel?' (my translation), Hans W. Thümmel, *Historische, Statistische und Topographische Beiträge zur Kenntniß des Herzogthums Altenburg* (Altenburg: [n. pub.], 1818), 'Dritter Abschnitt', pp. 1–8 (p. 8).
⁵⁴ See Joachim Emig, 'Die Altenburger Landesportion zur Zeit Ernst II', in *Ernst II. von Sachsen-Gotha-Altenburg*, ed. by Greiling, Klinger, and Köhler, pp. 101–28 (p. 108).
⁵⁵ See his many achievements listed in *Allgemeine Deutsche Real-Encyklopädie für die Gebildeten Stände: Conversations-Lexikon*, 12 vols (Leipzig: F. A. Brockhaus, 1827), XI, 235–36.
⁵⁶ 'mild and just' (my translation), Thümmel, p. 69.

such as Dorothea von Kurland in local politics served his own reform agenda, but von Kurland's political stage remained European.[57]

Dorothea von Kurland's economic patriotism complemented the reform efforts of Thümmel and Ernst II of Saxony-Gotha-Altenburg, which pre-empted later state-led reforms on serfdom and public welfare. As such she served well as an emblem of noble benevolence, charity and an understanding of the common good. But von Kurland's cosmopolitan outlook and sociability extended an economic patriotism, with its understanding of local/regional rootedness and indeed pride, into what Kwame Anthony Appiah calls 'rooted cosmopolitanism'.[58] Her commitment to both the local and the universal stemmed from her moral investedness in Enlightenment principles underlined by dynastic values of patronage and paternalism. The case studies of von Kurland and von Keyserling(k)'s *Musenhof* sociability suggest that though aristocratic in inception, their courts adapted more successfully than Anna Amalia's to the cultural, social and political demands of the late eighteenth century. The new *Musenhöfe* remained cultural brokers and mediators but developed a new 'bourgeois' form of sociability and patronage.

---

[57] Von Kurland moved to Paris in 1809 after her daughter Dorothea married Edmond de Talleyrand-Périgord, the nephew of the diplomat and politician Charles-Maurice de Talleyrand-Périgord (1754–1838). She was present at the Congress of Vienna. Initially a supporter of Napoleon, she quickly changed her mind. See letter by Elisa von der Recke to her nieces Wilhelmine von Sagan, Pauline von Hohenzollern-Hechingen and Johanna von Acerenza, of 6 May 1814, about their mother's political alliances, THUlB Jena, Nachl. Biron, Abt. B, Va, Bl. 4–5; <www.thulb.uni-jena.de/Objekt+des+Monats/Objekt+des+Monats_+Mai+2014.html>.

[58] See Kwame Anthony Appiah, *Cosmopolitanism: Ethics in a World of Strangers* (New York: Norton, 2006).

CHAPTER 5

Becoming Institutional
The Case of the Anacreontic Society

Ian Newman

For a brief period at the end of the eighteenth century, Anacreontic poetry was one of the most popular subgenres of the lyric. Inspired by the Greek poet Anacreon, whose celebrations of love and wine were written to honor Bacchus, writers took up the genre with renewed vigor in the context of the clubbable sociability of the late-eighteenth-century associational world, in which convivial bonds were celebrated, and wine and punch were understood as the fuel that powered the poetic muse and gave strength to the ties that bound social brotherhood together. Though frequently overlooked, Anacreontic verse has a notable presence in the poetry of many writers, including the Duchess of Devonshire, Robert Merry, Thomas Moore, Mary Robinson, John Thelwall, and the early experiments of William Wordsworth, among others. As I've argued elsewhere, the logics and locutions of the Anacreontic also provide an important structuring element in John Keats's 'Ode on a Nightingale'.[1] But besides its presence in familiar poetry collections, Anacreontic verse flourished in a variety of less traditional forms, in both print and performance. There were, for example, countless anonymous 'Anacreontics' that appeared in newspapers and as broadside ballads; they appeared too as sheet music and in convivial songsters, and these latter categories suggest a vibrant performance tradition, to which we only have partial access through printed versions of songs and reports of performances.

It is within this broad social field, one that traverses poetry, ballad, song, print, and performance, that we should place the Anacreontic Society, an

---

This chapter owes a considerable debt to Simon McVeigh, who generously shared a significant archive of notes and newspaper clippings relating to the Anacreontic Society with me. I am also grateful to Patricia Bredar for helping me to organize these notes and coordinate them with my own research.

[1] Ian Newman, *The Romantic Tavern: Literature and Conviviality in the Age of Revolution* (Cambridge: Cambridge University Press, 2019), pp. 172–74.

institution formed primarily to celebrate Anacreontic verse, but which mutated and became something quite different. The Anacreontic Society was one of the most prestigious of the tavern-based masculine convivial societies that flourished in the late eighteenth century. What began as a casual gathering of friends transformed into something more institutional, with a more rigid structure and a formalized set of practices. The society consequently provides an important case study for considering the evolution of literary institutions in the late eighteenth century, as it can illuminate how small groups developed into characteristically modern bureaucratic institutions. As a society named after a literary genre, the Anacreontic Society can also shed light on the relationship between literature and social gathering.

To suggest that the Anacreontic Society should be considered as an institution of *literature* is to recast it in the historiography, where it has most frequently been understood as a *musical* society. Brian Robins, for example, has discussed it in the context of eighteenth-century Catch and Glee culture, where he describes it as 'one of the earliest and most significant imitators of the original Catch Club'.[2] Indeed, one way of understanding the Anacreontic Society is to view it alongside the Catch and Glee Clubs, as a society dedicated to the appreciation of a single musical genre that combined words with music. Simon McVeigh has discussed the Anacreontic Society as one of the musical societies that helped shape middle-class tastes for what was emerging as a canon of 'classical' music, providing a proving ground for the works of composers such as Clementi (who regularly performed at the society), Haydn (who visited the society in 1791), Mozart, and Pleyel.[3] By considering the Anacreontics as a literary society, I do not mean to suggest that Robins and McVeigh are wrong – clearly the society had much to do with the musical culture of the period – so much as to suggest that this assessment is based on partial evidence, and fails to adequately explain the significance of the society's name. Furthermore, bringing the Anacreontic Society into closer proximity to Anacreontic poetry helps us see more clearly how closely connected musical and literary cultures were in the period, while also exposing the emerging logics at play in the development of 'literature' and 'music' as specialized disciplinary fields.

---

[2] Brian Robins, *Catch and Glee Culture in Eighteenth-Century England* (Woodbridge: Boydell, 2006), p. 72. For details of the origins of the Catch Club, see p. 32.

[3] Simon McVeigh, '"Trial by Dining Club": The Instrumental Music of Hayden, Clementi and Mozart at London's Anacreontic Society', in *Music and Performance Culture in Nineteenth-Century Britain: Essays in Honor of Nicholas Temperley*, ed. by Bennett Zon (Farnham: Ashgate, 2012), pp. 105–38.

The Society as Institution

Histories of the Anacreontic Society have been provided by several critics, so I will recap the salient details here only briefly and with an eye to its participation in the protocols of institutionality.[4] The Anacreontic Society began as a gathering of a small group of music-loving friends in 1766. By the 1770s it had around twenty-five members and was meeting regularly in the London Coffee House in Ludgate Hill. By 1773 the informal gathering regularly included concert performances that preceded dinner, and by 1780 the society had moved to a larger space, the Crown and Anchor Tavern in the Strand, to accommodate its growing membership. At its peak in the late 1780s, 200 people regularly attended its meetings and there was a waiting list beyond that. While there are no extant records of the society's early years, during the Crown and Anchor era its meetings took on a distinctive shape, consisting of a tripartite structure. They began with a formal concert of largely instrumental music – symphonies and chamber music by composers such as Haydn, Clementi, or Pleyel. This would typically last from 7:30 pm to about 10:00 pm, at which point they would move to another room for dinner; then after dinner they would return to the concert room, which had now been set up for convivial singing, and a succession of songs would then continue into the early hours of the morning, led by well-known singers from the London stage and pleasure gardens.[5]

The case of the Anacreontics is helpful for understanding the institutionalization process, because it rehearses many of the things one would expect to see in the development of an institution: it begins small, then grows into something much larger, with greater appeal; it develops a series of ritualized practices and repeated patterns of behavior, meeting on the same day every second week, at the same time, with a similar structure to the proceedings; it develops expectations for the behavior of its participants and begins to patrol and regulate them; it becomes increasingly reflexive, narrating the story of its own establishment; and it seeks greater public accountability, developing close relationships with newspaper editors, who would advertise meetings in advance and report retrospectively on the proceedings, developing an associated literature and interpellating the

---

[4] Stella Achilleos, 'The Anacreontic and the Growth of Sociability in Early Modern England', *Appositions: Studies in Renaissance/Early Modern Literature and Culture*, 1 (2008) <http://appositions.blogspot.com/2008/05/stella-achilleos-anacreontic.html>, paras 10–16 of 25; Robins, pp. 72–74; McVeigh, 'Trial by Dining Club', pp. 107–10; Newman, *Romantic Tavern*, pp. 98–106.
[5] Regular performers included Charles Bannister, Charles Dignum, James Dodd, Charles Incledon, and Thomas Sedgwick.

society into the bureaucratic regimes out of which histories might be written. But the Anacreontics provide an interesting case also, because in spite of successfully navigating all the bureaucratizing processes we might expect of institutionalization, the society collapsed in 1791 after a series of controversies concerning the permissibility of certain performances and the participation of women in their meetings. To put that another way, they got the form of institutionalization right, but they got the content wrong. The Anacreontic Society was, then, an exemplary *failed* institution – and it is in its failure that we can see most clearly the logics at play in the development of institutions, and the pressures exerted on them in the late eighteenth century concerning what was and was not permissible in the process of becoming institutional.

Characteristically, eighteenth-century institutionality bears an intrinsic relationship to the written word, and commonly to the printed word. In the transition from a meeting of friends to a formal institution, the club or society begins to get written into existence. Most frequently this involves reflexivity, with club members writing the history of the club, and often it involves keeping formal meeting minutes and proceedings. In the case of the Anacreontic Society, however, few such records have been found. Brian Robins reports, 'detailed records of the membership of the club have not survived, the only information relating to it being derived from contemporary observers'.[6] Robins's disappointment is palpable, but also telling. Histories of institutions are written using archival records, and so the institutions that feature in historical narratives are biased toward the ones with an enduring archival presence. We thus come to expect societies to keep detailed operational records, and Robins assumes that the absence of such records is surely because they are lost, not because they never existed, as history and historiography collapse into one another.

Mee and Sangster propose in the introduction to this book that an institution is 'an assemblage that organises, transmits, and validates, and that self-consciously represents itself as doing so'. In this account the reflexive practice of record-keeping is one of the defining qualities of an institution. Arguably, the absence of membership records in the case of the Anacreontic Society might mark it out as a club, rather than an institution. But a crucial aspect of institutional record-keeping was validation through the interface with a broader public. It was not enough for an institution simply to exist; it needed to be observed to exist, and to have that existence legitimated by public accountability. Groups like the Anacreontic Society often developed close relationships to the print public sphere, and so the

[6] Robins, p. 72.

absence of detailed operational records is considerably mitigated – at least in later years – by a considerable newspaper presence.

Newspaper advertisements for Anacreontic Society meetings were placed in advance, and quite detailed reports of individual meetings often appeared in the newspapers. A few notices were placed in the papers in the late 1770s, but the Anacreontic Society's relationship to print publicity began in earnest in 1780, when a history of the society was printed in *The Morning Chronicle*.[7] This account of its origins, discussed in detail by Stella Achilleos, ended with the full words of the Anacreontic Song, 'To Anacreon in Heaven' (the tune to which would later provide the melody for 'The Star Spangled Banner'), accompanied by the following preface: 'The following classical song, written by poor Ralph Tomlinson, their late President, is chorused by the whole company, and opens the mirth of the evening.'[8] The seven verses of this song took up more column space that rest of the history, suggesting how important this was as a statement of identity. This was a composition that was explicitly marked as both participating in and parodying the Anacreontic tradition. The substance of the song, which involves a comic squabble between the gods, hinges on Anacreon's willingness to 'lend his name' to the society and to teach them how to entwine 'The myrtle of Venus with Bacchus's wine', just as he himself had done. Sung after dinner, the song announced the commencement of the convivial part of the evening, and became a highlight of the meetings. The song would be principally sung by a well-known singer, and then, as the *Morning Chronicle* history indicates, 'chorussed by the whole company'. In his journals, John Marsh reported that all attendees would 'join hand in hand all round the table', as they sang the last verse together, a physical symbol of the convivial bonds the Anacreontics believed tied them together.[9]

Supplementing the connections forged among attendees, print productions associated with the society reached beyond the walls of the meeting space, potentially extending the convivial bonds of the physical meeting to the entire reading public, but at the very least calling for additional witnesses to legitimate their activities, something I want to suggest was a hallmark of the bureaucratic regime of institutionality. This attention to the importance of being represented in print marks an important phase in the development of institutions. It coexists with what Jon Mee has called 'print magic', defined as 'a faith that print could liberate mankind simply

---

[7] *Morning Chronicle*, 22 March 1780. [8] Achilleos, paras 10–12.
[9] John Marsh, *The Journals of John Marsh: The Life and Times of a Gentleman Composer (1752–1828)*, ed. by Brian Robins, 2 vols (Stuyvesant: Pendragon Press, 1998), I, 115–16. See also R. J. S. Stevens's account of an Anacreontic meeting, *Recollections of R. J. S. Stevens: An Organist in London*, ed. by Mark Argent (Basingstoke: MacMillan, 1992), p. 25.

by bringing ideas into circulation'.[10] There is ample evidence in the writings of popular radical societies of the French Revolution, Mee's primary focus, that attests to this phenomenon among societies with explicit political ambitions. But something similar happens elsewhere in the late eighteenth century, albeit in a more diffuse and indirect manner: a seemingly irresistible faith in print as itself salutary, and a desire for activities to be represented in print – even if these representations have no obvious purpose besides flattering those present with the gift of attention. Unlike the 'print magic' of the popular radical societies, which aimed at progress in direct political terms, many other societies, such as the Anacreontics, had few explicit aims beyond a vague shaping of 'middle-class tastes', a point that anyway must have been opaque to those involved at the time, becoming clearer in retrospect. And yet still, they were determined to be seen in print, as if demanding a form of witnessing that might be seen as the early stages of our own obsession with 'accountability'.

While Robins laments that in the absence of detailed records of the society, Simon McVeigh has extensively mined newspaper reports of meetings to rich effect.[11] While similarly regretting the 'scattered and incomplete newspaper reviews', McVeigh also points out the importance of musical sources such as 'set of printed part-books', at Cambridge University Library.[12] McVeigh's primary interest is in the development of the formal classical concert repertoire, but if we think of the Anacreontics not just as a musical society but also as a literary society, then we can considerably expand this list of sources to include an array of formats through which the popular songs performed at society meetings were made available in print. These would include broadside ballads, songbooks, or songsters, such as *The Festival of Anacreon,* and sheet music, printed both in codex form and as individual songsheets combining the intaglio engraved musical scores with relief letterpress words. In this latter category, I have found two collections especially helpful: one at the British Library, and the other at the Bodleian. They share the same title page: *A Collection of Favourite Songs Sung at the*

---

[10] Jon Mee, *Print, Publicity, and Popular Radicalism in the 1790s: The Laurel of Liberty* (Cambridge: Cambridge University Press, 2016), p. 8.

[11] In addition to *Concert Life in Eighteenth-Century London from Mozart to Haydn* (Cambridge: Cambridge University Press, 1993), McVeigh is the author of the database *Calendar of London Concerts 1750–1800* (Goldsmiths, University of London), drawn largely from newspaper records: <https://doi.org/10.25602/GOLD.00010342>.

[12] McVeigh, 'Trial by Dining Club', p. 119; see pp. 121–24 and 126–27 for a detailed discussion of the part-books.

Beefsteak Club and the Anacreontic Society by Messrs Edwin, Dodd, Dignum, Bannister, Sedgwick, Dighton, Hooke, Moss, Johnstone and Hewerdine (London: J. Fentum in the Strand, n.d.).[13] The content of each collection, however, is different, suggesting that Fentum printed this title page for patrons who bought individual songs but then wanted a formal title page when they bound them together into their own collections, indicating that these printed songs were intended to be preserved in libraries, and were not imagined as a kind of ephemera in the way that ballad sheets or slip songs often were. Not all of the songs in each collection were in fact printed by Fentum, and none of them bear a date, but many can be traced to specific performances that were mentioned in newspaper reports of society meetings. What follows is a discussion of two examples of the songs found in these collections, which have been selected not so much because they are representative (these songs were too numerous and too varied to attempt this in so short a space) so much as to give some insights into the kinds of song performed, with a view to exposing the society's more ludic impulses, indicating the limits of the institution, and showing what readers in the public sphere were being asked to witness.

Tho' Bacchus May Boast

The first of these songs, called 'The Triumph of Venus', with words by Captain Charles Morris, is one of many songs that was firmly in the Anacreontic tradition. 'The Triumph of Venus' circulated in numerous print formats, and could be found printed as a letterpress ballad with the words only; in songsters, including numerous editions of Morris's compositions as well as more general songsters such as *Calliope: Or the Musical Miscellany*;[14] and in printed sheet music, such as that printed by Fentum. Newspapers report that 'The Triumph of Venus' was performed at the Anacreontic Society numerous times over a twelve-month period between November 1786 and November 1787.[15] Captain Morris, though a well-known and much-admired performer himself, seems never to have appeared at the Anacreontic Society in person, though a number of his

---

[13] British Library H.1652 and Bodleian (W) Harding Mus. E 516.
[14] For a broadside ballad printing, see National Library of Scotland, Crawford EB 2394, <https://digital.nls.uk/74893873>.
[15] See *Morning Herald*, 17 November 1786; *Morning Herald*, 8 December 1786; *Morning Post and Daily Advertiser*, 5 January 1787; *Public Advertiser*, 1 February 1787; and *Morning Herald*, 9 November 1787.

songs were performed there by others, and it was the celebrated tenor and theatre actor Charles Dignum who performed 'The Triumph of Venus' there. It proved sufficiently popular that the words were printed in the *Morning Post and Daily Advertiser,* shortly after Dignum's 3 January 1787 performance:

> Tho' Bacchus may boast of his care-killing Bowl,
>   And folly in thought-drowning revel's delight;
> Such worship, alas! hath no charms for the soul,
>   When softer devotions, the senses invite.
> To the arrow of Fate, or the canker of Care,
>   His potion oblivious a balm may bestow;
> But to Fancy, that feeds on the charms of the fair,
>   The death of reflection's the spring of all woe.
>
> What soul that's possess'd of a dream so divine,
>   With riot would bid the sweet vision be gone;
> For the tear that bedews Sensibility's shrine,
>   Is a drop of more worth than all Bacchus's Tun.
> The tender excess, that enamours the heart,
>   To few is imparted to millions denied,
> 'Tis the brain of the victim that tempers the dart,
>   And fools jest at that for which sages have died.
>
> Each change and excess hath through life been my doom,
>   And well can I speak of its joys and its strife;
> The bottle affords us a glimpse through the gloom,
>   But Love's the true sunshine that gladdens our life.
> Come then, rosy Venus, and spread o'er my sight,
>   The magic illusions that ravish my soul;
> Awake in the breast the soft dream of delight,
>   And drop from thy myrtle one leaf in my bowl.
>
> Then deep will I drink of the nectar divine,
>   Nor e'er, jolly god, from thy banquet remove;
> But each tube of my heart ever thirst for the wine,
>   That's mellow'd by friendship, and sweeten'd by love.
> Then deep will I drink of the nectar divine,
>   Nor e'er, jolly God, from thy banquet remove;
> But each tube of my heart ever thirst for the wine,
>   That's mellow'd by friendship, and sweeten'd by love.[16]

---

[16] *Morning Post and Daily Advertiser*, 5 January 1787. There is some considerable variation in the different printed versions of this song. I have supplied the words as they appeared in the newspaper report.

For those who know Morris only as a writer of such pornographic verse as 'The Plenipotentiary' or political ballads such as 'Billy's Too Young to Drive Us', this song's overt participation in the culture of sensibility is perhaps a little surprising.[17] But the connection between the Anacreontic and sensibility is pervasive, and 'sensibility' provided a key term in understanding how the bonds of convivial friendship might structure social relations. The gaily circulating glass, which was passed from one person to another, or the punch bowl into which everyone might dip the ladle to fill their own glass, could provide a material metaphor for forms of connection that allowed a responsiveness to the emotions of others. One indication of the cross pollination of the culture of sensibility with the Anacreontic tradition is the fact that 'The Triumph of Venus' sometimes went by the title 'The Tear That Bedews Sensibility's Shrine', a notable line from the song's second stanza.[18]

'The Triumph of Venus' is in no sense the celebration of drinking that might be expected of the Anacreontic tradition (or of the Bacchanalian song, as it was sometimes later called, playing up the bibulous possibilities of the mode). Instead, the song is a genteel articulation of the limitations of wine, and of the greater attraction of love, suggesting that while drinking might brighten the gloom a little, love is a complete immersion in sunshine. The song ends by acknowledging that, in the absence of total sunshine, the punch bowl might be enhanced by a single leaf from Venus's myrtle. The song plays off the tropes made familiar by the Anacreontic Song, 'To Anacreon in Heaven', which proclaimed a desire to 'entwine/The Myrtle of Venus with Bacchus's wine' but had failed to adequately account for the role that women might play in the masculine convivial world.[19] 'The Triumph of Venus' redresses the imbalance in that song, tilting the scales away from Bacchus back toward Venus, while ultimately remaining irrevocably tied to masculine conviviality, the leaf of myrtle merely supplying a flavor enhancement to what is unequivocally the male world of the punch bowl.

What becomes clear from examining 'The Triumph of Venus', and the large number of Anacreontic songs like it that were performed at the society, is that the division of the meetings into the 'concert' at the beginning of the

---

[17] Both 'The Plenipotentiary' and 'Billy's Too Young to Drive Us' can be found in the Bodleian collection of *A Collection of Favourite Songs Sung at the Beefsteak Club and The Anacreontic Society*. Newspaper reports attest that 'Billy's Too Young to Drive Us' was performed by Hooke, on 18 January, 1 March, and 12 April 1786. See *Morning Chronicle and London Advertiser*, 21 January 1786; *Morning Herald*, 4 March 1786; and *Morning Herald*, 14 April 1786. 'The Plenipotentiary' was possibly too notoriously crude to be mentioned by name in the newspapers.
[18] See, for example, *The Universal Songster, or Museum of Mirth*, 3 vols (London: Jones, 1829), II, 34.
[19] For the role of women in the Anacreontic Song, see Newman, *Romantic Tavern*, pp. 103–07.

meeting and the 'convivial singing' after dinner does a significant disservice to some of the repertoire that was performed after dinner. While it is true that some of the songs that were performed were, as William Parke complained, 'very disgraceful to the Society; as the greatest levity, and vulgar obscenity prevailed', the Anacreontic songs themselves were by no means part of that 'improper' repertoire.[20] Indeed, they had much in common with glees (frequently ornate settings of secular lyrics) which, along with catches (which, like rounds, were arrangements of words and music that were staggered between singers to create novel harmonic and lyrical effects), were often included as part of the predinner concert performance. It would, then, be an oversimplification to suggest that the society collapsed because of the tensions between genteel concert and improper after-dinner bawdiness. This would fail to account for the genteel aspirations of masculine conviviality in general and of Anacreontic verse in particular. There was nothing intrinsic to conviviality or the Anacreontic that would associate it with the 'petty *ballad writers*' of which the newspapers complained at the time of the society's collapse.[21] For that we'll have to look elsewhere.

The Newly Dubb'd Jew

In December 1791, the songwriter and convivial entertainer William Hewerdine wrote a new song on the subject of Lord George Gordon's conversion to Judaism. Gordon is best known for his involvement with the Protestant Association, the organization that planned demonstrations in protest of Catholic emancipation, which broke out into violence in 1780, now known as the Gordon Riots. But Gordon, who was acquitted of treason for his involvement in the violence that was named after him, was embroiled in a series of controversies in the 1780s, including being found guilty of defaming Marie Antoinette, for which he was sentenced to five years imprisonment in Newgate. In prison, Gordon lived a devout life as a converted Orthodox Jew, undergoing brit milah at the age of thirty-six. As Iain McCalman has pointed out, 'by converting to Judaism in 1787, Gordon attracted

---

[20] William Parke, *Musical Memoirs; Comprising an Account of the General State of Music in England: From the First Commemoration of Handel, in the Year 1784, to the Year 1830*, 2 vols (London: Henry Colburn and Richard Bentley, 1830), I, 156.

[21] *Morning Post*, 12 December 1791.

almost as much attention as he had in 1780'.²² And it was this ceremonial circumcision that fired Hewerdine's poetic muse:

> My Muse t'other day, having laughter in view
> Selected George Gordon, the newly dubb'd jew
> Resolving to State with Mosaic precision
> What befell poor Crop's p–k on its late Circumcision.
>
> Derry Down &c &c.

> The rabbi appeared, and the Christian's foreskin
> Was about to be banish'd, to cleanse Crop of sin;
> But Gentiles and Jews, mark the cream of the joke,
> By Prometheus inspir'd, his P–K suddenly spoke.²³

Hewerdine's song was just one of a series of anti-Semitic satires across various media, both print and performance, that depicted Gordon as 'Lord Crop'. The trope began, perhaps, with the article 'The Loss of the Prepuce, or Lord George Riot Suffering a Clipping in Order to Become a Jew' in the September 1785 issue of the *Rambler's Magazine*.²⁴ The novelty of Gordon's genitals speaking, however, was all Hewerdine's own invention.

In the song, Gordon's penis initially shrinks, hiding 'like a snail in its shell' before threatening to urinate in the priest's face unless he put his knife away. This behavior startles both Lord Gordon and the priest. The former, alarmed at the 'damnable riot', attempts to silence the penis in a condom. Unperturbed, the penis begins making speeches, which Hewerdine uses as an opportunity to take a sideswipe at the government: 'his language was nervous, his reasoning clear, / And he spoke full as well as the *Members* elsewhere'. Finally, understanding Gordon's resolution to convert, his penis begins to weep and then finally falls asleep. As this summary illustrates, the song intertwines commentary on Gordon's conversion (taken here as elsewhere to be a sign of his madness) with reflection

---

²² Iain McCalman, 'Mad Lord George and Madame La Motte: Riot and Sexuality in the Genesis of Burke's Reflections of the Revolution in France', *Journal of British Studies*, 35.3 (1996), 343–67 (pp. 357–58).

²³ William Hewerdine, *A Complete Collection of the Convivial Songs Written by Mr. Hewerdine and Sung at the Je Ne Sçai Quoi, Anacreontic, Beef-steak Clubs, and the Strangers at Home* (London: D. Symonds, 1791), p. 16.

²⁴ *The Rambler's Magazine: Or, the Annals of Gallantry, Glee, Pleasure and the Bon Ton: Calculated for the Entertainment of the Polite World ; and to Furnish the Man of Pleasure with a Most Delicious Banquet of Amorous, Bacchanalian, Whimsical, Humorous, Theatrical and Polite Entertainment ; for the Year 1785* (London: G. Lister, 1785), pp. 342–43. See Marsha Keith Schuchard, 'Lord George Gordon and Cabalistic Freemasonry: Beating Jacobite Swords into Jacobin Ploughshares', in *Secret Conversions to Judaism in Early Modern Europe*, ed. by Martin Mulsow and Richard Popkin (Dordrecht: Kluwer Academic, 2004), pp. 183–231.

on his role in the riots of 1780, with general commentary of political power fueled by anti-Semitic humor. But the chief driver of the narrative is self-evidently a prurient enjoyment of representing a talking penis.

Hewerdine had a professional association with Captain Morris, and for a brief time moved in similar circles, including entertaining the Prince of Wales at his Je Ne Sçai Quoi Club and at the Sublime Society of Beefsteaks; he was also a fixture at the Humbug Club, for which he wrote several of his best-known songs. Hewerdine never attained the same status within these networks as Morris did, but his career coincided with the heyday of convivial culture, and in 1786 he made a number of appearances at the Anacreontic Society. On December 6, at a meeting in which Dignum sang Morris's 'Triumph of Venus', three of Hewerdine's songs were performed, two by himself, and one (*The High Mettled P____O* [Plenipo], to the tune of Charles Dibdin's *High Mettled Racer*) by Dignum. His songs were sufficiently popular that he made several subsequent appearances over the next three years, and Dignum continued to sing his songs thereafter.

The words to 'The Newly Dubb'd Jew' were written to the tune 'Derry Down', as indicated in the sheet music printed by Fentum preserved in the Bodleian library.[25] The name 'Derry Down' has been given to a large number of different ballad tunes, but the one that was most popular in the 1780s and 1790s, and the one that Fentum uses, is a lovely air in 6/8 time, in melodic G-minor, making distinctive use of the vacillation between minor and major on the seventh of the scale (F naturals and F sharps) in the verse, but with a strong G-major chorus (see Figure 5.1). The melancholy tonality in the verse compliments well the satirical 'complaint' of Gordon's member, but without ever straying far from the hearty and uplifting tonality reasserted with the perfect cadences of each refrain. The tune, which was frequently used for political satire, seems indeed to echo the structure of satire itself, with its glances at something serious that always, ultimately, are balanced by the overarching humor.

The song provides further evidence to support McCalman's discussion of Gordon's conversion as a multimedia event, which was referred to in newspapers, political documents (including Burke's *Reflections on the Revolution in France*), graphic satires, and in commemorative copper tokens. To this list we may now add song, which remains an important

---

[25] *A Collection of Favourite Songs Sung at the Beefsteak Club and the Anacreontic Society by Messrs Edwin, Dodd, Dignum, Bannister, Sedgwick, Dighton, Hooke, Moss, Johnstone and Hewerdine* (London: J. Fentum, [n.d.]), Bodleian (W) Harding Mus. E 516.

Figure 5.1 'The Newly Dubb'd Jew Written and Sung by Mr Hewerdine at the Beef Steak Club and the Anacreontic Society.' Bodleian Libraries, University of Oxford, Harding Mus. E 516 No. 53.

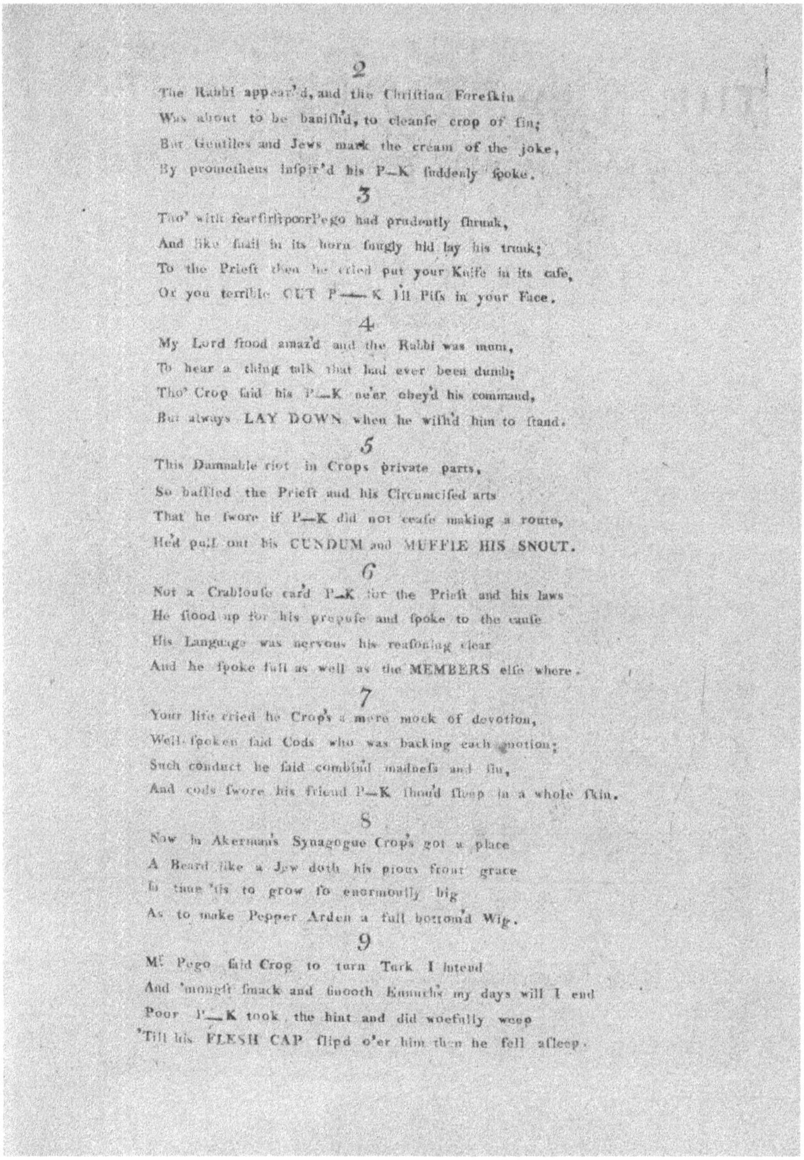

2

The Rabbi appear'd, and the Christian Foreskin
Was about to be banish'd, to cleanse crop of sin;
But Gentiles and Jews mark the cream of the joke,
By prometheus inspir'd his P—K suddenly spoke.

3

Tho' with fear first poor Pego had prudently shrunk,
And like snail in its horn snugly hid lay his trunk;
To the Priest then he cried put your Knife in its case,
Or you terrible CUT P——K I'll Piss in your Face.

4

My Lord stood amaz'd and the Rabbi was mum,
To hear a thing talk that had ever been dumb;
Tho' Crop said his P—K ne'er obey'd his command,
But always LAY DOWN when he will'd him to stand.

5

This Damnable riot in Crops private parts,
So baffled the Priest and his Circumcised arts
That he swore if P—K did not cease making a route,
He'd pull out his CUNDUM and MUFFLE HIS SNOUT.

6

Not a Crablouse car'd P—K for the Priest and his laws
He stood up for his prepuce and spoke to the cause
His Language was nervous his reasoning clear
And he spoke full as well as the MEMBERS else where.

7

Your life cried he Crop's a mere mock of devotion,
Well spoken said Cods who was backing each motion;
Such conduct he said combin'd madness and sin,
And cods swore his friend P—K should sleep in a whole skin.

8

Now in Akerman's Synagogue Crops got a place
A Beard like a Jew doth his pious front grace
Is thus 'tis to grow so enormously big
As to make Pepper Arden a full bottom'd Wig.

9

Mr Pego said Crop to turn Turk I intend
And 'mongst smack and smooth Eunuchs my days will I end
Poor P—K took the hint and did woefully weep
'Till his FLESH CAP slipd o'er him then he fell asleep.

Figure 5.1 (Cont.)

and underutilized resource for examining historical attitudes toward contemporary events. My primary concern here, though, is less with what the song can tell us about attitudes toward Lord George and more with what this, ludic, satirical, obscene piece of anti-Semitism can tell us about the ways institutions patrolled, or failed to patrol, the boundaries of taste.

If, as McVeigh has convincingly argued, the Anacreontic Society was a 'crucible for artistic judgement' of the emergent classical canon, what does it mean that they simultaneously performed such self-evidently tasteless, boundary-pushing repertoire?[26] What is most striking, when reviewing contemporary accounts of Anacreontic meetings, is the way this sort of political bawdry (of which 'The Newly Dubb'd Jew' is just one of many equally eyebrow-raising songs I could have focused on) was utterly unexceptional for the best part of a decade until suddenly in the early 1790s it became subject to intense scrutiny.

Institutionality and the Decline of the Anacreontics

The standard narrative of the decline of the Anacreontic Society, based on details provided in William Parke's account, involves the presence of women, and the Duchess of Devonshire in particular. Parke claims that the society folded after a visit from the Duchess, which inhibited the performance of the comic songs which were 'not being exactly calculated for the entertainment of ladies'. The members, displeased by these lacklustre performances that had wilted under the female gaze 'resigned one after another; and a general meeting being called, the society was dissolved'.[27] McVeigh is right to point out, however, that 'the seeds of decline had been sown much earlier, as the Society slipped into an awkward compromise between convivial male drinking club and public expression of genteel sociability: a hybrid that in its liminal ambiguities began to threatened established orthodoxies'.[28] This hybrid identity certainly contributed toward the society's collapse, but it is not clear that the fissure appears cleanly in the division between the largely instrumental classical repertoire of the early part of the evening, and the convivial song, associated with the spirit of Anacreon in the second part. Indeed, in his account of society meetings R. J. S. Stevens provides the added detail that the convivial singing continued until midnight, at which point the Chair would retire, leaving the remaining members to sing until the early hours of the morning, at

---

[26] McVeigh, 'Trial by Dining Club', p. 107. [27] Parke, pp. 83–84.
[28] McVeigh, 'Trial by Dining Club', p. 110.

which point, Stevens complains 'the proceedings were very disgraceful to the Society; as the greatest levity, and vulgar obscenity, generally prevailed. Improper Songs, and other vicious compositions were performed without any shame whatever'.[29] Stevens's detail about the Chair is significant. He explains that the president of the society would take the seat at 'the center of the elevated table, at the upper end of the room, supported on each side by the various Vocal performers' (25). Once the president had left the Chair, however, the remaining members' relationship to the society became more equivocal. Their activities were no longer sanctioned by the president, but were still nevertheless an extension of the gathering organized by the society – and, as Stevens's account indicates, were still understood as reflecting upon the society as a whole.

It is important to emphasize, then, that Hewerdine's performances were performed while the president was still present, before the postmidnight 'improper songs' had begun. In an account of the meeting of December 19, 1787, *The Times* reported:

> The signal being made by the President for introducing the laughable and less chaste productions, Mr Hewerdine, was requested to favour the company with a song. By his appearance he seemed to say, in the language of Horace,
> "Dincam insigne, recene adhue,
> "Indictum orc alio"
> [I will utter something striking, something fresh, something as yet unsung by another's lips.]
> Novelty of course ensued. The subject was the circumcision of Lord George Gordon, a composition that absolutely convulsed the company with laughter. The conclusion of one of the stanzas, which created such merriment, stated, that the beard of His Lordship was to grow until there was sufficient quantity of hair.[30]

The Public Advertiser presents Hewerdine's song with complete approval, speaking in superlatives of the 'unparalleled amusement' the evening afforded, and according to *The World* Hewerdine's performances of this song were sufficiently popular that several members of the society persuaded Fentum to purchase the copyright and print it.[31]

At stake here is the placement of the dividing line between appropriate and inappropriate repertoire. If, as McVeigh convincingly suggests, we are to understand the demise of the society as being bound up in the nature of

---

[29] *Recollections of R. J. S. Stevens*, p. 25.   [30] *The Times*, 21 December 1787.
[31] *The World*, 3 May 1788.

the compromise between 'convivial male drinking club and public expression of genteel sociability', then understanding where that line was located is crucial to grasping the characteristics of the modern institution, and what was and was not admissible. But what the evidence of the Anacreontic suggests is that there was no hard and fast dividing line between appropriate classical music and inappropriate drinking club, but a series of 'liminal ambiguities that began to threaten established orthodoxies'.[32] And we can begin to see now that those 'liminal ambiguities' involved a complex set of negotiations involving music, words, poetic genre, physical space, time of night, and membership.

It might be possible to read the example of the Anacreontics as successfully upholding the values of respectability we might expect: the more risqué songs were offered as part of the evening's entertainment and the audience tolerated them for a little while, until there followed a significant backlash which ultimately caused the society to collapse. However, this assessment can only be maintained with the benefit of hindsight, once the knowledge of their ultimate demise, and of a more stable set of 'middle-class values' is taken into account. But it fails to adequately explain what *at the time* the Anacreontics thought they were up to. And in particular, how and why they felt the need for these more ludic activities to be legitimized in print – why the significant focus on bawdy songs in newspaper reports, and why persuade Fentum to print songs like 'The Newly Dubb'd Jew' in much the same way that he would publish instrumental music by Haydn or Mozart?

What is most striking about the activities of the society is that they did not distinguish between the more respectable concertos, symphonies, and chamber music of the formal concert, the respectable form of Anacreontic convivial singing, and the lewd, improper songs of the unsanctioned ballad writers. They coexisted in the same meetings, and as such needed to be understood together as part of a continuum of performance and print, with the Anacreontic song located in the center as the respectable face of conviviality. As an informal meeting of friends, the members were free to enjoy the pleasures of a string quartet, an Anacreontic, or a bawdy satire, but once they began to desire the recognition that printed authority bestowed – once they began the transition into an institution – they became subject to the scrutiny that accompanies printed accountability. Newspaper reports could admire the 'laughable and less chaste productions', but they nevertheless made these performances public and exposed them to the judgment of a broad readership.

---

[32] McVeigh, 'Trial by Dining Club', p. 110.

In this sense, the Anacreontic Society provides further evidence for William Weber's influential account of the transformation of musical taste, in which a vast increase in the number of musical performances between the mid-eighteenth and the mid-nineteenth centuries resulted in the increase in the specialization of music programming.[33] In the mid-eighteenth century, Weber argues, the relatively small numbers of public performances of music meant that concerts tended to accommodate a wide variety of tastes. This tolerant regime of 'collegiality' had transformed by the mid-nineteenth century to much more specialized programs of music often focused on a single genre or composer, with a particular emphasis on music of the past, so that the notion of 'classical music' as we now understand it came into being, and grew increasingly separate from the ballad concerts and music hall entertainments that were offered to a broader public. This transformation in musical taste, then, is partly a result of the proliferation of institutions each dedicated to narrow areas, which developed specialist expertise and eroded the regime of tolerance.

Institutions can be seen as vehicles for establishing and maintaining boundaries of inclusion and exclusion. The case of the Anacreontic Society provides a concrete example of how this transformation worked in practice, demonstrating the particular pressures that were exerted as the broader social transformation occurred. The complaints about 'petty *ballad writers*', and ultimately the collapse of the society, demonstrates how institutional practice forced the collapse of societies that exhibited behavior that was deemed too tolerant of difference. Ironically, however, the Anacreontic Society (as far as we can tell from the spare records) was established with something very specialist in mind. Like the Catch Club and the Glee Club, the Anacreontic Society had been established to celebrate and promote a specific musical genre, as if in anticipation of the narrow focus required by the regime of the institution. The problem was that it was an anachronistically focused institution that operated at a time when tolerance was preferred, and by the time specialization had become mandatory, it had broadened out into areas beyond the Anacreontic. The degree to which they thrived as an institution dedicated to the promotion of classical music more generally is surely due to the growing cultural capital of the classical repertoire. When they began to stray in a different direction, toward the bawdy and obscene verses that

---

[33] William Weber, *The Great Transformation of Musical Taste: Concert Programming from Haydn to Brahms* (Cambridge: Cambridge University Press, 2008), pp. 13–39.

traversed both musical and literary domains, the spirit of tolerant collegiality could no longer be sustained.

In addition to shedding light on the development of the regime of specialization and the forms of behavior that were considered appropriate to the project of taste-making, the case of the Anacreontics also helpfully reveals the role that external validation played in shaping modern institutions. We know from elsewhere that the kinds of bawdy and obscene song performed at the Anacreontic Society were common features of life in the late-eighteenth-century metropolis and beyond, but what distinguishes the Anacreontic Society was their representation in print through newspaper reporting and the publication of their songs. When crowds of people gathered outside the Crooked Billet in the Strand to listen to two women sing the obscene ballad 'Sandman Joe', for example, they left no trace in print – and we only know about it because of the manuscript recollections of Francis Place.[34] But when the same song was sung at the Anacreontics, it was mentioned in newspaper reports and printed by Fentum. It was this form of validation through print witnessing, the same form of legitimation by which they attempted to fashion their institutional authority, that exposed the society's activities to the scrutiny of public opinion. It is, then, in the Anacreontics' failure that we can most clearly see the role that print played in the development of modern institutionality. By making the activities of a gathering available for broader public inspection, print exerted pressures of judgment on the institution. This, ultimately, was the consequence of a belief in print as intrinsically beneficial. Print could flatter the participants into thinking that their own activities had wider significance beyond their own amusement, but alongside flattery, external validation could also raise the possibility of illegitimacy. The failed institution did not live up to the standards the wider print readership wanted to uphold. A concert of instrumental music was legible and could be witnessed and legitimated through print. A concert of instrumental music that also included a song sung by a talking penis was less easy to validate and could not be assimilated into the logics of the institution.

---

[34] For a discussion of 'Sandman Joe', see Ian Newman, 'Civilizing Taste: "Sandman Joe," the Bawdy Ballad, and Metropolitan Improvement', *Eighteenth-Century Studies*, 48.4 (2015), 437–56.

CHAPTER 6

Circulating Libraries as Institutional Creators of Genres

Anne H. Stevens

> It's derivative, with a twist. That's what they're looking for.
> Don Draper, *Mad Men*[1]

In 'Three Sundays', from the second season of the television series *Mad Men*, a character describes to advertising executive Don Draper her pitch for a TV show that would be an imitation of *Candid Camera*, but hosted by her husband, Jimmy Barrett, a Don Rickles-style insult comic. Draper thinks the show has potential, and, indeed, *Grin and Barrett* gets picked up by a network shortly thereafter. I begin with this quote because 'derivative, with a twist' perfectly captures the essence of the institutional production of genres across a range of media.[2] Institutions create genres by a process of imitation (with a twist) of successful works, whether in literature, television, film, music, or other media.[3] In this chapter, I will discuss the role of institutions in creating popular genres. In particular, I am interested in the ways in which the interrelated institutions of publishing houses and the circulating library networks of the later eighteenth century facilitated the creation of new novelistic subgenres. The creation of genres is fundamentally a collective effort, one in which institutional actors play a significant role. Indeed, popular novelistic subgenres like the historical novel and the gothic novel emerge through the interrelations of individual creators and institutions such as

---

Thanks to Jon Mee and Matthew Sangster for putting this book together and for their attentive work editing and revising this chapter. Special thanks to Matthew for his contribution to this chapter's conclusion.

[1] 'Three Sundays', dir. by Tim Hunter, written by Andre Jacquemetton and Maria Jacquemetton, *Mad Men*, Season 2 Episode 4 (2008).

[2] The fictional example of *Grin and Barrett* has a real-life analog in the flourishing of hidden-camera prank shows modeled after the long-running success of *Candid Camera*: shows like MTV's *Punk'd*, *The Jamie Kennedy Experiment*, and even the unfortunate O. J. Simpson vehicle *Juiced*.

[3] See Ralph Cohen, 'Innovation and Variation: Literary Change and Georgic Poetry', in *Genre Theory and Historical Change: The Theoretical Essays of Ralph Cohen*, ed. by John L. Rowlett (Charlottesville: University of Virginia Press, 2017), pp. 215–46.

publishing houses, circulating libraries, and reviews. As books become more readily available to the public through libraries, this leads to a growth in readership and demand for new titles. Publishing houses then supply those titles, and the reviewers evaluate them. The creation of new categories or genres fuels this process: a new subgenre creates a template that novelists can follow, readers can identify, and reviewers can judge new works against. This process of category creation belongs to the interconnections among institutions rather than mere authorial invention.

In positing that institutions create genres, I am drawing upon my previous research on popular novelistic subgenres of the Romantic era. My book *British Historical Fiction before Scott* studies the way that the historical novel takes shape as a genre in the second half of the eighteenth century. In that study I look at the historical novels that preceded Walter Scott's *Waverley* alongside reviewers, publishers, libraries, and readers to contend that the conventions of the genre are codified through the interactions of these varied actors, institutions, and texts.[4] A later article, 'The Season Novel, 1806–1824: A Nineteenth-Century Microgenre', employs a similar method to examine a much more narrowly circumscribed group of texts.[5] These texts, with titles like *Autumn in Weymouth*, *A Winter in London*, *Summer in Brighton*, and *Six Weeks in Paris*, traffic in fashionable scandal, usually taking place within a set span of time (a season) and geographical location. In both of these examples, new subgenres emerge through the complex interplay of institutions and creators rather than springing fully formed from the mind of an individual author. I will return to these examples later in the chapter after first discussing in some detail the methodological work that informs it.

In these pieces and elsewhere, my method has been shaped by the work of other sociologically and historically minded critics who theorize the role of institutions in forming cinematic, television, and other genres. This model can be counterposed to other prevailing theories of the origins of genres. Most fundamentally, this stands in opposition to the received wisdom that individual innovators create genres: Horace Walpole as the inventor of the gothic novel, Edgar Allan Poe as the creator of detective fiction, Sir Walter Scott as the father of historical fiction, and so forth. In contrast to this model, narratologist Tzvetan Todorov contends that genres originate through a combinatory process. He argues that 'a new genre is always the transformation of one or several old genres: by inversion, by

---

[4] Anne H. Stevens, *British Historical Fiction before Scott* (Basingstoke: Palgrave, 2010), p. 2.
[5] See Anne H. Stevens, 'The Season Novel 1806–1824: A Nineteenth-Century Microgenre', *Victoriographies*, 7.2 (2017), 81–100.

displacement, by combination'.[6] Todorov here seems to attribute agency to the genres themselves: the genres invert, displace, and combine without that work being attributed either to an individual creator or to larger institutional forces. Similarly, Alastair Fowler in his seminal work of genre theory *Kinds of Literature* describes the way genres change through 'topical invention, combination, aggregation, change of scale, change of function, counterstatement, inclusion, selection, and generic mixture'.[7] Here too the agency resides either with individual creators or with the genres themselves as quasi-sentient beings. Fredric Jameson comes closer to an institutional model when he calls genres 'contracts between a writer and his readers; or rather ... they are literary *institutions*, which like other institutions of social life are based on tacit agreements or contracts'.[8] Although he uses the word 'institutions' here, Jameson is primarily interested in the relationship between the writer and the reader rather than the role of external institutions such as publishers and distribution networks in shaping generic production. All of these different models for describing the genesis of new genres have significant explanatory power. Individual creators play a significant role in creating new generic models, but genres are ultimately formed through processes of recombination and mutation, and genres vitally serve as implicit contracts between the producer and the consumer. However, I would contend that the role of institutions such as publishing houses and distribution networks in the process of genre creation (genrefication) has gone underanalyzed within literary studies as compared to studies of genres in other fields such as cinema and music, in part because literary studies remain invested in the idea of the author as an object of study.

In his *Course in General Linguistics*, Ferdinand de Saussure describes the way languages change over time. An individual can coin a new word, but that coinage does not become a part of a language until other members of the linguistic community utilize the word and institutions validate it: 'It must not be taken to imply that a signal depends on the free choice of the speaker ... the individual has no power to alter a sign in any respect once it has become established in a linguistic community'. Saussure continues, 'No individual is able, even if he wished, to modify in any way a choice already established in the language. Nor can the linguistic community

---

[6] Tzvetan Todorov, 'The Origin of Genres', *New Literary History*, 8 (Autumn 1976), 159–70 (p. 161).
[7] Alastair Fowler, *Kinds of Literature: An Introduction to the Theory of Genres and Modes* (Cambridge, MA: Harvard University Press, 1982), p. 170.
[8] Fredric Jameson, 'Magical Narratives: Romance as Genre', *New Literary History*, 7 (Autumn 1975), 135–63 (p. 135).

exercise its authority to change even a single word. The community, as much as the individual, is bound to its language'.[9] Thus, new words do not enter the system of language until they are collectively validated through repeated use. You can think of the controversies that recur each year as new terms like 'selfie' or the singular 'they' are added to dictionaries.[10] As much as an individual might want to complain that 'they' should be used only when a plural is intended, the gender-neutral singular 'they' has now entered English and is being used by millions of individuals.

Languages are the product of the collective, produced by a community of speakers but facilitated and shaped through the interactions of various institutions such as schools, universities, the media, and dictionaries. No individual speaker can just declare that a new word be added to the language without the participation of the collective and the help of educational institutions in teaching that language, dictionaries of codifying it, and the media of facilitating its spread. In the same way, no individual writer can declare the birth of a new genre unless other writers produce imitations of the work, publishers codify it into a category, reviewers recognize and evaluate that category, and readers consume the text. Sociologist Howard Becker has modeled a similar collectivist method for discussing works of art of various sorts, including literary works, as the product of collective rather than individual labor. In Becker's terminology, an 'art world' is comprised of a collection of actors performing various tasks that center around artistic production. From this perspective, 'Works of art ... are not the products of individual makers, "artists" who possess a rare and special gift. They are, rather, joint products of all the people who cooperate via an art world's characteristic conventions to bring works like that into existence'. Even seemingly autonomous, solitary art forms like poetry involve multiple workers: 'Poets depend on printers and publishers, as painters do on distributors, and use shared traditions for the background against which their work makes sense'.[11]

Just as languages and artworks are collective endeavors, so too are genres. An individual can claim to invent a new genre, but it does not become established until other creators imitate and vary a pattern and when

---

[9] Ferdinand de Saussure, *Course in General Linguistics*, trans. by Roy Harris (La Salle: Open Court, 1986), pp. 68, 71.
[10] See 'Miriam-Webster's Words of the Year: 2019', *Merriam-Webster Online* <www.merriam-webster.com/words-at-play/word-of-the-year/they> and Katy Steinmetz, 'This Is Why Singular "They" Is Such a Controversial Subject', *Time*, 13 December 2019 <https://time.com/5748649/word-of-year-they-merriam-webster/>.
[11] Howard S. Becker, *Art Worlds*, 25th anniversary edn (Berkeley: University of California Press, 2008), pp. 35, 14.

institutions recognize this pattern of imitation and variation and codify it into a recognizable, repeatable category. In John Rieder's words, 'there cannot be a first example of a genre, because the generic character of a text is precisely what is repeated and conventional in it'.[12] When Horace Walpole publishes the bizarre, striking novel *The Castle of Otranto* in 1764, 'the gothic' as a genre is not born at that moment. In fact, more credit may be given to Clara Reeve, whose novel *The Champion of Virtue* (1777), later renamed *The Old English Baron*, repeats the subtitle *A Gothic Story* that Walpole had added to later editions of his work.[13] By repeating that subtitle, Reeve changes the meaning of 'a gothic story' from a descriptor of an individual work into a category, albeit one with only two examples in 1777 (though drawing upon the older romance tradition, of course). That said, it isn't until the 1780s when many more titles are produced because of new markets for novels with the flourishing of the circulating library system and the 1790s with Ann Radcliffe's success that the gothic becomes a recognizable and indeed flexible genre or family of genres.[14] Similarly, Sir Walter Scott retrospectively becomes dubbed the inventor of the historical novel, even though he was writing within an established subgenre when he published his first novel, *Waverley: Or, 'Tis Sixty Years Since* (1814). In this case, because Scott's Waverley Novels were so commercially and critically successful, his reputation eclipses that of his predecessors, that 'long list of second- and third-rate writers (Radcliffe, etc.), who were supposed to be important literary forerunners of his', in Georg Lukács's memorably dismissive phrase.[15]

The success of the gothic and the efflorescence of other novelistic subgenres in the second half of the eighteenth century were spurred by the institution of the circulating library and the publishing houses that stocked the shelves of said libraries. In many cases, publishers and libraries were one and the same, as in the case of publisher William Lane, who opened a large London circulating library in 1770 and whose Minerva Press

---

[12] John Rieder, *Science Fiction and the Mass Cultural Genre System* (Middletown: Wesleyan University Press, 2017), p. 20.

[13] [Horace Walpole], *The Castle of Otranto, a Story. Translated by William Marshal, Gent. From the Original Italian of Onuphrio Muralto, Canon of the Church of St. Nicholas at Otranto* (London: Thomas Lownds, 1765). This work was later retitled *The Castle of Otranto: A Gothic Story* and Walpole admitted authorship. See also [Clara Reeve], *The Champion of Virtue: A Gothic Story. By the Editor of the Phoenix. A Translation of Barclay's Argenis* (Colchester: W. Keymer, 1777), later retitled *The Old English Baron: A Gothic Story*.

[14] See Frederick S. Frank, *The First Gothics: A Critical Guide to the English Gothic Novel* (New York: Garland, 1987).

[15] Georg Lukács, *The Historical Novel*, trans. by Hannah Mitchell and Stanley Mitchell (Lincoln: University of Nebraska Press, 1962), p. 30.

became synonymous with the more notorious gothic novels, such as the 'horrid' novels mentioned in Jane Austen's *Northanger Abbey*.[16] Before discussing in more detail the role of institutions such as circulating libraries in creating novelistic subgenres in the Romantic era, though, I want to pause for a moment to acknowledge the work of scholars in other fields in analyzing the ways that institutions create genres more broadly. In his influential text *Film/Genre*, Rick Altman has said that 'genres [are] not ... formal patterns or ... textual canons, but ... system and process. Every generic system is made up of an interconnected network of user groups and their supporting institutions, each using the genre to satisfy its own needs and desires'. He discusses genres as institutions that are 'in turn backed up by other institutions, far more material in nature. Among these material institutions, the most active are production companies, exhibition practices, the critical establishment and government agencies'.[17] The role of institutions in generic formation can be seen most vividly in the most commercial sectors of the culture industry. Film historian Thomas Schatz, for example, has analyzed the ways in which the studio system fostered the creation of genres or formulas during the Golden Age of Hollywood. Schatz does not see this as leading to inferior, 'formulaic' filmmaking; in fact, he titles his study *The Genius of the System* because he believes the system itself was generative. He discusses, for example, the way that Universal 'cultivated a few standard movie formulas like women's pictures and gangster sagas' to complement its 'signature genre in the early 1930s ... the horror film'.[18] Likewise, Jason Mittell, in his study *Genre and Television*, has examined industry's role in producing both film and television genres 'through techniques such as marketing (advertising campaigns, trailers, posters, press releases, star publicity, internet presence, merchandising), distribution ... exhibition ... and nontheatrical practices'.[19]

---

[16] Devendra Varma, *The Evergreen Tree of Diabolical Knowledge* (Washington, DC: Consortium Press, 1972), p. 38. On Lane, see Dorothy Blakey, *The Minerva Press, 1790–1820* (London: Bibliographical Society, 1939).

[17] Rick Altman, *Film/Genre* (London: British Film Institute, 1999), pp. 195, 91.

[18] Thomas Schatz, *The Genius of the System: Hollywood Filmmaking in the Studio Era* (Minneapolis: University of Minnesota Press, 1989; repr. 2010), p. 95. Elsewhere Schatz characterizes genre formation as 'a dynamic process of exchange between the film industry and its audience': *Hollywood Genres: Formulas, Filmmaking, and the Studio System* (Philadelphia: Temple University Press, 1981), p. vii.

[19] Jason Mittell, *Genre and Television: From Cop Shows to Cartoons in American Culture* (New York: Routledge, 2004), p. 57. See also Bryan Turnock, who contends, 'The major genres were created and evolved through the contributions of film-makers, publicists, audiences, exhibitors, and critics. Studios took note of which components of a film proved popular or effective, and through their re-use of these became generic "codes and conventions"': *Studying Horror Cinema* (Leighton Buzzard: Auteur, 2019), p. 2.

Sometimes genres even arise through unexpected institutional circumstances, such as the rise of reality television in the United States during writers' strikes.[20]

Although more common within media studies, literary scholars have also studied the role of institutions in shaping genres. Rieder, in his study of the genre system of science fiction (SF), contends that

> All those involved in the production, distribution, and consumption of SF – writers, editors, marketing specialists, casual readers, fans, scholars, students – construct the genre not only by acts of definition, categorization, inclusion and exclusion (all of which are important), but also by their uses of the protocols and the rhetorical strategies that distinguish the genre from other forms of reading and writing.[21]

Mark McGurl's influential work *The Program Era* studies the way MFA creative writing programs in the United States shaped the genres and aesthetics of the American short story in the second half of the twentieth century. Like Schatz and Mittell, McGurl doesn't denigrate the role of institutions in creating genres: 'It would in any case be a great loss to literary history if our disrespect for institutional relations as somehow embarrassing to art ... made us less than vigilant in remembering and understanding them'. He argues that institutions create genres like literary minimalism (as MFA students modeled their works on the short stories of Raymond Carver and that aesthetic became institutionalized) in the highbrow literary world, not just in commercial fiction, while stressing that minimalism can be seen as both a 'product of the corporate educational technology and textbook business of the 1960s and 1970s' and at the same time a 'singular aesthetic triumph of that enterprise'.[22] McGurl's study vitally contributes to the study of institutions in shaping literary production because of its focus on an area thought to be removed from the more commercial sphere of popular fiction.

All the examples described earlier that have informed my thinking on the role of institutions in establishing genres focus on the twentieth and twenty-first centuries. The role of institutions in genre creation has been relatively less frequently studied when it comes to earlier periods of literary

---

[20] Jim Rutenberg, '"Reality" Shows May Undercut Writers' Strike', *New York Times*, 23 April 2001, C1.
[21] Rieder, p. 2.
[22] Mark McGurl, *The Program Era: Postwar Fiction and the Rise of Creative Writing* (Cambridge, MA: Harvard University Press, 2009), pp. xii, 293. For a more recent work on the institutions that shape contemporary fiction, see Mark McGurl, 'Everything and Less: Fiction in the Age of Amazon', *Modern Language Quarterly*, 77 (September 2016), 447–71.

Circulating Libraries as Creators of Genres 127

history. Institutions shape the long history of the novel, in ways ranging from length (the triple decker, the railway novel) to subject matter (deeming certain subjects off limits or encouraging others) to modes of distribution (lending libraries, repackaging of 'classic' works, serialization). For British popular fiction of the Romantic era the most significant institutions include booksellers and publishers, reviews, and, most importantly, circulating libraries.[23] Circulating libraries proliferated in the second half of the eighteenth century, especially, as William St Clair has described, after the 1774 legal decision that ended perpetual copyright in Britain.[24] As Christopher Skelton-Foorde has argued, 'Any understanding of Romantic-era print culture must take into account the central role that circulating libraries exercised over the production, distribution, and reception of the novel'.[25]

An 1825 guide to London, *The Picture of London Enlarged and Improved*, lists twenty-seven circulating libraries in London alone, and every major British metropolis and spa town had multiple circulating libraries by the end of the eighteenth century.[26] Though these libraries contained works from a wide array of genres, including poetry, history, travel writing, and divinity, their bread-and-butter was the novel. As the circulating library system expanded, more readers had access to more novels than ever before. The nature of the system, where subscribers could borrow individual novels for a fee, led to increased consumption of novels and to reading practices that put a premium on novelty, disposability, and quantity, as has been well documented. As St Clair explains, because of these circumstances, in the 1780s and 1790s demand for new novels exceeded output. Publishers were in such need of new titles that they would advertise in the backs of books. For example, in the back of the 1790 Mary Anne Radcliffe

---

[23] In his history of British circulating libraries, Devendra Varma describes booksellers claiming that if they printed an edition of 1,000, circulating libraries would purchase 400 of those copies (*Evergreen Tree*, p. 39).
[24] See William St Clair, *The Reading Nation in the Romantic Period* (Cambridge: Cambridge University Press, 2004), esp. pp. 235–67.
[25] Christopher Skelton-Foorde, 'Economics, Expertise, Enterprise, and the Literary Scene: The Commercial Management Ethos in British Circulating Libraries, 1780–1830', in *Authorship, Commerce and the Public: Scenes of Writing, 1750–1850*, ed. by E. J. Clery, Caroline Franklin, and Peter Garside (Basingstoke: Palgrave Macmillan, 2002), pp. 136–52 (p. 136).
[26] John Feltham, *The Picture of London, Enlarged and Improved: Being a Correct Guide for the Stranger, and Useful Compendium for the Inhabitant, Relative to Every Object of General Curiosity, and Embracing Every Particular Connected Either With Business or Amusement, in the Metropolis of the British Empire* (London: Longman, Hurst, Rees, Orme, Brown, and Green, 1825), p. 316. St Clair estimates that there were 1,500 circulating libraries in Great Britain by 1820 (*Reading Nation*, p. 237). See also Jan Fergus, *Provincial Readers in Eighteenth-Century England* (Oxford: Oxford University Press, 2006), which studies the archives of several booksellers in five Midland towns, 1744–1807.

novel *Radzivil, a Romance*, William Lane of the Minerva Press ran an advertisement importuning, 'Any lady or gentleman having Novels, &c. in manuscript, which they would wish introduced to the public, on favouring a line, may depend on having them printed in the most correct and elegant manner'. This notice follows immediately upon a notice suggesting that 'any person ... desirous of commencing a Circulating Library' should contact Mr. Lane to receive 'an immediate supply of entertaining books'.[27] Thus in 1790, circulating libraries were a growth industry, and publishers like Lane were expanding the reach of the institution while struggling to have enough stock to keep up with demand.

As this desire for new titles intensifies during these decades, novelistic subgenres and formulas flourish. Genres like the historical novel and the gothic novel, examples of which pre-date the 1774 copyright decision, explode in popularity in the 1780s and 1790s, alongside many other subgenres and microgenres. Edward Jacobs, for example, argues that 'the Gothic romance genre was almost entirely underwritten by circulating library publishers'.[28] The speediest way to produce new works is to imitate existing works. Just as Hollywood studios in the 1930s kept pace with demand for new films by developing formulas like the gangster film, the Universal horror film, or the women's picture, or by cultivating franchises featuring Abbot and Costello or Andy Hardy, the circulating library system developed formulas that kept readers coming back for more. A page from William Earle's 1799 circulating library catalog suggests one way that generic formulas worked, where keywords in titles signal generic affiliation.[29] This page contains lists of titles available at the library, including long sequences of titles beginning with 'Castle of' and another with 'Child of'. In an exchange in the journal *Critical Inquiry*, Katie Trumpener responds to Franco Moretti's article about novelistic titles by

---

[27] Mary Anne Radcliffe, *Radzivil, a Romance. Translated from the Russ of the Celebrated M. Wocklow*, 3 vols (London: W. Lane, 1790), III, 180.

[28] Edward Jacobs, 'A Previously Unremarked Circulating Library: John Roson and the Role of Circulating-Library Proprietors in Eighteenth-Century Britain', *Papers of the Bibliographical Society of America*, 89 (March 1995), 61–71 (pp. 69–70). See also Edward Jacobs, 'Anonymous Signatures: Circulating Libraries, Conventionality, and the Production of Gothic Romances', *ELH*, 62.3 (1995), 603–29.

[29] William Earle, *A New Catalogue of the Extensive and Well-Chosen Collection of English Books; Being Part of Earle's Original French, English, Spanish and Italian Circulating Library; Established Upwards of 60 Years in Frith-Street, Soho. And Now Removed to no. 47 Albemarle-Street, Piccadilly; Where All New Books, in the Instructive and Entertaining Classes of Literature, are Constantly Added. Bookbinding in General. Libraries Repaired, Catalogued, Bought, or Sold by Auction* (London: W. Earle, 1799), p. 26. As John C. Cawelti has argued, formulas 'provide ... a means for the rapid and efficient production of new works': *Adventure, Mystery, and Romance: Formula Stories as Art and Popular Culture* (Chicago: University of Chicago Press, 1976), p. 9.

stressing the importance of subtitles as opposed to main titles specifically in relation to Romantic-era fiction as signaling generic affiliation.[30] Though this is certainly true, main titles also contain signaling language. In the example from Earle's catalog, the many titles beginning with 'Child of' indicate sentimental content, while the 'Castle of' sequence points to the gothic. With a title like *Children of the Abbey*, a sentimental gothic novel by Irish author Regina Maria Roche and published by the Minerva Press, you can see the place where these two generic clusters meet.[31] It is important to note, however, that novelistic formulae that spurred cultural production did not begin in the 1770s. Earlier in the eighteenth century, to cite just one notable example, the formula we now call the 'it-narrative', novels told from the point of view of an inanimate object or animal, flourished. The formula dates back at least as far as Charles Gildon's *The Golden Spy* (1709), but it really flourished in the 1750s and 1760s as dozens of narratives narrated by canes, fleas, corkscrews, coins, and animals were published.[32]

Turning back to early cinema as an analogous case, we can see that even earlier than the invention of sound and the development of the Hollywood studio system in the 1930s, genres coalesce around a new technology. Similar to William Lane's ad at the back of *Radzivil*, an 1897 Mutoscope ad for the short film 'Three Jolly Girls and the Fun they Had With the Old Swing' includes this solicitation of film scenarios: '$5.00 for an Idea.– The Proprietors will pay $5.00 for any suggestion of a good scene adopted and used by them in the Biograph or Mutoscope. Scenes submitted should be minutely described. Comedy scenes are preferred'.[33] Similar to the way publishers and circulating library catalogs used keywords in titles to signal generic affiliation, early film catalogs often arranged titles into generic categories quite different from the genres of the later sound era: 'Sports and Pastimes Views', 'Views of Notable Personages', 'Trick Pictures', 'Parade Pictures', etc.[34]

Just as circulating library catalogs helped make potential readers aware of the array of novels available, between 1894 and 1908 film catalogs documented the wares of the early silent film industry. In 1908, with the establishment of the Motion Picture Patents Company, trade journals and

---

[30] Katie Trumpener, 'Paratext and Genre System: A Response to Franco Moretti', *Critical Inquiry*, 36 (Autumn 2009), 159–71 (p. 163).
[31] Regina Maria Roche, *The Children of the Abbey: A Tale*, 4 vols (London: Minerva Press, 1796).
[32] See *The Secret Life of Things: Animals, Objects, and It-Narratives in Eighteenth-Century England*, ed. by Mark Blackwell (Lewisburg: Bucknell University Press, 2007).
[33] Kemp R. Niver, *Biograph Bulletins 1896–1908* (Los Angeles: Locare Research Group, 1971), p. 24.
[34] See the catalogs collected in Niver, *Biograph Bulletins*, and in the Thomas A. Edison Papers housed at Rutgers University and available through njdigitalhighway.org.

advertisements supplanted the early catalogs. Looking at the early catalogs one can observe the shift from film as a primarily scenic medium ('views') to a mature narrative art.[35] Some catalogs develop idiosyncratic categories such as 'Visions of art' in a Pathé catalog from 1903 or its 'Scenes for smoking concert', a risqué category that included such titles as 'The bride's first night', 'The prostitute's bath', and 'Caught in the act'. These categories, as defined by the industry, help consumers to make sense of the vast new world of possibilities within silent film. A list of titles can be overwhelming for accessing this newly emerging media form, so the institutions that mediate early cinema create categories that allow consumers to understand the different possibilities of this new art form. In the same way, keywords and genre labels in popular novel titles of the Romantic era help signal to readers the types of readerly experiences contained within – the pathos of the sentimental or the terrors of the gothic, for example. Not all these silent film categories survive as film develops into a narrative medium. Comic scenes, with their emphasis on slapstick and visual humor, form the basis for early silent comedies, while other genres develop by adapting other types of stories: adaptations of literary and dramatic works, for example, as the medium develops.

Turning back to the Romantic era, one such sub- or microgenre, the so-called season novel, provides a good illustration of the ways that institutions such as the circulating library helped to create genres. The season novel was a subset of the broader category of the fashionable novel, or novels depicting the lives of upper-class individuals and their fashionable amusements, that flourished between 1806 and 1824.[36] This microgenre took shape quick on the heels of the success of one work in particular, Thomas Skinner Surr's *A Winter in London* (1806). Surr's novel in itself is not particularly distinctive or innovative. It depicts fashionable London society, features a foundling young protagonist who after some setbacks marries his true love in the end, and contains a gothic interlude involving villainous Italians. It was highly successful, however, and that success spurred imitation, as successes often do.[37] Looking back upon this sequence of novels, a reviewer in 1827 lamented, 'about twenty years ago,

---

[35] See *A Guide to Motion Picture Catalogs by American Producers and Distributors, 1894–1908: A Microfilm Edition*, ed. by Charles Musser (Frederick: University Publications of America, 1985). See also Simon Popple and Joe Kember, *Early Cinema: From Factory Gate to Dream Factory* (London: Wallflower, 2004).

[36] See Stevens, 'Season Novel'.

[37] One possible reason for its spectacular success is its coded depiction of Georgiana Cavendish, Duchess of Devonshire, given the taste for fashionable scandal at that time (and indeed, our own).

in consequence of the success of a novel . . . called the Winter in London, the Town was inundated with a succession of the filthiest trash that ever disgraced the press of the country'.[38] These novels provide some insight into how institutions such as publishers and booksellers help to establish novelistic subgenres. In the case of the success of Surr's novel, publishers began producing works that mimicked *A Winter in London* through titles or subtitles within a year. The earliest such text, *A Summer by the Sea* (1807), bears little resemblance to the features of Surr's novel. While Surr's novel and its later imitators feature fashion, satire, and scandal in a distinct location, *A Summer by the Sea* is more standard courtship fare in a fictional rather than a real-world setting, 'Rockbeach'.[39] The five season novels published in 1807, however, imitate *A Winter in London* more closely by focusing on a fashionable season and recycling plot elements such as divorce and infidelity. Among these novels of 1807, the one most worth noting unfortunately has not survived to the present day: E. G. Bayfield's *A Winter at Bath; or, Love as It May Be and Friendship as It Ought to Be*, produced by the infamous publisher J. F. Hughes. An account from the time provides some context:

> The success of Mr. Surr's *Winter in London*, has, as is usually the case under such circumstances, called forth a herd of imitators. Amongst these, *A Winter in Bath* claims the first notice. Without the aid, however, of an imitative title, its intrinsic merit would have insured and commanded a gratifying reception from the public. The story is well written, the incidents are good, and the characters are excellently pourtrayed.
>
> About the same time that *A Winter in Bath* made its appearance, a Mrs. Bayfield had a novel ready for publication, under the title of *Love as it may be, and Friendship as it ought to be*. Her bookseller, however, imitating Mr. Surr's title, and perhaps conceiving that he might safely practise an imposition on the public, gave Mrs. Bayfield's novel the title of *A Winter AT Bath*. This circumstance excited much contention between the booksellers; and we are not certain whether some legal proceedings were not commenced upon the subject. Mrs. Bayfield very candidly declared, not only that the fraud was carried on without her approbation, but without her knowledge.[40]

---

[38] 'Fashionable Novels', *The London Literary Gazette and Journal of Belles Lettres, Arts, Sciences, Etc.*, 543 (16 June 1827), 364–75 (p. 374).

[39] Orlando, *A Summer by the Sea: A Novel*, 2 vols (London: Minerva Press, 1807).

[40] Francis William Blagdon, 'Introduction: Containing a General and Rapid View of the State and Progress of Literature, Foreign and Domestic. For 1805–1806', in *The Flowers of Literature, for 1806; or Characteristic Sketches of Human Nature, and Modern Manners. To Which are Added, a General View of Literature During That Period; Portraits and Biographical Notices of Eminent Literary, and Political Characters; with Notes, Historical, Critical, and Explanatory*, ed. by Francis William Blagdon (London: B. Crosby, 1807), pp. lxxviii–lxxix.

Hughes, publisher of such imitative works as *The Monk of Udolpho* (1807) and the novels of 'Caroline Burney', here retitles a completed novel in order to capitalize on a recent success. Bayfield's original title may have been more reflective of the contents of the novel (although because the text is lost we can never know for certain), but the publisher renames the text in order to affiliate his output with a recent success in a way that this reviewer saw as an 'imposition'. In the process, Hughes not only does what he can to promote one of his publications, he also helps to establish the season novel as a formula by mimicking the title of Surr's successful novel.

Titles were one of the most important ways that publishers and booksellers marketed their works, using keywords to try to capture readers' interest. A scene in Honoria Scott's *A Winter in Edinburgh* (1810) takes direct aim at Hughes's publishing practices (despite its own title that attempts to capitalize on the season formula). An advertisement at the start of the volume suggests that Hughes had advertised a book under the same title:

> The Publisher of the *Winter in Edinburgh*, feels himself called upon, however reluctantly, to make a Reply to an Advertisement of Mr. T. F. Hughes, Bookseller, Berner Street (late of Wigmore Street), in the *Morning Post*, wherein he asserts, that the title of *his* Book has been copied, and that he has no Connection with the Publisher of the present Work. – Should ever Mr. Hughes's Book appear, the Public will judge how far his statement is Consistent with Truth, should they be at the Trouble to look into it.[41]

Within the novel itself, a character named Owen plans to write a work called *A Winter in Wales*. After this work is advertised,

> [t]he morning brought forth a confirmation of the title being a taking one. Mr. Wigless, a bookseller, certainly of celebrity; for, under his guidance, the literary bantlings of the Miss Muffins were ushered into the world as follows;
> "The Horrors of the Church-Yard; by *Mrs. Radcliff.*"
> "Euphrosyne in Frocks, by *Miss Burney.*"
>   So delighted was he with every work of genius, and so desirous of making it his own, that when *The Autumn in Bristol* caught his eye, he embroidered it on his own foolscap; but dire mishap! apologies soon flew about, were posted in every blue cover, and appeared in every shape:–the Autumn in

---

[41] Honoria Scott, *A Winter in Edinburgh; or, the Russian Brothers: A Novel*, 3 vols (London: J. Dick, 1810), I, advertisement.

Bristol shed its fruit in other hands; and Mr. Wigless's book remained *as it may be*.[42]

Scott transforms the controversy over *A Winter at Bath* into *The Autumn in Bristol* and Mr Hughes of Wigmore Street into 'Mr Wigless'. In this incident, Wigless advertises a book using Owen's proposed title, just as Hughes had done with *A Winter in Edinburgh*. The fact that no record of a second novel called *A Winter in Edinburgh* survives suggests that he may have withdrawn the title from publication. In fact, a review published just a couple of months after the publication of *A Winter in Edinburgh* suggests that Hughes's name had just 'appeared in the Gazette, in the list of Bankrupts'. This reviewer in the *Satirist* takes credit for Hughes's bankruptcy, claiming 'we put a stop to the torrent of filth which issued from the Wigmore Street laboratory' and calling Hughes a 'nauseous reptile [who] could only exist amidst such filth', although those claims may be overstated.[43]

Other contemporaries made note of the derivative nature of publishing practices at this time. For example, an 1807 essay states,

> We mentioned on a former occasion the croud of servile imitators of the title (but alas! nothing but the title) of "*A Winter in London*", and we have now to add to that list, "*A Winter in Bath*", "*A Winter Bath*", "*The Winter in Dublin*", and by way of climax, we suppose, "*The Infidel Mother; or Three Winters in London*" ... at least two of these works were named, not by the author, but the bookseller.[44]

Here the essayist stresses the role of booksellers in retitling works in order to create commercially successful categories. Merely adding the word 'winter' to a novel's title affiliates the work with *A Winter in London* in the hopes of replicating its success. Another reviewer called this practice 'a *taking* title': 'The employment of what the booksellers quaintly, but expressively, call a *taking* title, is become a sort of fashion, among the novelists of England. The popularity of Mr. Surr's "Winter in London" has diffused winter all over the kingdom, and has generated a Winter in Bath, and a Winter in Kent, and Winter every where'.[45]

Though Hughes's career illustrates the extreme version of publishers creating genres by imitating recent successful works, in a broader sense all

---

[42] Scott, III, 196–97.
[43] Review of *A Winter in Edinburgh* by Honoria Scott, in *The Satirist, or Monthly Meteor*, 6 (February 1810), 193–97 (pp. 194, 193).
[44] 'Novels and Romances', *Monthly Magazine and British Register*, suppl. V., 23 (30 July 1807), 644–45.
[45] 'The Literary World', *The Port Folio*, new ser., 1 (April 1809), 342–45 (p. 342).

generic formations work in this way. It is my contention that literary scholars need to pay more attention to those aspects of the process of book publishing we often tend to dismiss as unworthy of our time – works that are derivative, imitative, and just plain bad – because it is only through the process of imitation, spurred by publishers, booksellers, and circulating libraries, that new genres are formed. While institutions' motives for creating and mediating genres are often to some extent self-interested – the propagation of authority, the reaping of profits – genres are also crucial for rendering cultural systems comprehensible and for opening such systems to new participants. Many of the Romantic-era readers who browsed the catalogs of the circulating libraries looking for associations with works they had enjoyed would have been priced out of novel-reading a generation before, and many new writers got their start by assaying imitations with twists. As the number of works, writers and audiences continued to expand, the shorthand conventions of genre became ever more important for rendering the cultural world navigable. In making genres, institutions also made maps that played substantial yet oft-occluded roles in determining both the lay of the land and how and by whom it could subsequently be traversed.

CHAPTER 7

Lecturing Networks and Cultural Institutions, 1740–1830

Jon Klancher

Until recently, networks and institutions appeared to be opposite kinds of social form. Networks are mobile, flexible, and do not often last beyond the figures traced by the actors who make them; institutions are hierarchical, imposing, and characteristically durable, gaining strength and authority as they become 'cognitive constructions ... imbued with legitimacy'.[1] Network-forming is a constant, widespread, and more highly self-conscious activity than perhaps it was before the concept 'network' began to take on an independent life of its own near the end of the last century.[2] But it is quite difficult to build an institution, a process that requires a great many already-existing elements and assemblages, including networks of many kinds: short or lengthy, flatter or thicker, smoother or more frictional, trustful or laden with suspicion. On this last point, however, the sociologists of organization have been asking more searching questions about how networks can be understood as imbricated in the making and effects of institutions. Walter Powell and Achim Oberg, for instance, propose thinking about networks as 'scaffolds for institutions', or even as 'co-evolutionary'. Networks do not simply connect their actors node to node; they also reveal an 'explosive organizing potential' that may give rise to institutions or indeed to whole fields of cultural production.[3]

---

[1] Walter W. Powell and Achim Oberg, 'Networks and Institutions', in *The SAGE Handbook of Organizational Institutionalism*, ed. by Royston Greenwood and others, 2nd edn (London: Sage, 2017), pp. 446–76 (p. 446).

[2] Luc Boltanski and Eve Chiapello date the emergence of a newly normative usage for 'network' to the late 1960s, noting in 2005 that 'the metaphor of the network is gradually taking on the task of a new general representations of societies ... taking for granted that the world is a network' (pp. 138, 151). See *The New Spirit of Capitalism* [2005], trans. by Gregory Elliott (New York: Verso, 2017), pp. xxxiv–xxxv, 138–43.

[3] For 'scaffolds of institutions', see Powell and Oberg, p. 447; for a 'co-evolutionary' relation between networks and institutions, see an earlier version of this argument in Jason Owen-Smith and Walter W. Powell, 'Networks and Institutions', in *The SAGE Handbook of Organizational Institutionalism*, ed. by Royston Greenwood and others (London: Sage, 2008), pp. 596–623.

This kind of institution-building power may also draw from the way networks become actants or active 'mediators' rather than mere 'intermediaries', if we adopt Bruno Latour's critical distinction, transforming what they transmit.[4]

In this chapter, I want to pursue such questions about networks for the cultural practices of lecturing, a medium which has been previously grasped only in terms of its institutional forms.[5] The new scientific and literary lecturing institutions that began appearing in the 1790s – Anderson's Institution in Glasgow (1796), the Pneumatic Institution in Bristol (1798), and the Royal Institution of Great Britain in London (1799) – presaged many more to come in the nineteenth century. Among these, the Royal Institution (RI) was pivotal for molding the scientific and literary lecturing institution as a major cultural force, and the only one to survive into the present to become what the BBC calls one of the 'most revered of scientific bodies' and others term 'one of the leading scientific institutions of the world'.[6] As Romanticists know, the Royal and its successors, like the Russell (1808) and Surrey (1809) Institutions, were not solely devoted to science; rather they featured a multeity of knowledge extending from the fine arts to the mechanical arts, from poetry to chemistry, and from moral philosophy to biology. The literary impact alone was immense. From 1800 to 1820, most of those we call Romantic writers either lectured or listened at a scientific and literary lecturing institution: Samuel Taylor Coleridge, William Hazlitt, Lord Byron, Thomas De Quincey, William Wordsworth, Percy and Mary Shelley, Thomas Campbell, Charles Lamb, William Godwin, John Keats, Henry Crabb Robinson, and others.[7] More widely, the complexity of the knowledge

---

[4] For Latour's distinction between mediators and intermediaries, see *Reassembling the Social: An Introduction to Actor-Network Theory* (New York: Oxford University Press, 2005), pp. 37–42. I am grateful to Emily K. Merchant for advice on the uses of actor-network theory in these contexts.

[5] In this chapter, I will rework my own earlier institutional analysis of the Romantic-age London lecturing venues (in *Transfiguring the Arts and Sciences: Knowledge and Cultural Institutions in the Romantic Age* [Cambridge: Cambridge University Press, 2013]) along the lines of network analysis. See also Sarah Zimmerman's stimulating work on lecturing performances and their institutions in *The Romantic Literary Lecture* (New York: Oxford University Press, 2018). For earlier institutional studies, see notes 34 and 35.

[6] Pallab Ghosh, 'Does the Royal Institution Have a Future?', *BBC News*, 1 December 2015 <www.bbc.com/news/science-environment-34699008>; Sanborn C. Brown, *Benjamin Thompson, Count Rumford* (Cambridge, MA: MIT Press, 1979), p. 213.

[7] Peter Manning shows the breadth and depth of these writers' attentiveness to lectures in 'Manufacturing the Romantic Image: Coleridge and Hazlitt Lecturing', in *Romantic Metropolis: The Urban Scene of British Culture, 1780–1840*, ed. by James Chandler and Kevin Gilmartin (Cambridge: Cambridge University Press, 2005), pp. 227–45 (esp. pp. 229–32).

on offer at these institutions roughly corresponded to the multiplicity of networks that converged to forge the RI and others like it.

One of those networks has been more difficult to study than others because it left so few marks in the archival record. The itinerant science lecturers crisscrossed Britain from the 1740s to the 1790s, appearing in large and small towns to enthused, diverse audiences that spanned a wide social range from artisans to gentry. They contributed immensely to an emerging culture of improvement grounded in a scientific, technical, and organizational process that social historians began to study in the 1960s and 1970s.[8] But the turn to cultural history around 1980 was also a turn toward London and its rich layering of scientific societies and literary lecturing institutions, a move that tended to leave the world of itinerant lecturing distantly in the shadows, seemingly unrelated to the high-profile institutionalized urban lecturing that became characteristic of the nineteenth century.

In what follows, I want to rethink the relation of both itinerant and metropolitan lecturing networks by making use of some classic network types – distributed, centralized, and decentralized (Figure 7.1). I will pay special attention to the decentralized network type as a useful heuristic for grasping the relation between the otherwise very different patterns that lecturing practices could take across diverging contexts. Among these patterns, I first consider the itinerant networks that were later reconfigured by the early lecturing institutions in Glasgow and London; the second half of the chapter turns to a particularly rich and well-documented case, the forming of the RI around 1800, an institution that has often been a historian's model for understanding how lecturing worked as a culturally influential medium. If institutions like the Royal and others can be shown to be both made up of converging networks and to generate more networks, I will also ask a larger question at the end of the chapter: is it possible to regard an institution as itself a complex network, and what is at stake in posing and trying to answer that question?

Itinerant Lecturing Networks

I begin with a brief thought experiment: suppose that Humphry Davy (1778–1829) was not hired to the RI in 1801 and therefore did not go on to

---

[8] A. E. Musson and Eric Robinson, *Science and Technology in the Industrial Revolution* (London: Gordon and Breach, 1969), pp. 101–12.

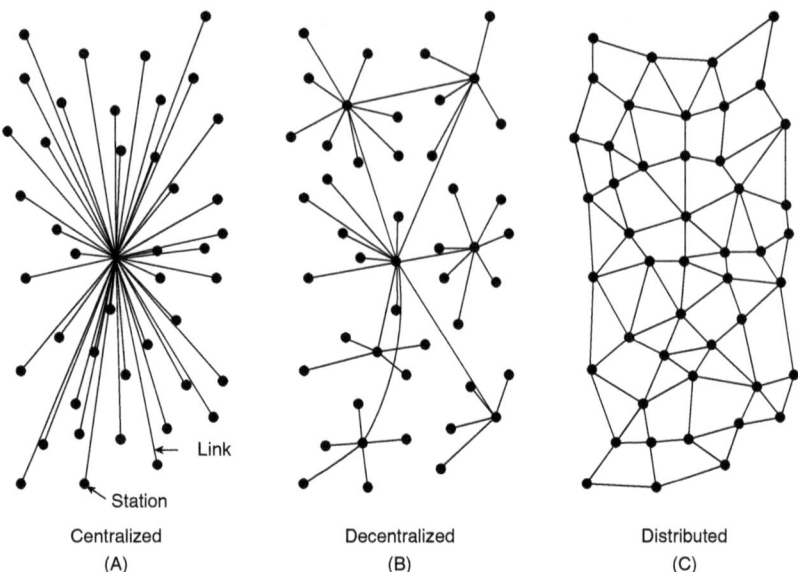

Figure 7.1 Three network types from Paul Baran's 1962 paper *On Distributed Communications Networks*. Reproduced with permission of the RAND Corporation.[9]

become the star scientific lecturer in London, from 1801 to 1812. After working briefly with Thomas Beddoes at the Pneumatic Institution in Bristol from 1798 to 1801, this scenario would go, Davy saw a new career path open for lecturing on chemistry in rented rooms at Bristol, then travelling either north to Birmingham and Derby or southeast to Bath and Reading as he became one of the itinerant science lecturers who had been flourishing across England since the 1740s to speak on natural philosophy, electricity, or chemistry (Figure 7.2). Had he been a more politically astute follower of Beddoes' radical social medicine, Davy might alternatively have followed the network paths traced by Adam Walker (1731–1821) from Liverpool to Manchester, York, and Newcastle along the curve of what Jon Mee has called the Transpennine Enlightenment.[10] Alternately, given what we know of Davy's social ambition, he could well have followed the

---

[9] Paul Baran, *On Distributed Communications Networks* (Santa Monica: RAND Corporation, 1962), p. 4 <www.rand.org/pubs/papers/P2626.html>.

[10] See Jon Mee and Jennifer Wilkes, 'Transpennine Enlightenment: The Literary and Philosophical Societies and Knowledge Networks in the North, 1781–1830', *Journal for Eighteenth-Century Studies*, 38.4 (2015), 599–612.

Lecturing Networks and Cultural Institutions, 1740–1830 139

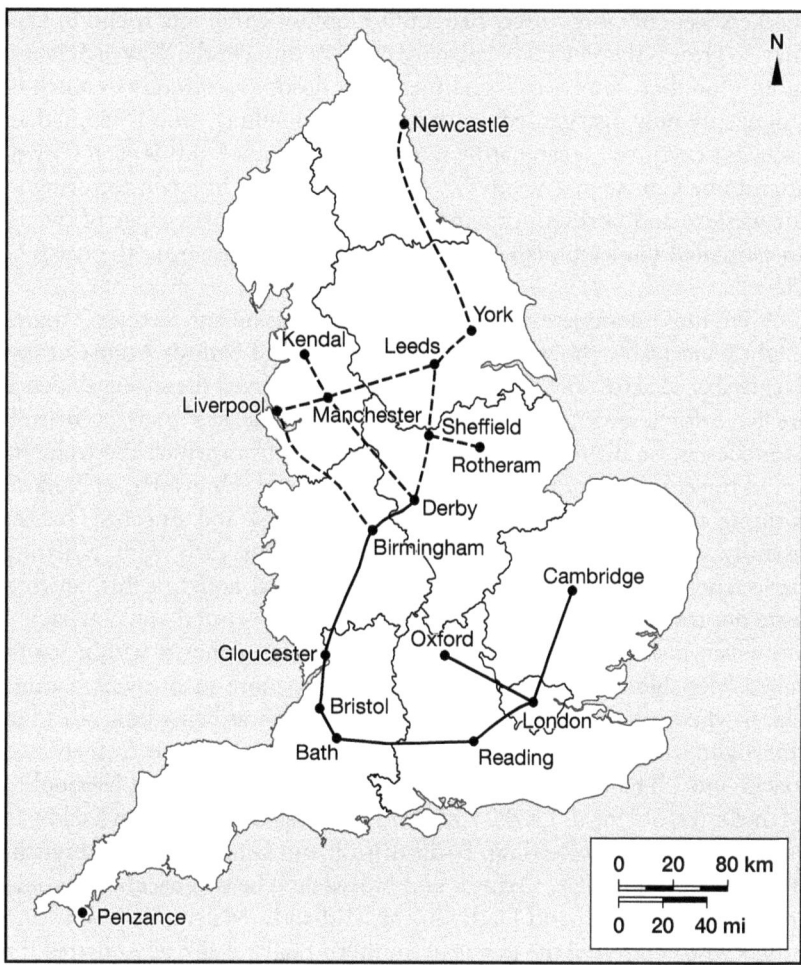

Figure 7.2 Map showing often-traveled itinerant lecturing routes of Adam Walker, Thomas Garnett, and others to the north; Benjamin Martin, James Ferguson, and others to the south.

paths of Benjamin Martin (1704–82), the electrical showman who linked the Midlands to the fashionable towns of southern England and basked in the admiration of wealthy subscribers from Reading to Bath, Bristol, and Birmingham.

While London had been a thriving center for lectures in natural philosophy that were offered variously by Francis Hauksbee, J. T. Desaguliers, James Stirling, and others until the 1740s, by the 1750s London lecturing markets were notably scarce. Benjamin Franklin wrote to a friend in 1759 that 'so great is the general Negligence of every thing in the Way of Science' in London that 'courses of Experimental Philosophy, formerly so much in Vogue, are now disregarded; so that Mr. Demainbray, who is reputed an excellent Lecturer ... can hardly make up an audience in this great City to attend one Course in a Winter'.[11] At the same time, itinerant lecturing in the western and northern provinces blossomed from an average of two to an estimated ten lecturers working in any given decade from the 1740s to 1800.[12]

A far more complete print record of these itinerant lecturers' routes might conceivably show a 'distributed' network of pathways more or less evenly spaced across Britain. But that is unlikely, given the strong evidence we have for a decentralized pattern instead. The key hubs at Bristol, Manchester, or Birmingham were intersections from which the lecturers could travel to nearby towns like Derby, Sheffield, Doncaster, or Bolton, forming the kind of pattern Alexander Galloway and Eugene Thacker usefully describe as 'a core "backbone" of hubs each with radiating peripheries'.[13] But we should be clear that the real nodes of this network were not towns themselves, but the audiences the lecturers could attract in any given place. The more often such audiences gathered within towns called Manchester, York, or Birmingham, the more such towns became places where a national audience for the sciences was being built. Read in this light, the itinerants' network patterns seem to have formed two 'backbones'. The northern network reached audiences from Liverpool to Manchester, Sheffield, Leeds, York, and Newcastle; the southern backbone ran from London to Reading, Bath, Bristol, and Gloucester, with branching trips to Cambridge, Oxford, and Norwich. The two backbones could meet at Birmingham and Derby in the Midlands. Martin, Ferguson, and others who connected the towns of southern England also accentuated the centripetal attraction to London as a center of polite culture that helped reestablish London scientific life by the end of the eighteenth century. 'Knowledge is now become a fashionable thing', Martin wrote in his widely distributed periodical, *The General Magazine of Arts and Sciences,* 'and philosophy is the science a la mode: hence to cultivate this study, is only to

---

[11] Benjamin Franklin (writing from London) to Ebenezer Kinnersley, 28 July 1759, in *Founders Online*, National Archives <https://founders.archives.gov/documents/Franklin/01-08-02-0107>.

[12] J. L. Heilbron, *Electricity in the Seventeenth and Eighteenth Centuries: A Study of Early Modern Physics* (Berkeley: University of California Press, 1979), p. 162.

[13] Alexander Galloway and Eugene Thacker, *The Exploit: A Theory of Networks* (Minneapolis: University of Minnesota Press, 2007), p. 32.

be in taste'.[14] But on the northern routes, lecturers like Walker, Henry Moyes (1750–1807), and Thomas Garnett (1766–1802) made the effort to break social barriers to scientific knowledge, joining artisans and mechanics to more highly educated audiences they were meeting from Liverpool to Newcastle.

The itinerants were not lonely travelers. They intersected with a growing cultural infrastructure that included theaters, circulating libraries, newspapers, assembly rooms, and booksellers in factory towns like Manchester or at resort villas in Bath. Many of their routes may also have been extended by the great push to create a new English infrastructure of roads and canals from the 1720s to the 1810s.[15] Though the lecturers advertised their courses in local newspapers, they also connected with their publics by way of recommendations from one 'man of science' to another, so that for Thomas Garnett to be assured of an audience in the Midlands, he needed a letter of introduction from Thomas Walker in Manchester to James Watt, Jr., in Birmingham.[16] The lecturers were often affiliated with schools, where local claims to expertise could be validated by wider institutional references. Caleb Rotheram (1694–1752) toured with electrical lectures in the north while serving as master of Kendal Dissenting Academy near Manchester, while John Arden (1721–91) taught experimental philosophy at Beverley in Yorkshire between lecture tours to Birmingham and Bath.[17] The affinity of public lecturing knowledge with established schools or academic routines was not an invention of the Romantic age or the RI but a feature of itinerant lecturing well before them.

These lecturers often competed with their peers to display the most advanced experimental apparatus for producing the most eye-filling effects.[18] While the London lecturers had apparatuses to display in their homes, the itinerant lecturers began buying and proudly carrying their own

---

[14] Quoted in John R. Millburn, *Benjamin Martin: Author, Instrument-Maker, and 'Country Showman'* [1976] (New York: Springer Netherlands, 2012), p. 44.

[15] 'The improvement of the road network allowed the conveyance of ever more elaborate [lecturers'] apparatus which added to the drama and spectacle': Paul A. Elliott, *The Derby Philosophers: Science and Culture in British Urban Society, 1700–1850* (Manchester: Manchester University Press, 2009), p. 41. On the wider infrastructural buildup in the eighteenth century, see Jo Guldi, *Roads to Power: Britain Invents the Infrastructure State* (Cambridge, MA: Harvard University Press, 2012).

[16] A. E. Musson and Eric Robinson, 'Science and Industry in the Late Eighteenth Century', *Economic History Review*, 13.2 (1960), 222–44 (p. 233, fn. 2).

[17] Musson and Robinson, *Science and Technology*, pp. 103–08.

[18] Simon Schaffer, 'The Consuming Flame: Electrical Showmen and Tory Mystics in the World of Goods', in *Consumption and the World of Goods*, ed. by John Brewer and Roy Porter (London: Routledge, 1993), pp. 489–526 (p. 490).

portable apparatuses from town to town.[19] We need to think of their networks as not only connecting speakers to audiences and towns but also as linking them to the prominent objects that defined them on their paths. In 1766, Adam Walker began his own lecturing tours across northern England by acquiring (or perhaps inventing) a gigantic astronomical apparatus that he named the Eidouranion, an elaborate orrery, twenty feet tall by twenty-six feet in diameter, that he outfitted to act something like the projector in a planetarium. The effects it could produce were analogous for audiences of astronomical lectures in Manchester to the spectacular effects later produced by the Voltaic battery apparatus on the stage of the RI in London. In both cases, as Jan Golinski points out in an essay on Walker's apparatus, the aesthetic language of the 'sublime' could be mobilized to imagine a swelling universe of meaning that emanated out of a material scientific instrument put into motion by a lecturer who could sometimes rise to the inspiring level of a poet.[20] In the early 1800s, Walker took his Eidouranion from the itinerant lecturing networks to the theaters of London, crossing what Golinski calls 'a chasm in British scientific culture', from the 1780s to the 1830s, that separated the DIY culture of itinerant lecturers from a new age of institutionalizing the sciences in urban societies, associations, and, not least, the new London scientific and literary lecturing institutions to which I will shortly come.

Perhaps more decisively crossing this chasm was Thomas Garnett. His career had begun with an Edinburgh medical degree that took him, by his mid-twenties, to practicing medicine in Yorkshire, then trying his hand at lecturing around Manchester, where he also affiliated with the Manchester Literary and Philosophical Society, reading at least two papers on climatology at the Society.[21] By 1795, newly married, Garnett set out to emigrate to America, where he was prepared to lecture and thus follow in the footsteps of Thomas Cooper and Joseph Priestley, whose dissenting republican views he broadly shared.[22] But a delay in the voyage from Liverpool

---

[19] Benjamin Martin was one of the first to carry his apparatus; see Millburn, p. 40. The difference between an immobile apparatus and a portable one is well illustrated by Jessie Molesworth in 'The Cosmic Sublime: Wright of Derby's *A Philosopher Lecturing on the Orrery*', *Lumen*, 34 (2015), 109–21 <https://doi.org/10.7202/1028514ar>.

[20] Jan Golinski, 'Sublime Astronomy: The Eidouranion of Adam Walker and His Sons', *Huntington Library Quarterly*, 80.1 (2017), 135–57 (p. 138).

[21] S. G. E. Lythe, *Thomas Garnett (1766–1802): Highland Tourist, Scientist and Professor, Medical Doctor* (Glasgow: Polpress, 1984), pp. 16–17.

[22] On Garnett's associations with the Manchester Literary and Philosophical Society, Cooper, and Priestley, see Arianne Chernock, *Men and the Making of Modern British Feminism* (Stanford: Stanford University Press, 2009), pp. 23–26.

prompted Garnett to unpack his lecturing apparatus and give local talks; soon he was persuaded to lecture more widely in Manchester, Warrington, Lancaster, and eventually Birmingham. Garnett's speaking style in these lectures was said to have 'a remarkable effect upon his audience'; word got around on the itinerants' network that he was no ordinary teacher of science but was unusually able to speak to the specialist and the popular audience alike, so that he was recommended to 'all who had been previously disgusted, or frightened by the difficulties they had before met with'.[23] Within a year, he became the first itinerant science lecturer to be hired as a professor at a new kind of educational experiment, the scientific and literary lecturing institution that came to be called Anderson's Institution in Glasgow.

Thus, Garnett's career might well crystallize *in miniatura* the interface of lecturing networks and cultural institutions addressed in this chapter. Coming to Glasgow six months after John Anderson's death in January 1796, he effectively became the co-creator of Anderson's Institution by being put in a position to interpret the lecturing remit of Anderson's posthumous bequest for founding a new institution. Richard Sher has placed Anderson's alternative university – as it was first envisioned – within a 'bifurcation of the Glasgow Enlightenment' in which 'a popular and evangelical Presbyterian Enlightenment of "useful knowledge"' led by Anderson, a professor of natural philosophy, divided itself from the polite Enlightenment of Francis Hutcheson, Adam Smith, and John Millar.[24] As John Gardner shows in Chapter 10, Anderson's passionate support for the French Revolution also gave his Institution a distinctly republican cast, where he would carry on the famous 'anti-toga' classes he taught at Glasgow University in which laboring men and women were invited to show up to higher education wearing their work clothes.[25] Garnett felt himself 'perfectly in unison' with Anderson's program and developed a curriculum of lectures that would address both the 'education of young gentlemen for manufactures or commerce' and the 'fair sex [who] have been admitted to the temple of knowledge on the same footing

---

[23] 'The Life of the Author', an anonymous biographical sketch prefatory to Thomas Garnett, *Popular Lectures on Zoonomia, or the Laws of Animal Life* (London: Press of the Royal Institution of Great Britain, 1804), pp. v–xxii (pp. xii–xiii).

[24] Richard Sher, 'Commerce, Religion, and the Enlightenment in Eighteenth-Century Glasgow', in *Glasgow, Volume 1: Beginnings to 1830*, ed. by T. M. Devine and Gordon Jackson (Manchester: Manchester University Press, 1995), pp. 312–59 (pp. 349–51). On the affinity of the Calvinists with radicalism in the early 1790s, see also Bob Harris, *The Scottish People and the French Revolution* (New York: Routledge, 2008).

[25] 'Memoir of Professor Anderson', *Glasgow Mechanics' Magazine*, 3 (1825), i–ix. I am grateful to John Gardner for this reference and for letting me see his chapter in this book as I revised mine.

as men'.²⁶ Structurally, Anderson's Institution featured all the elements — a lecturing room, a laboratory, a library, a museum, and practicing workshops — that would soon reappear at the RI in London and its successors. The RI's mimicry of Anderson's Institution helps explain why, within three years of successful lecturing in Glasgow, Garnett himself would receive an unexpected offer to become the RI's first Professor of Natural Philosophy and Chemistry, where he began lecturing on 4 March 1800.

The London Lecturing Empire

Garnett's moves from itinerant to institutional lecturing represented a leap of scale from loosely organized networks outside the metropolis to the far more highly integrated scene of new scientific and literary lecturing institutions, like the Royal, London, Russell, and Surrey Institutions in London. To see any degree of continuity between these provincial and metropolitan lecturing worlds has been difficult in the past. When historians of science turned from the towns to the great cities, as J. N. Hays did in an influential essay of the 1980s, 'The London Lecturing Empire 1800–1850', they argued that the new Romantic-age scientific and literary institutions, along with specialist societies like the Askesian or the Geological, formed a thick, far-reaching and London-centered scientific 'empire' lasting through much of the nineteenth century. With the metaphor of empire, Hays was also effectively portraying it as a centralized network of London scientific institutions, radiating power and knowledge to distant sites on the British periphery. Hays put the new lecturing institutions even more at the center of this world by noting that London scientific culture was 'dominated above all by the lecture'.²⁷ The effect of this and related pictures of British scientific production was to set back into the shadows the itinerant lecturing networks that had appeared prominently in earlier works like A. E. Musson and Eric Robinson's *Science and Technology in the Industrial Revolution* (1969). It was also to claim that at the watershed of 1800, with the rise of these institutions, British sciences became rapidly professionalized and disciplined, almost overnight, a view that no longer seems credible.²⁸

---

[26] Thomas Garnett, *Observations on a Tour through the Highlands* [1800], 2 vols (London: John Stockdale, 1811), II, 202–05.
[27] J. N. Hays, 'The London Lecturing Empire, 1800–1850', in *Metropolis and Province: Science in British Culture, 1780–1850*, ed. by Ian Inkster and Jack Morrell (Philadelphia: University of Philadelphia Press, 1983), pp. 91–119 (p. 94).
[28] Jan Golinski makes a persuasive case against grouping Humphry Davy's career or these lecturing institutions as 'professional' in the early nineteenth century in *The Experimental Self: Humphry Davy and the Making of a Man of Science* (Chicago: University of Chicago Press, 2016), pp. 3–4, 47–52; see

To think about the London scientific networks as decentralized instead will be to recognize they were often deeply and asymmetrically at odds as they competed for public legitimacy and acclaim. Who organized them and where they were situated were key to their identities. The RI was built by aristocratic improving landholders in the West End; the London Institution in the City was run by bankers and by colonial investors (and only the London Institution had palpable ties to Britain's actual empire abroad). The Russell Institution in Bloomsbury was organized by lawyers and one of the founders of the *Edinburgh Review*. As the most charming and sometimes raucous of these Institutions, the Surrey Institution on Blackfriars Road south of the Thames, Dissenters, literati, and commercial actors crowded its audiences and featured in its programs. Calling this institutional network decentralized will also underscore the point that Galloway and Thacker have made about networks in general – that they are often not free-flowing, but can be highly frictional between the nodes and will tend to reveal what they call 'antagonistic clusterings'.[29] As I will show in the next section, these antagonistic clusterings happened not only between institutions, but within an institution as well. The RI, which has been better documented than any other lecturing institution, is a telling case in point.

Building the Royal Institution: Converging Networks

The genesis of the RI has been told in two largely irreconcilable ways. In 1871, Henry Bence Jones published one of the great institutional histories in the annals of British science by telling a heroic founder story – how the RI was the brainchild of the Tory physicist and social engineer Count Rumford (*nee* Benjamin Thompson) with the purpose of educating British manual workers by using working models of the latest machines toward the ends of moral and economic improvement. Bence Jones's dramatic narrative turned on the way Rumford's project of improvement was betrayed by a cabal of fashion-seeking aristocrats who wrestled the RI away from him and presented to the public Humphry Davy, the purple-coated celebrity lecturer, in his place.[30] In the 1970s, Morris Berman refuted this account by mobilizing the tools of an emerging social history of science, arguing that

---

also Roy Porter, 'Gentlemen and Geology: The Emergence of a Scientific Career, 1660–1920', *Historical Journal*, 21 (1978), 809–36.
[29] Galloway and Thacker, p. 34.
[30] Henry Bence Jones, *The Royal Institution: Its Founder and Its First Professors* (London: Longmans, 1871).

Rumford was more a 'professional courtier' than a credible scientific innovator, while the true power behind the RI's throne were the improving landowners who established government boards and private societies in a united, class-based project.[31] Better than Bence Jones, Berman could explain how the RI was meant to lead England's landowning class to adopt scientific methods of agricultural improvement, and he put class analysis squarely in the midst of new attention to the Romantic sciences.

But from a network standpoint, Berman's picture looks quite different. If Rumford was not exactly the institutional 'founder' portrayed by Bence Jones, he was nonetheless a critically important network-builder – a 'mediator', in Latour's sense of the term, rather than a mere intermediary – who brought together no fewer than six networks that converged to form the RI around 1800:

- The British Board of Agriculture, founded in 1793 and joined by an array of landholders around London, several of whom also had investments in northern coal mining and canal-building;
- The Society for Bettering the Condition of the Poor (SBCP), organized in 1796 by a group of evangelical reformers led by Thomas Bernard, devoted to building workhouses and other means of 'scientifically' replacing old charity and poor law methods with self-help stratagems for alleviating forms of class conflict;
- The Royal Society network represented by Joseph Banks, whose own landholding interests also made him central to the Board of Agriculture;
- The dissident academics of Glasgow, whose radical educational experiment, Anderson's Institution, and its leading lecturer, Thomas Garnett, seemed to furnish a blueprint for a scientific lecturing institution in London;
- The Birmingham inventors and entrepreneurs, particularly Matthew Boulton and James Watt, whose uneasy relationship to the aristocratic landowners also suggested to Rumford that an unusually powerful deal might be struck to combine their powers;
- The Bristol network supporting Thomas Beddoes' Pneumatic Institution (1798), from which Humphry Davy, recruited by Rumford, would emerge by 1802 as the RI's leading public face.

---

[31] Morris Berman, *Social Change and Scientific Organization: The Royal Institution, 1799–1844* (Ithaca: Cornell University Press, 1978), p. 16.

These actors were themselves already embedded in networks, and it was largely Rumford, even more than the well-connected Joseph Banks, who associated these networks from 1796 to 1800. They composed an improbable mixture of tendencies and groups, with wealthy landowners jostling side by side with inventors and manufacturers, the commercial south with the industrial north. 'Novelty often emerges', as Powell and Oberg remark, 'at the intersection of two or more social worlds with divergent criteria of evaluation'.[32] Rumford's collaborations with Thomas Bernard and Joseph Banks cemented his plan to build a pedagogical institution that would incorporate the workhouses and soup kitchens he had famously engineered in Bavaria the preceding decade, but from Bernard he also gained moral energy from the evangelical mission to replace England's outdated poor laws by equipping workers and artisans with the means, or so Bernard believed, to better support themselves.

Meanwhile, Joseph Banks brought the Board of Agriculture's landholding interests to bear on their gestating plans along with the scientific authority of the Royal Society. As Berman shows, there was strong overlap between the Board of Agriculture, the SBCP, and eventual RI governance, but this was also a case of what the sociologist Mark Granovetter long ago called 'strong ties' – the dense and durable ties of class, family, and cultural community – rather than the more extended (or 'weak') ties that build larger networks.[33] Even then, it is unlikely that the interests of the landowners in scientific agriculture and the efforts of evangelical reformers like Thomas Bernard or William Wilberforce in the Bettering Society would have converged without Rumford, who formed a close collaborative relationship to Bernard through their shared interest in building hospitals, workhouses, and other institutional structures for accomplishing wider ideological aims.

Some of Davy's biographers credit Rumford with 'extraordinary organizational and administrative abilities', but it was equally his collaborations with Bernard and Banks that drove the project forward.[34] Banks himself had a double interest in the RI. First, he was a major landowner with keen interests in adapting scientific methods to traditional practices of agriculture and tanning, then as leader of the Royal Society at a time when it was widely seen to be losing direction and authority

---

[32] Powell and Oberg, p. 453.
[33] Mark Granovetter, 'The Strength of Weak Ties', *American Journal of Sociology*, 78.6 (1973), 1360–80.
[34] June Z. Fullmer, *Young Humphry Davy: The Making of an Experimental Chemist* (Philadelphia: American Philosophical Society, 2000), p. 30.

in the latter half of the eighteenth century.³⁵ Second, since he was intransigently opposed to the emergent specialist scientific societies like the Linnaean (1788), the Askesian (1796), and the Geological (1805), Banks saw the RI as a means to redouble the Royal Society's traditional remit to unify the sciences against the increasing tendency to recognize them as incipient disciplines. This resistance to specialization also meant the Royal Society would have to alter its earlier hostility to popular itinerant lecturing. A half-century earlier it had spurned Benjamin Martin's attempt to become a Fellow when the Society's Fellows, who were 'opposed to the rage for experiment' as Margaret Jacob and Larry Stewart remark, 'perceived him as pandering to the masses'.³⁶ To Banks the RI now represented a suitably measured effort, controlled from the top down, 'to place the Royal Society in a more popular Point of View'.³⁷

Banks also arranged Count Rumford's crucial meeting with Matthew Boulton on 5 March 1799, two days before the gathering that would formally found the RI, to present their case for making the steam engine the crown teaching machine for the institution's artisans and mechanics. Rumford and Banks were mindful in making their pitch that Watt's patent would expire in three months (on 27 May 1799) and that they were proposing to put the steam engine on public display for workmen to draw it, inspect it, and learn to run it – and for anyone, in fact, to imitate it. Without the steam engine included in its repertoire, the RI's array of teaching machines would have to remain backward and artisanal; hence much depended on its open availability to the workhouse reformers. This may be why, years later, Humphry Davy would refer to the steam engine question as pivotal to the RI's original mission. In 1799, though the meeting with Boulton seems to have gone well as he signed on to Banks and Rumford's agenda, this plan would go awry in less than eleven months.

Until he learned of Anderson's Institution in the north, Rumford's vision for the RI was still an idea without a method. He wrote in mid-1799 to Thomas Garnett, now its Professor of Natural Philosophy and Chemistry, to inquire about the institution's organizational logic, its

---

³⁵ John Gascoigne, *Joseph Banks and the English Enlightenment: Useful Knowledge and Polite Culture* (Cambridge: Cambridge University Press, 2003).
³⁶ Margaret C. Jacob and Larry Stewart, *Practical Matter: Newton's Science in the Service of Industry and Empire* (Cambridge, MA: Harvard University Press, 2004), p. 66.
³⁷ Joseph Banks, quoted in David Knight, 'Establishing the Royal Institution: Rumford, Banks, and Davy', in '*The Common Purposes of Life*': *Science and Society at the Royal Institution of Great Britain*, ed. by F. L. R. James (London: Routledge, 2002), pp. 97–118 (p. 106).

business model, and its success at teaching a curriculum of lectures and workshops that extended across social classes. For three years Anderson's Institution had been visibly successful, and Garnett himself wrote up a robust account of the Institution in his *Observations on a Tour through the Highlands* (1800). Soon Rumford tendered a job offer to him, and by March 1800 Garnett was delivering his first lectures as Professor of Natural Philosophy and Chemistry at the RI while newspapers reported that his lecture rooms, well before Humphry Davy arrived, were 'crowded with persons of the first distinction and fashion'.[38] In light of what would soon happen to him at the hands of the RI managers, though, it would be worthwhile to register the difference of institutional cultures he must have faced in coming to the RI from Glasgow. Far from the demotic Presbyterian radicalism Anderson's Institution inherited from its founder – the John Anderson who had stood alongside the French lustily singing *Te Deum* in Paris on Bastille Day, 1791, while the cannons roared – the RI's counterrevolutionary ethos was unstinting and frequently brutal to its lecturers.[39] Garnett got a taste of this in May 1800, when he introduced Alessandro Volta's new electrical pile to his audience and attributed the remarkable invention 'to the French'. Reports in the next day's newspapers carried wind of the remark to Joseph Banks, who demanded to Rumford that he discipline Garnett and require a retraction. Rumford dictated the text of apology that Garnett was forced to recite as a confession of mistake. Yet it was likely not a mistake. Giuliano Pancaldi's account of this episode shows that Garnett probably knew that Volta's home region of Lombardy had been under French rule since 1796, and in any case that the first reports of Volta's startling invention had been published in French.[40] Banks and Rumford's hair-trigger reaction owed in no small part to a determination that no scientific credit be associated with any part of France after the Revolution.

Garnett was already giving well-received lectures when Rumford invited Humphry Davy to interview in London during the winter of 1800–1. Having spent nearly three years at Thomas Beddoes' Pneumatic Institution trying to finish building a lecture theater, Davy excitedly wrote to his mother, 'My future prospects are of a very brilliant nature' because the RI will be 'a great instrument of moral and intellectual improvement'.[41] His brother John Davy later insisted that Rumford was attracted to Davy from

---

[38] Fullmer, p. 327.   [39] 'Memoir of Professor Anderson', p. viii.
[40] Giuliano Pancaldi, *Volta: Science and Culture in the Age of Enlightenment* (Princeton: Princeton University Press, 2003), pp. 217–18.
[41] Letters to Grace Davy, 27 September 1800 and 8 March 1801, *Davy Letters Project*, ed. by Tim Fulford and Sharon Ruston, <www.davy-letters.org.uk>.

reading his essays, but it was hardly probable that a cosmopolitan institution-builder like Rumford in London would have discovered a Cornish chemist working in Bristol without a thick mesh of intermediaries.[42] Davy's patron in Cornwall, the mathematician Davies Giddy, had introduced Beddoes to Joseph Banks in 1791, when Beddoes was still lecturing at Oxford, and Giddy again linked Davy to Beddoes in 1798. A year after arriving in Bristol, Davy was making trips to Birmingham to consult with Gregory Watt, Matthew Boulton, and James Keir. Watts's mentor in Glasgow, Charles Black, and Beddoes' collaborator in Edinburgh, Thomas Charles Hope, both became aware of Davy's precocious, home-schooled abilities, and Hope made a point of recommending him to Rumford.[43] By the time Davy reached the RI in June 1801, however, the networks that had converged to form it were already at odds with one another, mutating from collaborative labor toward becoming a particularly troubled 'antagonistic cluster'. Unlike Garnett, Davy would survive the mutation of networks that would make the RI an institution in more than name, and it was indeed Davy's own profile that would come to appear, as it does on the RI website's 'Historical Timeline' today, as the charismatic face of the institution itself.

The Mutation of Networks

By early 1800, the convergence of networks that had created the RI appeared complete. It was not only a fashionable new institution associated with top-drawer scientific authorities like Joseph Banks, it was also, as Rumford put it in his *Prospectus of the Royal Institution of Great Britain* (1800), a social experiment, treating the working relationships of everyday life as 'the great laboratory of civil society'.[44] Yet even at this moment of triumphal emergence, the RI's assembly of networks was already beginning to disperse. First to split off were the Birmingham machine makers – and thus the bridge Rumford had been trying to erect between manufacturers and landowners across England. Matthew Boulton's son stirred his father's misgivings about the RI, writing to him that 'an Institution for diffusing general Knowledge & Science may be usefull, but if the Manufacturers find

---

[42] John Ayrton Paris, *The Life of Humphry Davy* (London: Henry Colburn and Richard Bentley, 1831), pp. 76–77; on Beddoes and Banks, see Gascoigne, pp. 251–53.
[43] Fullmer, pp. 321, 328. Paris gave sole credit to Thomas Underwood and James Thomson in *Life of Humphry Davy*, pp. 76–89.
[44] Count Rumford, 'Prospectus of the Royal Institution' (1800), in *Collected Works of Count Rumford*, ed. by Sanborn C. Brown, 5 vols (Cambridge, MA: Belknap Press, 1970), V, 475.

it is intended to be a Vehicle for disclosing the particular Arts and Machinery employ'd by them, their Opposition to it will be pretty certain'.[45] Boulton himself later told the RI, in a statement reported by Davy, 'You would destroy the value of the labour of the industrious; by laying open his invention, you would take away the great stimulus to exertion.'[46] Hence, the RI would be denied a working model of the most dramatic invention of the age. Boulton's turnabout was doubly damaging to the agenda most important to Rumford himself, to build an institution for artisans and mechanics based on models and machines. But Joseph Banks also had chafed at the idea of educating working men who, he suspected, might be avid readers of Thomas Paine. The telling moment of dissolving the cross-class learning project came on the day when, as the architect Thomas Webster reported mournfully in his memoirs, 'my mechanics' stone staircase was pulled down at considerable expense.'[47]

While Boulton withdrew for his own reasons, Garnett had to be forced out the door. Notwithstanding his early success in lecturing to wealthy clients who formed the RI's main constituency, Garnett clashed with Rumford in ways that illuminate the frictional relationship between the institution and its network ties. The Volta episode had already frayed nerves, but the ensuing battle over curriculum undercut Garnett's position irrecoverably. In the fall of 1800, a still-confident Garnett published, on his own, two syllabi in the form of a 12-page and a 216-page outline of the London lectures he planned to give in early 1801. In so doing he followed the tradition of itinerant lecturers who created their own publicity and who made public records of their scientific discourse. But the RI responded harshly, averring that Garnett had published syllabi without consulting the Institution. The greater offense, however, may have been the evidence Garnett had inadvertently provided that his own program was so clearly at odds with the mission of the RI. For the 'popular' lectures on experimental philosophy, Garnett's twelve-page outline was brief and topical for a series to be given one afternoon a week. But the 216-page outline detailed a far more elaborate sequence of lectures for those who could follow mathematical reasoning, a smaller audience he expected to grow as he delivered its more demanding lectures three days each week.

---

[45] Matthew Robinson Boulton to Matthew Boulton, March 1800, cited in Brown, p. 229.
[46] Humphry Davy, quoted in Bence Jones, *Royal Institution*, p. 293.
[47] Webster, quoted in Bence Jones, *Royal Institution*, p. 184.

Neither syllabus corresponded to the Rumford program for the vocational education of artisans and mechanics, and especially not the long, thirty-lecture syllabus for those with serious interests in natural philosophy.

Unable to recall the now-published syllabi, the RI administrators responded by forming a committee to enforce a stern new policy stipulating that 'no syllabus of lectures ... at the Royal Institution be published by any person or persons without the permission of the committee'.[48] At least at the RI, there would be none of the autonomy the itinerant lecturers had enjoyed out on the trails, conceiving and publicizing their own lecture series, or, like Garnett at Anderson's Institution, boldly establishing his presence along the same lines. Within six months of this decision in February 1801, Garnett resigned from the RI, angry as well as despondent at the direction his once thriving career had now taken, while the autocratic Rumford, as Bence Jones put it, had now come to the point that he 'ordered and superintended *everything* in the house'.[49]

At this moment, when Rumford seemed to be reaching the peak of his authority, his network ties were rapidly collapsing around him. As early as July 1800, he suspected that Thomas Bernard and John Coxe Hippisley, two of the RI's most important aristocratic managers, were trying 'to wrest the direction of the affairs of the Institution out of my hands'. Those suspicions were shared by Joseph Banks and confirmed on the other side by Bernard's ally William Wilberforce, who later told Joseph Farington that 'the RI was almost ruined under the management of Sir Joseph Banks & Count Rumford, but Bernard recovered it & it was now more flourishing than before'.[50] Banks himself was approaching a state of despair by 1804 when it became clear to him that Rumford was not returning from his most recent trip to Paris. Rumford's decision was 'a material disappointment to me', Banks wrote to him, and the RI 'is now entirely in the hands of the prophane'.[51]

Being 'prophane' meant that Bernard, Hippisley, and other aristocratic managers were pushing back against Rumford's Tory paternalist utilitarianism and turning the RI into a center of 'fashion', 'amusement', and 'luxury'. When Rumford threw up his hands and left England, leaving Banks little choice but to withdraw as well, the mild-mannered Thomas Bernard became the most influential administrator of the RI. It was now

---

[48] Brown, p. 236.   [49] Bence Jones, *Royal Institution*, p. 163.
[50] Brown, p. 230; Joseph Farington, *The Farington Diary*, ed. by James Greig (London: Hutchinson, 1924), p. 285.
[51] Banks to Rumford, April 1804, quoted in Bence Jones, *Royal Institution*, p. 255.

Bernard, not Rumford, who would set the lecturing agendas and hire or fire the speakers. To indulge in 'fashion' and 'amusement' was also to open the RI to the fine arts and the humanities. During Bernard's period of power and at Davy's urging, the poets Samuel Coleridge and Thomas Campbell, the moral philosopher Sydney Smith, the Royal Academy painter John Opie, and the antiquarian bibliographer Thomas Frognall Dibdin, all shared Davy's lecturing platform, and Bernard himself would soon build the British Institution for the Fine Arts in 1806. This turn to the fine arts and humanities made a decisive break with Rumford's mechanical arts and constituted the most interdisciplinary moment, as we might now put it, in the RI's history. In all of this, Bernard made himself the consummate administrator. 'No important measure was thought of being carried into effect without his concurrence and guidance', reported Dibdin, as he showed 'the happiest tact in the management of bodies corporate – divested of the mace and the fur gown'.[52]

In Latour's terms, Bernard became a peculiarly effective mediator of networks even as those networks were now mutating, divesting, and concentrating in a nucleus of institutional identity. He put himself at the center of the RI's overlapping networks and weak-tie connections that through key moments of dissonance and reversal would finally crystallize into the powerful culture force represented publicly by Humphry Davy. What Latour and his collaborator Michel Callon call 'translation' seems especially suited to characterize Thomas Bernard's chameleon-like role in surviving and capitalizing on the intensive network changes that would result in the RI we have known since his day. By 'translation' Callon and Latour mean 'the negotiations, intrigues, calculations, acts of persuasion and violence, thanks to which an actor or force takes, or causes to be conferred on itself, authority to speak or act on behalf of another actor or force'.[53] In the RI's first decade, 1800–10, Bernard himself seemed to disappear into the shadows of the Institution as Humphry Davy surged forward in a glow of celebrity and growing scientific authority so powerful as to displace and render invisible any of his own institutional mediators. Thus, the RI could seem to become the center of London's leading scientific lecturing world that looked, according to social historians of science, like an 'empire' of British science forming

---

[52] Thomas Frognall Dibdin, *Reminiscences of a Literary Life*, 2 vols (London: John Major, 1836), I, 229–30. For Bernard's impact on lecturing agendas, see my *Transfiguring the Arts and Sciences*, pp. 72–84.

[53] Michel Callon and Bruno Latour, 'Unscrewing the Big Leviathan: How Actors Macrostructure Reality, and How Sociologists Help Them to Do So', in *Advances in Social Theory and Methodology: Towards an Integration of Micro- and Macro-Sociologies*, ed. by K. Knorr-Cetina and A. V. Cicourel (London: Routledge & Kegan Paul, 1982), pp. 277–303 (p. 279).

over the next fifty years. By the 1840s, 'Davy's story of spectacular self-improvement', as James Secord calls it, was well-placed to cement the scientific discovery narrative of the RI itself.[54]

The process of 'unrumfordizing' the RI, as Davy would call it in 1810, would complete its transformation, in the terms I am using here, from a cluster of networks to a full institution.[55] The issue was scientific credibility, which Davy had earned for himself with a series of remarkable discoveries, using the Voltaic battery as his apparatus to develop the field of chemistry by discovering eight new elements. But the RI's own reputation was now being compromised by the personal venality – Davy did not quite call it 'corruption' – of its oldest network members. On 20 March 1809, Davy published 'Sketch of a Plan for Improving the Royal Institution and Erecting It on a Permanent Foundation', arguing that the price of scientific authority would be the divesting of the RI's cobbled-together nature as a private institution by making it fully public. To create a 'public, national, and permanent establishment, devoted and dedicated to the cultivation of science' required proprietors to make a sacrifice of 'personal interest'. Hereditary shares had to be converted into publicly sold shares, and some proprietors from the original networks that founded the RI were suspected of having profited personally from their role in its history. 'Science can be exalted and promoted only by patronage and by sacrifices', Davy argued. 'It will not bear to be trafficked with', but requires 'disinterested persons' acting in the public good.[56] Following Davy's pronouncements, several members of the original networks resigned from the RI.

This transformational moment, in which the RI's earliest constitutive networks were now being called to account in the name of 'science', raises a final question for this chapter. If an institution like the RI can be shown to be so densely networked at its origins, is it possible to think of an institution as itself nothing but a network, or a cluster of networks? Does network analysis serve to undercut an institution's claim to authority, particularly a claim to the value of science? Since the nineteenth century the RI has been making a case that is now expressed on its website: 'Science lives here'. Arguably the RI outlived its early social origins to become

[54] James A. Secord, *Visions of Science: Books and Readers at the Dawn of the Victorian Age* (Oxford: Oxford University Press, 2014), p. 35.
[55] Davy advised Francis Jeffrey, the editor of the *Edinburgh Review*, of 'a sketch of a plan for unrumfordizing the royal Institution; our bill is passing through Parliament without opposition, & if a few words could be said in our favour in the *Edinburgh Review*, it would give us life and strength'. Quoted in 'An Editor's Letters', *The Living Age*, 204 (1895), 252–56 (p. 254).
[56] [Humphry Davy], *Annual Register*, 51 (1809), pp. 856–57.

identified with the disciplinary rigor of Victorian evolution, chemistry, geology, or thermodynamics, as well as twentieth-century physics. By the 1860s it had distanced itself far enough from Rumford's earliest aims for a teaching institution to declare, 'Research is the glory of the Institution'.[57] Later on it became a first-rate institutional exhibit of the ideological origins and bearings of the British sciences, one of the earliest and most compelling cases of the social studies of scientific knowledge in the work of Berman, Ian Inkster, and Hays.

Yet to identify an institution wholly with the networks that composed it would miss the fact that ultimately an institution must *stand* for something, and must do so over a long arc of time. It must make a claim to justice or a claim to truth. In the episode I have just cited, the RI appears to have been making both claims in 1809–10. Denouncing the members of its founding networks who had 'profited in a pecuniary way' by selling their shares on a private market, Davy could argue that a legitimate claim to scientific authority and truth required the corollary of just or noncorrupt character of the institution's material basis. He also invoked the principle of the common good – a national scientific institution famously dedicated to applying science to the 'common purposes of life'. Luc Boltanski and Eve Chiapello help clarify the distinction that I think is at stake here. This is a distinction between a world populated by institutions and a wholly networked world where 'there is no reason to pose the question of justice, because those of low status (who, as we shall see, can be very precisely characterized in such a framework as *excluded*) tend to disappear without a trace'.[58] Unlike the institutions of governance, or of the public sphere, networks in themselves, they argue, cannot give us a criterion of the 'common good'. Another way to put this, I would add, is to say that an institution's claim to justice or to truth – to equality, say, or to scientific truth – is also the basis for a *critique* of institutions when those claims become difficult or impossible to credit. The RI itself furnished the occasion for such critique when it became one of the first scientific institutions to be critically assessed in light of the new social studies of science in the 1970s.

At the same time, the RI's current slogan 'Science lives here' also matters.[59] Science is not an independent variable; it only works in environments

---

[57] [Henry Bence Jones], *Report on the Past, Present, and Future of the Royal Institution* [1861], quoted in *The Athenaeum*, 1796 (29 March 1862), p. 423.

[58] Boltanski and Chiapello, p. 106.

[59] The slogan 'Science Lives Here' is not a venerable institutional expression but was devised in 2012 for a rebranding campaign designed to refurbish the RI's public outreach. (Personal communication from Robert Davies, Head of Marketing and Communications, The Royal Institution,

designed for it, whether laboratories or institutions like the RI. The work of its early networks was to make the setting in which scientific work could happen. Writing as I do now, at a moment when institutions of science and of justice have been recently undercut in highly unprincipled ways by a venal presidential administration in the United States, it is worth insisting that an institution must be expected to stand for more than the interests of the networks that may compose it. My account of its converging and mutating networks has accentuated the contradiction between the RI's seemingly continuous identity as a scientific institution representing the field called 'science' and the discontinuous ferment of its networks.[60] Following its formative period, the RI helped create an influential network of lecturers and auditors across London, working to achieve a 'public understanding of science' as a fundamental part of scientific legitimacy that the Royal Society, rarely reaching out beyond its specialist circle, often fell short of attaining.[61] Such institutions also generate new networks and become themselves nodes in wider networks of the field of cultural production. By the early 1830s, as the Royal Society and RI both came under critical fire for being based in class deference rather than professionalism, the early British Association for the Advancement of Science turned away from London to construct a new network of scientific societies and institutions that would meet in the same provincial towns and cities where the itinerant lecturers had begun traveling a century before: York in 1831, Birmingham, Manchester, Bristol, Oxford, Cambridge, and others in the decades to come.

---

13 January 2021. The rebranding was conducted by Wiedemann Lampe; for an account of the process, see <www.wiedemannlampe.com/projects/ri>.) This moment seems entirely in keeping with the RI's mixed history of commercial outreach and institutional authority.

[60] In *An Enquiry into the Modes of Existence: An Anthropology of the Moderns* (Cambridge, MA: Harvard University Press, 2013), Latour makes a similar distinction between networks that run smoothly after they have been fully composed and networks that are more typically fragile and easily disrupted. The network 'establishes such a powerful constraint of continuity that a minor interruption can be enough to cause a breakdown' (p. 31). Following Boltanski, I have been proposing instead the distinction between institutions (composed of but not reducible to networks) and networks subject to breakdown.

[61] This recurring question of legitimating science for the public arose again in the 1980s when a faltering public confidence in science prompted a warning to the Royal Society to emulate examples of the Royal Institution and British Association. See 'The Public Understanding of Science', <https://royalsociety.org/~/media/royal_society_content/policy/publications/1985/10700.pdf>, p. 27.

CHAPTER 8

Catalogues as Instituting Genres of the Nineteenth-Century Museum
The Two Hunterians

Dahlia Porter

Like a library, bookshop, or art gallery, a museum is a particular kind of institution, one whose identity is fundamentally bound up with things. Museums are defined by their holdings – natural history museum, modern art museum, clock museum – which they conventionally endeavor to preserve, organize, and display.[1] Collections define museums and museums curate collections: how objects are classified and labeled; which items are accessioned and which sold or lent; how specimens and artifacts are displayed or otherwise made public – in aggregate, these acts comprise a museum's institutional identity. These are commonplace observations, but how does this process actually work? How do the myriad daily actions and decisions – made by a large number of individuals and groups, propelled by any number of internal and external factors from changes in the law to destruction by weather or war – coalesce over time to embody museums as institutions? This is the question I propose to answer here.

To begin with, a specific historical period, the nineteenth century, has conventionally marked the emergence of 'the modern museum'. This designation implies a distinction between the (supposedly) unruly and eclectic collections of early-modern *Wunderkammers* and private collections and the (supposedly) orderly and systematized museum born of eighteenth-century classificatory striving and embodying nineteenth-century disciplinary divisions.[2] This museum is conventionally 'modern' in its target audience as much as its methods of organization and

---

[1] This is not always the case; some museums don't survive, their collections unceremoniously carted off to the dump. See Steven Lubar and others, 'Lost Museums', *Museum History Journal*, 10.1 (2016), 1–14 (p. 1).

[2] This is a persistent claim, made so many times that it has become a given in much recent scholarship on museums. As my parentheticals suggest, I find this assumption suspect but also unhelpful, especially as a beginning point for understanding how institutionalization happens.

display: the 'Directors' Foreword' to a recent exhibition catalogue, *William Hunter and the Anatomy of the Modern Museum* (2018), describes the volume as an opportunity to 'assess fully the contribution made by Hunter to the development of the modern museum as a public institution'.[3] This is possible because 'Hunter sought to find an institutional form through which he could ensure the public utility, in perpetuity' of his collections.[4] This assessment of an eighteenth-century collection becoming a 'modern' (e.g. institutionalized) museum aligns with current definitions of museums more broadly: as the International Council on Museums codified it in 2007, 'a museum is a non-profit, permanent institution in the service of society' that is 'open to the public'.[5] Permanence and publicness are the defining pillars of the modern museum's institutional identity.

As scholars have noted, this definition is itself a nineteenth-century invention. As Steven Lubar, Lukas Rieppel, Ann Daly, and Kathrinne Duffy argue, nineteenth-century museums in Britain were 'public institution[s] ... designed to both symbolise and instil a particular set of social, moral, and epistemic virtues', namely to educate the public and elevate its tastes while preserving the material remnants of cultural and natural-historical pasts.[6] These 'virtues' were products of nineteenth-century European ideas of progress, with their attendant views on social improvement and the racial and cultural backwardness of working-class publics at home and of ethnographic and anthropological subjects across the globe.[7] The idea of a 'permanent' collection, and thus a permanent institution, derives from these nineteenth-century elitist and racist colonial ideologies: ascribing value to certain objects that must be preserved and displayed 'reinforce[d] the precise set of [cultural and social] distinctions these institutions had been designed to exhibit'.[8]

---

[3] Amy Meyers and Steph Scholten, 'Directors' Foreword', in *William Hunter and the Anatomy of the Modern Museum*, ed. by Mungo Campbell and Nathan Flis, with the assistance of María Dolores Sánchez-Jáuregui (New Haven: Yale University Press, 2018), pp. 7–10 (p. 7, my italics).

[4] Meyers and Scholten, p. 9.

[5] 'Museum Definition', International Council for Museums Statutes, 2007 <https://icom.museum/en/resources/standards-guidelines/museum-definition/>. This definition is currently in the process of being revised through consultation with member museums.

[6] Lubar and others, p. 5. See also Sharon Macdonald, 'Museums, National, Postnational and Transcultural Identities', *Museum & Society*, 1.1 (2003), 1–16.

[7] For discussions of the nineteenth-century museum's ideological agendas, see Tony Bennett's *Museums, Power, Knowledge* (Abingdon: Routledge, 2003); for the continuing presence of colonial and racial narratives in natural history museums, see Subhadra Das and Miranda Lowe, 'Nature Read in Black and White: Decolonial Approaches to Interpreting Natural History Collections', *Journal of Natural Science Collections*, 4 (2018), 4–14.

[8] Lubar and others, p. 5.

While the 'virtues' museums seek to instill are slowly shifting, many museums continue to rely on this nineteenth-century definition of the museum's objectives.[9] This reliance limits what stories are told – only recently have scholars begun to write on museums that have been destroyed, sold off or forgotten – and, perhaps more importantly for my concerns here, it limits how we pose questions about museums as institutions. For example, institutional histories of individual museums, which are often written or compiled by curators or other individuals internal to that museum, record change in the guise of progress toward the better fulfillment of the museum's mission as a permanent, public institution.[10] For this reason, they often describe – in minute detail – stabilizing forces such as buildings, regulations, governance structures, and the decisions of trustees, museum keepers, and curators.[11] This focus aligns with early sociological approaches to institutions (derived in large part from Max Weber's work on bureaucracy): mid-twentieth-century theorists considered institutions 'durable structures' that instill values while also directing, constraining, and often controlling behavior through rules and norms.[12] As W. Richard Scott summarizes Philip Selznick's work, 'by embodying a particular set of values, the organization acquires a *character structure*, a distinctive [institutional] identity. Maintaining the organization is no longer simply an instrumental matter of keeping the machinery working, but becomes a struggle to preserve a set of unique values'.[13] Institutional histories of museums script this struggle into a larger narrative of progress and permanence: by focusing on regulative

---

[9] For the many ways museums have begun to challenge the nineteenth-century ideologies embedded in their collections and to reinvent themselves as proponents of social change, see Sharon Macdonald, 'Introduction' to *Theorizing Museums: Representing Identity and Diversity in a Changing World*, ed. by Sharon Macdonald and Gordon Fyfe, Sociological Review Monograph Series (Oxford: Blackwell, 1996), 1–18, and Richard Sandell, *Museums, Prejudice and the Reframing of Difference* (London: Routledge, 2006).

[10] See, for example, Edward Miller, *That Noble Cabinet: A History of the British Museum* (London: Andre Deutsch, 1974), and Laurence Keppie, *William Hunter and the Hunterian Museum in Glasgow 1807–2007* (Edinburgh: Edinburgh University Press, 2007).

[11] This is particularly pronounced in Miller's and Keppie's histories, but it structures many discussions of museums, including exhibition catalogues. For example, the 'Directors' Foreword' and 'Introduction' to *William Hunter and Anatomy of the Modern Museum* equate the Hunterian's 'institutional form' with the opening of the purpose-built museum building in 1807: Meyers and Scholten, p. 9, and Mungo Campbell, 'William Hunter and the Anatomy of the Modern Museum: An Introduction', in *William Hunter and the Anatomy of the Modern Museum*, ed. by Campbell and Flis, pp. 25–47 (p. 25). Campbell reinforces this point with an image of the 1807 building and a discussion of Hunter's wills, which governed the bequest (pp. 26, 28–31).

[12] W. Richard Scott, *Institutions and Organizations: Ideas, Interests, Identities*, 4th edn (London: Sage, 2014), pp. 56–58.

[13] Scott, p. 24. Selznick describes the process of institutionalization as something that happens to organizations over time; his approach is to depict 'a natural history of a specific organization, a description of the processes by which, over time, it develops its distinctive structures, capabilities,

and normative structures — structures that have often molded the author's behavior, beliefs, and values as part of the institution — these histories prove what they have from the beginning assumed, namely the institution's long-term durability, the value of the objects it contains, and the principles it embodies and teaches.

While much can be learned by investigating regulative structures, recent neoinstitutional theory has begun to look more concertedly at the malleability of institutions. As Scott points out, 'although institutions function to provide stability and order, they themselves undergo change, both incremental and revolutionary'.[14] In concert with recent scholarship, I would extend this claim: institutions do not simply change, they evolve; they are dynamic structures, 'the unfolding outcome of people's and collective actors' continual efforts to maintain, modify, or disturb them'.[15] While institutional theorists have differing views on human agency within institutional frameworks, most would agree that institutionalization is an ongoing process.[16] However, again only recently have theorists taken up processes as *constitutive* of institutions (rather than simply tracking changes to existing entities).[17] Scholarship on process as an analytic has been hampered, as Francesca Polletta aptly puts it, because 'it is hard to tell new stories in which processes rather than people are what drive action'.[18] In this chapter, I want to excavate the processes of institutionalization, which means setting aside the stories museums tell about themselves and instead investigating the mechanisms and procedures by which the museum's day-to-day work is carried out, its values instilled, its knowledge consolidated.

Catalogues and Procedural Rhetoric

How does a historicist analyze process? First, let us return to where I began: museums carry out their work on or through objects. Processes can and do

---

and liabilities' (Scott, p. 25). More recent scholarship, discussed later in the chapter, takes a broader view of the relationship between institutions and organizations.

[14] Scott, p. 58.

[15] Trish Reay and others, 'Introduction', in *Institutions and Organizations: A Process View*, ed. by Trish Reay and others (Oxford: Oxford University Press, 2019), p. 1.

[16] Institutional theory diverges on how rules relate to people in institutions: for example, historical institutionalists see rules as constitutive — to the extent that the very nature of the actors, their capabilities but also preferences, is determined by the institutional framework — while rational choice theorists see regulative structures as constructed by actors to advance their particular interests. See Scott, pp. 40, 84.

[17] Reay and others, pp. 1–2.

[18] Francesca Polletta, 'Stories of (and Instead of) Process', in *Institutions and Organizations*, ed. by Reay and others, p. 62.

adhere in objects themselves: an accession number etched into wood or stone, a partially detached paper label, a coat of black lacquer – these are signs of particular acts of curation performed at specific historical moments.[19] However, not all (or even most) objects bear easily identifiable traces of their former lives.[20] Rather than reconstructing the lives of objects or trying to pin down specific curatorial decisions, I seek to unearth the ways objects were mobilized *procedurally* for institutional ends. To do this, I turn to the museum's documentary archive, a vast sea of paperwork including accession books, museum registers, inventories, shipping manifests, committee minutes, keeper's and curator's reports, and catalogues.

The most potent 'paper tool' in the process of the nineteenth-century museum's institutionalization was the catalogue.[21] As Geoffrey Swinney argues of museum registers, such documentary records are fundamentally 'a technology, by and through which the museum is constructed and constituted, its collections disciplined and its objects arrayed'.[22] Catalogues bring order and coherence to collections by labeling, organizing, classifying, and locating objects. This work depends on the formal elements of the genre. James Delbourgo and Staffan Müller-Wille point out that documents that list – catalogues, registers, inventories, logs – have a spatial logic; instead of linear narrative, lists draw things together by enumerating and abstracting, linking objects in non-syntactic formations that perform social, political, and cultural functions.[23] Furthermore, despite their utilitarian appearance, these genres are fundamentally rhetorical. As the Multigraph Collective argues, a catalogue's sequences and groupings can tell coherent, progressive stories, and this non-syntactic narrative mode

---

[19] While these could refer to any number of objects, I draw these examples from my interactions with the Glasgow Hunterian's collection of South Seas artifacts. For example, black lacquer was applied to objects in William Hunter's ethnographic collection and thus provides a mechanism for dating their acquisition.

[20] A rich field of scholarship on 'object biography' has undertaken such reconstructions; see, for example, the essays collected in *Biographies of Scientific Objects*, ed. by Lorraine Daston (Chicago: University of Chicago Press, 2000). For a discussion of writing the history of museums through objects, see Samuel Alberti, 'Objects and the Museum', *Isis*, 96.4 (2005), 559–71.

[21] For a survey of recent thinking on paper tools, see Boris Jardine, 'State of the Field: Paper Tools', *Studies in History and Philosophy of Science*, 64 (2017), 53–63. I use the term 'paper tools' here to describe the practices of inscription in catalogues, with the understanding that these practices are also the record of material processes carried out on objects and that they rely on the material affordances of paper, ink, printing, binding, and so on.

[22] Geoffrey Swinney, 'What Do We Know about What We Know? The Museum "Register" as Museum Object', in *The Thing about Museums: Objects and Experience, Representation and Contestation*, ed. by Sandra Dudley and others (Abingdon: Routledge, 2011), pp. 31–45 (p. 32).

[23] James Delbourgo and Staffan Müller-Wille, 'Introduction: Listmania', *Isis*, 103.4 (2012), 710–15 (pp. 711–12).

'stands behind many of the preeminent cultural institutions of the age'.[24] As such, catalogues are an example of what I call *instituting genres*: that is, genres of writing that, through 'the construction and interpretation of a symbolic system', transform a heap of material objects into a paper tool that supports and encodes the museum's institutional character and values.[25] Understood in this way, catalogues instantiate what Ian Bogost, writing about video games, has called 'procedural rhetoric', 'a practice of using process persuasively'.[26]

However – and this is true of both manuscript and printed catalogues – the genre does not always work as intended. Catalogues and inventories are purposefully designed and utilized by actors within organizations to integrate objects into systems of meaning, but they also inevitably record the innumerable things lost, out of place, detached from their provenance, unknown and unknowable. The catalogue's generic imperative to order, fix, stabilize, and name exists in tension with the equal pressure of disorder, of objects turning into 'things' unloosed from the system created to make them knowable as 'objects'.[27] Because of this tension, catalogues capture the dynamism of institutionalization as a process; rather than a narrative march toward order, stability, and permanence, catalogues make visible both the procedural consolidation of institutional identity and the continual dislocations and disorders that erupt to derail that process or alter its course.

A word on methodology and terminology: in what follows I employ a familiar historicist approach, the case study. There are many reasons for this, including my disciplinary training. That said, I am not writing a 'natural history' of how an organization becomes institutionalized and takes on a specific character. Following recent institutional theory, I understand institutions as comprised of symbolic systems (regulative, normative, and cultural-cognitive) that intersect with people's behavior

---

[24] The Multigraph Collective, *Interacting with Print: Elements of Reading in the Era of Print Saturation* (Chicago: University of Chicago Press, 2018), p. 70.

[25] Ian Bogost, *Persuasive Games: The Expressive Power of Videogames* (Cambridge, MA: MIT Press, 2007), p. 5. For a study of the 'fluidity' of catalogues and collections, and the centrality of catalogues to producing knowledge with pathological collections, see Tricia Close-Koenig, 'Cataloguing Collections: The Importance of Paper Records of Strasbourg's Medical School Pathological Anatomy Collection', in *The Fate of Anatomical Collections*, ed. by Rina Knoeff and Robert Zwijnenberg (Farnham: Ashgate, 2015), pp. 211–27.

[26] Bogost, *Persuasive Games*, p. 3. Bogost admits that procedurality can be seen in noncomputational structures; see also Ian Bogost, *Unit Operations* (Cambridge, MA: MIT Press, 2006).

[27] Here I am drawing on Bill Brown's distinction between objects and things: 'Things lie beyond the grid of intelligibility the way mere things lie outside the grid of museal exhibition, outside the order of objects': Bill Brown, 'Thing Theory', *Critical Inquiry*, 28.1 (2001), 1–22 (p. 5).

(their social activity, their compliance with or resistance to these systems of rules, norms, and beliefs) and material resources (in the case of museums, their collections, display cabinets, buildings, storage facilities, and so on).[28] Institutionalization will vary according to the specific elements (people, collections) comprising a particular museum at any point in time and across time. However, by analyzing the procedural form of the catalogue – the format and methods of which were standard across many nineteenth-century museums – I aim to describe processes of institutionalization that are also constitutive of museums beyond those treated in this chapter.

Other methods might support and extend the conclusions reached here. For example, digitization has driven new methodologies in institutional studies, including what Scott calls a 'new archival research' approach that employs 'formal analytical methodologies such as content, semiotic, sequence, and network analysis' to investigate various kinds of materials, including media accounts, reports, professional journals, and organizational documents. Applying such methods to a (currently unavailable but in progress) corpus of digitized manuscript and print catalogues would, I believe, generate complementary insights to those I develop here. Furthermore, materials related to the museum's public-facing activities – guidebooks, advertising leaflets, postcards, posters, webpages, and Twitter feeds – are fodder for what Ryan Skinnell identifies as 'institutional rhetoric', the investigation of 'how institutions shape public discourse in distinct and powerful ways'.[29] Analysis of these outward-facing materials might reveal either an alignment or a radical disjuncture between the procedural and the proclamatory, between what is done and what is said. However, for such comparisons to be possible, it is crucial to begin by recovering how procedural forms work as the paper tools of institutionalization and what they reveal about that process.

The Two Hunterians

I could have focused on any number of museums that took shape in the nineteenth century, but I have chosen the two Hunterian Museums, in

---

[28] See Scott, pp. 56–58. Regulative systems can work by incentives or sanctions but are generally defined by their high level of enforcement, while normative systems are often understood in conjunction with the roles people occupy within organizations; norms reflect 'the routine way in which people do what they are supposed to do' (Scott, p. 65). Scott's own neoinstitutional approach focuses on the cultural-cognitive aspects of institutions over the regulative and normative.

[29] Ryan Skinnell, 'Toward a Working Theory of Institutional Rhetorics', in *Reinventing (with) Theory in Rhetoric and Writing Studies: Essays in Honor of Sharon Crowley*, ed. by Andrea Alden and others (Logan: Utah State University Press, 2019), pp. 69–82 (p. 70).

Glasgow and London, for the correspondence of their core collections, the close proximity of their dates of formation, and the biographical connection between them. Each museum was formed from the private collections of an eighteenth-century surgeon-anatomist, William Hunter and his younger brother John Hunter, respectively, in the early decades of the nineteenth century (the Glasgow Hunterian opened in 1807, with the London Hunterian following in 1813). The conditions under which this transformation from private collection to public museum occurred were substantively different: William willed his collections more or less entire to the University of Glasgow and provided a lump sum to construct a purpose-built museum; John's collections were partially auctioned off before the residue (primarily anatomical preparations and drawings) was bought by the British Parliament and placed with the Royal College of Surgeons. Over the succeeding decades, each museum was shaped by its umbrella organization (a university and a professional society), and each was transformed by a host of other factors, including decisions made by trustees, keepers, committees, and boards; changes in location, buildings, and storage; damage to and purposeful destruction of collections; and continual influxes of new objects through various forms of accession, including creation, donation, and purchase.

In both cases, the name of the museum suggests an institutional identity closely aligned with the eponymous collector and his collections. This may well be the case for the Glasgow Hunterian in 2022, having celebrated the bicentenary of the museum's founding in 2007 with the publication of Laurence Keppie's institutional history, followed closely in 2013 by an exhibition focused on the Hunterian's first catalogue; the publication of an essay collection *William Hunter's World: The Art and Science of Eighteenth-Century Collecting* in 2015; and finally, in 2018, by a much larger, transatlantic exhibition and lavish, large format publication marking the tercentenary of William Hunter's death.[30] While William may be front and center now, this has not always been the case, as a wealth of recent scholarship attests in its quest to recover – by reconstructing from material evidence – the provenance of South Seas artifacts, antiquities, and anatomical preparations and casts in the Glasgow Hunterian collections.[31] The

---

[30] My first experience of the Glasgow Hunterian was through *This Unrivalled Collection: The Hunterian's First Catalogue*, the 2013 exhibition marking the 200th anniversary of the publication of John Laskey's catalogue. See also *William Hunter's World: The Art and Science of Eighteenth-Century Collecting*, ed. by E. Geoffrey Hancock, Nick Pearce, and Mungo Campbell (Farnham: Ashgate, 2015), and the aforementioned *William Hunter and the Anatomy of the Modern Museum*.

[31] See any of the essays included in the *William Hunter's World* volume and also Adrienne Kaeppler, '*Artificial Curiosities*': *Being an Exposition of Native Manufactures collected on the Three Pacific Voyages of Captain James Cook* (Honolulu: Bishop Museum Press, 1978), and N. A. McCulloch, D. Russell,

losses have been greater in the London Hunterian: not only was a large portion of the collection destroyed when the museum was bombed in the Blitz during World War II, but also a large part of the documentary archive containing John Hunter's papers was burned in 1823 by Sir Everard Home, Hunter's brother-in-law and one of the executers of his will. Despite these losses, a considerable number of manuscript catalogues have survived from both museums. In addition, catalogues of each museum, and specifically of the anatomical preparations, were prepared and published during the nineteenth century.

Manuscript and printed catalogues may look similar in format and in what information is presented, but they serve distinct functions vis-à-vis the process of institutionalization. Printed catalogues are public-facing; they might consolidate, articulate, and advertise an institution's identity, or they might display fissures in it by foregrounding internal conflicts between the symbolic systems that comprise it (e.g. rules, norms, and cultural-cognitive beliefs). Manuscript catalogues (and some printed catalogues that have been annotated), by contrast, are the working records of the museum; they show, in gritty detail, how the collections are mobilized procedurally. With their interlineations, notes, strikethroughs, paste-ins, and shorthand and technical language, manuscript catalogues comprise a system of organization; they materialize processes, 'the methods, techniques and logics that drive the operation of systems' integral to the museum's labeling, categorizing, storing, and displaying of objects.[32]

Like many of their contemporaries, both William and John Hunter put considerable time and effort (their own and that of various assistants and collaborators) into cataloging their collections.[33] Early surviving anatomical lists and catalogues in John Hunter's hand were copied during his lifetime and rearranged posthumously by his assistants William Bell and William Clift; catalogues of books in William Hunter's hand and a catalogue of anatomical preparations with his annotations survive, as do catalogues for various other parts of his collections (insects, shells,

---

and S. W. McDonald, 'William Hunter's Gravid Uterus: The Specimens and Plates', *Clinical Anatomy*, 15 (2002), 253–62.

[32] Bogost, *Persuasive Games*, p. 3.

[33] Both William and John employed assistants, including William Hewson, and William Bell and William Clift, respectively, to aid them in organizing and cataloging their collections; William also took advantage of the help of scientific visitors like Johann Christian Fabricius and Guillaume-Antoine Olivier, both of whom organized and used William's insect collections in their taxonomic research and publications. See Dominik Hünniger, '"Extolled by Foreigners": William Hunter's Collection and the Development of Science and Medicine in Eighteenth-Century Europe', in *William Hunter and the Anatomy of the Modern Museum*, ed. by Campbell and Flis, pp. 127–41.

minerals, coins, and medals) produced under the supervision of his trustees in advance of moving his collections from London to Glasgow. These early catalogues help us understand what the nineteenth-century museums inherited: not simply what objects but, equally importantly, the logics in place for keeping track of them and how those methods had developed and evolved. In what follows, I uncover the procedural rhetoric of manuscript catalogues by way of examples that cover the transition between private collection and public museum.

Elements of procedural rhetoric can be identified in the successive iterations of catalogues of anatomical preparations in John Hunter's museum, compiled by Hunter and his assistants between the 1777 and 1816, the date Clift began to rearrange the museum gallery twenty-four years after Hunter's death. The earliest extant 'catalogue' in the London Hunterian archives is titled 'Catalogue of the Preparations before entered into the Catalogue'.[34] This somewhat enigmatic title indicates the notebook's purpose as a chronological record of dissections: the entries in John Hunter's hand are organized by date and type of specimen, listing parts extracted and preserved. For example, one entry lists 'parts of a Lyon' dissected on 2 January 1779, including villi of the intestine, the perforated stomach, and a tumor from the abdomen, the cause of death. This dissection book uses a simple system of headings and numbering, but it also records the conceptual reorganization of objects as scribal practice. A series of strikethroughs signals redistribution and dispersal of the preparations: the sequence of 36, 37, 38, 39, 40 becomes 373, 509–514, 277, 516 and 276, unnumbered, 1248, unnumbered, 1591 and 1625, revealing how objects once united in a single body were reallocated into multiple other groupings.

The purpose of this reorganization emerges in the earliest museum catalogue (late 1770s/early 1780s): hearts join with hearts, stomachs with stomachs, regardless of what or who supplied them. In addition to grouping preparations by organ, each entry has been expanded to detail what each preparation is intended to 'show', underscoring how the objects are being mobilized as exempla.[35] In a third incarnation of the museum catalogue (in Clift's hand), preparations begin to illustrate conceptual categories like 'Muscular Arrangement' and 'The Absorbent System'.[36]

---

[34] *Anatomical Catalogue: October 17, 1777*, London, Royal College of Surgeons, Hunterian Museum and Library, MS 0189/2/1.

[35] *Brain, Hearts, Monsters Catalogue*, London, Royal College of Surgeons, Hunterian Museum and Library, MS 0189/2/10.

[36] *Catalogue of Anatomy and Physiology Forming the Original Catalogue of the Hunterian Museum*, London, Royal College of Surgeons, Hunterian Museum and Library, MS 0189/2/8.

These new categories correspond to the display of preparations in the museum: the west wall displayed organs of generation, the east wall was devoted to the senses, and the south-east corner populated by 'Absorbents', 'Intestines', and 'Stomachs'.[37] A fourth set of catalogues prepared in Hunter's lifetime (also in Clift's hand and titled *Catalogue of the Museum 1800: Gallery*, suggesting it continued to be used after Hunter's death in 1793) reiterate and expand the organization by function: the 'Absorbent System' is described in a long prefatory note supported by bare bones lists, stomachs and intestines lining pages and display cases. In this catalogue, description has by and large been stripped away from individual preparations and relocated into headnotes. For example, the 'Lion' dissected in 1779 has contributed a series of parts (still #509–517) that exemplify the Absorbent System, including a 'beautiful villous intestine' (see Figure 8.1).[38] The insertion of 'Lion' in Hunter's hand reminds us where this beautiful part came from, but his annotation also foregrounds the logic of the catalogue as a genre. The catalogue detaches the anatomical preparations from once-living animal and human bodies, rendering them freestanding objects that exist within (and materially support) conceptual systems. In other words, the process scripted by the catalogue renders the objects mobile and flexibly interpretable, available to be deployed strategically to support claims implicit in the museum's organizational schema (in this case, as I will discuss further in a moment, the 'principles of life' as Hunter conceived of them).

This process of erasing original context and scripting objects into the museum's episteme is certainly not exclusive to anatomical preparations; as scholarship has long underscored, 'the museum setting has become emblematic of the artifact's loss of original context', whether the artifact in question is a bottled intestine, a Polynesian tool, or a work of Medieval European art.[39] The Hunterian catalogues simply underscore that the decontextualization and recontextualization of objects happens

---

[37] See William Clift, 'Plan of the Museum', 1806. London, Royal College of Surgeons, Hunterian Museum and Library, MS 0007/1/4/5/3.

[38] Intestines, from *Catalogue of the Museum 1800: Gallery*, London, Royal College of Surgeons, Hunterian Museum and Library, MS 0007/1/1/1/7.

[39] Thelma K. Thomas, 'Understanding Objects', in *Reading Medieval Images: The Art Historian and the Object*, ed. by Elizabeth Sears and Thelma K. Thomas (Ann Arbor: Michigan University Press, 2002), pp. 9–15 (p. 10). There is a large body of scholarship on this topic across numerous disciplines; see, for example, Nicholas Thomas, 'Licensed Curiosity: Cook's Pacific Voyages', in *The Cultures of Collecting*, ed. by John Elsner and Roger Cardinal (London: Reaktion, 1994), pp. 116–36; Susan M. Pearce, *On Collecting: An Investigation into Collecting in the European Tradition* (Abingdon: Routledge, 1995); and Susan M. Pearce, *Museums, Objects, and Collections* (Leicester: Leicester University Press, 1992).

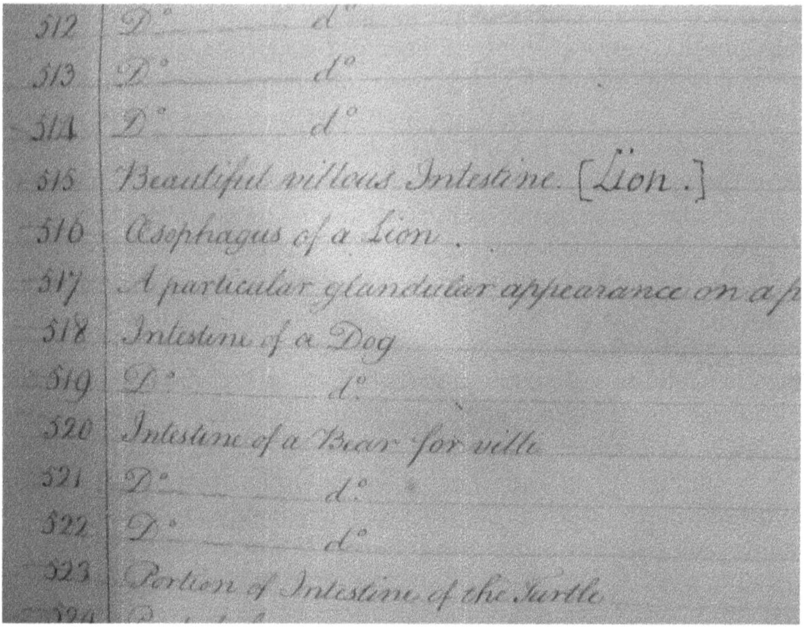
512 D° d°
513 D° d°
514 D° d°
515 Beautiful villous Intestine. [Lion.]
516 Œsophagus of a Lion.
517 A particular glandular appearance on a p
518 Intestine of a Dog
519 D° d°
520 Intestine of a Bear for villi
521 D° d°
522 D° d°
523 Portion of Intestine of the Turtle

Figure 8.1 Intestines, from *Catalogue of the Museum 1800: Gallery*, Hunterian Museum and Library, MS 0007/1/1/1/7. From the Archives of the Royal College of Surgeons of England.

procedurally: the processes of inscription, re-inscription, numbering, and renumbering deploy objects within a system of knowledge – a system that the objects in aggregate comprise and support. Other aspects of the catalogue's procedural rhetoric bolster this work of recontextualization. For example, note the pervasive use of 'D°', a shorthand for ditto (Figure 8.1). In the catalogue, 'ditto' linguistically means 'the same again', but it also functions to represent the process of sequencing: 514 is the same as 513, which is the same as 512, which is the same as 511, and so on. The 'beautiful villous intestine' interrupts this specific sequence by introducing an esophagus and a 'particular glandular appearance' before the list of intestines restarts with dog, ditto, bear, ditto, ditto, turtle, ditto. Setting the interruption aside for a moment, we can see how D° functions symbolically to represent the process of sequential ordering in which objects in a chain are coded as either the same or different. This instills a way of knowing the objects – the reiteration of sameness and difference foregrounds the comparative aspect of Hunter's anatomical investigations – while also directing what one does with the objects, for example, how the preparations should be arranged in the museum. In this way, the catalogue can be understood as what Bogost calls 'procedural expression': through manipulation of symbols like D°, the catalogue enacts 'the construction and interpretation of a symbolic system that governs human thought and action'.[40]

Let me now return to the Lion's beautiful villous intestine, which clearly derails the sequence with its call for aesthetic appreciation and the baggage it carries with it. Yet another early nineteenth-century catalogue in William Bell's hand, which Clift labeled 'Nov. 11th 1816. Began to re-arrange the Contents of the Gallery', attempts to correct this transgression by crossing out one interloper (the asophagus), but the 'particular glandular appearance' remains to interrupt the litany of intestinal villi (Figure 8.2). Something, Clift recognizes, is out of order here, intruding where it doesn't belong – except, of course, for Hunter it *did* belong, a consequence of the

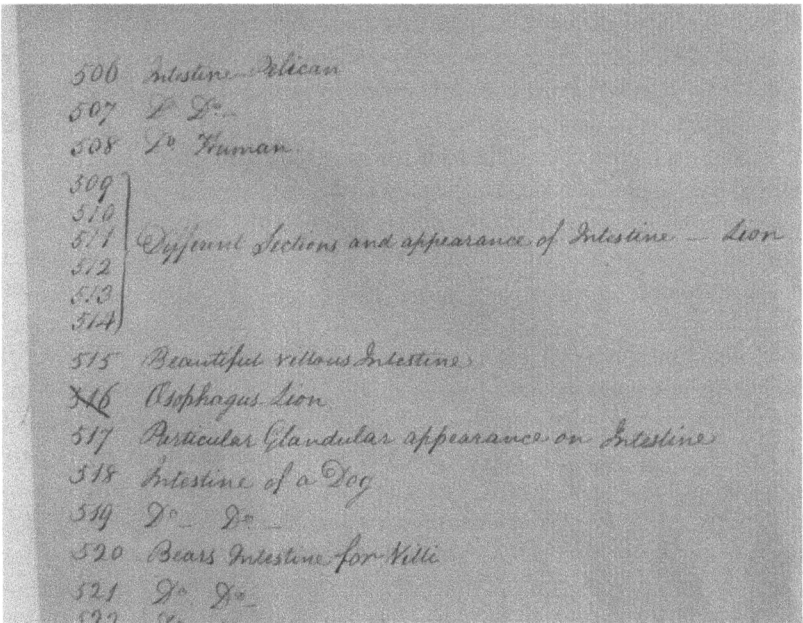

Figure 8.2 Intestines, from the *Original Fascicules of Hunterian Museum Catalogues, Bound in One Quarto Volume*, Hunterian Museum and Library, MS 0189/2/16. From the Archives of the Royal College of Surgeons of England.

---

[40] Bogost, *Persuasive Games*, p. 5.

history of the leonine subject that supplied the preparation in 1779. While this simple strikethrough may seem innocuous, the individuation of this preparation opens a gap in the catalogue's procedural rhetoric: when one actor (Hunter) refuses to strip an object of its context and allows it to be scripted into the catalogue, the object disrupts and thereby makes visible the processes that construct and uphold the museum's episteme, leaving other human actors (in this case Clift) unsure of how to proceed.

The early manuscript catalogues of the London Hunterian form an instructive instance of a nineteenth-century museum's procedural rhetoric at work. These manuscript catalogues register processes by which objects are mobilized on paper to form a symbolic system, which in turn is represented in the space of the museum. This system is governed by various rules (e.g. prohibiting the removal of objects), norms (the sanctioned role of the museum keeper to preserve and organize the objects), and cultural-cognitive beliefs (including the value ascribed to objects through their organization and display). But the processes of inscription are what *constitutes* the system and thereby the unique identity of the institution. In the case of the London Hunterian, this identity was codified and publicized through a series of catalogues published between 1830 and 1840 by William Clift and his then assistant Richard Owen.[41] Clift and Owen's six volume *Descriptive and Illustrated Catalogue of the Physiological Series of Comparative Anatomy* (1833–40) differs significantly from the manuscript catalogues produced by Clift and Bell. While the manuscript catalogues move seamlessly from pelican to human to lion to dog to bear, in the published version Owen divides the preparations according to class (i.e. mollusks, fishes, reptiles, birds, mammals) and sequences them in order of increasing complexity, often further subdividing them by genus and family: the pelican and turtle were moved out of the above sequence so it could represent *Mammalia*. Furthermore, the stripped-down lists of the late manuscript catalogues are replaced by detailed descriptive annotations that pinpoint exactly what each preparation shows. The preparations are not returned to their origin but rather made uniquely exemplary: for example, four preparations in the series (693–96, note the new numbering) are 'from the same Lion' but they are not 'the same again'; each now

---

[41] Clift and Owen began with pathological preparations, which were described in *Catalogue of the Hunterian Collection of the Museum of the Royal College of Surgeons of London*, 6 vols (London: Richard Taylor, 1830–31); this was followed by a separate set of catalogues devoted to comparative anatomy, *Descriptive and Illustrated Catalogue of the Physiological Series of Comparative Anatomy contained in the Museum of the Royal College of Surgeons in London*, 6 vols (London: Richard Taylor, 1833–40).

represents a slightly different (if 'similar') aspect of the intestine, and in aggregate they 'show the simple disposition and limited extent of the intestinal mucous membrane in this carnivorous animal'.[42] Clift and Owen's catalogue, in other words, draws finer, more copious divisions by multiplying both categories and narrative explanation (it also adds a good number of preparations 'prepared by Mr. Owen' to fill out the new categories). With these changes, the published catalogue stabilizes the relations between the objects themselves and between objects and the groups that contain them, minimizing disturbances in the (new) ordering schema. This six-volume catalogue codifies the Hunterian Museum London as an institution devoted to comparative anatomy, one that upholds an implicit evolutionary narrative in its selection, categorization, and organization of exemplary objects.[43]

Despite a holistic recasting and reorganization of the manuscript sources, Clift and Owen's published catalogues supplied evidence for arguments about the eponymous origin of the Hunterian Museum. In the Preface to his edition of *The Works of John Hunter* (1835), James Palmer argues that Hunter's writings are 'the text to his museum, – his museum the appropriate illustration of his writings'.[44] Palmer concludes his extensive life of Hunter (which opens the first volume of *Works*) with a chapter describing the Hunterian museum as Hunter's crowning achievement. Palmer quotes extensively from Clift and Owen's catalogues to argue that the 'original design of Hunter, in the formation of his museum, was to furnish an ample illustration of the phenomena of life exhibited throughout the vast chain of organized beings, by a display of the various structures in which the functions of life are carried on'.[45] This conclusion is speculative, Palmer admits, because Hunter did not finish a written account of the museum, and a large body of his preparatory material was lost when Home burned the 'ten folio volumes of MSS' in which Hunter had recorded his 'labours in the field of comparative anatomy'.[46] Nevertheless, Palmer confidently asserts that Hunter fully intended to organize his observations into 'one comprehensive work' in which he 'would have stated at large his views on the nature of animal life, on the particular uses of the several organs, and on

---

[42] *Descriptive and Illustrated Catalogue*, I, 209.
[43] Owen would later write critically of Charles Darwin's theories despite his own work proving evolutionary sequences, primarily because Owen saw transmutation as displacing humans from atop the order of nature.
[44] John Hunter, *The Works of John Hunter*, ed. by James F. Palmer, 4 vols (London: Longman, 1835–37), I, ix.
[45] Hunter, I, 148. [46] Hunter, I, 151.

their relations to one another'.[47] Palmer's confidence derives from his source: drawing on Owen's editorial work in the catalogues, Palmer lists the contents of the museum as a series of conceptual elucidations scripted by the spatial organization of the preparations. Both Clift and Owen's catalogue and Palmer's *Works* emphasize connections between sequences: in the category of locomotion, a series illustrating 'component parts' is succeeded by examples 'arranged according to their degree of vitality' and ascending through different types.[48] This rhetorical pattern of ascending sequence is repeated throughout Palmer's description. Palmer thus sutures Owen's elaborate descriptions into a coherent narrative that encourages viewers to see the museum's component parts as an expression of a unified theory. In doing so, he secures Hunter's reputation and extracts a unified theory of life out of a fragmentary archive.

Palmer's editorial project in *The Works of John Hunter* is an act of scientific canonization; the prefatory life and its culminating discussion of the museum demonstrates Hunter's original contribution to emergent biological science, despite the hodgepodge of fragmentary writings collected in the volume. Drawing on Clift and Owen's published catalogues, Palmer also presents this reconstitutive narrative of Hunter's theory of life as the public face of the London Hunterian, aligning the institution's name, the knowledge it conveys, and the (implicitly permanent) value it holds. The catalogue thus works as an instituting genre: the processes of ordering objects enacted by the manuscript catalogues form the material support for public-facing expressions of the institution's epistemic ends, values, and unique identity. While the Lion introduces a slight wrinkle in the catalogue's procedural rhetoric, it is but a momentary lapse. Deploying the catalogue's generic features, Clift and Bell (and later Clift and Owen) mobilize the objects (on paper and in space) to forge a symbolic system that institutionalizes the London Hunterian as a museum of comparative anatomy. In this case study, the catalogue's procedural rhetoric enables a relatively stable institutional identity to emerge in the first twenty years of the museum's public life, despite (or more likely enabled by) the loss of an immense part of the documentary archive.

I now turn to the Glasgow Hunterian as a counterexample, one that underscores the dynamism of the process of institutionalization rather than its culmination in order and stability. As will become clear, the greater scope and variety of the Glasgow Hunterian's collections – William Hunter's anatomical preparations arrived with a host of other objects,

---

[47] Hunter, I, 150.   [48] Hunter, I, 158.

supplemented from 1808 by donations of every imaginable type of object, from meteoritic stones to an African cap to stuffed birds to self-published poems – made the process of forging a stable institutional identity fraught and uneven.[49] What has become known as the first printed catalogue of the Glasgow Hunterian makes this patently obvious. Captain John Laskey's *A General Account of the Hunterian Museum, Glasgow: including Historical and Scientific Notices of the Various Objects of Art, Literature, Natural History, Anatomical Preparations, Antiquities, &c. in that Celebrated Collection* is more a museum guidebook than a catalogue proper: it is organized by room, allowing the reader to move through the museum virtually. Some 'departments' (such as the 'Conchological Division') are numbered, grouped by Linnaean classification, and described in detail, while others (e.g. the paintings and books) are simply listed by name of artist/author.[50] These gestures to the catalogue's procedural form, however, are embedded in a mass of dense descriptive prose, and Laskey's descriptions everywhere attest to various kinds of loss, both physical and contextual: beetles are wanting their heads; the identity of a prominently displayed terra cotta bust is 'unknown at present'; and ethnographic artifacts have become detached from geography, use, and name (here a spur 'probably from Mexico', there a fish hook whose operation is 'difficult to comprehend').[51] While these lapses might reflect the decontextualization of artifacts and their subsequent recontextalization in the museum order, it is also possible to read them as processes gone awry. Indeed, as I have argued elsewhere, in its haphazard organization, eclecticism and emphasis on the singular, unusual, and astonishing, Laskey's *General Account* has more in common formally with early accession books and inventories of goods packed for the move to Glasgow than with the procedural form of the London Hunterian catalogues.[52]

We might understand this as a case of 'messy beginnings', a period of disorder preceding the consolidation of institutional identity. However, examining manuscript and published catalogues of the Glasgow Hunterian collections indicates a more prolonged period of instability, one that signals a highly contested, dynamic process of institutionalization.

---

[49] For a discussion of the Glasgow Hunterian accession books, see Dahlia Porter, 'Catalogues for an Entropic Collection: Losses, Gains and Disciplinary Exhaustion in the Hunterian Museum, Glasgow', *BJHS Themes*, 4 (2019), 215–43 (pp. 230–33) <https://doi.org/10.1017/bjt.2019.15>.

[50] John Laskey, *A General Account of the Hunterian Museum, Glasgow* (Glasgow: John Smith, 1813), pp. 7–18, 98–106, 87–98.

[51] Laskey, pp. 29, 5, 19, 22.

[52] Porter, pp. 225–32. My argument here qualifies and revises my previous understanding of the disciplinary function of Laskey's *General Account*.

Specifically, the documentary archive reveals what Scott calls 'endogenous processes, involving conflicts and contradictions between institutional elements' of rules, norms, and cultural-cognitive beliefs.[53] These conflicts are nascent in the Trustee Catalogues produced in the 1780s, and which accompanied William Hunter's collections to Glasgow in 1807.

The Trustee Catalogues are often surprisingly sparse, comprised of long lists with minimal information. The 1785 Trustee Catalogue of printed books, for example, is organized alphabetically by author, with each letter subdivided by format (folios, quartos, octavos, pamphlets); individual books are recorded with one-line entries listing author's last name, abbreviated title, and so on. The Trustee Catalogue of anatomical preparations has considerably more detail: most entries provide a description of the preparation and what it is intended to 'show' while also (with preparations from human subjects) giving details of the medical case it derived from.[54] This manuscript catalogue incorporates aspects of the medical case history by explicitly naming the doctors whose cases are recorded and giving information about patients, such as Hunter's note to the preparation numbered 55.S, a stricture of the rectum: 'Lord T – Above a year's standing – dreadful case'.[55] Thus, while this catalogue makes extensive use of 'Ditto' (particularly in lists of the animal preparations) in combination with classificatory headings and numerical accounting, it also maintains a degree of individuation by linking many of the human-derived preparations to specific medical cases.

This aspect of the Glasgow Hunterian anatomical catalogue does not prevent it from functioning procedurally; however, it does mean that a large quantity of identifying contextual information is embedded, narratively, in the procedural rhetoric of a catalogue that is, ostensibly, devoted to an exploration of vitality by way of comparative anatomy. When a catalogue of anatomical preparations in the Glasgow Hunterian was published in 1840, it retained most of this information, effectively presenting the anatomical department of the museum as a mash-up of

---

[53] Scott, p. 58. Scott claims that endogenous processes are the most common drivers of institutional change while acknowledging that institutions are rocked by 'exogenous shocks, such as wars and financial crises'. The processes of institutionalization in both Hunterian museums were radically impacted by many exogenous factors, most obviously the decay of the Glasgow Hunterian building and its move to a new building in 1870 and the destruction of large portions of the London Hunterian during World War II.

[54] 'Catalogue of Anatomical Preparations', University of Glasgow Library, Special Collections, MR 20. MR 20 is a copy of MR 19, which is in an unknown hand with insertions and notes by William Hunter.

[55] 'Catalogue of Anatomical Preparations', p. 98.

comparative anatomy and medical case histories. This tension does not exist in the London Hunterian catalogues, in which pathological preparations are cordoned off in a separate publication. However, the difference between the published anatomical catalogues of the two museums is in fact starker: while the London Hunterian manuscript catalogues scripted objects into a specific, identifiable episteme that was then refined and codified in the published catalogue, the Glasgow anatomical catalogue was 'published for the use of the Medical Students at the University'.[56] Again, this innocuous statement belies specific tensions within the museum. After decades of disagreements between university faculty and the museum keeper over access to preparations for pedagogical purposes, in 1840 the Museum Committee resolved that 'the anatomical preparations in the Museum, should not on any account be removed from the room in which they are placed in the Museum'.[57] At a committee meeting the next year, keeper William Couper reported that 1,000 copies of the new catalogue were available for medical students to purchase; access to the museum was included in the three shilling purchase price. At the same time, Couper proposed 'that it would contribute to the security & usefulness of the anatomical preparations of Dr. Hunter as exhibited in the new room if they were protected by an Iron Trellice [sic]'.[58] As this evidence suggests, the catalogue's publication was directly attributable to a conflict between (1) the rules and regulations imposed by the museum keeper as part of his obligation (dictated by William Hunter's will) to preserve the objects under his care in perpetuity, and (2) the faculty's culturally sanctioned belief that students should have access to the preparations as part of their medical studies (an assumption also supported by Hunter's will).[59] Rather than codifying a stable institutional identity, both manuscript and published catalogues register an ongoing disruption in the process of institutionalization: are the preparations meant to elucidate medical conditions and facilitate diagnosis, or do they support a broader theory built on comparative anatomy?

---

[56] 'Advertisement', *Catalogue of Anatomical Preparations in the Hunterian Museum, University of Glasgow* (Glasgow: George Richardson, 1840).
[57] 'Minute book of the Committee of the Hunterian Museum, 2 Aug. 1820–31 Dec. 1842', Glasgow University Archives, GUA 11563.
[58] 'Minute book of the Committee of the Hunterian Museum, 2 Aug. 1820–31 Dec. 1842'.
[59] Hunter's London will and testament explicitly states that his collections should be 'kept and preserved' by the University 'for ever'; it also states that the collections were bequeathed to the university for the 'improvement of knowledge' and specifically for 'the Improvement of the Students'. See 'MS copy of William Hunter's will and codicil. 19th century', University of Glasgow Library, Special Collections, MS Gen 1000. Quoted in Keppie, p. 32.

This is, of course, a false dichotomy: a collection of objects can be deployed to do two, or four or ten, things at once. My point here is that a dual agenda does not lend itself to the consolidation of a particularly stable institutional identity. In this case, the procedural rhetoric of the catalogue could not surmount and stabilize the conflict of interests registered in the descriptions, and thus the published catalogue displays a tension in the ongoing process of institutionalization. This conclusion is supported by the Advertisement to the 1840 publication, which explicitly undermines the catalogue's work as an instituting genre. While stating that the catalogue was printed from one of the two manuscript catalogues of anatomical preparations, the Advertisement also claims that these catalogues 'abound with errors of every kind, rendering the descriptions often obscure and sometimes quite unintelligible'. Furthermore, the Advertisement admits that the work of correcting these errors by consulting the physical preparations was not done carefully in several sections, such that 'some Preparations have been wrong described, and some not described at all; while some descriptions have been printed, to which no Preparation corresponds'. These errors, the editor admits, will 'prove embarrassing to the student' who tries to use the catalogue to study the preparations, but the printing was too far advanced to allow for corrections.[60] As this indicates, the printed catalogue was a rather slipshod affair, a plaster on an open conflict of interests rather than a strategic deployment of the genre's procedural rhetoric.

The fate of the Glasgow Hunterian's anatomical collections usefully qualifies the case of the London Hunterian. The anatomical preparations, so long contested, were eventually ceded to the Anatomy Department in 1912 – ironically (or predictably) once they were no longer at the core of medical research or teaching.[61] This decision was spurred by the acquisition of a large group of more publicly engaging ethnographic objects, which arrived around the turn of the century – a moment which also witnessed a stream of published catalogues of the Glasgow Hunterian's varied collections, including the pictures, sculptures and other works of art (1880), coins and medals (1899–1905), manuscripts (1908), and the anatomical preparations (1900–01). While the other catalogues mention William Hunter's foundational collections, John Teacher's anatomical catalogue specifically set out to identify which preparations originated with William Hunter; as such, it treated a subset of the museum's objects as a unique, historically singular collection rather than a working collection of

[60] 'Advertisement', *Catalogue of Anatomical Preparations*.
[61] For an extended discussion of this decision, see Porter, pp. 215–16 and 240–43.

medical knowledge.[62] Read alongside John Young's scientific biography of Hunter, *William Hunter: Physician, Anatomist, Founder of the Hunterian Museum* (1901), Teacher's catalogue constitutes an attempt to deploy the genre's procedural rhetoric to frame the Glasgow Hunterian as a historically significant medical museum – an identity that, a little more than ten years later, would be soundly rejected by the transfer of the anatomical preparations out of the museum entirely.

While much more can be said about how the nineteenth-century manuscript catalogues function within the two Hunterian museums, my analysis demonstrates both the drive to order and fix and the dynamism of institutionalization as a process. By analyzing the procedural rhetoric of the catalogue, I have identified both stabilizing and destabilizing forces that contributed to actors' attempts to consolidate particular institutional identities for each museum, or to reroute or thwart that process. Despite the contrast developed here, the institutional identity Clift and Owen established through the published catalogues was neither unequivocal nor permanent. Likewise, the Glasgow Hunterian has had swings of greater and lesser institutional stability. Celebrations of each museum's permanence and the enduring value of the objects it contains paper over a much more dynamic process of invention and reinvention – a process that depends on the mundane, everyday work of listing, organizing, numbering, of inscription and reinscription, undertaken with and through the museum's paper tools.

---

[62] For a discussion of this distinction, see Boris Jardine, Emma Kowal, and Jenny Bangham, 'How Collections End: Objects, Meaning and Loss in Laboratories and Museums', *BJHS Themes*, 4 (2019), 1–27.

CHAPTER 9

Charles Lamb and the British Museum as an Institution of Literature

Gillian Russell

In an 1808 letter to his friend Thomas Manning in Canton, China, Charles Lamb asked: 'Does anyone read at Canton? I think public reading rooms the best mode of educating young men. Solitary reading is apt to give the headach. Besides who knows that you *do* read?' Lamb explained 'public reading rooms' as the 'ten thousand institutions similar to the Royal Institution that have sprung up from it. There is the London Institution, The Southwark Institution, The Russell Square Rooms Institution &c – *College* quasi *Con-lege*, a place where people read together'.[1] The proliferating 'Institutions' of the early nineteenth century had made visible a new form of male homosociality devoted to reading as a performative practice in the service of knowledge, one which could logically be extended beyond London to the far corners of the world as part of the expansion of imperial knowledge and influence: Lamb ventures that Thomas Manning might suggest to Sir Joseph Banks, the president of the Royal Society, the setting up of a 'similar institution' in Canton.[2] Another important site in this period, which is relevant to the institutionalisation of knowledge after 1800 and also foundational in the expansion of empire, was the library of the British Museum. Unlike the Institutions referred to by Lamb that were organised by paid subscription, access to the printed books and manuscripts in the Museum was free, though it was strictly regulated and limited, as I shall go on to discuss. Opened in 1759, the British Museum

---

[1] Charles Lamb, *The Letters of Charles and Mary Anne Lamb*, ed. by Edwin W. Marrs Jr., 3 vols (Ithaca: Cornell University Press, 1975–78), II, 274. The Royal Institution was founded in London in 1799 and the London Institution in 1806, followed by the Surrey Institution (which Lamb referred to as the Southwark Institution) in 1808 and the Russell Institution (also in 1808). See Jon Klancher, *Transfiguring the Arts and Sciences: Knowledge and Cultural Institutions in the Romantic Age* (Cambridge: Cambridge University Press, 2013).

[2] Lamb, *Letters*, ed. Marrs, II, 274. A subscription library was established in Canton in 1806: see John M. Carroll, *Canton Days: British Life and Death in China* (London: Rowman & Littlefield, 2020), p. 127. I am grateful to Caroline Stevenson for this reference.

was the only state institution of knowledge, insofar that it was established by an act of parliament in 1753 and funded by public monies, subject to parliamentary review. It was dedicated by law 'not only for the inspection and entertainment of the learned and the curious, but for the general use and benefit of the publick'.[3] The role of the library of the Museum in shaping and developing the Romantic period literary field paralleled, intersected with, and sometimes competed with the Institutions mentioned by Lamb, as well as with the discursive institutions and networks constituted by periodicals and newspapers.[4] In this chapter, I will discuss the use Charles Lamb made of the British Museum library and its reading rooms in relation to his own book collecting and sociable reading practices, and the increasing identification of the British Museum as a distinctively 'literary' institution in the 1820s and 1830s.[5]

Charles Lamb's experience as a reader in the library of the British Museum was confined to two distinct periods: 1804–7 and 1826–7. In early 1804 he left off writing for newspapers to attempt other literary projects that would supplement his income as a clerk in the East India Office. Using a recommendation from William Godwin, he applied for a reader's ticket which he received on 12 May 1804, initially with the intention of finding material for William Wordsworth, who was planning an anthology of poetry, including dramatic poetry.[6] Lamb acted as a book broker by scouring the dealers and bookstalls for 'old plays' to dispatch to the Lake District. Warning his friend that 'Ben Jonson' was now a 'Guinea Book' and 'Beaumont & Fletcher in folio, the right folio, [was] not now to be met with', Lamb noted the enjoyment of book-hunting on his

---

[3] Geo. II. Cap. 22, *Statutes at Large from the 26th to the 30th Year of George II*, vol. 21 (London: Bathurst, 1766), pp. 66–85. The Museum was governed by forty-one trustees, 'a body politick and corporate in deed and name', appointed by the Crown: *Statutes*, p. 65. Other comparable 'public' libraries in London were Lambeth Palace Library, Archbishop Tennison's library at St Martin-in-the-Fields, Dr Williams's library, and the libraries of Sion College and St Paul's Cathedral: see David McKitterick, 'Wantonness and Use: Ambitions for Research Libraries in Early Eighteenth-Century England', in *Enlightening the British: Knowledge, Discovery and the Museum in the Eighteenth Century*, ed. by R. G. W. Anderson and others (London: British Museum, 2003), pp. 37–47 (p. 40). See also P. R. Harris, *A History of the British Museum Library 1753–1973* (London: British Library, 1998); Martin Spevack, 'The Impact of the British Museum Library', in *The Cambridge History of Libraries in Britain and Ireland, vol. 2: 1640–1850*, ed. by Giles Mandelbrote and K. A. Manley (Cambridge: Cambridge University Press, 2006), pp. 422–37.

[4] By 'literary field', I follow the Bourdeuvian model of cultural production, as outlined by Ina Ferris and Paul Keen in their 'Introduction: Towards a Bookish Literary History', in *Bookish Histories: Books, Literature, and Commercial Modernity, 1700–1900*, ed. by Ina Ferris and Paul Keen (Basingstoke: Palgrave, 2009), pp. 1–17 (pp. 7–8).

[5] The most comprehensive account of Lamb at the British Museum is the relevant entry in Claude A. Prance's *Companion to Charles Lamb* (London: Mansell, 1983), pp. 38–40.

[6] G. F. Barwick, *The Reading Room of the British Museum* (London: Ernest Benn, 1929), p. 54.

behalf: 'next to the pleasure of buying a bargain for one's self is the pleasure of persuading a friend to buy it. It tickles one with the image of an imprudency without the penalty usually annex'd'.[7] After his farce *Mr. H* failed disastrously at Drury Lane in December 1806, Lamb concentrated on his collaboration with his sister Mary on the *Tales from Shakespeare* (published 1807), and in 1807 worked more intensively at the Museum on his own anthology of extracts from early modern plays, which was eventually published in 1808 as *Specimens of English Dramatic Poets Who Lived about the Time of Shakspeare.*

The British Museum that Lamb first entered as a reader in 1804 was housed in Montagu House, a mansion in Bloomsbury dating from 1678. The provision of access to books and manuscripts was prominent in the Museum's remit, as indicated by the Act establishing it in 1753 as 'a general repository' for the collections of Sir Hans Sloane, the Harleian manuscripts, and the Cottonian library.[8] The reading room that Lamb used in 1804–7 had been set up in 1803 and held up to thirty people: according to James Peller Malcolm, it contained shelves of books protected by wire, 'a vaulted cieling, a handsome cornice, and large marble chimney-piece, a West window and three North, with several portraits on the walls', as well as two long tables for readers.[9] The process of ordering a book entailed consulting the catalogues in the room, writing down a title, and then summoning a servant by means of a bell-rope: ideally 'a messenger instantly obeys the summons, and in as short a time as possible returns with the wished for book'.[10] Although catalogues for collections such as the Harleian were available for consultation, there was no up-to-date comprehensive general catalogue: in 1804, an article in the *Times* complained about the lack of 'opportunity [for inspection] of the immense accumulation of works' that had been acquired since 1787, when the first catalogue of printed books was published. The writer complained that 'half the advantage of this great national depôt of general talent, [was thereby] lost to the public'.[11] By 1804, when Lamb first began to use the reading room, the British Museum was no longer regarded as a repository or 'hospital' for discrete collections but rather as a 'national depôt' that was being tested in its capacity to meet the demands of a burgeoning knowledge economy.

The year 1803 also marks the first time that rules for the use of the Museum reading room were published. Readers could visit it between 10

[7] Lamb, *Letters*, ed. Marrs, II, 146, 147. [8] *Statutes*, p. 66.
[9] Harris, p. 54; James Peller Malcolm, *London Redivivium or, an Ancient History and Modern Description of London*, vol. 2 (London: John Nichols, 1803), p. 500.
[10] Malcolm, p. 500. [11] *The Times*, 24 September 1804, p. 3.

and 4 on Monday to Friday only: it was closed for a week at Christmas, Easter, and Whitsuntide, and on thanksgiving and fast days. Those who wished to use the library were required to produce a recommendation letter because 'it might be dangerous, in so populous a metropolis as London, to admit perfect strangers'.[12] This provision was a sign of the expansion of the idea of the public served by British Museum, as well as how reading practices, especially those of the lower orders, had become a focus of anxiety for the political elite in the 1790s.[13] The idea of the public served by the Museum was predominantly male. Though Catharine Macaulay used the Museum library soon after it was opened, as did later Eliza Ryves, Elizabeth Benger, and Matilda Betham, and possibly others, women readers there were few and far between.[14] P. R. Harris's 1998 history of the library does not indicate that a woman was granted a ticket between 1804 and 1827.

Because of the opening hours, Lamb's capacity to read at the British Museum in 1804–7 was limited to his holidays from his salaried job at the East India Office, for which, by around 1802, he was receiving annual leave of four weeks.[15] Lamb and his sister usually journeyed outside London, meaning that using his holidays to work in the British Museum encroached upon these periods of travel and recreation. In December 1806, Mary Lamb

---

[12] For a report on the British Museum's new 'printed directions' for the reading room, see the *Gentleman's Magazine*, 73 (February 1803), pp. 99–100 (p. 99).

[13] For the expansion of the radical reading public in the 1790s, see Paul Keen, *The Crisis of Literature in the 1790s: Print Culture and the Public Sphere* (Cambridge: Cambridge University Press, 2004) and Jon Mee, *Print, Publicity, and Popular Radicalism in the 1790s: The Laurel of Liberty* (Cambridge: Cambridge University Press, 2016).

[14] Macaulay was granted a ticket in 1763: Barwick, p. 34. Isaac D'Israeli recalled seeing Eliza Ryves 'conning' manuscripts in the reading room: *Calamities of Authors*, 2 vols (London: John Murray, 1812), I, 301. Ryves died in 1797. In 1825, Elizabeth Benger, a friend of the Lambs, was described as 'a lady we have often seen in the Reading Room of the British Museum': *The Literary Chronicle*, 6.340 (19 November 1825), p. 746. See also Grace Wharton and Philip Wharton, *The Queens of Society* (London: James Hogg, [1860]): 'Those who remember the reading-room in the days of Sir Henry Ellis – that dingy room, in which one took leave of cleanliness and light when one put off one's clogs at the door – will recall Miss Benger ... patiently reading through dusty tomes to compile her "Elizabeth of Bohemia"' (p. 509). Matilda Betham, who was also a friend of the Lambs, was described in the 1870s as a 'constant student in the old Reading-rooms of dismal memory': *The Academy*, 14 (28 September 1878), p. 317. For the importance of the reading room to women writers in the nineteenth and twentieth centuries, see Susan David Bernstein, *Roomscape: Women Writers in the British Museum from George Eliot to Virginia Woolf* (Edinburgh: Edinburgh University Press, 2013).

[15] See Samuel McKechnie, 'Charles Lamb of the India House, No. IV', *Notes and Queries*, 191.12 (14 December 1946), 252–56 (p. 253). For a useful summary of holidays taken by Lamb, see Prance, pp. 149–51. For changes in privileges at East India House in 1816–17, which ended holidays on Saints' Days and made Saturday a full working day rather than a half day, see H. V. Bowen, *The Business of Empire: The East India Company and Imperial Britain, 1756–1833* (Cambridge: Cambridge University Press, 2009), p. 149.

wrote to Catherine Clarkson, wife of Thomas Clarkson, that her brother 'sometimes threatens to pass his hollidays [sic] in town hunting over old plays at the Museum. ... The Museum is only open during his office hours'.[16] She also expressed her hope that eventually her brother would be 'able to borrow the books of some good old collector of those hidden treasures' so that he could copy them 'at home'.[17] The following summer of 1807, Charles and Mary Lamb spent a period visiting the Clarksons at Bury St Edmunds, on return from which Mary became ill. Lamb wrote to the Clarksons asking for some manuscript books that Mary had 'left behind', 'in particular, the Dramatic Extracts, as my purpose is to make use of the remainder of my holydays in completing them at the British Museum, which will be employment & money in the end', indicating that he had been trying to work on the *Specimens* project while in Bury (and also that Mary Lamb had responsibility for their papers).[18] He later (in July 1807) wrote to Catherine Clarkson that he had after all 'made good use of my holydays in town. I still go to the Museum, and shall to the end of the week, which closes my vacation'.[19] The time spent at the Museum on the *Specimens* during 1804–7 was therefore intermittent, brief, and constrained by obligations to both his job in the East India Office and to Mary Lamb: it was truly a time of 'holyday' in the sense of being a time of exception, Lamb's use of that term, and especially the spelling of 'holyday', evoking the idea of a day marked for a religious festival as opposed to the more secular connotations of 'vacation'.

Charles Lamb's experience at the British Museum was only part of a repertoire of his reading practices that included reading for the purposes of his work at the East India Office, as well as reading alone at home, in company with Mary Lamb or friends and acquaintances, in booksellers or at outdoor bookstalls, or even in the midst of a heaving crowd waiting to go into a theatre.[20] Reading at the British Museum was different in that it was publicly sanctioned by institutional authority and the rules and rituals that regulated it: Lamb's ticket of admission interpellated him among a class of literary men (and the occasional woman) participating in a particular form of knowledge 'work'. Throughout the eighteenth century, venues such as

---

[16] Lamb, *Letters*, ed. Marrs, II, 253. [17] Lamb, *Letters*, ed. Marrs, II, 253.
[18] Lamb, *Letters*, ed. Marrs, II, 258. [19] Lamb, *Letters*, ed. Marrs, II, 259.
[20] In 'Detached Thoughts on Books and Reading', Elia describes himself conspicuously reading *Hamlet* 'by the lamp-light' in an octavo volume outside Covent Garden Theatre while waiting to see Master Betty perform the role. On Lamb's reading practices and his representations of reading, see Lee Erickson, 'Charles Lamb on Romantic Reading and Social Decorum', *The Wordsworth Circle*, 39.3 (2008), 79–85.

coffee houses and taverns, as well as more heterosocial spaces such as circulating libraries and assembly rooms, many of which had news rooms, offered spaces in which reading could be conducted outside the home and in the company of others.[21] In such contexts, the distinction between reading for the purposes of utility and reading for leisure (or as a pretext for meeting others, or for not reading at all – dozing over a newspaper or the latest Scott novel, for example) was often obscured. With the development of the new Institutions of the first decade of the nineteenth century and the growth of club libraries, opportunities for male homosocial reading, especially in the metropolis, expanded significantly. The provision of libraries and facilities for reading were highlighted in commentary on the new Institutions, the *Gentleman's Magazine* reporting in 1805 that the three objects of the London Institution were (1) 'a library, to contain every work of intrinsic value'; (2) 'reading-rooms for the daily papers, periodical publications, interesting pamphlets, and foreign journals'; and (3) 'a lecture-room' for 'lectures and experiments'.[22] In their libraries of books, newspapers, periodicals, and pamphlets from both England and abroad, the Institutions were responding to the increase of print information in the 1790s and after, as well as to the expense of books, even for the privileged.[23] The Institutions acted as filters or clearing houses of knowledge, in contrast to the initial conception of the British Museum as a repository, part of how, as Jon Klancher observes, they 'became adept at cross-hatching the mediatic with the institutional'.[24] Not only did the Institutions work in tandem with the periodical press, which publicised and commented on them, but they also performed a similar mediatory role to the periodical press by assembling, disseminating, and regulating access to reading matter of all kinds. Such a role was particularly significant at a time of national crisis such as the early 1800s when the threat from

---

[21] Scholarship on 'reading communities' in Britain and Ireland – e.g. book clubs, circulating libraries, subscription libraries, reading societies, and those constituted by Institutions, Lit and Phil societies, and Mechanics' Institutes – is growing: there is still, however, relatively limited work on spaces for public reading such as designated 'reading rooms' within these spaces or how leisure facilities such as assembly rooms facilitated public reading. See e.g. Markman Ellis, 'Coffee-house Libraries in Mid-Eighteenth-Century London', *The Library*, 7th ser., 10.1 (2009), 3–40; James Raven, 'Libraries for Sociability: The Advance of the Subscription Library', in *The Cambridge History of Libraries in Britain and Ireland, vol. 2: 1640–1850*, ed. by Giles Mandelbrote and K. A. Manley (Cambridge: Cambridge University Press, 2006), pp. 239–63; Ina Ferris, 'Recovering the Country Book Club', in *Sociable Places: Locating Culture in Romantic-Period Britain*, ed. by Kevin Gilmartin (Cambridge: Cambridge University Press, 2017), pp. 33–50.

[22] 'New Institutions', *Gentleman's Magazine*, 75 (August 1805), p. 747.

[23] On the expense of books, see William St Clair, *The Reading Nation in the Romantic Period* (Cambridge: Cambridge University Press, 2004).

[24] Klancher, p. 6.

Napoleon was pressing: in 1805 the *Gentleman's Magazine* commented that the London and other Institutions of the period signalled to 'foreigners' 'the voluntary acts of a free people' rather than 'glittering appendages of despotism'.[25]

The British Museum differed from the Institutions in being theoretically free to the public, though access, as we have seen, was strictly controlled and limited. Lamb was able to use the library partly because of his friendship with Godwin but also because he did not have to pay. His experience contrasts with that of Thomas Moore, who was both a British Museum ticket holder and a subscriber to the British Institution. Moore had 'a long spell of research' one morning in the British Museum in 1834, after which he went to the British Institution and 'read for two hours'.[26] Moore differentiates between the British Museum as a place for 'research' and reading at the British Institution as more informal, in a similar way to Henry Crabb Robinson's characterisation of his reading at the Surrey Institution as 'lounging'. In 1818, Crabb Robinson 'lounged at the Surrey Institution till it was time to go to Covent Garden Theatre', suggesting that the Surrey functioned for him as a de facto club.[27] On a visit to the Lambs at Enfield in 1829, he took the opportunity to 'lounge' with his friends' books: 'I spent the whole of the day with him and his sister, without going out of the house. ... I had plenty of books to lounge over. I read Brougham's Introduction to the Library of Useful Knowledge.'[28] The accessibility of the Lambs' books to Crabb Robinson suggests firstly how important books and reading were to the domestic life of the Lambs, and secondly how 'lounging' with books conflated the more public space of the Surrey with book-reading practices in the domestic sphere. As a professed man of letters, Crabb Robinson could in effect 'lounge' anywhere with books: the denizens of the Surrey Institution, Charles and Mary Lamb, and the pages of his diary were the necessary witnesses to this performance. As Lamb had remarked to Manning in 1808, 'who knows that you *do* read?'. Making one's reading visible as an object of knowledge as well as a cultural practice was becoming increasingly important to the Romantic period

---

[25] 'New Institutions', p. 747.
[26] Thomas Moore, *The Journal of Thomas Moore, vol. 4: 1831–1835*, ed. by Wilfred S. Dowden (Cranbury: Associated University Presses, 1987), p. 1620.
[27] Henry Crabb Robinson, *Diary, Reminiscences, and Correspondence*, 3 vols (London: Macmillan, 1869), II, 95. For the sociability of the Institutions linked with lecturing, see Gillian Russell, 'Spouters or Washerwomen: The Sociability of Romantic Lecturing', in *Romantic Sociability: Social Networks and Literary Culture in Britain, 1770–1840*, ed. by Gillian Russell and Clara Tuite (Cambridge: Cambridge University Press, 2002), pp. 123–44.
[28] Crabb Robinson, *Diary*, II, 415.

literary sphere, a visibility manifested in spaces such as the British Museum and the Institutions, and in discursive contexts, such as the periodical press, letters, and diaries.

At one end of the spectrum of these reading practices was Thomas Moore's idea of the British Museum library as a place of 'research'. The *OED* ascribes the earliest example of the use of 'research', meaning 'investigation undertaken in order to obtain material for a book, article, thesis, etc.', to 1818, specifically in a letter from Robert Southey to John Taylor Coleridge, the nephew of S. T. Coleridge. Southey advised the young man that it was now possible to establish a career as a professional writer, which he opined was a better guarantee of future happiness than marrying for money. 'The most profitable line of composition', he claimed, was reviewing, while translation was 'of all literary labours the worst paid'.[29] Biography was 'the most likely to succeed; and, with the London libraries at hand, the research for it would be rather pleasurable than toilsome'.[30] By 'London libraries', Southey was referring to the libraries of the Institutions as well as the British Museum, highlighting the significance of an emerging infrastructure for literary sociability and networking that could align 'pleasure' with 'toil'.

The research commended by Southey and practiced by Thomas Moore at the British Museum used the resources of these institutions to create 'product' – histories, biographies, translations, editions – to be sold in the literary marketplace. In this sense, the British Museum was not just a repository or even a trading 'depôt' for the goods of knowledge, but also a resource or mine of raw material that could be repurposed or remediated in other genres and formats. The kind of 'literary labour' signified by Southey's idea of 'research' was distinct from the conventional view of 'antiquarian research' as conducted for its own sake by scholars of independent means who focused on the minute, the anecdotal, and the recondite rather than more scientific systems of knowledge. Exponents of antiquarian research were notable for their carelessness with the boundaries of time, both in the scope of their studies and their freedom to conduct them, unconstrained by opening hours. The 'researches' of Moore, Godwin, and Lamb were timebound, not only by the circumstances of employment elsewhere, as in Lamb's case, but also by the need to produce

---

[29] On the wages for reviewing for the quarterlies, see Matthew Sangster, *Living as an Author in the Romantic Period* (Cham: Palgrave Macmillan, 2021), pp. 129–35, 249–50.
[30] Robert Southey, *The Life and Correspondence of Robert Southey*, 6 vols (London: Longman, Green, Brown, and Longmans, 1850), IV, 331–32.

a literary work to sell, which would both enhance their literary reputation and remunerate them.

The late Romantic period is therefore significant for laying the groundwork for the identification of reading in public in an institutionalised setting as 'research', distinct from, though inevitably contingent on, reading for casual information, for pleasure, or simply for lounging. This development represented a refinement of what Vicesimus Knox, in 1788, had defined as the three divisions of readers: the professional, the philosophical, and the miscellaneous. Professional readers were those who 'read either to qualify for the assumption of a profession, or to regulate the conduct and exercise of one readily assumed'; 'philosophical readers' were those dedicated to 'improvements in science', who would 'come forth at last as Bacons, Boyles, Lockes and Newtons', while 'miscellaneous readers', the most numerous, consisted of 'all conditions, of the young and the old, the gentleman and the merchant, the soldier, the mariner, the subordinate practitioner in medicine and law . . . the philosopher and professor, in their leisure; and lastly though not the least numerous and important, of the *ladies*'.[31] In gaining a reader's ticket to the British Museum, Godwin and Lamb were acting primarily as 'philosophical' readers in search of truth but also as readers working 'to qualify for the assumption of [a] profession', that of authorship, in service of the third category of reader, the miscellaneous readers of 'all conditions' for whom they were writing.

Lamb's career exemplifies how the classification of both reading and readers, a process of distinction in a Bourdeauvian sense, was still inchoate in the early decades of the nineteenth century. Lamb's own bookishness, conflating and confusing Knox's categorisation of readers and definitions of reading was supposed to be for, was one way in which this inchoateness was manifested. Ina Ferris has highlighted Lamb as exemplifying a cultural category that has lost its currency – 'the bookman' – that is, someone 'designating a hinge figure in contentious relation to a literary sphere intent on separating itself from the wider culture of books'.[32] The figure of the bookman and 'the wider culture of books' represented the vital connection between books as material objects, on the one hand, and as vehicles for meaning and aesthetic value, on the other, as well as practices associated with that connection – such as book-collecting, the nascent discipline of bibliography, the organisation of libraries, institutions, and discourses of

---

[31] Vicesimus Knox, *Winter Evenings: Or Lucubrations on Life and Letters*, 3 vols (London: Charles Dilly, 1788), I, 74–75.
[32] Ina Ferris, *Book-Men, Book-Clubs and the Romantic Literary Sphere* (Basingstoke: Palgrave, 2015), pp. 1–2.

criticism in the periodicals, as well as more informal, personal modes of book talk, book circulation, and sociability (including lounging with books). This connection also sometimes extended to an excess of bookish affect, what Ina Ferris calls the queer 'dandiacal register' of 'book fancy', or what Jon Klancher characterises as the 'wild bibliography' of the bibliomaniacs, something that was both formative in the discipline of literary studies and what it was ultimately compelled to disavow.[33] As Klancher memorably states, in considering 'wild bibliography' we can identify 'new orders of book knowledge that carve out histories and futures for the humanities' amidst 'the cut-ups of the crazed bibliophiles, who tell a truth unintelligible to the same orders of emerging knowledge'.[34]

Lamb played an important role in the Romantic period and after in promoting bookishness, what Denise Gigante terms the 'living aesthetic' of books, as worthy of cultural attention.[35] His was the poor man's bookishness, far from the ostentation of the aristocratic bibliomaniac, though sharing the same investments in the pleasure of acquisition and possession, as shown by his excitement in acting as a book-broker for Wordsworth in 1804. The publication of Thomas Noon Talfourd's *Letters of Charles Lamb, with a Sketch of His Life* in 1837, just three years after Lamb's death, amplified his reputation with reference to his letters, making public the now often quoted letter to Wordsworth of 1801, in which Lamb declares his preference for London over the Lake District. Books feature in that letter in the form of Lamb's celebration of book sociability out of doors: 'the print-shops, the old book-stalls, parsons cheapening books'.[36] Books in Lamb's life were always on the move – precious folios carried from Covent Garden to Islington, as he recounts in the essay 'Old China'; disappearing, sometimes forever, into the collections of friends such as Coleridge; or literally flying through the air when he was disposing of unwanted presentation volumes.[37]

---

[33] Ferris, *Book-Men*, p. 5; Klancher, p. 88.   [34] Klancher, p. 99.
[35] Denise Gigante, 'On Book-Borrowing: Forming Part of Literary History Seen from the Perspective of a Book from Charles Lamb's Library', *Studies in Romanticism*, 55.3 (2016), 369–91 (p. 388).
[36] Thomas Noon Talfourd, *The Letters of Charles Lamb, with a Sketch of His Life*, 2 vols (London: Edward Moxon, 1837), I, 213, 214. See also the edition of the letter in Lamb, *Letters*, ed. Marrs, I, 267. On the Lamb's library, see E. V. Lucas's 'Appendix III: Charles Lamb's Books' to his *The Life of Charles Lamb*, vol. 7, 2nd edn (London: Methuen, 1905), pp. 304–26. For the dispersal of the library after Lamb's death, see Joseph Rosenblum, 'Lost Lambs; or, the Dispersal of Charles Lamb's Library: An Essay in Reconstruction', *The Charles Lamb Bulletin*, new ser., 86 (April 1994), 47–55.
[37] Lamb's Enfield neighbour Thomas Westwood reported that 'A Leigh Hunt would come skimming to my feet through the branches of the apple trees ... or a Bernard Barton would be rolled downstairs after me from the library-door': W. Carew Hazlitt, *Mary and Charles Lamb: Poems, Letters, and Remains* (New York: Scribner, Welford and Armstrong, 1874), p. 211.

For his contemporaries, Lamb's bookishness was a criterion by which institutions such as the British Museum library could be defined. In an 1823 essay 'My Books', Leigh Hunt wrote that the British Museum was not conducive to literary labour: he hated 'to read in a public place and in strange company. The jealous silence, – the dissatisfied looks of the messengers, the inability to help yourself... with a variety of other jarrings between privacy and publicity, prevent one's settling heartily to work'.[38] Reading in public makes Hunt uncomfortable, self-conscious, and exposed. In contrast, Lamb's library is unaffected, welcoming, and sets Hunt at his ease: 'It has... an handsome contempt for appearance. It looks like what it is, a selection made at precious intervals from the book-stalls; now a Chaucer at nine and twopence; now a Montaigne or a Sir Thomas Brown at two shillings.'[39] Lamb's library, moreover, was arranged according to idiosyncratic notions of book sociability, 'Mr. Southey', according to Leigh Hunt, taking 'his place again with an Radical friend: [while] there Jeremy Collier is at peace with Dryden'.[40] Leigh Hunt's preference for the informality (and catholicity) of Lamb's bookishness over the discomfort of the reading room suggests that Romantic-period writers needed to learn how to adapt to the kind of public space for reading and writing that the British Museum reading room represented: Charles Lamb was a useful 'hinge figure' in which the relationship between 'private' and institutionalised reading could be gauged. In 1805, William Godwin made a case to the librarian that he should be allowed to take books away because reading in public was inimical to 'deep & concentrated attention': 'The majority of the frequenters of such a room will always be persons who read more from a spirit of vague curiosity, & that they may spend their time agreeably to themselves, than from any other motive.'[41] Both Hunt and Godwin seem reluctant to stage themselves as authors in the space of the reading room, where 'jarrings between privacy and publicity' make proper literary 'work' impossible.

Lamb's cultivated bookishness, his careless booklove, would thus seem to be antithetical to the ideals of cultural authority and stability associated with a national library.[42] Though Henry Crabb Robinson permitted himself to 'lounge' with the Lambs' books, he described them as 'finest

---

[38] Leigh Hunt, 'My Books', *The Literary Examiner*, 1 (5 July 1823), 1–6 (p. 2).   [39] Hunt, p. 3.
[40] Hunt, p. 3.
[41] William Godwin, *The Letters of William Godwin*, vol. 2, ed. by Pamela Clemit (Oxford: Oxford University Press, 2014), p. 355.
[42] On Lamb and book love, see Deidre Lynch, *Loving Literature: A Cultural History* (Chicago: University of Chicago Press, 2015), pp. 120–23.

collection of shabby books I ever saw . . . filthy copies, which a delicate man would really hesitate touching'.[43] Lamb's tattered and 'filthy' volumes never lost their connection with the street bookstall, the ultimate free library of the period where people could read, and browse among (or even steal) books that were open to all weathers, in contrast to the security and dignity of the books within the walls of Montagu House.[44]

However, the British Museum library of the early decades of the nineteenth century was not as stable or authoritative as we might suppose: it was itself experiencing the inchoateness and flux that characterised print and literary spheres as a whole in this period. The lack of a union catalogue, for example, meant that it was difficult to know what books the Museum actually held. In 1805, Godwin wrote to the Assistant Keeper of Printed Books, Henry Ellis, to ask if he could help him with a query about French law in the *Code Criminelle* which he could not locate in the British Museum catalogue. Ellis helpfully suggested some relevant titles that the Museum held, adding that if Godwin would 'take the pains to call at any time during the Museum hours', he would 'readily show' [him] 'everything' they had 'on the subject'.[45] The library also underwent significant upheaval between 1804 and 1826, both in terms of content and its physical structure. The donation to the nation of the library of George III in 1823 led to the building of a new east wing to house it, part of the construction of a new museum building, designed by Robert Smirke, that would eventually replace the increasingly decrepit Montagu House. Two new reading rooms accommodating up to 120 people were included in the new east wing in order to meet a growing demand, opening in mid-1826. According to Harris, the number of new readers increased tenfold between 1805 and 1827.[46]

The construction of these rooms signified a change in the kind of reading being undertaken there and by whom, leading to debates in the newspaper and periodical press about the purpose of the library as a publicly funded institution, and also, implicitly, of the new phenomenon of 'institutionalised' reading more generally. A persistent theme in this commentary was how the library's opening hours restricted access to the ever-widening reading public, the 'miscellaneous readers' of 'all conditions', as Knox had categorised them in 1788. A writer to the *London Medical and Physical Journal* in 1819 expressed a 'feeling of shame' that

---

[43] E.V. Lucas, *The Life of Charles Lamb*, 2 vols (London: Methuen, 1905), II, 121.
[44] See the entry on 'Bookstalls' in Prance, pp. 34–35.   [45] Godwin, *Letters*, II, 335, fn. 3.
[46] Harris, p. 54; see also Robert Cowtan, *Memories of the British Museum* (London: Richard Bentley, 1872), p. 205.

the British Museum, as 'the only public library in London', was 'entered with some difficulty, and is rather suited to antiquarian research than to the purposes of general study' (indicating that antiquarian research was being distinguished from 'general study').[47] A letter to the *Times*, reprinted in the *Examiner* in 1825, made a specific case for attornies' clerks with 'serious duties to perform' who needed access to information: 'When, then, are they to acquire this? . . . Institutions are daily rising, but which of them will delay its sittings to accommodate the attorney's clerk?'[48] Also in 1825, the *London Magazine*, in which Lamb's Elia essays appeared, and with which he was closely associated, highlighted the 'inutility' of the library's opening hours of ten to four:

> These are the hours of actual business in the metropolis – the marrow of the day which none but professed authors or loungers can give to reading. To the immense number of individuals who, being engaged in the middle of the day, might beneficially pursue their studies in the morning or evening, the great building in Russel-street is a blank – rubbish – a heap of bricks and mortar.[49]

Sometimes the 'loungers' of the reading room were too much for the 'professed authors'. Using the 'nom de plume' of 'Tom Hearne', referring to the notable antiquarian, a writer to the *Gentleman's Magazine* complained in winter 1822 about the space around the reading room fire being taken up by 'Bond-street Dandies, enveloped in fur and lamb's wool' and 'tall school-boys, at home for the holydays, with dictionaries on their laps, and *Virgils* in their hands!' 'The Reading-room ought not to be used merely as a library at a watering place', humphed 'Tom Hearne', 'notwithstanding ignorant young men may so conduct themselves'.[50]

By 1837, however, the atmosphere of the reading room and the kind of work done within it had been transformed. In an essay in the *Metropolitan*, James Grant (1802–79) described the reading room as identified primarily with 'literary men' and the occasional woman. It was a 'literary workshop' or 'manufactory', a hive of intellectual labour where individuals worked in collective immersion in their solitary endeavours.[51] Though Grant commended the support of the British Museum by 'public money', he does not disguise the pointlessness of much of the work conducted there due to the

---

[47] *London Medical and Physical Journal*, 41.243 (May 1819), p. 371.
[48] 'Attornies' Clerks', *Examiner* (4 December 1825), p. 771.
[49] 'The Library of the British Museum', *London Magazine*, new ser., 3 (1825), 533–36 (p. 534).
[50] *Gentleman's Magazine*, 92 (1822), p. 112.
[51] [James Grant], 'The British Museum', *The Metropolitan*, 20 (1837), 337–48 (p. 339).

failure to find publishers, readers, or sometimes simply an answer to a research query. The dogged single-mindedness of the literary researcher was embodied above all for Grant by the women of the reading room whose 'moral fortitude', he claimed, was greater than that of their fellow male readers.[52] Forever 'hoping against hope' that they might find success, these women turned up at the Museum every day, 'living on little better than chameleon's fare'.[53] 'Little do the readers of works requiring research know', Grant writes, 'what amount of labour is sometimes required before the authors have succeeded in ascertaining or clearing up a certain point . . . People talk of manual labour: it is not half so exhausting or oppressive as this'.[54] Within the space of a few decades then, a new kind of institutionalised reading as a form of literary labour, with implications for the social status of those undertaking it, had become visible, with profound implications for the development of the literary sphere in the Victorian period – Grant's essay anticipates the depiction of the drudgery of a literary career in George Gissing's *New Grub Street*. It differs remarkably from Hunt and Godwin's concerns about the British Museum library as not being conducive to 'work'.

Charles Lamb's return to the British Museum library in 1826, nearly twenty years after he had last spent his holidays working there, therefore occurred in the midst of an alteration in the character of the library and a wider debate about its utility as a public institution. In 1826, Lamb was established as the celebrated 'Elia', no longer constrained by his hours of work at the East India House, from which he retired in March 1825. A month after his retirement, 'The Superannuated Man' was published in the *London Magazine*, setting forth his condition as living in a new configuration of time: 'I am in no hurry. Having all holidays, I am as though I had none.' Even his habits of reading had changed: 'I do *not* read in that violent measure, with which, having no Time but my own but candlelight Time, I used to weary out my head and eye-sight in by-gone winters.'[55] However, a continuity with his former life at the East India House persisted in his old habits of book browsing: 'I digress into Soho, to explore a book-stall. Methinks I have been thirty years a collector. There is nothing new nor strange in it.'[56]

Lamb's return to the British Museum library in 1826 was sponsored by his friend, the Dante scholar Henry Francis Cary, whom Lamb had known

---

[52] [Grant], pp. 346, 344.   [53] [Grant], p. 345.   [54] [Grant], pp. 345, 346.
[55] Charles Lamb, 'The Superannuated Man', *London Magazine*, new ser., 2 (1825), 67–71 (p. 70).
[56] Charles Lamb, 'The Superannuated Man No. II', *London Magazine*, new ser., 2 (1825), 71–73 (p. 71).

from about 1819–20. Cary was appointed assistant keeper of the department of printed books in June 1826 and both Charles and Mary Lamb socialised in Cary's apartments at the Museum, very close to the reading rooms, until Lamb's death in 1834.[57] Whereas in 1807 reading in the British Museum had been a time of 'holyday', Lamb's period of work there in 1826–7 represented a return to the routine of East India House, in spite of the freedom celebrated, albeit ambivalently, in 'The Superannuated Man'. In September 1826, he wrote to his friend Bernard Barton that the reading room was 'a sort of Office to me; hours, 10 to 4, the same. It does me good. Man must have regular occupation, that has been used to it'.[58]

Lamb's 'course of reading', as he described it to Barton, was a resumption of the work he had undertaken in 1807 for the *Specimens*, based in one of the Museum's foundational collections, the 'Garrick Plays'.[59] Compiled by the actor David Garrick and bequeathed to the Museum after his death in 1779, the 'Garrick Plays' consisted of over 1,300 items of rare early modern drama, only a small part of which Lamb had been able to 'mine' for the *Specimens*, due largely to time constraints.[60] The plays that he encountered in his periods in the reading room were still primarily identified as Garrick's personal collection (in spite of disposals and interpolations), thus bearing a connection with the theatre and also intersecting with Lamb's similar collecting interests in plays and playwrights that had been neglected or forgotten. Lamb was thus visiting a library within a library in a topological sense, socialising with Garrick's books, in other words, meaning that his own 'shabby' playbooks were metaphorically visiting the British Museum with him.

Lamb's goal was not a more comprehensive selection of the texts in the Garrick Plays that would supplement the *Specimens*. Instead, in the form of what he called 'mere after-gleanings', he submitted extracts from the plays and brief comments on them as a weekly column for William Hone's *The Table Book*, published between January and December 1827.[61] Like Cary, Hone belonged to the network of friends associated with the penultimate decade of Lamb's career. They first met in 1819 and Lamb later contributed to Hone's *Every-Day Book*, which Hone dedicated to him. Lamb offered

---

[57] Prance, p. 55.
[58] Charles Lamb, *The Letters of Charles and Mary Lamb*, ed. by E. V. Lucas (London: J. M. Dent and Methuen, 1935), III, 61.
[59] Lamb, *Letters*, ed. Lucas, III, 61.
[60] On the Garrick Plays, see George M. Kahrl (with Dorothy Anderson), *The Garrick Collection of Old English Plays* (London: British Library, 1982).
[61] Lamb, *Letters*, ed. Lucas, III, 62.

Colebrooke Cottage for Hone's use in the summer of 1825, while the Lambs were at Enfield, describing for him where he could find '*Cibber's Apology*, octavo, facing the window': he also tried to support Hone after he was imprisoned for debt in the King's Bench Prison in 1826.[62] In 1827, Lamb told Bernard Barton that he was 'giving the fruit of [his] Old Play reading at the Museum to Hone, who sets forth a portion weekly in the Table Book'.[63] In a letter to Hone that was printed as an introduction to the *Table Book*, Lamb asked him to 'Imagine the luxury of one like me ... of sitting in the princely apartments, for such they are, of poor condemned Montagu house, which I predict will not speedily be followed by a handsomer, and culling at will the flower of some thousand Dramas. It is like having the range of a Nobleman's Library, with the Librarian to your friend.'[64] (As Cary, the assistant keeper of printed books, was Lamb's friend, the latter was literally the case.)

Lamb's version of the British Museum library was not that which figured in contemporary debates about its utility, nor does it resemble the 'literary manufactory' of Grant, but rather harks back to what Mary Lamb had envisaged for him – the support of a 'good old collector' whose loans of rare books would have enabled Charles to work, privately, at home. Lamb elaborates this prospect as he contemplates reading in the 'princely apartments' of old Montagu House, in a fantastic scene of intimacy with books and his own private enjoyment of an imaginary patron's largesse. One of the luxuries of being a 'superannuated' man in 1826 was that Lamb could replicate the timetable of the working day without being bound to it. Similarly, he could afford to circumvent a literary economy whereby writers were labourers in the mine of knowledge, producing goods to be sold in the marketplace, as he had done with the *Specimens* in 1808, by donating his 'after-gleanings' to Hone, moreover, in a format – cheap sixpenny weekly sheets – that was as different as it was possible to be from the single-authored codex-form book. Outside the East India Company and the immediate pressure of writing for money, Lamb could experience an exceptional independence and reading as a kind of 'jouissance': 'I read without order of time', he wrote to Hone and indirectly the readers of the *Table Book*: 'I am a poor hand at dates; and for any biography of the Dramatists, I must refer to writers who are more skilful in such matters. My business is with their poetry only.'[65]

---

[62] Lamb, *Letters*, ed. Lucas, III, 13; Prance, p. 153. [63] Lamb, *Letters*, ed. Lucas, III, 75.
[64] Lamb, *Letters*, ed. Lucas, III, 62. [65] Lamb, *Letters*, ed. Lucas, III, 62.

Lamb's exceptionalism in this second period as a reader in the British Museum library becomes clear in the context of the rapidly changing and often shifting identities of the public reader that the reading room housed and enabled in the first three decades of the nineteenth century: the antiquarian, the lounger, 'the professed author', the researcher, the leisure reader passing the time, the aspiring attorney's clerk or medical man, the female scholar of sterling 'fortitude'. These are all prototypes of the professional reader of today who occupies the reading rooms of the British Library at St Pancras, such as the humanities academic subject to the time pressures of the modern university.[66] The emergence of the British Museum library as a key literary institution of Victorian Britain, promoted by the monumental beauty of Panizzi's round reading room, was therefore based in deep-seated anxieties about what literary research was for in the 1820s, anxieties about whether it was sign of privilege or self-indulgent lounging, labour for the good of the nation, a form of anti-work, self-punishing drudgery, or the sometimes perverse labour of booklove, the joy of simply doing it for the sake of it, of spending a brief time in the company of books. The two periods that Lamb spent in the British Museum illustrate some of these tensions: in 1804–7, as someone who could not use the library during the working day, he was anticipating the class of people who in the 1820s and 1830s became a focus of struggle over the meaning of the British Museum as a public institution. In 1826, Lamb did not return to the library as an active 'professed author' like Thomas Moore, though his success as Elia entitled him to such status. Nor was he in solidarity with the attorneys' clerks who did not have access to the library: rather, by imagining himself a lone reader in the vestige of a nobleman's library, and not the modernising institution of the British Museum, Lamb indulged in the fantasy that he did not belong to these categories of reader and the historical developments that they represented. In his arch anachronism, his desire to read without the order of time, and his conferring of his authorial 'name' on a work of cheap, fugitive print, Lamb articulated a resistance to the alienation of labour entailed in the new definition of literary research – whether by the attorney's clerk or those in the 'literary manufactory'. Such a resistance can be seen as 'Romantic' in gesturing to the possibility that the profession of the author could be something other than a job of work, unconstrained by the discipline of time or the need to earn an income. Was the public library a place where

---

[66] In this context, it is appropriate that the portrait of Lamb by Henry Meyer, painted in 1826, should be in the foyer of the Rare Books room in the British Library at St Pancras.

one could momentarily experience the luxury of being truly solitary, truly free, in the company of books, or equally also a place where one experienced the acquisition of knowledge as supremely sociable, a communion with both the living and the dead? What does it matter, ultimately, who knows you *do* read, when the 'business' is with 'the poetry only' (whatever 'the poetry' might be)?

CHAPTER 10

A Disruptive and Dangerous Education and the Wealth of the Nation
The Early Mechanics' Institutes

John Gardner

This chapter examines the formation of mechanics' institutes in the first quarter of the nineteenth century and how members and governors clashed, creating new breakaway institutions. These institutes fought to include literary and historical studies despite opposition from bodies such as sections of the established Church. I begin by focussing on the foundation of John Anderson's university in Glasgow in 1798, looking specifically at the Mechanics' Class, which was established by George Birkbeck there in 1800, and which split in 1823 (Figure 10.1). I argue that there were three main drivers behind this democratisation of education: free lectures given to workers by the likes of John Anderson, George Birkbeck and Andrew Ure; agitation by workers to set up their own institutes rather than relying on benevolent enlightened individuals giving what they could; and finally the 1819 'tax on knowledge' that came in with the Six Acts. My argument is that the suppression of people in terms of their political agency caused politics more readily to find expression in technical publications and educational institutes. Innovation and demand for education came from those literally at the cutting edge of society: the turners, millers, fitters and millwrights who created and drove scientific and educational progress through practice, improvement and invention. As L. J. Henderson said, these workers, and not theoreticians, were the agents behind Britain's industrial progress: 'until 1850 the steam-engine did more for science than science did for the steam-engine'.[1] The most celebrated engineer of perhaps all time, James Watt, was an inspiration to craft engineers, being, as Eric Robinson and Douglas McKie write, 'largely self-educated'.[2]

Research for this chapter was completed thanks to a grant from the Leverhulme Trust.
[1] L. J. Henderson, quoted in R. J. Forbes, 'Power to 1850', in *A History of Technology*, ed. by Charles Singer and others, 5 vols (Oxford: Oxford University Press, 1958), IV, 148–67 (p. 165).
[2] *Partners in Science: Letters of James Watt and Joseph Black*, ed. by Eric Robinson and Douglas McKie (London: Constable, 1970), p. 4.

Figure 10.1 Mechanics' class ticket from the Andersonian Institution, 1812. Reproduced with thanks to Special Collections at the University of Strathclyde.

There was a notion that giving workers a greater technical education to help understand more about their trades would boost innovation and the wealth of the nation. The period of the literary and philosophical societies and mechanics' institutes was also one during which the majority of modern machine tools were invented.[3] There were demands for a broader education that would allow workers to understand the principles behind the machines they were making. The new mechanics' institutes could also give artisans greater access to wider varieties of literature, and not all of it was judged safe to read.

There had been earlier examples of institutions where the labouring classes could enhance their educational opportunities, such as at Spitalfields Mathematical Society, founded for weavers and shopkeepers to work out problems on slates in 1717. The Manchester Literary and Philosophical Society, founded in 1781, seems to have played a part in sponsoring the College of Arts and Sciences that began providing evening courses for tradesmen from 1783 and carried on for around four sessions.

[3] K. R. Gilbert, 'Machine-Tools', in *History of Technology*, IV, 417–41 (p. 417).

Largely the brainchild of Rational Dissenters, the College was designed for the children of manufacturers.[4] The less-exclusive extra-mural initiative seems to have folded with the College itself after only a few years, partly because of opposition from Anglican members of the Society.[5] A more substantial link between these late eighteenth-century initiatives and mechanics' institutes comes in the figure of the Thomas Garnett, a corresponding member of the Manchester Lit. Phil., whose work as an itinerant lecturer around Manchester and at the Royal Institution is discussed in Chapter 7.

Garnett was appointed as the first Professor of Natural Philosophy at Anderson's Institution in September 1796. Admission to his lectures was expensive at £1/1s., but nearly a thousand people attended, with half the audience made up of women.[6] More significant for the history of mechanics' institutes were the free Saturday evening lectures for workers that George Birkbeck gave in the Institution from 1800. Birkbeck's lectures, which ran for another twenty years under the care of Andrew Ure, were the precursors of a new mechanics' institute, set up in 1823, the first to be initiated by members of the working classes. Thereafter, mechanics' institutes were founded around Britain, but the Scottish example was crucial.[7] By 1850, there were around 120,000 individuals in over 700 institutes in the United Kingdom alone, and the Glasgow institute model was soon adopted around the world.[8]

John Anderson, the founder of Anderson's Institution, was a person of many parts. He served as a Hanoverian officer defending Stirling during the Jacobite Rebellion. In 1753, he became a member of Glasgow's Literary Society, where he lectured on the poet George Buchanan as 'a writer in defence of liberty'.[9] By 1757, he had become Professor of Natural Philosophy at Glasgow University, a post he held until 1796. Benjamin Franklin became a lifelong friend after he met Anderson in 1759 on his first visit to Scotland, renewing their intimacy when he visited Glasgow in 1771. In 1760, Anderson

---

[4] Thomas Barnes, 'A Plan for the Extension and Improvement of Liberal Education in Manchester', *Memoirs of the Literary and Philosophical Society of Manchester*, 2 (1785), 16–29.

[5] See W. V. Farrar, Kathleen R. Farrar, and E. L. Scott, 'The Henrys of Manchester Part 1: Thomas Henry (1734–1816)', *Ambix*, 20.3 (1973), 184–208 (pp. 192–95).

[6] University of Strathclyde Archives, GB 249 OB/1/1/1, Anderson's Institution Minute Book, 1796–1799, Entry for 28 April 1797.

[7] See Mabel Tylecote, *The Mechanics' Institutes of Lancashire and Yorkshire before 1851* (Manchester: Manchester University Press, 1957), p. 18.

[8] J. W. Hudson, *The History of Adult Education in Which is Comprised a Full and Complete History of the Mechanics' Institutions, Athenaeums, Philosophical, Mental and Christian Improvement Societies, Literary Unions, Schools of Design etc. of Great Britain, Ireland, America, etc., etc.* (London: Longman, Brown, Green, 1851), p. vi.

[9] John Butt, *John Anderson's Legacy: The University of Strathclyde and its Antecedents, 1796–1996* (Edinburgh: Tuckwell Press, 1996), p. 11.

published *A Compendium of Experimental Philosophy* and, anticipating his new institute, offered free lectures to skilled workers.[10] Using early steam engines to teach, in 1763 he sent James Watt a Newcomen engine to repair, and a friendly correspondence on mechanics began between them.[11] In 1791, Anderson presented his design for a six-pound field cannon to the French nation, and celebrated when King Louis XVI 'took the oath to the Constitution'.[12] Anderson's time at Glasgow University was eventful. After a tavern fight that resulted in a jug of beer being smashed over Anderson's head by James Moor, the Professor of Greek, Anderson challenged Moor to a duel. Both were fined £20.[13] Moor later assaulted a student with a candlestick and was reprimanded by the university. Nonetheless, he rose to Vice-Rector and later Clerk, keeping his university emoluments even after he resigned his chair. These sorts of incidents give some clue to the motivations behind Anderson's will.

Three days after Anderson died on 13 January 1796, his executors met to discuss the terms of his will, including his wish for a new university to be established in his name.[14] The new university was to have the same schools as Glasgow University with Colleges of Arts, Medicine, Law and Theology, although the Law and Theology colleges never got off the ground, partly because there were insufficient funds to fulfil the founder's vision.[15] The will stipulated that the university should have thirty-six named professors, but Anderson's deep distrust of his former employer dictated that no person connected with the University of Glasgow could be appointed: 'The Professors in this University shall not be permitted, as in some other Colleges, to be Drones, or Triflers, Drunkards, or negligent of their duty.'[16] Although Anderson seems to have hated Glasgow University with the ferocity that only an employee could, his Institution's 1796–7 session followed the model of his previous lectures closely, with the exception that the audience was also open to women.[17] A few years into the life of the new university, Garnett approached the Quaker George Birkbeck, who had been lecturing at the Sunday Society in Birmingham, to take up the post of Professor of Chemistry and Natural Philosophy. Supported by John Playfair and Dugald Stewart, who had taught both Birkbeck and

---

[10] Butt, p. 6. [11] Butt, p. 4.
[12] *Glasgow Mechanics' Magazine*, vol. 3 (Glasgow: M'Phun, 1825), p. viii.
[13] Butt, p. 5.
[14] Anderson's Institution Minute Book, 1796–1799, p. 10. Anderson's Institution became Anderson's University in 1828.
[15] See Thomas Kelly, *George Birkbeck, Pioneer of Adult Education* (Liverpool: Liverpool University Press, 1957), p. 25.
[16] Anderson's Institution Minute Book, 1796–1799, p. 11.   [17] Kelly, p. 25.

Garnett at Edinburgh University, Birkbeck took up his post in November 1799.[18]

After his election, it became apparent there was no money to pay Birkbeck. The minute book entry for 21 June 1800 thanks him 'for the handsome manner in which he conducted himself, in not only lecturing gratis this last session, but also proposing to defray out of the proceeds of next session'.[19] On starting at Anderson's Institution, Birkbeck found himself scouring the workshops of Glasgow for new suppliers of the apparatus he needed for his teaching. From these journeys he observed: 'I had frequent opportunities of observing the intelligent curiosity of the "unwashed artificers", to whose mechanical skill I was often obliged to have recourse'.[20] Setting a model of a centrifugal pump in motion, Birkbeck realised that despite their thirst for knowledge, these skilled workers found 'the avenues to science barred against them because they are poor'.[21] He began delivering his free Saturday night lectures in the autumn of 1800. The first lecture attracted an audience of 75 men, the second 200 and the third 300. When attendance reached 500 at the fourth, people had to be turned away.[22] Birkbeck believed that no detractor could 'rob me of the gratification, which to the last hour of my conscious existence, I shall derive from the part which I have taken in the education of the working classes'.[23] The arrangement lasted only two years as the Institution's managers brought in a 5s. fee, although it was reduced to 2s. 6d. after Birkbeck intervened.[24] Despite the great popularity of the lectures, the minute books show that the Institution was in over £200 of debt to Birkbeck by 1803.[25] The university authorities tried to get Birkbeck to drum up more custom and return earlier in the summer to attract more paying students to lectures that were advertised in the *Glasgow Courier* and *Glasgow Advertiser*. Birkbeck told the Institution that he was not 'able to discover any alteration or addition having the apparent advantage of rendering the Lectures more attractive, and consequently more productive', also revealing that he was thinking about leaving because 'the institution cannot afford a very considerable remuneration to the Professor'.[26] He resigned in August 1803,

---

[18] *Scots Mechanics Magazine*, 1 (January 1825), p. 4.
[19] University of Strathclyde Archives, GB 249 OB/1/1/2, Minutes of Anderson's College, 1799–1810, p. 12.
[20] *Mechanics' Magazine, Museum, Register, Journal and Gazette*, 1.12 (15 November 1823), p. 17.
[21] *Mechanics' Magazine*, 1.12 (15 November 1823), p. 17.
[22] Forbes Winslow, *Physic and Physicians: A Medical Sketch Book*, 2 vols (London: Longman, 1839), p. 311.
[23] Cited in Kelly, p. 32.   [24] Kelly, p. 33.   [25] Minutes of Anderson's College, 1799–1810, p. 44.
[26] Minutes of Anderson's College, 1799–1810, p. 59.

and the university immediately advertised for a new professor, boasting it possessed 'the most complete apparatus in Britain'.[27] Birkbeck's replacement, Andrew Ure, lasted more than twenty years at Anderson's Institution and arguably made a greater contribution to the success of the Mechanics' Class. However, Ure also helped create a fracture in the composition of the Class that resulted in the formation of the Glasgow Mechanics' Institute in 1823.

Ure continued Birkbeck's Saturday night lectures, but his surviving reputation has been tarnished for many scholars by his enthusiasm for factories.[28] Karl Marx famously dismissed Ure as 'the Pindar of the automatic factory' in *Capital* for his defence of the moral order of the factory in *The Philosophy of Manufactures*.[29] Nevertheless, the evidence in the Andersonian minute books is of someone warmly committed to Anderson's Institution. Ure spent a deal of his own money and time in advocating for improvements to the Mechanics' Class. After Birkbeck's departure, Ure tactfully, and over some time, managed to persuade the Institution's governors that a library was needed for the mechanics and even paid for the furniture himself. In 1805, Ure fitted gas lighting to the lecture theatre, which was said to be the first time this lighting had been seen in Glasgow. After its foundation in 1817, the Glasgow Gas Light Company supplied Ure's theatre with gas for free as a reward for this innovation.[30] Ure also inspired other educators such as Baron Charles Dupin, who met Ure in 1818 and later founded the École des Arts et Métiers in Paris in 1825 on the model of the Andersonian. Ure tried to encourage the young to attend his classes. By 1823, for every 100 tickets sold to Ure's Mechanics' Class five apprentices over the age of fourteen went free.

Ure became famous enough to find his way Byron's *Don Juan* after conducting experiments on the corpse of hanged murderer, Matthew Clydesdale, in Glasgow on 4 November 1818. To reanimate the corpse, Ure used his 270 plate galvanic battery, which was almost as powerful as the one at the Royal Institution.[31] In a talk that was read at the Glasgow Literary Society on 10 December 1818, Ure described how he, like

---

[27] Minutes of Anderson's College, 1799–1810, pp. 65, 71.   [28] Butt, p. 35.
[29] Karl Marx, 'Section 4: The Factory', in *Capital: A Critique of Political Economy*, trans. by Ben Fowkes, 2 vols (London: Penguin, 1990), I, 339.
[30] University of Strathclyde Archives, GB 249 OB/1/1/3, Minutes of Anderson's College, 1811–1830, p. 300.
[31] W. V. Farrar, 'Andrew Ure, F. R. S., and the Philosophy of Manufactures', *Notes and Records of the Royal Society of London*, 27.2 (February 1973), 299–324 (p. 307).

a playwright, reanimated Clydesdale after he had been cut down from the gallows, 'hideous smiles passed over the murderer's face, surpassing far the wildest representations of Fuseli or a Kean'.[32] Byron noted drily that 'galvanism has set some corpses grinning'.[33] On the basis of the incident, Edwin Morgan called Ure 'the Glasgow Frankenstein' in his poem '1818'.[34] Ure's experiment occurred a few months after the publication of Mary Shelley's book, and he is reminiscent of Victor when he claims that if he had continued with Clydesdale, 'there is a probability that life might have been restored. This event, however little desirable with a murderer, and perhaps contrary to law ... would have been highly honourable and useful to science'.[35] This kind of sensationalism found its way into later mechanics' institute exhibitions, such as at Leeds, where it was advertised that 'Mr Potts announced that next Tuesday he shall deliver a lecture on Galvanism, and though he might not have an executed criminal to operate upon, yet he hoped to be able to procure some animal of sufficient size'.[36] Later mechanics' institutes held exhibitions that were designed to amaze the public and encourage membership. Like some elaborate university open day, they would publicise their institutions with exhibits like the acoustic 'Invisible Girl', where a girl appeared to be trapped in a steel ball, when in reality she was in another room.[37]

The Andersonian minute books confirm that classes contained a significant proportion of women who wanted a better education in the Sciences and Arts. Ure was proud that his class was 'attended by Ladies and Gentlemen, the average number of Auditors, being about Four hundred'.[38] Even before the Saturday night Mechanics' Class started, Anderson had stipulated that women would be taught at his new university in a course on Experimental Philosophy, and another on Experimental Physics, to be known as the Ladies Course of Physical Lectures.[39] Anderson instructed

[32] Andrew Ure, 'Dr Ure's Account of Experiments on the Body of a Criminal Immediately after Execution', *Quarterly Society Journal*, 6 (1819), 283–94 (p. 290). For more on the Glasgow Literary Society, see Thomas Atkinson, *Sketch of the Origin and Progress of the Literary and Commercial Society of Glasgow* (Glasgow: [n. pub.], 1831), held in University of Glasgow Archives and Special Collections, Sp Coll Mu22-b.25.
[33] Lord Byron, *Don Juan* (London: Davison, 1820), I, CXXX (p. 68).
[34] Edwin Morgan, '1818', in *Virtual and Other Realities* (Manchester: Carcanet, 1997), pp. 54–55.
[35] Ure, p. 292.
[36] *Journal of Leeds Polytechnic Exhibition*, 30 June 1845. Cited in *The Steam Intellect Societies: Essays on Culture, Education and Industry, c.1820–1914*, ed. by Ian Inkster (Nottingham: University of Nottingham, 1985), p. 28.
[37] See Alexander Jamieson, *A Dictionary of Mechanical Science*, 2 vols (London: Fisher, 1817), I, 9.
[38] Minutes of Anderson's College, 1799–1810, 21 March 1806, p. 107.
[39] See Jon Mee, '"Some Mode Less Revolting to Their Delicacy": Women's Institutional Space in the Transpennine Enlightenment', *Journal for Eighteenth-Century Studies*, 24.4 (2019), 541–56.

that the 'intention of this Course of Lectures is, that the Ladies in Glasgow, may have an opportunity for a small sum ... of being at several of these Courses of lectures ... as will make them the most accomplished Ladies in Europe'. There was no bar on the class of people allowed other than 'no men may be admitted who are disorderly, talkative, ill-bred, or intoxicated; and no women that are giddy or incorrect in their manners'.[40] At the Manchester Mechanics' Institution in 1839 women seem to have made up around 20 per cent of the audience.[41] Mechanics' institutes provided women with a post-school education that vied with that offered by universities, which were largely closed to women until the twentieth century. By 1851, there were 5,710 women and 55,239 men attending mechanics' institutes in England and Wales.[42] Harriet Martineau felt 'more respect and affection for the studies which are going forward within a Mechanical Institution than for a university, or any other place, where intellectual luxury was reserved to pamper the few while the many starve'.[43] There were two important female-only institutes in Bradford and Huddersfield.[44] In *Mary Barton* (1848), Elizabeth Gaskell has Margaret earn half a sovereign each night she sings at the Manchester Institute. Furthermore, a number of women became teachers at Institutes where they had studied.[45]

Prior to the formation of mechanics' institutes, education for the masses was patchy, with no compulsory schooling until the Elementary Education Act of 1870, which only provided for children aged between five and thirteen. There were of course church schools, dame schools, private schools, charity schools and the schools of industry, but by 1800 it is probable that around 40 per cent of men and 60 per cent of women were illiterate.[46] In the aftermath of post-Waterloo radicalism, Farrar has argued, 'artisans began to look upon education as a right, rather than as a charity for which they should be grateful'.[47] To Ure and the governors of Anderson's Institution, though, it may have seemed ingratitude when on 10 May 1823 the Mechanics' Class carried a resolution to split. Those

---

[40] *Glasgow Mechanics' Magazine*, 2.55 (15 January 1825), p. 414.   [41] Tylecote, p. 264.
[42] June Purvis, *A History of Women's Education in England* (Milton Keynes: Open University, 1991), p. 37.
[43] Harriet Martineau, *The Scholars of Arnside* (London: Fox, 1834), pp. 112–13.
[44] Ruth Watts, *Gender, Power and the Unitarians in England 1760–1860* (London: Routledge, 1998), p. 187.
[45] See Martyn Walker, *The Development of the Mechanics' Institute Movement in Britain and Beyond* (Abingdon: Routledge, 2016), p. 85.
[46] See Amy J. Lloyd, 'Education, Literacy and the Reading Public', in *British Library Newspapers* (Detroit: Gale, 2007) <www.gale.com/intl/essays/amy-j-lloyd-education-literacy-reading-public>.
[47] Farrar, p. 309.

leaving did not want to cut off their noses though, as the minutes of 10 July show that the new class still wanted access to the library that Ure had lobbied hard for. The break had been coming for some time, and, after teaching the class for almost twenty years, Ure played a significant part in its arrival. The year before the rupture some of Ure's pupils wrote to him scornfully about the quality and content of his teaching:

> We have been prompted to write this letter to you, not by a desire to know, whether tea, sugar, or milk, should be first put in our cups; what is the cause of our breath appearing, in a foggy wintry season ... nor indeed, to ask so puerile and contemptible questions, at a period of knowledge and refinement, equall to the present; but by a wish to remind you, in a humble and polite manner, of a promise which you gave in the last session, of giving us a few words concerning Lithography.[48]

That the students' perceived Ure's paternalism is evident, as they charge that he is trying to teach them 'puerile' gentlemanly affectations. After the break, twin mechanics classes existed, with the one Birkbeck set up in 1800 continuing with Ure in parallel with the new Glasgow Mechanics' Institute, where they chose their own lecturers. A split occurred at Manchester for similar reasons. The Manchester Mechanics' Institute started with a library at King Street, under the aegis of members of the Literary and Philosophical Society. From 1825, a lecture series, patronised by wealthy Society members, began with Andrew Wilson from Edinburgh School of Art lecturing on Mechanics and Richard Philips on Chemistry. However, this institution, like Anderson's, broke over the curriculum and the running of the place. A 'New Mechanics' Institute was formed in 1829 led by Rowland Detroisier, and this ran until 1835. Two issues divided the Manchester Institute. According to Eileen Yeo, they were 'the autocratic government of the Institute' and 'the content of the education' designed to 'enable [mechanics] to "get on" in their jobs as rational competitive atoms'.[49] Keeping people in their place and addressing the division of labour seem to have been the issues that led to the break-up. These splits at Glasgow and Manchester attest to tensions between paternalist governors at institutes, and students who wanted something more than an education designed just to 'improve' them in the eyes of employers.

---

[48] Cited in Farrar, p. 310.
[49] Eileen Yeo, 'Robert Owen and Radical Culture', in *Robert Owen: Prophet of the Poor: Essays in Honour of the Two Hundredth Anniversary of His Birth*, ed. by Sidney Pollard and John Salt (Lewisburg: Bucknell University Press, 1971), pp. 84–114 (p. 90).

Byron warned of such problems when he pledged £50 to the London Mechanics' Institute, writing, 'unless all the offices in such an institution are filled with real practical mechanics, the working classes will soon find themselves deceived ... they will only become the tools of others'.[50] Nevertheless, Helen Flexner has suggested that 'the London Mechanics' Institution (in its first seven years) deserves to be considered a progressive institution run substantially by working-class men for working-class men'.[51] Flexner does much to show the diversity of workers at the London Institute, but the picture seems to have been different elsewhere. Henry Brougham described the opening of the Sheffield Mechanics' Library in 1823 'under the able and zealous super-intendence' of James Montgomery, the poet and hymn writer, the then vice-president of the Sheffield Literary and Philosophical Society.[52] Montgomery observed two cardinal rules: first, the exclusion of any book 'suspected of containing principles subversive to the Christian religion', and second, a ban on novels and plays as they were 'superficial and unrewarding'.[53] The restrictions in the library at Sheffield were not unusual, but the library in December 1823 and the Mechanics' Institute that followed in 1832 were clearly responsive to local circumstances. Minute books show they wrote to the new Glasgow Mechanics' Institute for advice, giving some insight into the networks that fledgling institutes worked within. The Mechanics' and Apprentices' Library and Reading Room at Sheffield followed the one in Liverpool in July 1823, which was inspired by the Apprentices' Library that had been formed in New York in 1820.

A meeting to set up the library took place at Sheffield Town Hall on 27 December 1823 with the 'Master-Cutler' in the Chair. Here, the physician Arnold Knight talked of the 'necessity there exists in Sheffield, more than perhaps in most other places, of providing books calculated to improve the minds and morals of apprentices'. The pressing issue in Sheffield, as Knight well knew as a local physician, was the early death of grinders in the cutlery trade, many leaving young children behind 'when their passions are strong' and 'deprived of their natural guardians'.[54] The

---

[50] William Parry, *The Last Days of Lord Byron* (London: Knight and Lacey, 1825), pp. 204–05.
[51] Helen Hudson Flexner, 'The London Mechanics' Institution: Social and Cultural Foundations 1823–1830' (unpublished doctoral thesis, University College London, 2014), pp. 36, 261.
[52] Henry Brougham, *Practical Observations upon the Education of the People Addressed to the Working Classes and Their Employers* (London: Longman, 1825), p. 26.
[53] John Salt, 'The Creation of the Sheffield Mechanics' Institute', *The Vocational Aspect of Secondary and Further Education*, 18.40 (1966), 143–50 (p. 144).
[54] Sheffield City Archives, MD187, Sheffield Mechanics' and Apprentices' Library Minutes, 30 August 1823 to 18 September 1838, p. 12.

average ages of death for Sheffield grinders are a shocking reminder of the pollution faced by certain classes of workers. J. C. Hall found that

> the average age of fork-grinders does not exceed thirty years ... the poisonous atmosphere ... produces a complication of diseases, of which the most formidable is the asthma and dry cough, known by the name of the "grinders' complaint", attended as it is by consumption, which no medical man can cure. In such cases, life is a burden to the poor sufferers, and their frames are gradually emaciated and wasted by a repetition of slow tortures.[55]

In short, Knight was proposing that the Library take the place of these dead fathers.

Alison Twells argues that the urban elites who founded literary and philosophical societies, mechanics' institutes, statistical societies and city missions were concerned with the 'reform of the working-class man'.[56] After these workers left to form their own institutes, the changing syllabus and questions attest that they had more pressing concerns than middle-class ideas of reform. Questions set by the Glasgow Mechanics' Institute between 1823 and 1835 mix practical and written assessments and speak to conditions faced by people working and living in industrial areas. There are questions on whether 'Mechanics or Chemistry had contributed much to the Arts and to the comfort of civilised life'. A gold medal was awarded for the best essay on the question of 'whether it would be more advantageous to Society, if less of the time of the generality of young men were devoted to the study of Dead Languages, and more to the study of the laws of nature as developed in the Sciences of Natural Philosophy and Chemistry'. Another question addresses economy and air pollution:

> A GOLD MEDAL, value £5: 5s., for the best Essay on the Manufacture of Gas for Lighting towns and factories, as regards economy, quality, and the means of protecting from offensive effluvia those who live in the neighbourhood of the works where the Gas is made.[57]

This question about lighting, economy and 'quality' finishes with an environmental problem that shows concern for communities living near a gasworks. Coal gas was first manufactured in Britain in 1792 by Ayrshire engineer William Murdoch, who then went on to light the Soho factory of

---

[55] J. C. Hall, *Prevention and Treatment of the Sheffield Grinders' Disease* (London: Longman, Brown, Green, 1857), p. 24.

[56] Alison Twells, *The Civilising Mission and the English Middle Class* (London: Palgrave, 2009), pp. 215–16.

[57] University of Strathclyde Archives, GB 249 OC/1/1, Glasgow Mechanics' Institute Minute Book, July 1823–May 1834.

Bolton and Watt in 1802. The process produced much pollution. Once coal tar and ammoniacal liquor was removed, the coal gas was purified from hydrogen sulphide and hydrogen cyanide by passing it over beds of slaked lime. The resulting waste material, 'gas lime' or 'blue billy', was often used as a building filler. In damp weather the mix gave off toxic sulphur and cyanogen.[58] A more useful by-product of producing coal gas was coke, which was used in iron smelting. Questions about things that affected working-class people jar with the actions of a government that was, at that time, trying to police the knowledge economy of the poor.

Among the Six Acts of 1819 was the 'tax on knowledge'. That is, 'pamphlets and papers containing any public news, intelligence, or occurrences, or any remarks or observations thereon, or upon any matter in church or state' could now not be sold 'for a less sum than sixpence'.[59] The circulation of popular papers such as William Cobbett's *Political Register* and Thomas Wooler's *Black Dwarf* sank as their price rose from twopence to sixpence. The aim of the act was quite simply to take such papers beyond the means of the masses.[60] The penalty for publishing or selling an unstamped newspaper was £20 per violation. The Bill, not fully repealed until 1855, was thoroughly enforced. Patricia Hollis finds that 'between 1830 and 1836 at least 1130 cases of selling unstamped papers were considered by London magistrates' and over 800 people found themselves in prison for the offence in this period.[61] Political discussion, denied to many through the newspaper tax, consequently found its way into the pages of the new mechanics' magazines. In the introductory address of 'The Glasgow Gas Workman's Institution', published in the threepenny *Glasgow Mechanics' Magazine*, radical politics can be seen at work as the workmen attack British class structures:

> No nation can be called rich, merely because a few ancient families have annexed immense treasures to their overgrown estates; nor can a country be famed for its knowledge, which has merely a few richly endowed seminaries. This, however, is a maxim that has been tardily acknowledged. That proud aristocratic feeling, which would elevate the few by the oppression of many, has strained every nerve to keep things as they were.[62]

---

[58] See Farrar, p. 324, fn. 70.
[59] T. C. Hansard, *The Parliamentary Debates from the Year 1803 to the Present Time, vol. 41: Comprising the Period from the Twenty-Third Day of November 1819 to the Twenty-Eighth Day of February 1820* (London: Hansard, 1820), p. 575.
[60] G. D. H. Cole, *The Life of William Cobbett* (London: Collins, 1924), p. 240.
[61] Discussed in Martin Hewitt, *The Dawn of the Cheap Press in Victorian England* (London: Bloomsbury, 2014), p. 5.
[62] *Glasgow Mechanics' Magazine*, 4.97 (29 October 1825), p. 171.

There seem to be echoes of Edmund Burke and William Godwin here, suggesting just how far their works reached through the classes. Burke's famous section of *Reflections* where he writes that 'never more, shall we behold that generous loyalty to rank and sex, that proud submission, that dignified obedience, that subordination of the heart' can be detected in the letter from the gasmen.[63] So can an allusion to Godwin's political novel *Things as They Are; or, The Adventures of Caleb Williams* (1794). The writer goes on:

> It is a melancholy fact that in this city (a city that has arisen from a paltry village to be the second city in the empire, solely by discoveries in the arts and sciences) there are thousands who revel in the wealth these discoveries have produced, and yet remain ignorant of the nature and principles of those sciences and machines which have thus enabled them to acquire their fortunes! How many hundreds do we find weekly emigrating to their bathing quarters in that delightful conveyance the steam-boat, who know ... little of its machinery.[64]

Again, class is the issue. There are the people who have toiled and used their ingenuity to produce the wealth of the nation – set against those who 'revel in the wealth' they created. Nonetheless, the workers are often as ignorant as the rich who enjoy their creations: 'Nor is this ignorance alone chargeable on those who have a means of enjoying the labour of others; but even in our workshops and manufactories will we find many who are little better than parts of the machines around them.'[65] To an extent Marx's theories on the alienation of the worker are anticipated, along with the distinction between those who create and those who consume wealth made by the working classes. In 1800, Birkbeck identifies the same estrangement between the thing produced by workers and their knowledge of its usage, stating that there are many cases 'where the manual part alone is known, the artist remaining entirely ignorant of everything besides'.[66] In a manifesto for the London Mechanics' Institute, published in the 3d. *Mechanics' Magazine*, Thomas Hodgskin sounds like the Glasgow gas workers when he writes that 'Even in the arts which mechanics themselves practice ... of the principals of the operations they know little or nothing'.[67] Hodgskin makes the point that 'the upper classes, can know little or nothing of what the lower classes need, nor what is fitting for them. They know, indeed, too well what is

---

[63] Edmund Burke, *Reflections on the Revolution in France* (London: Dodsley, 1790), p. 113.
[64] *Glasgow Mechanics' Magazine*, 4.97 (29 October 1825), p. 171.
[65] *Glasgow Mechanics' Magazine*, 4.97 (29 October 1825), p. 171.
[66] Cited in Kelly, p. 30.   [67] *Mechanics' Magazine*, 1.7 (11 October 1823), p. 99.

proper for them as subjects, as tax-paying machines, as slaves, but not what is suitable to them as labourers and men'.[68]

Nevertheless, there were issues around which the 'upper classes' and workers might unite, especially when it came to engineering. Evidence of these can be found in questions set by the new breakaway Glasgow Mechanics' Institute. There are gold medals offered for 'the best scientific account of steam power and the instruments by which it operates, as applied to cotton factories, to the propelling of steam boats and railway carriages'; practical exercises such as building models of steam engines; and also competitions to make aspirational household items more accessible:

> Prize of £5:5s., for the best and cheapest Clock, of British manufacture, in imitation of German Clocks, so much used in this country, £3:3s. for the best, and £2.2s. for the second. The object in offering this premium is to encourage the manufacture of an article for which we are largely indebted to other countries. The competition will not be confined to students of this Institution.[69]

These 'German Clocks' are frequently referred to in literature concerned with working- and middle-class life in the nineteenth century. Charles Dickens mentions 'Dutch clocks' (Deutsch clocks) fifteen times in his novels alone, and Mary Elizabeth Braddon mentions them three times in *Lady Audley's Secret* (1862). However, this desirable commodity was foreign made and the gold medal competition links the aspirations of working-class people with those of British industrialists. People wanted jobs and their own clocks at home; and the nation needed to cut down on imports from abroad. At Leeds, Edward Baines warned that 'we must strain every nerve to keep clearly ahead of our competitors'.[70] John Martineau, an engineer from the firm Taylor and Martineau, proposed the fourth resolution for a London Mechanics' Institute to over 2,000 people at the Crown and Anchor Tavern on 11 November 1823, stating it 'was to the superiority of our mechanics that this country was indebted for the pre-eminent rank which it held in the scale of nations, and it behoved us to do all in our power to retain that pre-eminence'.[71] In the same meeting, Benjamin Rotch, a patent lawyer, identified an economic war with

---

[68] *Mechanics' Magazine*, 1.7 (11 October 1823), p. 100.
[69] Glasgow Mechanics' Institute Minute Book, July 1823–May 1834.
[70] Cited by John T. Bradshaw, 'Social Club Perspectives on Steam Intellect: The Case of Leeds 1824–1905', in *Steam Intellect Societies*, ed. by Inkster, pp. 73–79 (p. 74).
[71] *Mechanics' Magazine*, 1.12 (15 November 1823), p. 186.

Europe that Britain was winning as 'the sailors and mechanics may alike be denominated heroes of Trafalgar' as both 'deserve almost equal glory'.[72]

Similar to Glasgow, the London Mechanics' Institute had annual prizes for students. The Reverend Robert Fellowes offered, from 1826, and for five years, two annual prizes of £10 each, one for 'the best Essay on one of the Mechanical Powers' and the other 'for the best Model of a new or improved machine'. The first stipulation for entrants was that 'Candidates must be actual Mechanics'; however, this title seems to have been synonymous with 'tradesman'.[73] In 1826, a journeyman shoemaker, Thomas Holmes, won for an essay on 'The Lever', and the other was won by a machinist for a model of a comb-cutting machine. These innovative assignments that mix practical and theoretical questions addressed issues that were not being examined at British universities. They responded to the allure and potential of new technologies as well as environmental pollution and other consequences of industrialisation. Questions set by the new mechanics' institutes speak of the desire of people to advance themselves intellectually and economically, along with environmentally improving their quality of life.

At this political moment, some sections of the established Church countered labouring-class claims to an education. The conservatism of the Church as a blocker of education and reform can be seen throughout the 1820s and 1830s. Mabel Tylecote claims that the new mechanics' institutes faced persistent opposition from the Tory party and the Church of England.[74] J. W. Hudson finds that 'MECHANICS INSTITUTIONS established in England during the years 1824 to 1835, with few exceptions, received the most direct opposition from that powerful section of the community the clergy of the established church.'[75] In Aberdeen, the Reverend Dr Forbes told the members of that city's institute that 'Belles lettres, Political Economy, and even History, were dangerous studies'.[76] The *Mechanics' Magazine* of 19 November 1825 quotes Dr Magee, the Archbishop of Dublin, saying that 'over-educating ... will make the people uneasy and unmanageable'.[77] E. P. Thompson cites a Yorkshire clergyman who predicted in 1826 that mechanics' institutes would 'in time degenerate into Jacobin clubs and become nurseries of disaffection'. Thompson also writes that 'in the early 1830s a curate attacked the

---

[72] *Mechanics' Magazine*, 1.12 (15 November 1823), p. 182.
[73] Thomas Holmes, *An Essay on the Principles and Application of the Lever* (London: for the Author, 1827), p. 23.
[74] Tylecote, p. 63.   [75] Hudson, p. 201.   [76] Hudson, p. 59.
[77] *Mechanics' Magazine*, 6.117 (19 November 1825), p. 76.

management of the Leicester Mechanics' Institute for perverting it into a school "for the diffusion of infidel, republican, and levelling principles".[78] The established Church opposed the 1832 Reform Bill with twenty-one bishops voting against the Bill, six abstaining and only two in favour.[79] What was being taught worried sections of the Church, governors of institutes and Tories who opposed an education for the masses on the basis that it could lead to radicalism and more calls for parliamentary reform. These issues can be detected in the running of libraries at institutes and debates about their contents.

Among the Whigs, radicals and emerging liberals who championed the new mechanics' institutes, William Huskisson was one of the few Tories who supported them. However, Huskisson wanted teaching limited to 'such branches of science as will be of use to mechanics and the artizans in the exercise of their respective trades'.[80] That sort of benevolent but paternalistic governance of the new institutes was widespread. As John Seed points out, 'Mechanics Institutes in the 1820s rigorously barred not only religion and politics but also newspapers and fiction – anything in fact which stimulated the feelings or the imagination. Intellectual "self-improvement" via hard scientific discipline was the medicine.'[81] Hudson writes that at Sheffield Mechanics' Library there was 'the exclusion of *novels and plays*', but not all fiction:

> For many years the members annually agitated for the abrogation of the law which prevented them from reading novels of acknowledged excellence, but successive committees held that there is a real distinction between the tales of Miss Martineau, illustrating some principle of political economy, and Sir Walter's Scott's novels.[82]

Harriet Martineau was deemed intellectual, improving and acceptable, but Scott, amongst others, was banned at Sheffield. In 1833, at Ipswich Mechanics' Institute, members lobbied for three years to get the works of Scott accepted by their governors. Herbert Walker writes that 'after a battle royal, that the matter was settled by the casting vote of the Chairman of the Committee and the Waverley novels admitted. To mark the victory an

---

[78] E. P. Thompson, *The Making of the English Working Class* (Harmondsworth: Penguin, 1980), p. 809.
[79] D. G. Wright, *Popular Radicalism: The Working-Class Experience 1780–1880* (London: Routledge, 2014), p. 96.
[80] *Glasgow Mechanics' Magazine*, 3.80 (2 July 1825), p. 348.
[81] John Seed, 'Unitarianism, Political Economy and the Antinomies of Liberal Culture in Manchester, 1830–50', *Social History*, 7.1 (1982), 1–25 (p. 12).
[82] Hudson, pp. 159–60.

enthusiastic Scottite presented a bust of the author and a neat bookcase to hold the books'.[83] The library at Sheffield, as at Ipswich, was to be a moral guardian. Regulations dated 27 December 1823 state that 'any subscriber may propose such Books (except Novels and Plays) as he may deem proper'.[84] 'Shakespeare's Works' made it into Sheffield's Library in April 1831. However, the governors allowed only works that they deemed would 'provide suitable mental food to the mechanics and artizans of Sheffield'.[85] The governor of Manchester Mechanics' Institute negatively responded to 'a letter from several members of the institution requesting permission to meet every Saturday evening for the study of history', as it would 'lead to the introduction of political debates in the Institution, which cannot be allowed'.[86] At Ipswich there were complaints that people at the library 'resorted to it for political discussion'.[87]

Ipswich Mechanics' Institute evidently had little money. By 1827 the society had a librarian, Robert Franklin, and the books were 'almost entirely scientific, historical and philosophical works'.[88] The library took a daily newspaper, the *Times*, 'obtained second-hand the day after publication', from 1831. Members had to write their names on a slate, and ten minutes of reading time was allowed with a sand-glass.[89] Matilda Betham-Edwards's novel *The White House by the Sea* (1864) briefly documents the value of yesterday's newspaper at the Ipswich library. In the novel it becomes Ingham Town-Hall Library, and Franklin's character, Mr Binnie, breaks the rules by giving the sixteen-year-old heroine half of the subscription fee back and lets her 'carry all the second day's *Times* for papa to read'.[90] The notion that there was a proliferation of cheap print available to the poor from the 1820s on has to be reined in by the fact that cheap news was not all that available after the Six Acts. It is apparent that with the demise of radical papers, the new mechanics' magazines, priced at half the cost of newspapers, became important sources for political discussion. The short extracts I have included from the Glasgow gas workers, Hodgskin and Birkbeck all attest to how politically radical discussion in mechanics' magazines could be. Mechanics' magazines, due to their status as technical

---

[83] Herbert Walker, *The Ipswich Institute 1824–1924: An Historical Sketch*, Suffolk Archives, Ipswich Branch, GC1/6/3, pp. 4–5.
[84] Sheffield Mechanics' and Apprentices' Library Minutes, 30 August 1823 to 18 September 1838, p. 20.
[85] Sheffield Mechanics' and Apprentices' Library Minutes, 30 August 1823 to 18 September 1838, p. 142.
[86] John Rylands Library, MMI/1/2, Manchester Mechanics' Institute Minute Book, 31 May 1838.
[87] Walker, *Ipswich Institute 1824–1924*, p. 4.   [88] Walker, *Ipswich Institute 1824–1924*, p. 4.
[89] Walker, *Ipswich Institute 1824–1924*, p. 4.
[90] Matilda Betham-Edwards, *The White House by the Sea* (London: Smith, Elder, 1864), p. 15.

publications, managed to evade the minimum price of 6d. for publications that contained news or politics, thereby allowing a vent and access to political discussion for the working classes.

Maybe the Church was right to worry about the links between the new institutions and radicalism, as mechanics' magazines could provide a gateway to political extremism. Colonel Francis Macerone, a Mancunian Italian engineer who had been aide-de-camp to Napoleon's brother-in-law Murat, gets a chapter in William Hazlitt's 1819 publication, *Political Essays*. Later, Macerone was known for letters and articles in *The Mechanics' Magazine,* covering subjects from paving London to a steam carriage that he invented and manufactured with his partner Squires.[91] Macerone, a revolutionary ultra-radical, produced works that would be banned today, such as *Defensive Instructions for the People*, published by William Benbow in 1831. Released on the eve of the Reform Bill, this pamphlet shows amateurs how to make pikes, bullets, incendiary devices and bombs, as well as the best ways to engage in street-fighting against soldiers. Extracts of the pamphlet were reprinted in Heatherington's one-penny *Poor Man's Guardian*, advertising this dangerous information to the masses. A review in *The United Service Journal and Naval and Military Magazine* gives a flavour of its contents: 'It professes to contain the explanation of a certain system of organization, by which a mob can be enabled to beat an army.'[92] The writer notes that Macerone provides 'observations on the best means for the defense of a city, not against a foreign enemy, but against its own natural protectors and constitutionally appointed forces'. Most offensive for the reviewer, Macerone has a chapter on 'Burning Acids' and the 'effect of aqua fortis and glass bottle grenades'.[93] Macerone, the engineer who published in mechanics' magazines, was evidently a dangerous revolutionary who advocated violent insurrection. It can be concluded that mechanics' magazines not only engaged in the kinds of levelling discussion that had been found in pre-Six Acts radical papers, but also provided a route to more violent radical publications.

The new Mechanics' Institutes, which emerged from the Mechanics' Class run by Birkbeck and Ure at Anderson's, challenged, from the outset, conservative notions of who should be educated and what the content of that education could be. The Mechanics' Class and most of the early

---

[91] *Mechanics' Magazine*, 20.539 (7 December 1833), pp. 164–66.
[92] 'Colonel Macerone's Defensive Instructions for the People', *United Service Journal and Naval and Military Magazine*, 46 (May 1832), 50–56 (p. 50).
[93] 'Colonel Macerone's Defensive Instructions', p. 56.

institutes began with benevolent paternalism, set up, as Maxine Berg writes, 'on the basis of a passionate concern among middle-class reformers for providing a scientific education for the artisan'.[94] That circumscribed education, paternalism and workers' own insights into what they wanted to learn caused friction and sometimes ruptures in those early institutions. The new institutes tested the patience of governors and members alike, as each tried to limit the power of the other. Notions that Mechanics' Institutes, unchecked, could be breeding grounds for radicalism were tangible. The post-Peterloo crackdown on political activism among the poor led to political engagement being sought in libraries, syllabi and publications such as technical magazines that evaded the new 'tax on knowledge'. That period between Peterloo and the rise of Chartism in the 1830s saw disenfranchised working-class people pursue their own representational interests in innovative ways, combining professional, educational and personal aspirations. Occasionally though, behind the technical publications, radical figures from that violent post-Waterloo period of protest, such as Macerone, can be glimpsed still working towards the revolution that did not arrive in 1819.

[94] Maxine Berg, *The Machinery Question and the Making of Political Economy 1815–1848* (Cambridge: Cambridge University Press, 1980), p. 146.

CHAPTER II

'The Ladies' Contribution'
Women and the Mechanics' Institute on the Goldfields of Victoria

Sarah Comyn

During an 1859 soirée commemorating the third anniversary of the Beechworth Athenaeum in the goldfields town of the colony of Victoria (Australia), the Athenaeum's honourable secretary acknowledged the 'immense influence exercised by the ladies in the success or decline of an institution of this nature', noting that 'before the ladies gave their support the attendance at the weekly meetings and lectures was small'. Framing the Athenaeum as an alternative to the 'play house, or the billiard room', the speakers at the soirée viewed it as 'particularly well suited ... to the requirements of the class of people in the colony, where, and more particularly in a mining district, the great proportion had no other home but a tent, and which generally did not glow with the sunny smiles of the fairer sex'. Accommodating women in the institution was, the speakers argued, crucial to the success of future generations: 'considering the influence exercised by the mother in succeeding generations, we should do all we could to aid in the intellectual culture of the fair sex'.[1] A rather different view of women's presence in the institute is evident in an 1878 report, with the Athenaeum's library and museum subcommittee complaining that 'patterns and fashion plates belonging to the ladies newspapers are frequently abstracted' and that accordingly 'no cut paper pattern, pattern sheet, or fashion plate belonging to "The Queen", or "Englishwoman's Domestic Magazine" be laid upon the table, but that such shall be retained by the Curator and only issued by him on application'.[2] In another goldfields town,

---

This research was funded by the Irish Research Council.
[1] 'Beechworth Athenaeum: Soiree', *Ovens and Murray Advertiser*, Saturday 28 May 1859, p. 3 <http://nla.gov.au/nla.news-article117927364>.
[2] Report of Library and Museum Sub-Committee, Monday 4 February 1878, Records 1877–1878, Beechworth Athenaeum Archives, Burke Museum, Mechanics' Institutes of Victoria.

the committee of the Ballaarat Mechanics' Institute (BMI, established in 1859) voted in favour of the following motion: 'That the pages of the Ladies Suggestion Book be pasted together and a notice written on a fresh page requesting the ladies not to allow the Book to be made the receptacle of idle and impertinent remarks.'[3]

These moments – one an example of the mediated accounts representing the social respectability lent to the colonial institutes by the presence of women; one an example of the disruptive potential and policed presence of women in the institutes; and the final an act of foreclosing the textual interventions by women into the organisational print culture of the institution – demonstrate the varied and conflicting positions of women in the institutes. Like the 'frequently abstracted' patterns of the Athenaeum's newspapers, the presence and role of women in the colonial mechanics' institute often takes the form of an elision, allusion, or even an active erasure in contrast to the named accounts of men serving on the committees. This chapter aims to trace these diverse (and often fleeting) instances of women's appearances in the archival records of goldfields mechanics' institutes and athenaeums in order to reassess the role they played in these literary institutes and, correspondingly, the opportunities the institutes offered to women in what was viewed as a 'masculine society untempered by the feminine': the Australian goldfields.[4] An analysis of committee minute books and local newspaper reports demonstrates how the social respectability of colonial women and the mechanics' institutes could be mutually constitutive, providing women with opportunities and platforms for public and political engagement, while also revealing the acts of resistance to institutional forms of surveillance and moral policing.

Following the emergence of mechanics' institutes in Great Britain in the early 1820s, the institutes soon proliferated in the Australian colonies, with the Van Diemen's Land Mechanics' Institute established in Hobart Town only six years later in 1827. The number of institutes in the colony of Victoria rapidly increased with the discovery of gold in 1851 and the ensuing goldrush.[5] The assumed hyper-masculinity of this dual setting –

---

[3] Ballaarat Mechanics' Institute Minute Books, 12 April 1875. For a discussion of this incident, see Peter Mansfield, 'Public Libraries in Ballarat: 1851–1900' (unpublished PhD dissertation, Deakin University, 2000), p. 166 <https://dro.deakin.edu.au/eserv/DU:30023527/mansfield-publiclibraries-2000.pdf>. The BMI follows the original spelling of the town (with four a's), whereas the town changed its spelling to Ballarat in 1863, hence the varied spelling throughout.

[4] David Goodman, *Gold Seeking: Victoria and California in the 1850s* (Stanford: Stanford University Press, 1994), p. xxviii.

[5] Pam Baragwanath, 'The Origins and Growth of Mechanics' Institutes in Victoria', in *Mechanics' Institutes: The Way Forward Conference Organised by the Kilmore Mechanics Institute, 18–19 April 1998*

Women and Mechanics' Institute in Victoria 217

the overwhelmingly male demographic of the colonial goldfields and the ostensibly male-focused educational remit of the mechanics' institute – has meant that women's involvement in the institutes has received comparatively little attention.[6] As recent feminist scholarship has shown, however, women played an important role in the social, economic, political, and cultural life of the goldfields despite representing a much smaller proportion of the population than men.[7] The digitisation of Australian newspapers through the Trove database and the ongoing project of digitising surviving archival material of mechanics' institutes by Mechanics' Institutes of Victoria Incorporated provides an opportunity to identify when and how women enter a male-dominated organisational archive and reassess the role women played in these goldfields institutions.[8] Drawing on Australian women's history scholarship and examining the archival material of goldrush-era institutes in the goldfields towns of Ballarat and Beechworth in the colony of Victoria, this chapter demonstrates the associative power of women's domesticity and gentility, emphasising how the institutes mobilised, appropriated, and reinforced the improving sociability and colonial domesticity of women for the purposes of maintaining the institutions' reputations of social respectability and ensuring

(Kilmore: Department of Infrastructure, 1998), pp. 7–12 (p. 11); Sarah Comyn, 'Literary Sociability on the Goldfields: The Mechanics' Institute in the Colony of Victoria, 1854–1870', *Journal of Victorian Culture*, 23.4 (2018), 447–62.

[6] For accounts of women's involvement in goldfields mechanics' institutes, see, for example, Jennifer Hazelwood, 'The Unseen Influence of Women in the Institute', in *Under Minerva's Gaze: 150 Years at the Ballaarat Mechanics' Institute*, ed. by Jill Blee and Phil Roberts (Ballarat: Ballaarat Mechanics' Institute, 2010), pp. 110–21; and Mansfield. For a good study of women's relationship to the mechanics' institutes movement in Britain, and the Huddersfield Mechanics' Institute and Yorkshire Union of Mechanics' Institutes in particular, see Martyn Walker, *The Development of the Mechanics' Institute Movement in Britain and Beyond: Supporting Further Education for the Adult Working Classes* (London: Routledge, 2017), pp. 82–99; and Teresa Gerrard and Alexis Weedon, 'Working-Class Women's Education in Huddersfield: A Case Study of the Female Educational Institute Library, 1856–1857', *Information and Culture*, 49.2 (2014), 234–64.

[7] See, for example, Margaret Anderson, 'Mrs Charles Clacy, Lola Montez and Poll the Grogseller: Glimpses of Women on the Early Victorian Goldfields', in *Gold: Forgotten Histories and Lost Objects of Australia*, ed. by Iain McCalman, Alexander Cook, and Andrew Reeves (Cambridge: Cambridge University Press, 2001), pp. 225–49; Catherine Bishop and Angela Woollacott, 'Business and Politics as Women's Work: The Australian Colonies and the Mid-Nineteenth-Century Women's Movement', *Journal of Women's History*, 28.1 (2016), 84–106; Lorinda Cramer, 'Making a Home in Gold-rush Victoria: Plain Sewing and the Genteel Woman', *Australian Historical Studies*, 48.2 (2017), 213–26; Patricia Grimshaw and others, *Creating a Nation, 1788–1990* (Ringwood: Penguin Books, 1994), see especially pp. 79–105; Clare Wright, '"New Brooms They Say Sweep Clean": Women's Political Activism on the Ballarat Goldfields, 1854', *Australian Historical Studies*, 39 (2008), 305–21, and *The Forgotten Rebels of Eureka* (Melbourne: Text, 2013).

[8] The Trove newspaper database is accessible at <https://trove.nla.gov.au/newspaper/?q=>; more details of the digitising programme of Mechanics' Institutes of Victoria Inc. can be found at <www.mivic.org.au/scanning-project.html>.

their financial viability during the turbulent decades following the discovery of gold in Australia. Examining what Jennifer Hazelwood refers to as the 'unseen influence of women' in the goldfields mechanics' institutes, this chapter reveals the 'ladies' contribution' to the intellectual and material culture of the institutes while also exploring the oscillating support and involvement of the mechanics' institutes in the nascent women's rights movement of Australia.[9]

A Ladies' Room on the Goldfields

The presence of women in mechanics' institutes, as the speakers at the 1859 Beechworth Athenaeum soirée attest, was frequently welcomed and viewed as adding to the institutes' public appeal. Acknowledging and remarking on women's attendance at lectures, soirées, conversaziones, and other events celebrating the literary sociability of the institutes was a strategy often used by mechanics' institutes to market themselves as respectable alternatives to venues such as the public house. As I have argued elsewhere, women were crucial in 'defining the respectability of the mechanics' institutes and their rational recreations' on the goldfields, with their attendance at events signalling respectable sociability, while their absence, in contrast, could be a viewed as a sign of 'unsuitable sociability or controversy'.[10]

Admitting the importance of women to the institutes' reputation, many of the committees recognised the need to provide suitable and often separate spaces as a means of attracting more women subscribers. A report of the BMI in May 1875, for example, noted that a room 'fitted up for the accommodation of lady members' offered 'the utmost privacy and comfort' which they believed would 'result in a large accession of lady members'.[11] Committee minutes and reports indicate the efforts of the institutes to maintain and improve the rooms for the comfort of women as well as stocking periodicals they deemed appropriate for women readers, such as the *Ladies' Magazine*, *Victoria Magazine*, *The Queen*, *London Society*, and *All the Year Round*. Women's periodicals were a proliferating aspect of middle-class life as advertisers started to target female consumers,

---

[9] Hazelwood, p. 110; 'Mechanics' Institute: The Ladies' Contribution', *Bairnsdale Advertiser and Tambo and Omeo Chronicle*, Thursday 11 June 1896, p. 2 <http://nla.gov.au/nla.news-article84825482>.
[10] Comyn, p. 457.
[11] 'Mechanics' Institute', *Ballarat Star*, Friday 21 May 1875, p. 2 <http://nla.gov.au/nla.news-article208328891>.

contributing to stereotypes of female domesticity and expanding the women's sphere by 'aggressively examin[ing] topics such as women's work, philanthropy, education, equality, and social issues'.[12] Magazines like the *Englishwoman's Domestic Magazine* (to which the Beechworth Athenaeum restricted access due to theft) were part of a new literary culture that celebrated domestic management as a professional activity and emphasised the need for 'literacy and print-based knowledge'.[13]

As 'muddled social spaces of gentlemen and laborers', the colonial goldfields presented new sites of negotiation for women where forms of industriousness and 'colonial femininity' could align.[14] This colonial reassessment of the norms of female gentility applies not only to the scenes of domestic utility promoted by the women's periodicals stocked by the institutes' libraries, but also to the opportunities the mechanics' institutes provided for women to perform genteel acts such as charitable works and fundraising, sitting on the 'ladies committees' associated with institutes, assisting in the organisation and hosting of events, and performing at literary and sociable gatherings. The ladies' rooms of the mechanics' institutes were therefore participating in and encouraging a literary culture of useful and enterprising domesticity in keeping with the needs of the growing goldfields settlements, while also providing access to a print culture advocating for women's equality, with the *Victoria Magazine* explicitly involved in the women's rights movement in Britain.[15] This seeming contradiction in purpose demonstrates the capacity of the colonial literary institutes to also provide spaces where the engagement with a gendered print culture could potentially escape the authoritarian tendencies and surveillance of the institutes' governing committees.

Despite the literary, intellectual, and domestic space ostensibly offered to women through these rooms, the minute books nonetheless reveal the secondary status of 'lady members' in comparison to male subscribers. The BMI committee's response to a 'lady member' requesting the removal of the 'daily papers' from the primary reading room show where the priority

---

[12] Kathryn Ledbetter, 'Periodicals for Women', in *The Routledge Handbook to Nineteenth-Century British Periodicals and Newspapers*, ed. by Andrew King, Alexis Easley, and John Morton (London: Routledge, 2016), pp. 260–75 (p. 260). See also Alexis Easley, 'Gender, Authorship, and the Periodical Press', in *The History of British Women's Writing, 1830–1880: vol. 6*, ed. by Lucy Hartley (London: Palgrave Macmillan, 2018), pp. 39–55 (p. 41).

[13] Margaret Beetham, *A Magazine of Her Own? Domesticity and Desire in Women's Magazine, 1800–1914* (London: Routledge, 1996), p. 65.

[14] Lorinda Cramer, 'Diggers' Dress and Identity on the Victorian Goldfields, Australia, 1851–1870', *Fashion Theory*, 21.1 (2018), 85–108 (p. 103).

[15] Beetham, p. 171.

of access lay: 'the committee is not in a position to supply the daily papers to the ladies' room, and that the removal of the copies from the desks in the reading room cannot be permitted. Instructions were given to place yesterday's *Argus* in the ladies' room'.[16] Constantly faced with tight budgets and limited space, the ladies' room was often the first to feel the effects of financial restraints. In 1881, for example, the Beechworth Public Library (BPL) acknowledged that 'for over four months' they were 'compelled to deprive the ladies of the room set apart for their use' because 'contributions' to the institute's museum were being stored and sorted in this room. While the committee emphasised the 'necessity that exists for the creation of an additional room', the museum's collection was nonetheless given precedence and a billiards room was mooted as the suitable additional room.[17]

Faced with dwindling funds in the 1890s, the BPL committee responded by applying the 'pruning knife' to the ladies' room again, but this time with the library keeping company, stating that neither of the rooms 'be lighted with gas or that fires be used in either of these apartments in future except such as is necessary to prevent damp'.[18] These 'pruning' efforts by the committee met resistance, however, with 'DISGUSTED' writing to the *Ovens and Murray Advertiser* editor to complain: 'Such lunacy in the working of an institution by a section of committee calls for the utmost contempt from any right minded person. For the ladies – no light, no fire; for the non-subscribers – plenty of everything.'[19] Although seen as necessary for securing women's support of the institute, the institute's support of ladies' rooms was not, therefore, always guaranteed and thus women's status in the library proved unstable.

Nor were the rooms themselves uncontested spaces, a fact that fits with Kate Flint's analysis of the woman reader in British public libraries. Like the debates Flint identifies as animating British public libraries, the ladies' rooms of the institutes were seen as both inviting for women subscribers and places 'in which to giggle and gossip and pick up fashion hints', while the 'gendering of reading spaces in the [colonial] public library meant that

---

[16] 'Mechanics' Institute', *Ballarat Star*, Wednesday 26 January 1876, p. 4 <http://nla.gov.au/nla.news-article200187177>.
[17] 'The Beechworth Free Public and Burke Museum', *Ovens and Murray Advertiser*, Saturday 30 July 1881, p. 4 <http://nla.gov.au/nla.news-article199459909>. The Beechworth Athenaeum became the Beechworth Public Library in 1872.
[18] 'Beechworth Public Library', *Ovens and Murray Advertiser*, Saturday 13 April 1895, p. 7 <http://nla.gov.au/nla.news-article201541747>.
[19] 'Beechworth Public Library Retrenchment', *Ovens and Murray Advertiser*, Saturday 20 April 1895, p. 7 <http://nla.gov.au/nla.news-article201546372>.

the spaces themselves became coded by the types of reading associated with them'.[20] The abstraction of paper patterns at the Beechworth Athenaeum demonstrates how literal the taking of 'fashion hints' could be, while the BMI identified the ladies' room as a site of theft and destruction with a copy of the *Argus* newspaper 'destroyed . . . by some lady tearing out the advertisement inviting applications for the position of governess to a family near Sandhurst' and the '*London Society* and Godey's "Ladies' Book" . . . abstracted from the ladies' room'.[21] Flint has noted in the British context how separate ladies' rooms resulted in demands for more supervisory staff, and the BMI equally expressed frustration at the constant thefts across the library, giving their 'officers' instructions to 'give the first person detected into custody'.[22]

Complaints about noise were frequently associated with the presence of women. A letter to the *Ovens and Murray Advertiser* editor reveals the gendered and class-based tensions that could manifest at the library. 'SUBSCRIBER' complains that 'certain ladies and gentlemen (save the mark!) claiming to be members of the "upper class," . . . make a constant practice of talking aloud'. Berating these people for believing that 'their subscriptions have greater privileges and liberties attached to them than those of the common people', the writer identifies the 'offenders against common politeness' as 'principally ladies, young and old'.[23] The perception that women were not properly educated in the social norms of the institute meant that they were occasionally accused of disrupting orderly processes. In a lengthy editorial celebrating the BPL, the *Ovens and Murray Advertiser* singled out women readers and their social networks as disrupting the supply of new books by borrowing them 'immediately after they are received' and not returning them to the 'institution for several months, though there may be scores of other subscribers constantly inquiring for them'. Describing this process, the *Advertiser* characterised the woman reader as a bad member of the institute, creating gossipy and privatised circles of self-interest in contrast to the manly communal interest the institute aimed to create:

> Mrs A. gets the new book first and, when she has done with it, instead of returning it to the institution, as is the rule, passes it on to Mrs

---

[20] Kate Flint, *The Woman Reader, 1873–1914* (Oxford: Clarendon Press, 1993), p. 175; Lara Atkin and others, *Early Public Libraries and Colonial Citizenship in the British Southern Hemisphere* (London: Palgrave Macmillan, 2019), p. 64.

[21] 'Mechanics' Institutes', *Ballarat Star*, Wednesday 28 March 1877, p. 4 <http://nla.gov.au/nla.news-article199827912>; 'Mechanics' Institute', *Ballarat Star*, Tuesday 13 August 1878, p. 2 <https://trove.nla.gov.au/newspaper/article/199326155>.

[22] Flint, p. 172; 'Mechanics' Institutes', *Ballarat Star*, Wednesday 28 March 1877, p. 4.

[23] 'An Objectionable Practice', *Ovens and Murray Advertiser*, Saturday 26 February 1881, p. 6 <http://nla.gov.au/nla.news-article199460361>.

B. who is so anxious to see 'that dear Mrs So-and-so's new –,' Mrs C. gets it next and in turn passes it over to Mrs D. and so on. When the capitals of the alphabet have thus 'rung the changes' and are satisfied, and not till then, the small letters have a chances of scrambling for a prize which is no longer new, and hardly worth the winning.[24]

Drawing on the common tropes of woman readers' habits as preoccupied, voracious, and 'manifest[ing] no self-awareness', the *Advertiser* is also alert to the different claims of social status being exacted by the capital letters to the detriment of those 'small letters'.[25] Given the frequent accusations that mechanics' institutes were becoming sanctuaries for the colonial middle class instead of serving the working classes as they were intended, this preferential treatment of the 'capitals' was viewed as a worrying trend and, like 'SUBSCRIBER' who referred to the needs of the 'common people', the *Advertiser* condemned these borrowing practices as 'keep[ing] a good many names off the subscription list' and recommended that the borrowing rules be 'rigorously and impartially enforced'.[26]

If the institutes' respectable reputations were reliant on the presence, custom, and support of women, then any disreputable behaviour by women could have damaging effects on the perceived character of the institute itself. The above examples suggest that while women's involvement in the institutes was actively encouraged by the committees, their presence simultaneously occasioned disciplinary practices of surveillance, policing, and even – as the pasting shut of the offensive pages of the 'ladies suggestion book' at the BMI indicates – punishment. As spaces where men, women, and youth mixed, it was crucial that the institutes monitored and mediated the interactions between the sexes. During a committee meeting at the BMI in 1875, it was noted, for example, that 'annoyance to ladies was caused by the misbehaviour of certain young men' and it was resolved that the president of the institute would 'communicate with the friends or employers of some of the offenders'.[27] Despite the institute's efforts, the mixing of 'youth' nonetheless occasionally attracted controversy, as a letter to the *Ballarat Star*

---

[24] 'The Beechworth Public Library', *Ovens and Murray Advertiser*, Saturday 20 July 1872, p. 2 <http://nla.gov.au/nla.news-article196856861>.
[25] Flint, p. 3.
[26] 'The Beechworth Public Library', *Ovens and Murray Advertiser*, Saturday 20 July 1872, p. 2.
[27] 'Mechanics' Institute', *Ballarat Star*, Wednesday 11 August 1875, p. 4 <http://nla.gov.au/nla.news-article208330826>.

in 1883 reveals. Fearing the 'noble' mechanics' institute is becoming a 'courting saloon', 'Observer' writes:

> On Saturday evenings the library of the Institute is patronised to a great extent by bits of boys and girls. These youths, it appears to me, congregate solely for the purpose of going through a kind of flirtation, which in some instances occasions a good deal of loud talk, much to the inconvenience of the adult and more staid section of the visitors. The recesses on the northern side of the library are often used by youths as a place in which to secret themselves from the secretary's view for the purpose of having a 'lark' with the girls, who stand with their backs against the bookshelves on the opposite side, and who thereby prevent subscribers from having recourse to many of the literary works.[28]

This letter not only points to the irritation caused to subscribers by the flirtatious behaviour of the 'youths', but also identifies the institute as a site of appropriate and improving sociability that must be strictly maintained.

The most radical action taken by the BMI in response to the socially threatening behaviour of what it identified as 'larrikinesses' was to shut the ladies' room entirely. Associating these young women with the figure of the 'larrikin' – a term that emerged in the 1870s 'to describe rowdies who hung about the streets, aged anywhere between about twelve and their early twenties' who became 'a repository for anxieties about sexuality and urban life' – demonstrates the social, cultural, and economic danger these youth presented to the committee.[29] With 'no fewer than four books ... ruined, pictures and reading matter having bean ruthlessly cut out wholesale', the committee resolved to offer a reward of £5 'for such information as will lead to the conviction of the thieves' and suggested that the 'separate room for ladies be abolished and one of the library tables set apart' for them instead.[30] Over the next month the committee continued to discuss what to do about the room as 'the destruction of magazines, &c. in the ladies' room continued' and with 'nearly all last month's numbers having been destroyed', the committee finally 'unanimously resolved "that the

---

[28] 'A Courting Saloon', *Ballarat Star*, Thursday 18 October 1883, p. 4 <http://nla.gov.au/nla.news-article201616752>.
[29] Melissa Bellanta, 'The Larrikin Girl', *Journal of Australian Studies*, 34.4 (2010), 499–512 (p. 500) and 'The Larrikin's Hop: Larrikinism and Late Colonial Popular Theatre', *Australian Drama Studies*, 52 (April 2008), 131–47 (p. 132).
[30] 'News and Notes', *Ballarat Star*, Wednesday 1 January 1879, p. 2 <http://nla.gov.au/nla.news-article199346874>.

present ladies room be closed at the end of the month and that the large table at the last end of the library be reserved for the exclusive use of ladies'".[31] A letter to the editor of the *Ballarat Star* hints at the additional offence caused by these 'larrikinesses' that did not make it into the official institutional record:

> The mere fact of a number of young girls having free access to its shelves and reading the works of 'Ouida,' and other abominations of a similar nature, where young minds are perverted by being introduced to the 'scenes' behind the scenes of a theatre (and, such a theatre as could only exist in the imagination of a novelist), the billiard-room, the racecourse, the gambling hell, and heaven knows where besides, may account for the fact that it was found necessary to paint the walls of a certain portion of the ladies' rooms black so that the disgraceful (to use the mildest term) pencil marks made by these juvenile larrikinesses might not shock the sight of modest women. Is this what a Mechanics' Institute is intended for?[32]

This behaviour seemed to prove the danger of that long-feared literary figure, the young woman novel reader. Fuelling the sexual anxieties associated with fiction reading that were exacerbated by a colonial setting, these reading activities potentially compromised the status of the 'modest women' subscribers of the institute.

The 1881 engraving 'Reading-room, Ballarat Mechanics' Institute' (Figure 11.1), originally published in the *Australasian Sketcher*, enacts the implicit surveillance of the women reader and female presence in the institute achieved through the closure of the ladies' room. Illustrating the 'Ladies Only' table, which is indeed located 'at the last end of the library', the women patrons nonetheless remain within full observation of the viewer, the secretary, and the other readers. The rules of the library are foregrounded and centred and thereby code the image with order and respectability, though a pair of women are still seen to be conversing with one another while all the men are pictured as reading alone.

Feeling sufficiently punished, a prospective woman subscriber wrote to the editor of the *Ballarat Star* in 1885, arguing that the BMI did not treat its women subscribers with 'extravagant generosity', and blamed the closure of ladies' room on the committee's policy of allowing 'troops of State school girls' into the rooms, who with other non-subscribers 'annoyed and often

---

[31] 'Mechanics' Institute', *Ballarat Star*, Tuesday 14 January 1879, p. 4 <http://nla.gov.au/nla.news-article199347161>; 'Mechanics' Institute', *Ballarat Star*, Tuesday 28 January 1879, p. 3 <http://nla.gov.au/nla.news-article199347535>.

[32] 'Billiards at the Mechanics' Institute', *Ballarat Star*, Thursday 13 February 1879, p. 4 <http://nla.gov.au/nla.news-article200132845>.

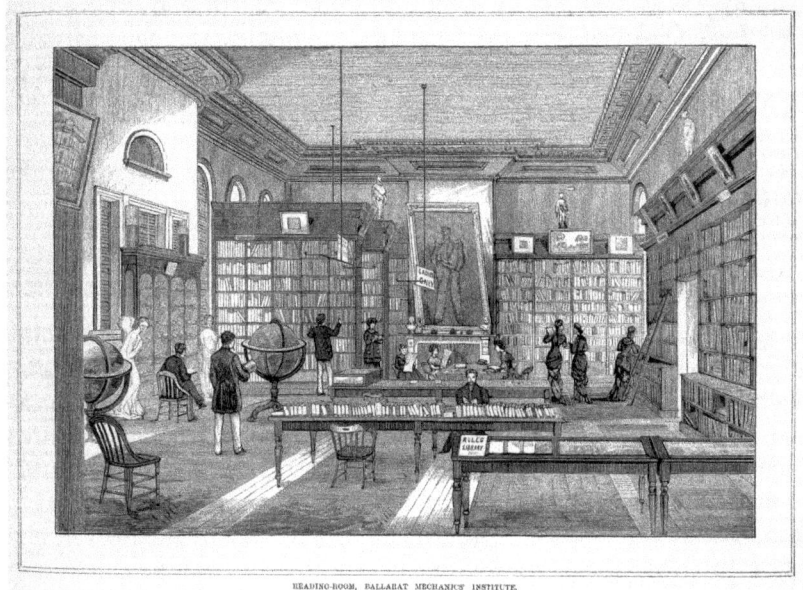

Figure 11.1 Alfred May and Alfred Martin Ebsworth, 'Reading-Room, Ballarat Mechanics' Institute', 1881. Courtesy of the State Library of Victoria, <http://handle.slv.vic.gov.au/10381/257858>.

disgusted' members. The writer ended her letter by hoping that as she had 'broken the ice' she could rely upon the wives of the institute's committee members to 'use their powers of persuasion to get what we require'.[33] A rare publicised example of a woman trying to intervene in the management of the institute, this letter – through its appeal to both public and domestic networks of influence – demonstrates the mediated access and fragile authority women had within the institutes. With no representation on the governing committees, women were reliant on local newspapers or their husbands to intervene on their behalf and defend their interests.

The presence of women in the goldfields institutes was therefore conditionally welcomed by the governing committees. Given the social and class anxieties associated with the goldfields as a 'society dangerously out of balance' with the need for domestic ideals to be reasserted, the mechanics' institute could provide a space of rational recreation in which women's

[33] 'The Mechanics' Institute', *Ballarat Star*, Saturday 2 May 1885, p. 4 <http://nla.gov.au/nla.news-article203306201>.

gentility was assured and in which they could exercise and express their enterprising colonial domesticity and industriousness through charitable acts.[34] Despite this promised associative gentility, however, some women within the institutes performed undomesticated and ungenteel acts that resisted the attempts by the male-dominated committees to surveil, govern, and police their behaviour, thereby disrupting the social order of the institutional space.

A Debt of Gratitude to the Ladies

Recognising the potential of the mutually constitutive respectability attached to women involved in the institutes, committees frequently called upon women in their communities to assist them with their fundraising and philanthropic endeavours as 'ladies committees'. In 1860, the BMI committee was facing a debt of almost £2,000 and called upon the 'Ladies of Ballarat' to assist them, and through their help in organising a bazaar, managed to raise £1,000.[35] A similar appeal was made by the BMI in 1871 when '[b]urdened with the pressure of a debt of £6,500' the committee, 'with a wise instinct as to what was essential to success, sought to enlist the ladies in the movement'. In an extensive report of the fancy bazaar held for these purposes, the *Ballarat Star* reported the degree of women's involvement in the event with the 'leading ladies ... attend[ing] business meetings and sewing meetings regularly from the first, and a host besides' working at home in addition to 'making collections of money and goods in aid'.[36]

A collective noun, the 'Ladies of Ballarat', though indisputably tied to the success of the institute, remain anonymous: 'The ladies have been the soul of the organisation and yet so great is their modesty, they do not appear on the list of committees in the books of Mr J. B. Ross, the very active and shrewd secretary of the general bazaar committee.' It is only by turning to the descriptions of various stalls that we get an indication of the over 100 women involved in managing them. The 'A' stall, for example, is managed by a 'Mrs Thomas, and Misses Errington, Jordan, and Bain', while at 'B' 'Mesdames Batten and Aldred and Misses Rix, Abrams, Cowe and Harrington' oversee the stall's affairs. The list also signifies the importance of married women to the institute's performance of respectability, with the

---

[34] Goodman, p. xxviii.
[35] For a more detailed account of this fundraising event, see Comyn, p. 459; and Hazelwood, pp. 113–14.
[36] 'The Mechanics' Institute Bazaar', *Ballarat Star*, Thursday 7 September 1871, p. 2 <http://nla.gov.au/nla.news-article197565713>.

Ballarat Star at pains to stress how the bazaar was a continuance of a tradition begun in 1860 when 'with only £30 in bank a move was made to obtain the present site, and at length the ladies – mostly married ones too – got up a bazaar which yielded a £1000 clear profit'.[37] Married women's involvement emphasised the domesticating potential of the institute and domesticity, as Goodman argues, was seen as 'an antidote to intemperance', which was considered one of the primary social afflictions facing goldfields settlements.[38]

Symbols of respectability, married women also signalled a maturing goldfields colony no longer overrun with unmarried men or as the destination solely for assisted single-women's emigration strongly associated with domestic service work. Unless they were taking up positions as domestic servants, single women were often viewed as undesirable in the colonies.[39] The marriage market of the goldrush was nonetheless a 'seller's market' and with the privilege and 'anonymity' of distance, single women could be selective about the future they chose, as satirised by John Leech's 'Alarming Prospect The Single Ladies off to the Diggings' (Figure 11.2).[40] Leech depicts the arrival of single women who haughtily dismiss and reject the offers of the men waiting for them as 'Twopenny Ha'penny Fellows!' With pleading, beseeching, and confused men all around them, the unimpressed women instead rely on one another, forming a self-sufficient female community and economy with no need for a man's proposal of a cottage or their hundred pounds – 'a likely start indeed!'[41] By highlighting the role of married women in its social activities, the BMI distances itself from this marriage economy and instead advertises itself as a venue in which women – single and married alike – can suitably perform acts of gentility and sociability.

In acknowledging their 'debt of gratitude to the ladies', the BMI explicitly tied the women's support of the bazaar to the institute's mutual support of women, stating in their annual report in 1872 that as a result of the successful bazaar 'the committee decided to carry out some long needed improvements in the library and ladies' room, having special reference to their comfort and convenience'.[42] With this financial and philanthropic history to the ladies' room, the women may have felt

---

[37] 'The Mechanics' Institute Bazaar', *Ballarat Star*, Thursday 7 September 1871, pp. 2–3.
[38] Goodman, p. 176.
[39] Lisa Chilton, 'A New Class of Women for the Colonies: The Imperial Colonist and the Construction of Empire', *Journal of Imperial and Commonwealth History*, 31.2 (2003), 36–56 (pp. 41, 40).
[40] Wright, *Forgotten Rebels of Eureka*, pp. 166–69. [41] Wright, *Forgotten Rebels of Eureka*, p. 166.
[42] 'Ballarat Mechanics' Institute: Annual Meeting', *Ballarat Star*, Wednesday 29 May 1872, p. 3 <http://nla.gov.au/nla.news-article197629108>.

Figure 11.2 John Leech, 'Alarming Prospect The Single Ladies off to the Diggings', 1853. Courtesy of the State Library of Victoria, <http://handle.slv.vic.gov.au/10381/93216>.

justifiably chagrined when the room was closed by the institute seven years later. The BPL took this philanthropic exchange a step further when (through the medium of the *Ovens and Murray Advertiser*) it connected the institute's provision of 'comfort' for women to those women's fund-raising support. After highlighting the improvements the BPL committee had made to their facilities, including the provision of a 'room specially for ladies', the newspaper report proceeds to 'suggest that the ladies, who lately so delighted the people of Beechworth at a concert in St. George's Hall, should be asked to give a similar entertainment for the benefit of an institution in which they have always taken so lively an interest, and the Committee of which has done so much in providing for their comfort'.[43] The charitable acts of women thus became an interchange that secured the financial interests of the institute, emphasised the comfort and respectability of women members through the provision of suitable facilities, and reinforced the associative propriety attached to women in the institute. The relationship of charitable exchange between women and

---

[43] 'The Beechworth Public Library', *Ovens and Murray Advertiser*, Saturday 1 August 1874, p. 4 <http://nla.gov.au/nla.news-article197296676>.

the mechanics' institutes on the goldfields could also extend beyond the benefits of the institute. If we examine adjacent charities, we can see the support provided by the BMI, for example, to the fundraising activities of the Ladies' Benevolent Clothing Society, with the 'gratuitous use' of a room offered to them for their weekly meetings.[44]

The reliance of the institutes on women's support was not, however, always gracefully acknowledged, even though the committees not only depended on women's involvement in the cultivation of literary sociability attached to events like bazaars, but also called on 'influential ladies' to act as canvassers for new member subscriptions and the supply of donations.[45] The BMI faced criticism for not managing their finances properly and instead 'when pushed for funds' did not 'consider it beneath their dignity ... to solicit their lady friends to beg and bother subscribers for money and presents'.[46] When the BMI 'got in a fix', its strategy seems to have been to 'ask ladies to beg'.[47] This behaviour clearly annoyed some members of the public; it also jeopardised the reputation not only of the institute but also of the women. An institute could, therefore, be deemed *too* reliant on the charitable and 'industrious behaviours' of colonial women on the goldfields in ways that undermined the gentlemanly masculinity of the committee members.

A sociable space of practiced gentility and charitability, 'Ladies' Committees' could also be a means of assertion by women members in opposition to the governing committee. In the 1890s, when a disagreement between the BPL committee and its curator, Mr Ballard, intensified, the women members chose to give Mr Ballard a public display of support. In 1892, they held a 'very pleasing ceremony' in the ladies' room convened and attended by the 'majority of the lady members' and Mrs G. F. Cross expressed 'their appreciation of the courtesy with which he had uniformly fulfilled his duties'.[48] The tension between Ballard and the committee continuing until his retirement, 'A LADY SUBSCRIBER' felt the need to write to the *Ovens and Murray Advertiser* in 1895, suggesting the 'justice

---

[44] 'Ladies' Benevolent Clothing Society', *Ballarat Star*, Tuesday 18 December 1866, p. 2 <http://nla.gov.au/nla.news-article112860150>.
[45] 'Beechworth Public Library and Museum', *Ovens and Murray Advertiser*, Saturday 29 September 1888, p. 2 <http://nla.gov.au/nla.news-article198925870>.
[46] 'Our Ballarat Mechanics' Institute and Its Balance Sheet', *Ballarat Courier*, Monday 22 May 1871, p. 2 <http://nla.gov.au/nla.news-article191430292>.
[47] 'The Mechanics' Institute: A Suggestion', *Ballarat Star*, Saturday 27 May 1871, p. 4 <http://nla.gov.au/nla.news-article197563057>.
[48] 'Beechworth Public Library: Presentation to the Curator', *Ovens and Murray Advertiser*, Saturday 17 December 1892, p. 6 <http://nla.gov.au/nla.news-article199734951>.

of some public recognition of Mr. J. H. Ballard, on his retirement from the faithful service of ten years. Whatever may be thought as to his disagreement with the present committee, it is universally admitted that he has been most courteous and obliging in his official capacity', and urging the women members to 'take the initiative', the letter writer felt 'certain they would, with their usual energy, bring the affair to a successful termination'.[49] The loss of Ballard occasioned the need for a new curator, and for the first time, perhaps in recognition of the women's energised involvement in the institute's affairs, the committee debated and agreed upon opening up the curator position to women applicants. Prompted by the observation that 'ladies of a kindred institution' in Shepparton had women serving on their governing committee, a member, Mr Warren, asked whether it 'might not be advantageous to them to follow this example'. Though women had been invited to attend the annual meeting since at least 1880, Warren was 'not just then prepared to move in this direction but he hoped members would think over the matter' and eventually 'such a change would commend itself to their approval'.[50] The meeting then closed and the issue was not discussed further, but records show that a Miss Alderdice was appointed as the curator in 1896 and that she carried out her duties 'in a manner that gave every satisfaction to the subscribers and others frequenting the institution'.[51] While this reveals a changing attitude towards the role women could play in these institutions as paid members of staff, the committees remained dominated by men. It was not until 1984, for example, that a woman, Mary Lillian McArdle, became president of the BMI.[52]

The Novelty of Listening to a Lady Lecturer

In October 1884, a letter appeared in the *Ballarat Star* from Helen Hart, accusing the BMI of refusing her access to the institute's newspapers, 'order[ing] her out' and 'threat[ening] to fetch a constable'.[53] Hart, who later marketed herself as the 'Founder Women's Suffrage, New Zealand

---

[49] 'Beechworth Public Library', *Ovens and Murray Advertiser*, Saturday 13 July 1895, p. 2 <http://nla.gov.au/nla.news-article201541402>.
[50] 'Beechworth Public Library', *Ovens and Murray Advertiser*, Saturday 6 July 1895, p. 10 <http://nla.gov.au/nla.news-article201541501>.
[51] 'Beechworth Public Library', *Ovens and Murray Advertiser*, Saturday 18 April 1896, p. 3 <http://nla.gov.au/nla.news-article199696736>.
[52] Hazelwood, p. 120.
[53] 'The Mechanics' Institute', *Ballarat Star*, Wednesday 22 October 1884, p. 4 <http://nla.gov.au/nla.news-article201120124>.

and Australia', was correct in asserting her right to browse the newspapers without a subscription, but the BMI was steadfast in their refusal to allow her entry to the institute, and earlier, in July of that year, had rejected Hart's request to hire the hall for the delivery of a lecture on women's rights.[54] Although not mentioned in the official committee records, Hart's notoriety within the institute is perhaps traceable to an incident the year before during a lecture by Rev. Charles Strong on the subject 'Women, her place and power', when Hart is reported as taking up a 'position at the Galloway monument' located not far from the BMI and addressing 'a somewhat numerous gathering on the temperance question'. 'During her remarks the lady lecturer' is reported to have given the 'Rev. Charles Strong a decided "hit." She broadly hinted that the Rev. lecturer would be more profitably occupied in discussing men and their evil habits of drinking than talking of women and the place they should hold in the social world.'[55]

Refused entry at the BMI, Hart was nonetheless able to lecture at a number of institutes in the colony of Victoria, including Williamstown, Traralgon, and Kyneton. A fairly divisive figure, even within the women's suffrage movement, it is not certain whether the institute's dismissive response to Hart was due to her subject matter as a 'lady lecturer' or the aggressive manner in which she approached the institute.[56] The fact that the institute hosted a soirée and concert in celebration of the passing of the 'Female Employment Regulation Act' in 1873 would suggest that the BMI was supportive of improving the employment conditions of working-class women even if it is unclear whether this support extended to women's suffrage. The legislation limited the working hours of seamstresses and female factory workers to eight hours per day and the celebration at the institute was attended by almost 200 seamstresses. Speaking at the event, Joseph Jones (member of the legislative assembly and president of the BMI, 1868–70) made his commitment to the employment act clear, stating that 'he had great pleasure in coming forward and identifying himself with this movement, as he had given it his best support in Parliament'.[57] While their support may have been targeted, it appears

---

[54] Mansfield, p. 166. For Hart's self-styling, see *Ballarat Star*, Tuesday 19 July 1898, p. 3 <http://nla.gov.au/nla.news-article215227348>.
[55] 'News and Notes', *Ballarat Star*, Tuesday 15 May 1883, p. 2 <http://nla.gov.au/nla.news-article202505167>.
[56] Helen D. Harris, 'Hart, Helen (1842–1908)', *Australian Dictionary of Biography* (Canberra: Australian National University, 1966) <http://adb.anu.edu.au/biography/hart-helen-12966>.
[57] 'The Female Employment Regulation Act', *Ballarat Courier*, Wednesday 10 December 1873, p. 2 <http://nla.gov.au/nla.news-article192285089>.

that the BMI did not hesitate in associating themselves with political causes it believed of benefit to the women in their community.

It is also evident that, although considered a 'novel' event, institutes were not completely averse to women lecturers.[58] Martha Turner delivered a lecture on 'Ill-used Men' at both the BPL and the BMI in the late 1870s. Celebrated in both instances for her 'good and clear delivery', her 'expressive face', and her 'breadth of thought and keen insight into human nature', Turner's lecture dealt with a range of 'ill-used men', including Socrates, Columbus, Captain Flinders, Robert Burns, and John Keats, and drew upon the works of Charles Dickens and John Stuart Mill to illustrate her accounts of these men's personal and professional histories.[59] A pastor of the Unitarian Church in Melbourne and the first woman minister of a church in Australia, Turner explicitly began her lecture by stating her intention 'not to trespass on the rights of women, not knowing what they were, though for the past fifteen years she had been trying to find them out'.[60] She would continue to search for these rights, and as the married Mrs Webster, she was 'present at the meeting which resolved to form the Victorian Women's Suffrage Society', becoming an active member in the Australian Women's Suffrage Society.[61] Turner would also prove to have a lasting influence on the Scottish-Australian author and suffragist, Catherine Helen Spence, who in listening to Turner speak in Adelaide wrote that she 'felt how much the world had been losing for so many centuries' because of the absence of women preachers.[62] In the following decades more women lecturers would follow, though they remained in the minority, and in 1903 (following the achievement of women's suffrage at the federal level in Australia in 1902), a leading Victorian suffragist, Vida Goldstein, addressed a packed and welcoming audience in the BMI to 'explain why she should be elected a member of the Federal Senate'.[63] Notwithstanding the frequent ambivalence of their support for women, the colonial mechanics' institutes

---

[58] In reporting the large audience, including women, attending Martha Turner's lecture at the BMI, for example, the *Ballarat Courier* explained the phenomenon as partly due to 'the novelty of listening to a lady lecturer' ('Ill-Used Men', *Ballarat Courier*, Tuesday 5 February 1878, p. 4 <http://nla.gov.au/nla.news-article211537341>).

[59] 'Ill-Used Men', *Ballarat Courier*, Tuesday 5 February 1878, p. 4; 'Ill-Used Men', *Ovens and Murray Advertiser*, Saturday 20 October 1877, p. 5 <http://nla.gov.au/nla.news-article199685278>.

[60] 'Ill-Used Men', *Ovens and Murray Advertiser*, Saturday 20 October 1877, p. 5.

[61] The Australian Women's Register <www.womenaustralia.info/biogs/AWE3761b.htm>.

[62] Spence cited in Susan Magarey, *Unbridling the Tongues of Women: A Biography of Catherine Helen Spence* (Adelaide: University of Adelaide Press, 2010), p. 53. Spence is also famous for insisting on delivering a lecture at the South Australian Institute in 1871 (p. 131).

[63] 'The Federal Elections. The Contests for the Senate. Miss Vida Goldstein's Candidature', *Ballarat Star*, Tuesday 8 December 1903, p. 1 <http://nla.gov.au/nla.news-article208359214>.

provided a platform for women's public and political engagement pre- and post-Australian Federation and as Victorian women continued to demand suffrage at the state level.

Women's involvement in these goldfields mechanics' institutes demonstrates the complexity of social access and denial offered by the institutes. In the rapidly growing and changing setting of the goldfields the institutes could provide a mediated space of genteel and respectable expression for women, but this was also a space that could provoke policing, censure, and even erasure. The support of women was crucial to the financial sustainability of the institutes as well as reinforcing their reputations as morally respectable and socially improving institutions. This synergistic relationship between women and the institutes provides an opportunity to reassess the social, political, and economic prospects open to women on the goldfields of Australia, but also, more broadly, the place of women in the seemingly male-dominated literary institutes of the nineteenth century. Our attention should not only be turned to the narrative of the woman reader entering literary institutes, but also to that of the woman committee member and her growing associative power through acts of fundraising, literary sociability, and domesticity, while also being attuned to the ways women could use literary institutes and their networks for political purposes. Even the moments of 'pasting shut' women's writing in the literary institutional archive can provide glimpses of women-authored disruption. While our access to the accounts of women's participation in male-dominated literary institutions is frequently mediated by newspaper editors or institutional committee men, the records provided by local newspaper reports and committee minute books nonetheless provide fruitful sites of investigation for the active presence of and resistance by women, demonstrating their role not only in contributing to but also reshaping the literary institution.

CHAPTER 12

'[L]etters Must Increase'
Reading and Writing the Post Office as a Literary Institution

Karin Koehler

To begin: two institutions. In 1858, senior staff of the General Post Office in London established the London Post Office Library and Literary Association, which installed a permanent reading room and lending library.[1] Until the end of the century, it provided both a communal space and literary material to 'the gentlemen' employed in the postal service, with a view to cultivating in them the habit of 'systematic reading'.[2] It also organised public cultural activities, including a series of *conversazioni*, to raise funds for the collection. Three decades later, between 1885 and 1890, postal employees contributed to and published *Blackfriars*, a magazine featuring poetry, prose sketches, and serial fiction alongside travel reports, political discussions, and general interest articles. This periodical, Laura Rotunno explains, conceived itself as a network of public servants that resisted the competition and class division underpinning civil service examinations and employment practices, promoting a more inclusive and participatory model of culture.[3]

These institutions bear testimony to the ways in which a Victorian government department that 'entered into the life of every town and village in the kingdom' formalised its commitment to literary culture and education.[4] In the case of the Library and Association, this commitment was made by the leadership of the General Post Office to a relatively narrow section of the workforce. One speaker at the initial meeting argued that 'one of the greatest advantages this Society holds out will be, that Controllers and Presidents, Secretary's men and Circulation men, in fact, every one in the Post Office from end to end, will come into this room on

---

[1] Post Office Library and Literary Association, *Proposal to Establish a Post Office Library and Literary Association* (London, 1858).
[2] Post Office Library and Literary Association, *Proposal*, p. 8.
[3] Laura Rotunno, '*Blackfriars: The Post Office Magazine*: A Nineteenth-Century Network of "The Happy Ignorant"', *Victorian Periodicals Review*, 44 (2011), 141–64.
[4] Martin Daunton, *Royal Mail: The Post Office since 1840* (London: Athlone, 1985), p. 271.

an equality', but the group he addressed consisted exclusively of higher-ranking postal servants.[5] Frederic Hill, assistant secretary to the Postmaster General, hoped 'that when your own Society shall be well-established, at some future time, a similar Society (though adapted to the peculiar circumstances of the case) may be established for the benefit of the letter carriers', whom he described as 'a most respectable body of men deserving our sympathy, support, and consideration'.[6] But while the benefits of literature were to be disseminated beyond the upper ranks of the institution, Post Office leaders also took it for granted that letter carriers' literary sensibilities differed, and needed to be cultivated separately, from those of higher-ranking employees. *Blackfriars*, though endorsed by the Post Office administration, was more genuinely egalitarian in its aims and operations, inviting contributions from anyone in the service of Her Majesty's Mails. It not only reflects an alternative understanding of who may speak for an institution, but also signals a more inclusive conception of the literary public sphere – a conception which, as I will argue, nineteenth-century postal reforms helped to shape.

In themselves, the two institutions are not remarkable. Many professional groups conducted their own periodicals, and the Post Office Library and Literary Association were modelled on similar clubs and societies within the Admiralty and the Bank of England, as well as smaller groups in individual Post Office branches.[7] Britain's political and professional institutions encouraged the development of collectives that, by promoting reading and the exchange of literary ideas, strove to elevate their members' character. Literary education and sensibility were desirable attributes in the public servants who embodied the 'soft power' of liberal government.[8] And yet, as speakers noted during the 'meeting to establish a Post Office Library and Literary Association' on 6 November 1858, it felt *especially* appropriate for 'Post Office people' to promote the 'love of literature'; the project, assembled members affirmed, would accelerate the 'progress of *mind*' to which the 'progress of intercommunication in this great nation' had already materially contributed.[9] The cultivation of literary sensibilities and improvement of facilities for communication were, for these officials,

---

[5] Post Office Library and Literary Association, *Proposal*, p. 12.
[6] Post Office Library and Literary Association, *Proposal*, p. 20.
[7] On similar associations, see Post Office Library and Literary Association, *Proposal*, pp. 1, 3, 10.
[8] On character and Victorian liberalism, see Lauren M. E. Goodlad, *Victorian Literature and the Victorian State: Character and Governance in a Liberal Society* (Baltimore: Johns Hopkins University Press, 2003).
[9] Post Office Library and Literary Association, *Proposal*, pp. 4–5, 21.

connected, jointly advancing the 'march of intellect'. In this chapter, I trace how this conceptual link came about, arguing that the 1830s campaign for postal reform, and the subsequent changes to the postal service it triggered, ought to be understood in reciprocal relation to the operations and ideologies of other literary institutions – and to the institution of literature. The literary assemblages that emerged within the Post Office in the later nineteenth century, I suggest, were products of an ongoing process of organisational change defined by the institution's central place in the literary economy.

In thinking about the Post Office as a literary institution, I build on scholarship that demonstrates the fruitfulness of reading nineteenth-century literature through a postal lens.[10] I pursue two broad lines of enquiry: first, I consider how changing Post Office regulations and policies shaped literary production, consumption, and circulation. Second, I examine the significance of literary idea(l)s to the institutional reinvention of the Post Office from the 1830s onwards. Since the nineteenth-century Post Office 'knitted together', to borrow a popular contemporary metaphor, geographically disparate as well as culturally, socially, and linguistically diverse communities, these lines of enquiry may yield different answers depending on the vantage point from which they are addressed.[11] Nevertheless, the Post Office is ever-present in the background or just beneath the surface of nineteenth-century literary activity, if only as an obstacle or source of frustration, imbricated with the operations of other literary and cultural institutions.

Literary Infrastructure

The *Literary Gazette*, an important literary tastemaker during the 1820s and 1830s under William Jerdan's editorship, offers a prominent, if indirect, acknowledgement of the Post Office's literary significance. Original poetry was central to the weekly journal's success, but those who contributed verse were styled 'correspondents' rather than 'poets'. If that term still carried lingering associations of the 'democratic "exchange" of reading and

---

[10] See Bernhard Siegert, *Relays: Literature as an Epoch of the Postal System*, trans. by Kevin Repp (Stanford: Stanford University Press, 1999), p. 113; Richard Menke, *Telegraphic Realism: Victorian Fiction and Other Information Systems* (Stanford: Stanford University Press, 2008); Kate Thomas, *Postal Pleasures: Sex, Scandal, and Victorian Letters* (New York: Oxford University Press, 2012); Laura Rotunno, *Postal Plots in British Fiction, 1840–1898: Readdressing Correspondence in Victorian Culture* (Basingstoke: Palgrave, 2013).

[11] See Ruth Livesey, *Writing the Stage Coach Nation: Locality on the Move in Nineteenth-Century British Literature* (Oxford: Oxford University Press, 2016), pp. 218–19.

writing' it had evoked in eighteenth-century periodicals (where, as Jon Klancher argues, readers were also always potentially writers), in Jerdan's publication it primarily served to conceal the professionalism and commercial interests of the most successful – often female – *Gazette* poets, especially Letitia Elizabeth Landon.[12] In either case, the term also foregrounds the material process by which a writer's words reached periodical pages, directing attention to the fact that the post provided a vital infrastructure for professional literary activity. Correspondence between authors, publishers, editors, reviewers, booksellers, printers, and readers – in all the configurations that structure the creation of literary value and meaning – depended on the postal service. In addition, the post became increasingly important for the circulation of books and other printed matter, especially as infrastructure improved and prices decreased during the nineteenth century. This point may appear self-evident but deserves careful consideration; it clearly mattered to literary actors as well as to advocates of postal reform. To consider literary actors' and institutions' interactions with the postal system not only sharpens our understanding of how texts were made, circulated, and used, as book historians like Stephen Colclough and Robert Patten demonstrate, it also reveals the importance of literature to the Victorian Post Office's institutional self-understanding and public image.[13]

During the *Literary Gazette*'s heyday, literature's postal infrastructure was expensive and, in Jerdan's words, 'tedious'.[14] A tax levied by the government for the conveyance of the mails, postage was usually paid by the recipient and calculated based on the distance a letter travelled, multiplied by the number of sheets included (or the weight of communications exceeding an ounce). A letter's arrival, especially if it contained any kind of enclosure, could place the recipient under considerable financial strain. Political newspapers – when approved by the Postmaster General,

---

[12] Jon P. Klancher, *The Making of English Reading Audiences, 1790–1832* (Madison: University of Wisconsin Press, 1987), p. 22. On poetry in the *Literary Gazette*, see Susan Matoff, 'William Jerdan and "The Literary Gazette"', *The Wordsworth Circle*, 46.3: Romanticism and Experiment (Summer 2015), 190–97. On the poetess and literary professionalism, see Anne K. Mellor, 'The Female Poet and the Poetess: Two Traditions of British Women's Poetry, 1780–1830', *Studies in Romanticism*, 36.2 (1997), 261–76.

[13] Stephen Colclough, 'Distribution', in *The Cambridge History of the Book in Britain, vol. 6: 1830–1914*, ed. by David McKitterick (Cambridge: Cambridge University Press, 2009), pp. 238–80; Robert L. Pattern, 'The New Cultural Marketplace: Victorian Publishing and Reading Practices', in *The Oxford Handbook of Victorian Literary Culture*, ed. by Juliet John (Oxford: Oxford University Press, 2005), pp. 481–506.

[14] William Jerdan, *The Autobiography of William Jerdan*, 4 vols (London: Arthur Hall, Virtue, 1853), IV, 379.

put in an open packet, and correctly stamped by the publisher – circulated 'free of postage', but other printed and manuscript texts were expensive. Contemporary writers were acutely aware of the costs of correspondence. Jerdan deplored that Landon's letters demonstrated a 'terrible economising about franks and postages'.[15] In fretting over postages, however, Landon was unexceptional, in good company with Samuel Taylor Coleridge, who, according to Anne Fadiman, was 'famous for approaching MPs, who had the privilege of free postal franking, and badgering them into signing his mail', and even the significantly better-off Percy Bysshe Shelley, whose manuscripts and notebooks evince great care to minimise the cost of exchanges with publishers.[16] As new institutions, including literary periodicals, reconfigured authorship and audiences, navigating postal charges and etiquette was a necessary but expensive part of literary labour. Accordingly, the reform of postal arrangements and postage costs in 1840 significantly changed the economic, material, and social contexts in which literary activity took place, for individuals and institutions alike.

But although tedious postal arrangements clearly inconvenienced those who made their living by literature, a vital argument in the 1830s campaigns for postal reform focussed on the reading public. A frequently quoted passage from Rowland Hill's 1837 pamphlet *Post Office Reform: Its Importance and Practicability* captures this literary case for reform. Despite the pamphlet's evident focus on economics, Hill – whose earlier life had been dedicated to educational reform and to running the progressive Hazelwood school in Warwickshire – claims that '[t]he loss to the revenue is' not the greatest evil 'inflicted on society by the high rates of postage'.[17] By preventing the 'circulation of letters and of the many cheap and excellent non-political publications of the present day', he writes, expensive postage hinders the 'religious, moral, and intellectual progress of the people'. Reform of 'erroneous financial arrangements' would allow the Post Office to fulfil its potential as a 'a powerful engine of civilization; capable of performing a distinguished part in the great work of National education'.[18] For readers unimpressed by Hill's financial rationale, his

---

[15] Jerdan, III, 191.
[16] Anne Fadiman, 'The Oakling and the Oak: The Tragedy of the Coleridges', in *Letter Writing among Poets*, ed. by Jonathan Ellis (Edinburgh: Edinburgh University Press, 2015), pp. 95–110 (pp. 97–98); on Shelley, see Donald R. Reiman, 'Shelley's Manuscripts and the Web of Circumstance', in *Romantic Revisions*, ed. by Robert Brinkley and Keith Hanley (Cambridge: Cambridge University Press, 1992), pp. 227–42 (p. 227).
[17] See Daunton, pp. 12–13.
[18] Rowland Hill, *Post Office Reform: Its Importance and Practicability* (London: C. Knight, 1837), p. 8.

arguments about education – and thus the moral fabric of the nation – were harder to dismiss. In an age of growing literary rates and educational standards among the middle and working classes, obstacles to the distribution of literature appeared increasingly problematic, both to reformers seeking to extend the benefits of learning and to publishers who perceived new commercial opportunities and markets.[19]

Hill's campaign was successful, and on 10 January 1840, several key changes took effect. The cost of inland letters weighing up to half an ounce, irrespective of the number of sheets or distance between sender and recipient, fell to one penny. For letters weighing up to an ounce, the cost increased to twopence, with a further two charged for each additional ounce. Prepayment became, along with the use of postage stamps, customary. Sending manuscripts and printed texts in parcels was never exactly cheap after 1840, but it became a good deal more affordable. Correspondence, by contrast, came within reach of a much larger section of society, as the penny rate encouraged the public to consider themselves as part of one broad discursive community.[20]

Entangled Institutions

Changes to the postal infrastructure found reflection in the forms of literary texts, inspiring new plot structures, tropes, and models for imagining social relations.[21] Moreover, a wealth of archival evidence bears witness to the increase in personal and professional correspondence between literary actors, and to the proliferation of such communications as publishers' circulars, fan letters, payments, and receipts for subscription fees, among others. As noted earlier, public reform propaganda focussed on the reading public, but those who made, marketed, and sold literature stood to benefit in similarly important – and more tangible – ways. Cheaper postage cost, and an expanding postal infrastructure, opened up new markets and created opportunities for increased profits. It would be a mistake, therefore, to consider literary institutions, or the individuals who ran or interacted with them, as passive beneficiaries or victims of postal arrangements. In his classic 1982 essay on the history of books, Robert Darnton argues that 'The wagon, the canal barge, the merchant vessel, the post office and the railroad may have influenced the history of literature more than one would

---

[19] See Alan Rauch, *Useful Knowledge: The Victorians, Morality, and the March of Intellect* (Durham: Duke University Press, 2001), pp. 1–39.
[20] See Thomas, p. 22.   [21] See Menke; Rotunno, *Postal Plots*; Thomas.

suspect.'²² At first reading, the post office here appears as one more system of literary dissemination, alongside several other private and public infrastructures. But Darnton's shorthand, the 'post office', evokes both an elaborate infrastructural system and a set of centralised institutions, usually associated with nation-states, which organised postal services in Europe. In the United Kingdom at least, the General Post Office had its own agenda and investment in literary culture. Hence, the reverse of Darnton's statement also applies: the nineteenth-century Post Office not only shaped literary history, its institutional development is also marked by the interventions of literary actors.

Hill's above-cited pamphlet, for instance, was published by Charles Knight, who also ran the *Penny Magazine* of the Society for the Diffusion of Useful Knowledge and numerous other publishing ventures targeting working-class readers.²³ The *Penny Magazine*, in turn, was an important advocate of postal reform propaganda throughout the 1830s. As Catherine Golden has shown, other newspapers and periodicals, too, enthusiastically joined in the promotion of Post Office reform, while Henry Cole's 'Scene at Windsor Castle', which imagines Queen Victoria's discovery of the suffering inflicted on her subjects by high postage, was sown into the serial instalments of Dickens's *Nicholas Nickleby* (1838–9), published by Chapman and Hall.²⁴ J. C. Loudon, the editor of the *Gardener's Magazine*, took the more conventional route of writing to the editor of *The Times* to share his views about the 'influence of that measure on periodical literature', hoping to 'induc[e] the supporters of Mr. Hill's measure to persevere'.²⁵ If 'reformers attested to the salutary effects of cheap postage on literature', as Richard Menke argues, publishers and booksellers were actively involved in the campaigns for cheap postage, working to create an infrastructure better adapted to the exigencies of their trade.²⁶

The influence of literary actors – individual and institutional – emerges yet more clearly in the history of the Inland Book Post, a reduced rate for the transmission of printed matter. In 1847, Rowland Hill wrote to the

---

²² Robert Darnton, 'What is the History of Books?', *Daedalus*, III (1982), 65–83 (p. 77).
²³ On the relationship between Hill, Knight, the S.D.U.K, and the *Penny Magazine*, see Menke, p. 37.
²⁴ Catherine Golden, *Posting It: The Victorian Revolution in Letter Writing* (Gainesville, FL: University Press of Florida, 2009), pp. 58–73.
²⁵ J. C. Loudon, 'The Effect of A General Penny Post on Periodical Literature', *The Times*, 9 May 1839, p. 5.
²⁶ Menke, p. 39.

Postmaster General affirming the 'expediency of still further facilitating the transmission of Books or other printed matter by means of the Post office'.[27] His minute not only predicts the profits the Book Post will generate for his department, but also links the measure to the 'present state of the public mind on the important subject of Education', reactivating Post Office reform rhetoric by suggesting that any 'arrangement' designed to advance 'intellectual progress' would likely be 'valued'. On the one hand, Hill claims that by facilitating 'the transmission of scientific & literary Reports and of other documents tending to the extension and diffusion of knowledge', the proposed 'privilege' would assist 'Literary & Scientific Societies'. On the other hand, Hill affirms the benefits of the newly affordable rate for 'residents in remote Country places, many of which are scarcely reached by any other system of conveyance'. Hill thus pre-empts the counterargument that parcels did not fall under the Post Office monopoly, so that the book trade and periodical publishers could use private companies with competitive pricing structures. By distinguishing the Post Office's expansive (and constantly expanding) infrastructure from 'any other system of conveyance', he implies the need for a government-subsidised service supplying Britain's rural readers 'with much valuable matter, which, under present circumstances, can seldom reach them'.[28] Here, the free trade disciple Hill not only argues for a nationalised infrastructure to support the work of 'Literary & Scientific Societies', he also positions the Post Office itself as one such society, claiming the transmission of literary matter and information as a central part of its public institutional purpose and identity.

The Postmaster General was unenthusiastic, but Hill succeeded again. From 21 February 1848, the public could take advantage of a book post rate of sixpence for packets weighing up to one pound. Colclough demonstrates the importance of these regulations for the book trade, major circulating libraries such as Mudie's and Smith's, and smaller but influential libraries beyond London.[29] What is less well documented, however, is the fact that a variety of literary actors successfully lobbied the Post Office to change Book Post arrangements. Following some letters to the editor of *The Times*, for example, the initial prohibition on enclosures and on writing on the material in book packets was abandoned, because it prevented trade in second-hand and antiquarian books.[30] From 1852, book packets were no longer restricted to 'a single printed book, or printed

---

[27] Rowland Hill, 25 October 1847. London, Postal Museum Archive, Post 30/112, E183/47.
[28] Hill, 25 October 1847. [29] Colclough, pp. 241–42, 247, 254.
[30] J. O. Halliwell, 'To the Editor of the Times', *The Times*, 15 May 1851, p. 8; 'A Sufferer', 'Books by Post', *The Times*, 19 May 1851, p. 8.

magazine, or printed review, or printed pamphlet', but could 'contain any number of separate books, maps, or prints, and any quantity of paper, vellum ... either printed, written, or plain, or any mixture of the three'.[31] This new regulation bore the imprint of those members of the public, presumably linked to the publishing world, who had called for 'the transmission of printed proofs and of the copy, whether M.S or print, which is in almost all cases necessarily sent therewith, to & from their authors'.[32] In the 1860s, the impetus for the creation of a halfpenny stamp (which would pay for the carriage of two ounces' worth of books) came from the educational publishers Cassell, Petter, and Galpin, who affirmed that such a measure would bring an 'enormous' increase of postal business.[33]

Network Culture

Mary Mullen's remark that 'although institutions act as forms, they also foster relationships that undermine the stability of these forms' illuminates the Post Office's complex position as both shaping and shaped by multiple, shifting assemblages of literary actors.[34] Rather than exercising unilateral influence on other literary institutions, the Post Office constantly negotiated its relationship with the 'many overlaid networks' in which, as Caroline Levine notes, 'acts of reading and writing in Victorian Britain routinely took shape'.[35] However, as Andrew Winckles and Angela Rehbein argue, the shape and operations of literary networks, especially outside the institutional public sphere, are also contingent upon the 'technologies and means of mediation' available to specific groups in specific spatio-temporal settings.[36] Given the Post Office's monopoly on letter carrying in nineteenth-century Britain, changes to the cost of postage, or to delivery routes and patterns, directly impacted possibilities and processes of network formation.

The study of literary networks and sociabilities – recently boosted by the growing sophistication of digital humanities methods – has enabled

---

[31] Treasury Warrant, 7 February 1848 and Notice to Public, 25 February 1852. Post 30/112.
[32] Hill, 30 May 1851. Post 30/112, E1089/51.
[33] Letter from Messrs. Cassell, Petter & Galpin, 11 September 1867. Post 30/204a.
[34] Mary Mullen, *Novel Institutions: Anachronism, Irish Novels, and Nineteenth-Century Realism* (Edinburgh: Edinburgh University Press, 2019), p. 5.
[35] Caroline Levine, 'From Nation to Network', *Victorian Studies*, 55.4 (2013), 647–66 (p. 664).
[36] Andrew O. Winckles and Angela Rehbein, 'Introduction: "A Tribe of Authoresses"', in *Women's Literary Networks and Romanticism*, ed. by Andrew O. Winckles and Angela Rehbein (Liverpool: Liverpool University Press, 2017), pp. 1–16 (p. 3).

reinvigorating and sometimes canon-defying accounts of literary influence, production, and reading.[37] Moving the focus from canonical writers and prestigious institutions to processes of mediation and points of connection, scholars working on different periods have embraced an understanding of literature as 'an aggregated ecosystem or "economy" of texts'.[38] But consideration of Victorian literary networks in particular raises additional questions. First, to what extent, and in what ways, do they differ from the patterns of literary sociability and networking that characterised earlier historic moments?[39] Second, how did Victorian literary networks – social and professional – differ from, and interact with, more formal institutional structures, especially the institutions of the liberal state?[40] In pursuing these questions, it is not only important to consider material and infrastructural factors such as postage costs or delivery patterns and routes, but also to acknowledge that the postal reform of 1840 normalised a relatively new way of thinking about networks, which hinged on this form's imagined capacity to weave the nation's individual subjects into an apparently inclusive community.

The General Post Office had already sustained the work of cultural institutions, the networked communities they contained, and more informal correspondence and manuscript networks for two centuries prior to the introduction of universal penny postage. At a local level, cultural actors could also frequently take advantage of penny or twopenny postage rates. What changed after 1840, however, was the scale and scope of the networks – or rather *the network*, singular – woven by correspondence.

---

[37] See *Romantic Sociability: Social Networks and Literary Culture in Britain, 1770–1840*, ed. by Gillian Russell and Clara Tuite (Cambridge: Cambridge University Press, 2002). On Victorian networks, see essays in *Victorian Periodicals Review*, 44 (2011) (a special issue on 'Victorian Networks and the Periodical Press', edited by Alexis Easley); the chapters in *Virtual Victorians: Networks, Connection, Technologies*, ed. by Veronica Alfano and Andrew Stauffer (Basingstoke: Palgrave Macmillan, 2015); Nathan K. Hensley, 'Network: Andrew Lang and the Distributed Agencies of Literary Production', *Victorian Periodicals Review*, 48 (2015), 359–82; Andrea Stewart, '"The Limits of the Imaginable": Women Writers' Networks during the Long Nineteenth Century', *Victorian Review*, 45 (2019), 39–57.

[38] Matthew L. Jockers, *Macroanalysis: Digital Methods and Literary History* (Champaign: University of Illinois Press, 2017), p. 32.

[39] See, for instance, *Romantic Sociability*; Lindsay O'Neill, *The Open Letter: Networking in the Early Modern British World* (Philadelphia: University of Pennsylvania Press, 2015); Paul Trolander, *Literary Sociability in Early Modern England: The Epistolary Record* (Cranbury: University of Delaware Press, 2014).

[40] Simon Potter argues that it is important for scholars to distinguish between 'informal, open, multiple, competing, and dynamic' networks and 'more formal, entrenched, and limited patterns of interconnection': 'Webs, Networks, and Systems: Globalization and the Mass Media in the Nineteenth- and Twentieth-Century British Empire', *Journal of British Studies*, 46 (2007), 621–46 (p. 622).

Newly accessible means of mediation reduced, at least conceptually, the distance between cultural centres and readers and writers who found themselves at the margins because of class, gender, language, or geography. More 'delivery and access' points were constantly being added to the postal infrastructure in the four nations of Victorian Britain, so that conceptions of remoteness and centrality were redefined, while transnational agreements and imperial infrastructure facilitated connection across national borders.[41] Inexpensive prepayment of postage made it more plausible for aspiring writers to address a stranger with an expectation of being read. For the price of a penny, they could correspond with editors, publishers, or established authors, and try their luck even without a name, fame, or recommendation to precede the message. Those who were not quite bold enough for such initiative could at least look for support from a mediator in their local network.[42] As a result, networks were becoming more spatially dispersed, socially heterogeneous, and densely interconnected, as the postal system – propped up by railways and steam packets – encouraged the literate public to consider themselves as part of one vast 'small world network', where degrees of separation appeared to be shrinking and where, as Walter Bagehot commented, one could never be sure 'what effect any force or any change may produce on a frame work so exquisite and so involved'.[43]

Despite its centralised bureaucracy and uniform institutional regulations, the Post Office decentred existing models of literary sociability and necessitated new models of the literary public sphere, echoing the effects – real and imagined – of the periodical's rise a century earlier. Eighteenth-century periodicals, Klancher argues, cultivated the faith that 'readers might exchange roles with writers', and this 'freedom of access to writing gives periodical writing the aura of the democratic and communal'.[44] Similarly, though on a larger scale, postal reform allowed an ever-growing number of correspondents to imagine themselves as members of a democratic community of writers and readers. As Kate Thomas suggests, it encouraged the public to consider '"everyone" as communicative

---

[41] Menke, p. 41.
[42] On the notion of a mediator, see Nathan K. Hensley, 'What is a Network? (And Who is Andrew Lang)?', *Romanticism and Victorianism on the Net*, 64 (2013), para. 5 <https://doi.org/10.7202/1025668ar>.
[43] Walter Bagehot, 'The Character of Sir Robert Peel', in *The Collected Works of Walter Bagehot*, ed. by Norman St John-Stevas, 15 vols (London: Economist, 1965–86), III, 255.
[44] Klancher, p. 22.

subjects' and as parts of 'a network designed to connect that same "everyone" to anyone', an idea that was as exhilarating to some as it was unsettling to others.[45] But this nineteenth-century postal network also differs significantly from the ideal periodical community of the eighteenth century. Before the 1790s, Klancher explains, 'the social text of periodical writing ... joins two dissonant orders: inside the text, a communal, democratic exchange; outside the text, a hierarchically ranked world'.[46] But the Victorian postal network, instead of 'effacing social differences', accentuated the sheer diversity of the correspondents that had been enfranchised as 'communicative subjects'.[47] The fact that everyone's letters, provided they carried a penny stamp, received the same treatment from the postal service was remarkable precisely because these letters displayed 'the same sort of variety that marks society', as William Lewins noted in 1865.[48] Thus, the imaged community fostered by the postal service did not counteract those processes of differentiation and hierarchisation – between audiences, between genres, between tastes – that, as Klancher and Clifford Siskin show, shaped literary culture and literary institutions in the wake of the French Revolution.[49] Rather, the apparently all-inclusive postal network interacted with a literary culture that was, on the one hand, accessible to a growing and increasingly diverse section of the population while, on the other hand, distinguishing carefully between different types of texts, writers, and readers.

The declared commitment to constructing a more broadly inclusive and democratic national culture did not, of course, dismantle existing hierarchies in a literary marketplace dominated by men with the requisite financial and cultural capital. But improved access to long-distance communication helped women 'bec[o]me more accepted and embedded within the publishing industry'.[50] Likewise, the increasing affordability of correspondence supported the 'social networks that were so vital in assisting working-class poets to publication and recognition'.[51] In a sense, then, the Victorian Post Office challenged the power of socially – and, to a lesser extent, sexually – exclusive institutions to broker and regulate literary networks; by the same token, it claimed kin with associations that championed a more inclusive –

---

[45] Thomas, p. 4.   [46] Klancher, p. 23.   [47] Klancher, p. 23.
[48] William Lewins, *Her Majesty's Mails: A History of the Post-Office, and an Industrial Account of Its Present Condition*, 2nd edn (London: Sampson, Low, Son, and Marston, 1865), p. 266.
[49] See Klancher; and Clifford Siskin, *The Work of Writing: Literature and Social Change in Britain, 1700–1830* (Baltimore: Johns Hopkins University Press, 1998), especially Chapter 6.
[50] Stewart, p. 42.
[51] Kirstie Blair, *Working Verse in Victorian Scotland: Poetry, Press, Community* (Oxford: Oxford University Press, 2019), p. 16.

if not always more equal – model of culture: the local 'Literary and Scientific Societies' that would, in Hill's view, benefit from affordable postage and rates for transmitting printed matter as well as national ventures, including the Society for the Diffusion of Useful Knowledge. As suggested earlier, this identification ran deep: reformers not only self-consciously advertised the benefits these societies would derive from cheaper postage, they also considered their own department to perform a similar function – albeit on a larger scale – by transmitting information and ideas. Some commentators went even further, however: they compared the services of the Post Office not only to the operations of other literary institutions but also to the work of literature itself.

Literary Institution: 'Postmen are Men of Letters, Too'

As the idea of a national network gained traction, local institutions played a vital role in connecting marginal writers and readers to national and transnational networks. The career of Edward Capern, the 'postman poet' of rural Devonshire, illustrates the kinds of networking processes that could create a national audience for a provincial working-class writer while also revealing him as a hinge figure between two different kinds of literary institutions. William Frederick Rock, a banker-turned-philanthropist with humble beginnings, took it upon himself to 'introduce a man of genius to the world' and champion the 'rural letter carrier' who earned 'ten shillings and sixpence per week' for his daily thirteen-mile walk around Bideford. Having returned from London to his native Barnstaple, Rock founded the Barnstaple Literary and Scientific Institute in 1845.[52] Members had access to a reading room, a library, public lectures, and evening classes, and also benefited from the Institute's affiliation with the London Society of Arts. The institution aimed '[t]o place within the reach of the Public, the best and most recent information on all subjects, Literary, Scientific, Commercial, and Political'; 'to accumulate a supply of Entertaining as well as Instructive Reading for the Public generally'; and 'to provide means of extending their Education to Young Men and Adults, by affording facilities for Systematic Study'.[53] In line with his commitment to 'the mental improvement of the humbler classes of society', its founder also 'munificently subscribe[d] £100 per Annum, with a view of rendering

---

[52] William Frederick Rock, 'Preface to the First Edition', in *Poems*, ed. by Edward Capern, 2nd edn (London: Bogue, 1856), pp. v–vi.
[53] 'Barnstaple Literary and Scientific Institution', Barnstaple, North Devon Athenaeum Document Archive, B01F-003–02.

the full benefits of the Institution available to a large class of Society, whom the Ordinary Terms of Subscriptions might otherwise debar therefrom'.[54] Capern was among the beneficiaries.

In 1855, Rock began to use not just money but also influence to facilitate Capern's participation in literary culture. He activated his network of 'literary friends' to procure subscriptions for Capern's first volume of verse, demonstrating the growing reach of a much older practice.[55] Charles Kingsley was among those who furthered this cause, writing to Frederick James Furnivall, his collaborator in the London-based Working Men's College, with the request to 'obtain ... 2 or 3 subscriptions to the poetry of the poor fellow herewith enclosed'.[56] Many subscribers to Capern's *Poems* were North Devonians, but the eventual list also connected Capern's name to such nationally renowned figures as Alfred Tennyson, Charles Dickens, J. A. Froude, and Rowland Hill. Thanks to the network Rock had established, the first edition sold out in three months; it was soon followed by a second edition and, in due course, three further collections of poems. Capern was granted a civil service pension by Palmerston's government in 1857 and enjoyed a modest career as a poet and lecturer until his death in 1894.[57] His trajectory provides insight into the changing conditions of access to publishing and reflects the increasing social heterogeneity of literary networks. It also made a peculiar kind of sense in relation to the Victorian Post Office's institutional ideology.

Capern's example delivered on the promise that postal reformers had made two decades earlier: that improved intercommunication, and improved facilities for the transmission of 'useful knowledge', would disseminate the benefits of learning, so that even those who carried Britain's mail could become active participants in, as well as servants of, the nation's cultural life. But Capern's career and public image as 'postman-poet' was also significant because it embodied a second idea central to the public image of the post: the idea that postal work was somehow akin to literary work. In *Postal Pleasures* (2013), Kate Thomas discusses an anecdote popular among proponents of the penny post, featured in Harriet Martineau's *A History of England During the Thirty Years Peace*

---

[54] 'Barnstaple Scientific and Literary Society', *North Devon Journal*, 10 April 1845, p. 2; North Devon Athenaeum, B01F-003–02.
[55] Rock, p. v.
[56] Charles Kingsley, letter to Frederick James Furnivall, 6 May 1855, San Marino, The Huntington Library, MSS FU460.
[57] For a recent popular biography, see Ilfra Goldberg, *Edward Capern: The Postman-Poet* (Cambridge: Vanguard Press, 2009). For a Victorian account, see W. Ormond, *Recollections of Edward Capern* (Bristol: W. Mack, 1860).

(1849).⁵⁸ Martineau's version follows a young Hill who, while 'walking through the Lake district', sees the 'postman deliver a letter to a woman at a cottage door'. Moved by her inability to 'pay the postage, which was a shilling', Hill pays on her behalf, only to discover that 'the sheet was blank', a strategy devised by the woman and her brother to ensure 'she had tidings of him without expense of postage'. The encounter becomes an origin myth for Hill's ambitious plans to reform the corrupt 'system which drove a brother and sister to cheating, in order to gratify their desire to hear of one another's welfare'.⁵⁹

The one problem with Martineau's account: it was Samuel Taylor Coleridge who had experienced and recorded the incident in 1822.⁶⁰ Other writers who 'celebrated the liberating effects of the Penny Post' made the same error, however, and, according to Thomas, 'this particular switch' – between postal servant and poet – may have been a 'natural cultural slip'.⁶¹ Using the specific term 'postman' to refer to postal work more broadly, Thomas argues that 'the figures of the poet and postman were more easily mistaken for each other than the twenty-first century reader might imagine', since both 'could – through the texts they put into circulation – enable a reader to experience correspondence with someone or something outside of themselves, to imagine themselves in another place or time, or to feel the feelings of somebody else'.⁶² In tracing instances of this 'cultural slip', focussing on contemporary periodical poetry, it becomes clear how strongly contemporary theories about the power and purpose of literature shaped the institutional mythology of the Post Office.

Like many other public events, the introduction of penny postage (and its anniversaries) inspired poetry, much of which appeared in newspapers and periodicals. Some of these poems directly engage – often not wholly seriously – with contemporary claims for the reform's literary effects. For instance, 'The Penny Post-Age', printed in the *Norwich Mercury* on 25 January 1840, praises Hill's invention as the 'pride of modern times', imagining its positive impact on the law, medicine, religion, and romantic love. It ends, however, with '[t]he literary man who loves in learning's path to walk / And makes *belles lettres* and the art his common table-talk'. This figure, according to the anonymous poet, '[r]egards the Postage Act, and cries, "enough" I am at peace; / The *Hill* of learning rears its head, and *letters* must

---

⁵⁸ Thomas, pp. 21–22.
⁵⁹ Harriet Martineau, *The History of England during the Thirty Years' Peace, 1816–1846* (London: C. Knight, 1850), p. 425.
⁶⁰ Golden, p. 48-9.   ⁶¹ Thomas, p. 22.   ⁶² Thomas, p. 22.

increase'.[63] Using the kinds of puns that characterised newspaper poems about postal reform, the poet frames cheap postage as a boost to literary learning. The predicted growth in the number of post letters implicitly heralds an expansion of literary sensibilities and productivity. A comic song by James Bruton, printed in several provincial newspapers in the late summer of 1839 and early months of 1840, similarly imagines the proliferation of texts – and prodigious use of paper and ink – after postal reform, before going on to satirise the possibility (turned reality in Capern's case) that those who deliver the nation's correspondence will now become participants in the exchange of literary ideas:

> Mail coachmen are improving much in the knowledge of the head,
> For like the letters which they take they're themselves all over *red*:
> Post-men are 'men of letters,' too, each one's a learned talker –
> And 'cause he reads the diction'ry, the people call him '*Walker!*'[64]

Bruton's portrayal of postmen as 'men of letters' is facetious, exploiting the juxtaposition of prosaic labour and poetic language for comic effect; nevertheless, the song anticipates more earnest affirmations of the poetic spirit underpinning postal services. These affirmations, I argue, served to reinforce the claim that, as one of the founding members of the Post Office Library and Literary Association put it, 'the progress of intercommunication' brings 'great good to humanity'.[65]

In *Romantic Correspondence*, Mary Favret describes the network of 'reform societies' that, at the end of the eighteenth century, claimed the ostensibly private letter as a means of building egalitarian, sympathetic, and mutually improving communities.[66] She explains that, far from being state-sanctioned, the national network of Corresponding Societies, who looked to the London Corresponding Society as their parent, were perceived as a threat, since 'friendly' correspondence served to disseminate radical and revolutionary thought. Cheap and efficient means of mass communication appeared more likely to undermine than strengthen social cohesion.[67] After the end of the Napoleonic Wars, however, perceptions of

---

[63] 'The Penny Post-Age', *Norwich Mercury*, 25 January 1840, p. 2.
[64] Bruton's song appeared, for instance, in the *Worcester Journal* on 22 August 1839, the *Derbyshire Courier* on 31 August 1839, the *Preston Chronicle* on 21 September 1839, the *Cheltenham Chronicle* on 3 October 1839, the *Bolton Chronicle* on 11 January 1840, and even – via the *Cheltenham Chronicle* – in *The Perth Gazette and Western Australian Journal*, 16 May 1840.
[65] Post Office Library and Literary Association, *Proposal*, p. 21.
[66] Mary Favret, *Romantic Correspondence: Women, Politics, and the Fiction of Letters* (Cambridge: Cambridge University Press, 1993), pp. 26–29.
[67] Favret, p. 29.

'intercommunication' underwent a radical transformation. Hill's own parliamentary testimony in 1843 about the early effects of postal reform reveal, in Favret's word, a 'confident approval of "large societies" brought together via correspondence'.[68] By 1865, when William Lewins described the Post Office as 'eminently a democratic establishment, conducted on the most approved *fraternité et egalité* principles', the words were calculated to inspire national pride rather than alarm.[69] An understanding of 'intercommunication' as a public good and source of moral improvement had become commonplace, thoroughly absorbed into the mainstream of liberal discourse.[70] The early-Victorian campaigners who worked to legitimise claims about the benefits of living in a postally networked world, I suggest, found welcome material in contemporary theories about the power of written texts to generate sympathy, disseminate knowledge, and foster moral communities. Specifically, postal reform propaganda bore the influence of the Wordsworthian poetics which, in their turn, left a strong imprint on George Eliot's theory of the novel.[71]

Introducing his 1879 edition of Wordsworth's selected poems, Matthew Arnold claims that Wordsworth had 'never ... been so accepted and popular ... as he was between the years 1830 and 1840' – years profoundly marked by the spirit of liberal reform.[72] Stephen Gill convincingly traces the appropriation of Wordsworth by liberal thinkers like Arnold and J. S. Mill to the reappraisal by a new generation of readers of the poet's 'radical humanitarianism', captured in the declaration in the *Cumberland Beggar* that 'we all of us have one human heart'.[73] The moral and political imperatives that shaped the earlier Wordsworth's reception in the 1830s, I suggest, also formed the basis of contemporary reform movements; more specifically, they created fertile grounds for a scheme like Hill's, which sought to turn the postal service into the arterial network that would keep the 'one human heart' pumping. Three ideas that were central to the early-Victorian 'idea of Wordsworth' – articulated in the 1802 preface to *Lyrical Ballads* – found reflection in the popular, affective discourse about the postal service: first, that 'incidents and situations from common life' are

---

[68] Favret, p. 205. [69] Lewins, p. 266.
[70] On the positive connotations of the network for the Victorians, see Laura Otis, *Networking: Communicating with Bodies and Machines in the Nineteenth Century* (Ann Arbor: University of Michigan Press, 2001), p. 8.
[71] See Stephen Gill, *Wordsworth and the Victorians* (Oxford: Clarendon, 1998), pp. 145–67; and Otis, pp. 117–19.
[72] Matthew Arnold, *Poems of Wordsworth* (London: Macmillan, 1879), p. v. [73] Gill, p. 27.

worthy of poetic treatment; second, that such treatment is no less poetically valuable for being expressed in a 'language really used by men'; third, and most important, that the poet's mission is to 'carry everywhere with him relationship and love', 'bin[ding] together by passion and knowledge the vast empire of human society'.[74] Wordsworth may have been unimpressed with Hill's reform, expressing the view that 'letters are sure to be impoverished by the change' and complaining that 'the penny postage has let in an inundation of complimentary letters upon me'; nevertheless, this reform was a product of the same cultural and political climate that had given new currency to his earlier poetry and poetics.[75]

Hill's own arguments and motivations for postal reform were rooted, above all, in economic considerations, regarding both the affordability of penny postage and the stimulus it would provide to commerce. Never losing sight of profit margins, Hill believed that intellectual, moral, and religious improvement would naturally follow in the wake of free trade and material prosperity.[76] But the celebrations of the penny post that found a wider readership in newspapers and periodicals – in articles, tales, sketches, cartoons, and poems – favoured a different and ultimately more influential narrative.[77] 'Lines on the Penny Post', a poem that appeared in the *Literary Gazette* on 27 August 1842, contends that the 'mystic import' of 'those little words' – penny post – lies in the 'world of ties' fostered by correspondence. The poet declares:

> They say that commerce to thine aid
> Owes much of fostering speed and ease;
> That thou, good post, art 'good for trade'—
> But what are services like these
> The generous commerce of the heart,
> This forms thy dearest, noblest part.

Here, the 'commerce of the heart' is elevated above 'trade', and the postal service is framed as a social service and public good rather than a mechanism for generating revenue – an idea which, as the speeches held during the opening meeting of the Post Office Library and Literary Association confirm, also took hold within the postal bureaucracy.

---

[74] William Wordsworth, 'Preface to *Lyrical Ballads, with Pastoral and Other Poems* (1802)', in *The Major Works*, ed. by Stephen Gill (Oxford: Oxford University Press, 2000), pp. 595–615 (pp. 596–97, 606).
[75] *The Complete Letters of William and Dorothy Wordsworth*, ed. by Ernest de Selincourt, 2nd edn, rev. by Chester L. Shaver, Mary Moorman, and Alan G. Hill, 8 vols (Oxford: Clarendon, 1967–93), VII, 49, 20.
[76] See Daunton, p. 32. [77] See Golden, p. 46.

Another set of 'Lines on the Penny Post', written by Alexander Smart and initially published in the *Scotsman* in 1845, demonstrates how closely such celebrations of the Post Office's noble mission could reflect language habitually used to theorise the power of literature, specifically poetry. Addressing Rowland Hill, the 'king of reformers', Smart writes:

> Not reckoned by pennies, thy glory and gain is:
> A great moral engine we find
> In love's golden fetters, thou true man of letters,
> That links the republic of mind.
>
> To each heart and each home do thy benefits come,
> With blessings untold in their train:
> Though distance divide from a father's fireside,
> We're link'd by thy magical chain.
>
> The ties of the heart 'tis thy bountiful part
> To strengthen and cherish and bind;
> And waft o'er the land, at thy wizard command,
> The beauty and light of the mind.[78]

Far more earnestly than Bruton, Smart frames postal work as literary work, celebrating Rowland Hill, the most prominent among the nation's postmen, as a 'true man of letters'. His language stresses that the penny post is not just a utilitarian socio-economic reform, 'reckoned by pennies', but the product and expression of a public and poetic spirit. Hill is credited with creating a 'great moral engine' that will 'strengthen and cherish and bind' 'the ties of the heart' and carry 'the beauty and light of the mind' to all corners of the nation, 'linking' its subjects in a 'republic of mind'. A Wordsworthian conception of the poet as one who carries 'everywhere relationship and love', and who disseminates the 'breath and finer spirit of all knowledge', reverberates loudly in this appraisal of Hill's achievement.

Hardwicke Rawnsley, a Victorian Wordsworthian and co-founder of the National Trust, was not wholly fanciful, then, when he linked Wordsworth to the Post Office in his 1881 sonnet 'On Seeing a Telegraph Wire and Pillar Post below Wordsworth's House'. Rawnsley writes:

> The Poet he who strikes a Prophet's lyre
> And to his own day's ear will tune its chimes;
> For while this quick world jars there shall be Rhymes,
> And while men love they will Love's Song require.

---

[78] Alexander Smart, 'Lines on the Penny-Post, Addressed to Rowland Hill, Esq.', *The Scotsman*, 25 December 1844, p. 4.

> So thought I, as I spied the humming wire
> Whose sound was as bee-music in the limes,
> And that grim letter-post, that held betimes
> The peasant's missive and the lord's desire
> Is it not well the Eolian harp should sing
> Down the white road that gave the sage his thought?
> And well the post should back to memory bring
> The man whose sympathy to concord wrought
> The poet's passion and the postman's lot,–
> Who lived, and loved, and sang in yonder humble cot?[79]

The speaker's encounter with this 'grim' prospect is less jarring than the title might suggest, because the pillar-post comes to recall a view of Wordsworth that was articulated by a contributor to *Fraser's Magazine*, who praised the poet's capacity to 'break down ... the conventional barriers that, in our disordered social state, divide rich and poor into two hostile nations'.[80] In Rawnsley's poem, 'two hostile nations' come into direct contact, as 'the peasant's missive and the lord's desire' mingle in the shared space of the pillar-post, from which both will travel to their destinations at the uniform cost of one penny. The poem imagines the power of the pillar-post – a metonym for the postal infrastructure – to erase difference and distance, challenging 'conventional barriers' in a manner that recalls Wordsworth's politically charged challenge to poetic conventions. The tensions in its title are resolved because the postal service, which forges sympathetic connections between socially and geographically distant individuals, becomes an emblem for the poetic legacy of '[t]he man whose sympathy to concord wrought/ The poet's passion and the postman's lot'. In Rawnsley's sonnet, both structures – poetry and post – are similarly capacious, accessible, and capable of 'working concord'.

The significance of Rawnsley's poem derives neither from its aesthetic qualities nor from providing insight into the literary significance of the Post Office; rather, it derives from what it reveals about the transformation of the Post Office's institutional identity during the preceding decades – a transformation driven partly from within and partly from without, by journalists, petitioners, tradesmen, and periodical poets. The association between Wordsworth's poetry and the postal service is not random, like the placement of a pillar-post beside the poet's cottage, but

---

[79] H. D. Rawnsley, *Sonnets at the English Lakes* (London: Longmans, Green, 1881), p. 35.
[80] 'Wordsworth, Part 1', *Fraser's Magazine*, 44 (1851), 101–18 (p. 106). See Gill, p. 27.

responds to a cultural narrative about the postal service that, in turn, came to shape the stories this centralised institution told about itself.

Since both literature and the postal service are fundamentally concerned with the transmission of texts, the operations and institutional logic of the nineteenth-century Post Office were firmly linked to the literary economy. From the moment the Post Office became a public institution in the seventeenth century, postal policies, regulations, and infrastructure shaped processes and networks of literary production, dissemination, and reception. In the early Victorian years, however, the General Post Office re-built its identity and mission in explicit relation to literature. It self-consciously presented itself as a literary actor, a macroscopic counterpart to those localised institutions working towards educational, intellectual, and moral improvement by facilitating the dissemination of information, ideas, and texts. Additionally, in their largely successful efforts to popularise the belief that increased connectivity would improve morality, education, and fellow-feeling throughout Britain and its empire, postal reformers adapted claims about the power of written texts to foster sympathy and community. In this light, even material infrastructure, and the individuals who kept this infrastructure running, could appear to perform a function that was not only intertwined with but also analogous to the cultural work of literature.

CHAPTER 13

Networks, Nodes, and Beacons
Cultural Institutions in Nineteenth-Century Southeast Asia

Porscha Fermanis

In 1878, the president of the newly formed Straits Branch of the Royal Asiatic Society, Archdeacon George F. Hose, noted the special importance of literary and scientific societies in underpopulated colonial settlements, where 'men who may have much to communicate to, or learn from one another, are likely to meet very rarely unless there are fixed times and places of meeting'.[1] Hose's tribute to the society's monthly meetings at the Raffles Library and Museum in Singapore underscores the extent to which colonial institutions invested in models of social clubbability, as well as encouraging bridging connections to influential parent organisations in metropolitan and regional centres: in this case, the Asiatic Society of Bengal and the Royal Asiatic Society of Great Britain and Ireland.[2] Modelled on precedents that aimed to harness the social power of the educated male middle classes, these institutions helped to weave together the fabric of atomised colonial communities and connect settlers back to their counterparts in Britain. Yet they also enabled more than just 'the reproduction of one's own society through long-range migration', simultaneously mobilising networks within and between various settlements in Southeast Asia – horizontal connections that bypassed London, Edinburgh, and even to some extent Calcutta in their intellectual remit, practical operations, and reading audiences.[3]

Drawing on networked conceptualisations of empire that imagine the imperial world system as a series of multi-directional webs, circuits, or chains, this chapter considers the contribution of a range of cultural institutions, such as schools, libraries, and learned societies, to the ways

---

This research was funded by the European Research Council under the Horizon 2020 research and innovation programme (grant agreement no. 679436).

[1] *Journal of the Straits Branch of the Royal Asiatic Society (JSBRAS)*, 2 (1878), p. 3.
[2] For conversations and spoken papers, see *JSBRAS*, 1 (1878), p. 11, and *JSBRAS*, 2 (1878), p. v. On parent organisations, see *JSBRAS*, 1 (1878), pp. vi–vii.
[3] James Belich, *Replenishing the Earth: The Settler Revolution and the Rise of the Angloworld* (Oxford: Oxford University Press, 2009), p. 21.

in which people, knowledge, and cultural goods circulated in the entrepôt cities of the British Straits Settlements in the long nineteenth century.[4] I use the term 'network' here not in the strict sense of social network analysis and its visualisations, but rather as a way of understanding institutions as nodal points for intersecting 'circle[s] of persons' instead of just as static, place-based repositories of knowledge and its material forms.[5] While these institutions were key sites for social aspiration, embracing the peculiar 'social and cultural plasticity' of colonial settlements, my concern in this instance is primarily with the ways in which institutional frameworks converted informal associative practices into structurally embedded pedagogic systems involving particular forms of reading, authorship, and taste formation.[6] I therefore understand colonial cultural institutions as achieving their institutional identity not just by being more 'heavily administered spaces' than other associative groups, but also by being essential to the standardisation, authorisation, and diffusion of cultural goods and practises, as well as enabling the transmission of what Andrew Sartori has called a global 'culture concept' – or the Herderian idea that culture could be a discrete category of autonomous meaning – that was so central to the development of anti-colonial nationalism and pan-Asian internationalism in Southeast Asia.[7]

Taking as its primary case study a cluster of interrelated cultural institutions, including the Singapore Institution (est. 1823), the Singapore Free School (est. 1834), the Singapore Library (est. 1844), the Raffles Library and Museum (est. 1874), and the Straits Branch of the Royal Asiatic Society (est. 1877), this chapter focusses on these institutions and their medial forms on multiple scalar and conceptual levels: first, as local, regional, and transnational networks of people, enabling both bonding networks with local and regional institutions and bridging networks with metropolitan institutions; second, as geographical nodes and/or centres of regional knowledge collection, production, and accumulation that extend and disseminate knowledge gathered in the colonies to metropoles and regional centres via

---

[4] See, e.g., Alan Lester, 'Imperial Circuits and Networks: Geographies of the British Empire', *History Compass*, 4.1 (2006), 124–41.
[5] Ina Ferris, *Book-Men, Book Clubs, and the Romantic Literary Sphere* (Basingstoke: Palgrave Macmillan, 2015), p. 152.
[6] Tony Ballantyne, 'Placing Literary Culture: Books and Civic Culture in Milton', *Journal of New Zealand Literature*, 28.2 (2010), 82–104 (p. 99).
[7] Jon Mee and Jennifer Wilkes, 'Transpennine Enlightenment: The Literary and Philosophical Societies and Knowledge Networks in the North, 1781–1830', *Journal for Eighteenth-Century Studies*, 38.4 (2015), 599–612 (p. 607); Andrew Sartori, 'The Resonance of "Culture": Framing a Problem in Global Concept-History', *Comparative Studies in Society and History*, 47.4 (2005), 676–99.

journals, publication exchanges, and printed works; and third, as perceived beacons attracting both European and non-European knowledge producers and consumers within a global system of useful knowledge societies for the diffusion of moral and intellectual improvement.[8] In each case, I understand these interconnected circles as what Raymond Williams has called 'cultural formations', which can at varying times be dominant, residual, or emergent, but following Mrinalini Sinha, I also think of them as distinctively imperial cultural formations mediated by their location within a heterogeneous colonial public sphere that is neither entirely European nor entirely Asian.[9]

Shaped by this mixed public sphere and by an emerging regional identity formed by lateral connections between British, Chinese, and Malay interest groups, I consider British and vernacular cultural institutions as mutually informing platforms that enabled opportunities for both coercion and dissent. The cultural discourses that emanated from British and/or British-sponsored institutions could be used to argue for the deferral of individual and collective self-determination for 'unenlightened' colonial subjects in need of 'cultivation', but they were also mobilised by non-European groups to promote conceptions of 'autonomous agency' and to provide a 'philosophical foundation for ethical and political action'.[10] Moreover, British cultural institutions relied on the information capital of non-European knowledge-brokers for the collection and dissemination of knowledge, as well as for financial and other supports in alleviating anxieties about institutional durability in settlements with mobile populations and minimal civic infrastructures. Despite their claims to originary status and their pervasive diffusionist rhetoric, British cultural institutions were defined by relationships of dependency and contingency even as they had a profound effect on the construction of cultural and linguistic capital in Southeast Asia.

Networks

Following the 1833 Charter Act, the East India Company pursued a policy of non-intervention in the British Straits Settlements, alienating European

---

[8] On knowledge accumulation, see, e.g., Bruno Latour, *Science in Action: How to Follow Scientists and Engineers through Society* (Cambridge, MA: Harvard University Press, 1987), p. 220.
[9] Raymond Williams, *Marxism and Literature* (Oxford: Oxford University Press, 1977), pp. 118–20; Mrinalini Sinha, 'Teaching Imperialism and a Social Formation', *Radical History Review*, 67 (1977), 175–86.
[10] Sartori, p. 680.

trading communities in Singapore, Malacca, and Penang through its failure to invest in long-term financial planning and civic infrastructures, and effecting what one historian has described as 'a half-century of inactivity'.[11] Early library development and education policy in the Straits was therefore 'haphazard and uncoordinated', funded mainly by a combination of self-governing voluntary initiatives and small public grants known as grant-in-aids.[12] This made the informal social networks of non-state actors surrounding schools, libraries, associations, and presses critical to the development of the region's cultural life – a role that was partly assumed by Christian missionary networks, partly by Malay, Chinese, South Indian, and Arabic vernacular schools and presses, and partly by the group of educators surrounding the Singapore Institution and the associated Singapore Institution Free School (later the Raffles Institution).[13]

First proposed by Stamford Raffles in 1819 as a revivalist project that would restore a perceived Malay literary 'golden age' free from 'foreign' Islamic influences, the Singapore Institution sought to develop a purposeful framework for centralising the region's production and diffusion of knowledge by providing a 'centre or nucleus ... which shall be placed on a footing beyond the reach of contingencies or accidents'.[14] Its stated aims included collecting 'the scattered literature and traditions of the country', 'educating the higher classes of the native population', instructing East India Company officers in 'native languages', and facilitating research into the region's 'history, condition and resources'.[15] While couched in an expansive 'civilising' rhetoric that imagined the institution's role in improving the condition of millions, Raffles' brief suggests the extent to which the region's ethnic diversity necessitated a 'language technocracy ... shaped and underpinned by linguistic needs'.[16]

---

[11] Emerson Rupert, *Malaysia: A Study of Direct and Indirect Rule* (New York: Macmillan, 1937), p. 91. On anti-East-India-Company sentiment, see Anthony Webster, 'The Development of British Commercial and Political Networks in the Straits Settlements 1800–1868: The Rise of a Colonial and Regional Economic Identity?', *Modern Asian Studies*, 45.4 (2001), 899–929.

[12] Edward Lim Huck Tee, *Libraries in West Malaysia and Singapore* (Kuala Lumpur: University of Malaya, 1970), p. 12.

[13] Mark Ravinder Frost, '*Emporium in imperio*: Nanyang Networks and the Straits Chinese in Singapore, 1819–1914', *Journal of Southeast Asian Studies*, 36 (2005), 29–36; Jan van der Putten, 'Abdullah Munsyi and the Missionaries', *Bijdragen tot de Taal-, Land-en Volkenkunde (BKI)*, 162.4 (2006), 407–40.

[14] Syed Muhd Khairudin Aljunied, 'Sir Thomas Stamford Raffles' Discourse on the Malay World: A Revisionist Perspective', *Sojourn*, 20.1 (2005), 1–22 (pp. 15–16); Thomas Stamford Raffles, *Minute by Sir T. S. Raffles on the Establishment of a Malay College at Singapore* (Singapore: [n. pub.], 1819), p. 23.

[15] Raffles, *Minute*, p. 17.

[16] Rachel Leow, *Taming Babel: Language in the Making of Malaysia* (Cambridge: Cambridge University Press, 2016), p. 55.

In particular, Raffles hoped his 'Malayan College', with its English, Chinese, and Malay branches and its liberal 'arts and sciences' curriculum, would encourage an elite class of multi-lingual non-European teachers and professionals, the want of which 'is owing to the absence of any centre or seat of learning to which they could resort'.[17]

Without drawing too sharp a distinction between institutions and associations, Raffles' nascent endeavour to centralise education, language acquisition, and information gathering in the Straits is suggestive of the ways in which institutions could coordinate and assimilate the more random or spontaneous social ties of self-organising associational culture and align them with imperial state machinery. Like British-sponsored institutions of higher learning in India such as the Hindoo College (est. 1817), the Singapore Institution was closely intertwined with British expansionism, simultaneously aiming to consolidate British state power against the Dutch via various forms of soft cultural influence, to mitigate the influence of Islamic, Malay, and Chinese vernacular institutions in what were effectively multi-imperial port cities, and to aggregate the work already achieved by the region's missionary schools.[18] Raffles thus intended to use his institution to wrest control from proselytising missionary-controlled educational establishments that were primarily interested in religious conversion, such as his co-founder Robert Morrison's Anglo-Chinese College in Malacca (est. 1820), while nonetheless allowing a British liberal education to indirectly diffuse its 'scriptural morality'.[19]

If Morrison was himself broadly in favour of a centralised 'literary Christian institution', he presciently noted that it was 'difficult, if not impracticable', to bring 'different nations together amicably in one College'.[20] By the 1830s, when Raffles and his co-founders had either died or returned to Britain, the Singapore Institution's centralising arts and sciences vision amounted to a partially completed building, a local elementary free school, and a small school library. As the Singapore Free School committee report put it in a melancholic reflection on the contingency of colonial institutions in 1835, 'nought remains but an unfinished building of eleven years standing to remind us that such a project was ever

---

[17] Raffles, *Minute*, p. 17.
[18] On cultural institutions in Bengal, see Raffles, *Minute*, p. 24. Raffles was instrumental in reviving the Dutch Batavian Society of Arts and Sciences in 1813. See Lady Sophia Raffles, *Memoir of the Life and Public Services of Sir Thomas Stamford Raffles* (London: John Murray, 1830), p. 141.
[19] Raffles, *Minute*, pp. 18, 21; Gauri Viswanathan, *Masks of Conquest: Literary Study and British Rule in India* (New York: Columbia University Press, 1989), p. 86.
[20] Quoted in R. L. O'Sullivan, 'The Anglo-Chinese College and the Early "Singapore Institution"', *JMBRAS*, 61.2 (1988), 45–62 (p. 49).

contemplated'.[21] While Raffles' ambitious idea of a multi-ethnic cultural institution loosely anticipated later understandings of British Southeast Asia as a distinct commercial and geographic zone, it was not until the 1850s that a renewed attempt was made to gather a collection of research sources on South and Southeast Asia, with the Singapore Library noting in 1850 that they were 'to have the first consideration on all occasions'.[22]

Like many other subscription libraries in the colonies, this library was organised and funded by the group that Peter Cain and Tony Hopkins have called 'gentlemanly capitalists', those 'modular men' who were bound together by 'specific-purpose, ad-hoc' ties of business and ethnicity, and increasingly by institutional loyalties to a variety of civic bodies and associations.[23] In this case, nearly 50 per cent of the library's founding proprietary shareholders were merchants or traders (many of them Scottish Presbyterian), such as William H. M. Read of A. L. Johnston & Co and James Guthrie Davidson of Woods & Davidson, who were united in their collective, Scottish Enlightenment-derived belief that commercial sociability was key to the formation of civic society.[24] A small group of white middle-class male professionals therefore 'set the tone' of social, political, and cultural life in Singapore and the Straits Settlements more broadly, ensuring that cross-institutional membership, network density, and group cohesion between the Singapore Library, the Singapore Institution, and the Singapore Free School was high.[25] Two of the earliest trustees of the Singapore Institution and founders of the Singapore Free School, for example, were also subscribers to and shareholders of the Singapore Library: the influential Scottish Presbyterian merchants Alexander Laurie Johnston and Alexander Guthrie.[26]

The Free School itself is an apt model of how inter- and intra-colonial networks in Southeast Asia were mobilised and drawn together into a collective interest group. Notwithstanding donations of books and tracts from metropolitan organisations such as the Religious Tract Society and

---

[21] *The First Report of the Singapore Schools* (Singapore: Mission Press, 1835), p. 6.
[22] *The Sixth Report of the Singapore Library, 1850* (Singapore: Free Press Office, 1850), p. 10.
[23] Peter Cain and A. G. Hopkins, 'Gentlemanly Capitalism and British Expansion Overseas I: The Old Colonial System, 1688–1850', *Economic History Review*, 39.4 (1986), 501–25; Ernst Gellner, *Conditions of Liberty: Civil Society and its Rivals* (New York: Allen Lane/Penguin, 1994), pp. 97–108.
[24] Only two shareholders out of a total of around thirty-five were non-European. See, e.g., *The Second Report of the Singapore Library, 1846* (Singapore: G. M. Frederick, 1847), p. 2. On Scottish ethnic associationalism, see Tanja Bueltmann, *Clubbing Together: Ethnicity, Civility and Formal Sociability in the Scottish Diaspora to 1930* (Liverpool: Liverpool University Press, 2015), esp. pp. 106, 163.
[25] Webster, p. 910.
[26] For a list of early trustees, see 'The Singapore Institution', *The Chinese Repository*, 4.11 (1836), 528.

the Royal Dublin Society, equipment and expertise in the form of teachers, superintendents, books, maps, slates, globes, and grammars for the school were obtained largely through an informal network of educators, booksellers, and London Missionary Society employees, including Revs Samuel Dyer and Thomas Beighton in Penang, Rev. Josiah Hughes in Malacca, and the British booksellers Ostell & Lepage (who had large eastern distribution networks), as well as organisations such as the Calcutta School-Book Society, the Calcutta School Society, and the Calcutta General Committee of Public Instruction.[27] The Free School's networks thus coalesced towards regional bonding networks between Singapore, Penang, Malacca, and Calcutta rather than towards bridging networks with British or other European metropoles.

Since appeals to 'our more distant readers' in Britain were largely unsuccessful, both the Free School and the Singapore Institution courted subscriptions and donations from wealthy non-European benefactors in Singapore, Malacca, and Penang, such as leading Arab Muslim merchants, as well as engaging with intermediaries in China and India.[28] In 1858–9, the Institution and School received a large increase of ongoing monthly subscriptions in the form of around thirty Chinese subscribers.[29] A sizeable donation also came from HRH the Temenggong of Johor, who donated an annual sum of $1,500 for the support of the vernacular schools from 1855–6 onwards.[30] British cultural institutions in the Straits Settlements therefore drew on dense pre-existing networks of Chinese, Malay, Indian, and Arab maritime traders and ruling elites in the Indian Ocean, described by Sugata Bose and others as involving bazaar systems of trade and finance, as well as indirectly relying on the proceeds of revenue gained from Chinese-owned opium and pepper farms, sugar plantations, and tin-mines for their financial stability and longevity.[31]

---

[27] *First Report of the Singapore Schools*, p. 4; *Singapore Institution Free School Sixth Annual Report, 1839–40* (Singapore: Free Press Office, 1840), p. 19; *Report of the Singapore Institution Free Schools for the Year 1853* (Singapore: Mission Press, 1854), p. 13.

[28] *Singapore Institution Free School Sixth Annual Report*, p. 20. In 1839–40, the list of donors includes seventeen Chinese and three Malay donors, *Singapore Institution Free School Sixth Annual Report*, p. 24. Of the twenty-eight monthly subscribers collected in China by Rev. Morrison in 1836–37, ten were of Indian descent, *The Third Report of the Singapore Free School, 1836–37* (Singapore: Free Press Office, 1837), p. 16.

[29] *The Report of the Singapore Institution Free Schools for the Year 1858–59* (Singapore: J. P. Hanzen, 1859), pp. 17–20.

[30] *The Report of the Singapore Institution Free Schools for the Year 1855–56* (Singapore: G. M. Frederick, 1856), p. 3.

[31] See, e.g., Sugata Bose, *A Hundred Horizons: The Indian Ocean in the Age of Global Empire* (Cambridge, MA: Harvard University Press, 2006), p. 73.

In recognition of this financial support, British officials and merchants, in turn, attempted to mitigate what one Chinese contributor to the *Straits Chinese Magazine* (est. 1897) called a 'colonial policy which persistently declines to recognise any just aspirations of a political nature in its alien subjects' by facilitating British-sponsored 'improving' associations, such as the Chinese Christian Association (est. 1889), the multi-ethnic Straits Philosophical Society (est. 1893), and the Straits Chinese Literary Association and Reading Club (est. 1911).[32] Adopting the Enlightenment model of separating the intellectual and cultural sphere from politics and religion, the Straits Philosophic Society had less of a religious emphasis than the Chinese Christian Association, promoting comparative discussions on western and eastern philosophy, literature, and science (albeit within British state-approved forms), and contributing to the formation of Chinese-only useful knowledge associations such as the Chinese Philomathic Society (est. 1896), and Malay societies and clubs, including *Persekutuan Dar-ukk-Taadzim* (est. 1894) and the *Perkseutuan Jawa Almasakin* (est. 1901).[33]

The European model of the literary and philosophical society – and the medial and cultural forms it pioneered – came to shape the cultural life of elite Straits Chinese and, to a lesser extent, elite Malay communities by the turn of the twentieth century, drawing networks of wealthy merchants, literate Chinese and Malay teachers and intelligentsia, and western-educated cosmopolitan men of letters, such as Song Ong Siang, Tan Teck Soon, and Lim Boon Keng, into a mutually constituted colonial public sphere, despite the operation of otherwise highly segregationist and ethnocentric colonial policies.[34] While the view of literary culture promoted by these British-sponsored societies was largely a Calvinist one, demarcating a disciplined and 'cultivated' Straits Chinese or Malay self from the 'natural' or 'native' self of the peasant worker and sojourning indentured labourer, the nature/culture oppositions of European-style associationalism nonetheless provided Chinese and Malay communities

---

[32] 'Local Chinese Social Organization by a Straits Chinese', *Straits Chinese Magazine (SCM)*, 3.10 (1899), 45, 43. On the CCA, see Song Ong Siang, *One Hundred Years' History of the Chinese in Singapore* (Singapore: Oxford University Press, 1984), pp. 59, 254.

[33] On Malay associations and presses, see William R. Roff, 'The Malayo-Muslim World of Singapore at the Close of the Nineteenth Century', *Journal of Asian Studies*, 24.1 (1964), 75–90 (esp. pp. 86–87). On literary and philosophical societies in a colonial context, see Peter Hill, *Utopia and Civilization in the Arab Nahda* (Oxford: Oxford University Press, 2020), esp. pp. 31–34.

[34] Tomáš Petrů, 'A Curious Trajectory of Interrace Relations: The Transformation of Cosmopolitan Port Polities into the Multiethnic Divisions of Modern Malaysia', *Asian Ethnicity*, 19.1 (2018), 59–80 <https://doi.org/10.1080/14631369.2017.1307688>.

with forums for progressive social reform, vernacular language education, and cultural revivalism, as well as in some cases encouraging the kinds of anti-colonial nationalism and pan-Asian internationalism that would eventually sweep through Southeast Asia.[35]

It was these very assumptions of intellectual and participatory parity that worried some British observers. The municipal engineer Samuel Tomlinson claimed in an address to the Chinese Christian Association in 1897, for example, that 'the task of Eastern peoples is not ended by mere imitation of the lives of their Western brethren'. For Tomlinson, the introduction of European-style institutions, clubs, and other forms of associational life had 'created inevitably the thirst for acquiring knowledge regarding politics and science and the treatment of social questions' among non-European populations. Worried about the speed with which western knowledge was being consumed by eastern audiences, Tomlinson attributes the 1857 uprising in India to 'the feverish anxiety of some to realize in their own lifetime the ideals which in England had been the growth of centuries'.[36]

British concerns about the galvanising role of vernacular associations and institutions were countered by frustrations from Malay and Chinese intellectuals. Upon its closure in 1907, the editors of the *Straits Chinese Magazine*, Lim Boon Keng and Song Ong Siang, noted that in the Straits Settlements 'almost every venture of an intellectual or literary character has been short-lived'.[37] Yet if these kinds of voluntary and often broadly secular cultural formations lacked longevity, they nonetheless encouraged an institutionalising ethos that was increasingly applied in the service of new kinds of ethnic nationalism.[38] More specifically, these publications and associations fostered the culturalist idea that reading, self-cultivation, and vernacular language acquisition were key to the rejuvenation of national interests. National culture, a concept that combined both 'humanistic and ethnographic discursive functions', would become an essential element of Malay nation-building (*bangsa Melayu*) and Chinese empire-building ideologies as the twentieth century progressed, contributing to the development of schools, libraries, book clubs, and reading rooms, such as the *Hu Yew Seah* (est. 1914) and the numerous offshoots of the *Tong de shu bao she* (United Chinese Library) established by the *Kuomintang* from 1910.[39]

---

[35] Viswanathan, pp. 18, 7. On pan-Asian internationalism, see, e.g., Mark Frost, '"Wider Opportunities": Religious Revival, Nationalist Awakening and the Global Dimension in Colombo, 1870–1920', *Modern Asian Studies*, 36.4 (2002), 937–67.
[36] *SCM*, 1.3 (1897), pp. 102, 103.   [37] *SCM*, 9.1 (1907), p. 95.
[38] The magazine was itself something of a centralising force, with numerous societies adopting it as their mouthpiece. For reports on the CCA and SCPS, see, e.g., *SCM*, 3.9 (1899), p. 73.
[39] Sartori, p. 698. On Chinese-language libraries, see *Xinjiapo Tong de shu bao she shi hua* (Singapore: Tong de shu bao she, 2015). On Malay and Chinese ethnic and national identities, see

Nodes

Raffles' early vision of the Singapore Institution as a centralised repository of knowledge on Southeast Asia was substantially accelerated in the 1840s and 1850s by James Richardson Logan, one of the Singapore Library's subscribers and shareholders. Logan was the owner of the *Penang Gazette*, the founder of the *Journal of the Indian Archipelago* (*JIA*), a member of the Royal Asiatic Society of Bengal, a fellow of the Royal Geographical Society of London, and a corresponding member of the Batavian Society of Arts and Sciences and the Ethnological Society of London. Drawing on the scholarly networks and knowledge technologies enabled by these inter-continental and trans-imperial affiliations, Logan was determined to develop Singapore into a regional node in Britain's imperial system, describing the intellectual brief of the journal he founded in 1847 as an attempt to connect the Straits Settlement into a pre-existing network of British useful knowledge and learned societies that encompassed 'Calcutta, Madras, Bombay, Ceylon, and Hong Kong'.[40]

Cognisant of the ways in which print culture could mediate and in some ways even actualise the institutional domain, Logan declared that his journal would be of a 'more mixed character than may be acceptable to any one class of readers', embracing 'a wide and singularly varied field' of both 'humanist' and 'purely scientific interests' along the lines of a 'popular miscellany'.[41] Encouraged by Raffles' original plan for the Singapore Institution and by his strong personal connections with the Batavian Society of Arts and Sciences, Logan conceived of the *JIA* as a virtual society that in many ways sought to approximate the dialectical model of the arts and sciences that Jon Klancher has identified as *the* modern category of institutional organisation in the early nineteenth century.[42] The *JIA* was therefore strongly shaped by Logan's desire to unite 'subjects generally kept separate' and his recognition of 'the growing tendency to treat all kinds of subjects in a scientific or accurate and thoughtful spirit', combining a qualitative and humanistic mode of intellectual inquiry with a concern for methodological rigour and quantitative data.[43]

Anthony Milner, *The Invention of Politics in Colonial Malaya: Contesting Nationalism and the Expansion of the Public Sphere* (Melbourne: Cambridge University Press, 1994).

[40] J. R. Logan, *The Prospectus of the Journal of the Indian Archipelago* (Singapore: [n. pub.], 1847), p. iv.

[41] Logan, pp. iv, v.

[42] Jon Klancher, *Transfiguring the Arts and Sciences: Knowledge and Cultural Institutions in the Romantic Age* (Cambridge: Cambridge University Press, 2013), p. 6.

[43] Logan, p. v; Klancher, *Transfiguring the Arts and Sciences*, p. 18.

In keeping with this directive to understand knowledge in 'the widest sense', the *JIA*'s primary aims were to reprint European scholarship on a wide range of topics; to collect, record, and disseminate primary data from the Malay Archipelago; and to revive an earlier scholarly undertaking by Raffles, John Crawford, William Marsden, and other philologists by collecting, translating, and reproducing Malay letters.[44] Logan added to these inherited and racialised philological master tropes a new emphasis on the emerging 'scientific' discourse of ethnography, publishing a 'Prospectus' and detailed 'Scheme of Desiderata' (1847), which was modelled on the ethnological questionnaire developed by James Pritchard and Richard Cull for the British Association for the Advancement of Science in 1841.[45] Attempting to guide the amateur gentlemen scientists that gathered around the journal via the Singapore Institution's associational networks, Logan hoped to establish appropriate category formations or the 'topics on which [his contributors] should treat', and to promote a methodology that would allow for 'the reduction of every species of information that admits it, into an arithmetical or accurate quantitative form'.[46] Conscious of the journal's reputation in European metropoles, Logan thus aspired to integrate the observations of amateurs on the ground into a categorical taxonomy that could contribute to developing academic structures of knowledge, while also encouraging the schematising of raw data into maps, diagrams, tables, catalogues, and other 'immutable mobiles' that could move from regional to metropolitan centres and in the process be ratified as imperial knowledge.[47]

As well as functioning as a 'space-binding technology' between colony and metropole, Logan's journal also provides an illuminating case study of the ways in which the cross-disciplinary, modernising but primarily humanist discourses of the arts and sciences remit increasingly butted heads with the quantitative methodologies and differentiating systems of disciplinary formation that emerged from scientific institutions such as the Ethnological Society.[48] What is remarkable about the *JIA* is not just its precociousness, but also its sustained application of quantitative methodologies to what would formerly have been observation-based discursive

---

[44] Klancher, *Transfiguring the Arts and Sciences*, p. 2; Logan, pp. v–vii. On philology, see Martin Muller, 'Manufacturing Malayness: British Debates on the Malay Nation, Civilisation, Race, and Language in the Early Nineteenth Century', *Indonesia and the Malay World*, 42.123 (2014), 170–96 (esp. pp. 170, 177).

[45] Logan, pp. 1–6. On Logan and ethnology, see Lara Atkin and others, *Early Public Libraries and Colonial Citizenship* (Cham: Palgrave Macmillan, 2019), pp. 111–14.

[46] Logan, pp. v, 1, 5.   [47] Latour, p. 226.

[48] Tony Ballantyne, 'Mobility, Empire, Colonisation', *History Australia*, 11.2 (2014), 7–37 (p. 25); Klancher, *Transfiguring the Arts and Sciences*, p. 11.

domains: for example, interviews and descriptions of encounters with Indigenous peoples are either replaced or supplemented by statistical tables and graphs showing anatomical measurements or demographic spreads. The ways in which this methodology worked to abstract the life worlds of the Indigenous subjects of the Malay Archipelago into numerical data and statistical demonstration – in other words, to reduce the corporeal to the semiotic – was increasingly vital to racialised understandings of colonial institutions as 'comparative instrument[s]' for measuring social development, as well as ultimately compounding the conceptual distance between humanist and scientific methodologies that the journal ostensibly sought to unite.[49]

While the *JIA* considered itself to be 'well-received' in Britain and America, Logan's legacy was primarily achieved by the endorsement of his journal and research endeavours by institutional bodies within the Straits Settlements.[50] A few years after the publicly funded Raffles Library and Museum replaced the Singapore Library in 1874, it purchased Logan's collection of ethnographic and philological books, beginning the process by which it became an 'institutional node designed to sustain colonial endeavours' and a 'centre of calculation ... for the South East Asian region' as a whole. It achieved this status by purchasing collections of ethnographic material; supporting societies such as the Straits Branch of the Royal Asiatic Society and the Hakluyt Society; increasingly holding scientific as well as literary periodicals; and becoming a copyright library for the Straits Settlement via the Book Regulation Ordinance of 1886, from which a major archive would emerge. By the end of the nineteenth century, the Raffles Library contained 13,103 volumes and was the largest library in Southeast Asia, forming an institutional node from which radiated several smaller institutions, including the Straits Branch of the Royal Asiatic Society (SBRAS).[51]

Closely associated with the network of scholars and librarians surrounding the Raffles Library,[52] the SBRAS conceived of itself as

---

[49] Klancher, *Transfiguring the Arts and Sciences*, p. 42.
[50] See, e.g., the positive reception of the *JIA* in 'Bibliographical Notices', *Annals and Magazine of Natural History*, 20 (1847), 422–23.
[51] *JSBRAS*, 4 (1879), p. xiv; Brendan Luyt, 'Centres of Calculation and Unruly Colonists: The Colonial Library in Singapore and its Users, 1874–1900', *Journal of Documentation*, 64.3 (2008), 386–96 (p. 391); Tee, pp. 70, 71; Porscha Fermanis, 'British Cultures of Reading and Literary Appreciation in Nineteenth-Century Singapore', in *The Edinburgh History of Reading: Subversive Readers*, ed. by Jonathan Rose (Edinburgh: Edinburgh University Press, 2020), pp. 116–37.
[52] On links with the Raffles Library, see J. M. Gullick, 'A Short History of the Society', *JMBRAS*, 68.2 (1995), 67–79 (p. 71).

part of a multi-generational network of scholars in a direct lineage of filial descent that stretched from Raffles to Logan to the present day so that those of the 'present generation' who now 'contribute something to the common stock' may 'be stirred up by the example of those who have gone before'. Acknowledging Logan's great contribution to the principles of association, organisation, and collaborative labour as opposed to the individual or private scholarly pursuit of knowledge practised by Raffles, Marsden, and others, the society's president, Archdeacon Hose, identified the 'weak point' in Logan's scheme as his failure to instantiate the informal associative group gathered around his journal into an institutional form, resulting in a publication that depended primarily upon the unsustainable 'energy and enthusiasm of a single individual'.[53] Logan, it seems, had succeeded as an organiser, writer, and scientist, but had failed as an institutor and long-term producer and transmitter of information on the Malay Archipelago, allowing many great minds to 'have passed away "mute and inglorious" for the lack of such an organisation'.[54]

If Hose's comments register an undercurrent of anxiety about the durability of colonial institutions, he nonetheless sees his society as Logan's institutional successor, providing the formal framework that the *JIA* had lacked by 'uniting its members into a society' and endowing them not just with regular meetings, a fixed address, a library, and a journal but also with a 'meta-medial' identity.[55] Hose thus understands the act of institution-building both as 'transmitting an inheritance' of 'successively realized knowledge' and as a way of systematising the productions of looser and more ephemeral associational bodies: 'we are a Society, and ... when one man fails or drops away, another will be found to fill up his place in the ranks, and the work will go on'.[56] The SBRAS also conceived of itself as a more specialised society than the circle of amateurs that had surrounded Logan, drawing a distinction between the *JIA*'s compilation of observations and its own more systematic approach to knowledge formation.[57] As Tim Harper has noted, the SBRAS was largely concerned with realising statistical data into a series of cultural goods that could be stamped with its institutional

---

[53] *JSBRAS*, 1 (1878), pp. 3, 2, 10.   [54] *JSBRAS*, 4 (1879), p. xix.
[55] *JSBRAS*, 1 (1878), pp. iv, iii, ix; Klancher, *Transfiguring the Arts and Sciences*, p. 18.
[56] Klancher, *Transfiguring the Arts and Sciences*, pp. 10, 3, 39; *JSBRAS*, 4 (1879), p. xx.
[57] For the SBRAS's membership of colonial officials, scholars, and scientists connected with the Raffles Museum, see Wai Sin Tiew, 'History of the *JMBRAS* 1878–1997: An Overview', *Malaysian Journal of Library & Information Science*, 3.1 (1998), 43–60. On prominent Malay and non-European members, see *JSBRAS*, 1 (1878), p. vii.

endorsement and transmitted to other learned societies and schools in the region, with its energies directed towards the compilation of word lists, bibliographies and other morphological schema, linguistic standardisation via grammars and dictionaries, the indexing and organisation of collections of research material, and the publication and reprinting of Malay letters.[58]

As the diversity of this work suggests, the SBRAS had a cross-disciplinary agenda and, like Logan's journal, it was firmly imbricated in the arts and sciences domain. Like other arts and sciences institutions, it was also determinedly modern in its approach to Malay culture. Seeing Malay literature as an ethnographic referent and mirror of the state of Malay society, it heavily promoted Abdullah bin Kadir Abdul's famous *Hikayat Abdullah* (1849) – a travel narrative and autobiography that self-consciously adopts and reproduces what Sanjay Krishnan has called the 'universal metric' of European representative structures – by securing a large subscription grant from the Straits government and bringing out a new edition in 1879 at a low price aimed mainly at local Malay populations.[59] The SBRAS thus inaugurated the institutionalisation of Munsyi Abdullah as the almost single-handed progenitor of Malay literary modernity and promoted the canonisation of the *Hikayat Abdullah* as the first realist Malay work that could teach 'the natives to value other remains of their own literature'.[60] Members of the SBRAS, such as the colonial officials R. O. Winstedt and R. J. Wilkinson, subsequently integrated these orientalist principles into the Malay vernacular school system during a series of state education reforms in 1906, when they primarily reprinted those Malay texts that would provide their students with useful knowledge, and promoted a newly standardised Malay language and script as the colonial *lingua franca* in the region.[61]

British cultural institutions thus played what they saw as an important modernising role in Southeast Asia, enabling the learning of Malay and Chinese languages by Europeans, the collation of information on local races and peoples, linguistic standardisation, and the promotion of modern canons of Malay literature. In this way, they helped to valorise European

---

[58] T. N. Harper, 'Globalism and the Pursuit of Authenticity: The Making of a Diasporic Public Sphere in Singapore', *Sojourn*, 12.2 (1997), 261–92 (pp. 266–67); *JSBRAS*, 1 (1878), p. 5.

[59] Klancher, *Transfiguring the Arts and Sciences*, p. 10; Sanjay Krishnan, 'History and the Work of Literature in the Periphery', *Novel: A Forum on Fiction*, 42 (2009), 482–89 (p. 482); *JSBRAS*, 4 (1879), pp. viii, xv, xxi.

[60] *JSBRAS*, 4 (1879), pp. xxi.

[61] Jan van der Putten, 'Bangsawan: The Coming of a Malay Popular Form', *Indonesia and the Malay World*, 42.123 (2014), 268–85 (p. 283).

models of individual authorship and genres such as the autobiography and short story as markers of a modern subjectivity, as well as standardising the Malay language and script while barely acknowledging the native-speaker language collaborators who made this possible.[62] Eventually receiving state endorsement and in some cases public funding, the aggregating efforts of the Singapore Library, the Singapore Institution and Free School, Logan's *JIA*, the Raffles Library and Museum, and the SBRAS demonstrate how colonial cultural institutions worked alongside or in tandem with the state to collect, collate, codify, and disseminate information, and to create centralised nodes of knowledge production driven and underpinned by expansionary imperial endeavours.[63] In so doing, they redirected circulating culturalist discourses surrounding self-cultivation towards a form of power whose 'normalizing function was strategically directed to the production of a manageable population'.[64]

Beacons

Reflecting on the successes of the British Empire in a speech on the formation of the Singapore Institution in 1819, Raffles argued that Britain must continue to 'lay the foundations of our dominion on the firm basis of justice and mutual advantage, instead of the uncertain and unsubstantial tenure of force and intrigue' and, in doing so, should not neglect to cultivate literature and the liberal arts: 'shall we not consider it one of our first duties to afford the means of education to surrounding countries and thus render our stations not only the seats of commerce but of literature and the arts?'[65] Raffles' distinction between coercion and consent is, as Gauri Viswanathan has noted, key to understanding British education policy in South and Southeast Asia, which aimed to establish administrative and social control in the guise of 'civilising' education and culture.[66] In this instance, Raffles' view of Singapore as a 'seat of commerce' united by exchange rather than by force is enhanced by his recognition of its potential status as a cultural centre from whence 'its influence may be diffused and its sphere gradually extended'.[67] Metaphors of enlightened diffusion abound in Raffles' speech but coalesce in a striking sentence in which he imagines Singapore as a beacon that will call 'forth the literary spirit' of the Malay people and awaken its 'dormant energies': 'The rays of intellect now divided and lost, will be concentrated into a focus

---

[62] Van der Putten, 'Bangaswan', p. 123; Leow, p. 86. [63] Harper, p. 265. [64] Sartori, p. 693.
[65] Raffles, *Minute*, pp. 14–15. [66] Viswanathan, p. 20. [67] Raffles, *Minute*, p. 23.

from whence they will be again radiated with added lustre, brightened and strengthened by our superior lights.'[68]

Extending his vision from the regional to the global, Raffles recognises that literary, philosophical, and scientific institutions are a key conduit for British expansionism by providing a means to reinforce cultural and commercial ties to non-European communities and their resources: 'Thus will our stations not only become the centres of commerce and its luxuries, but of refinement and the liberal arts.'[69] This is a point made more explicitly by his respondent Rev. E. S. Hutchings, founder of the Penang Free School (1816), who notes that the Singapore Institution will not only act as a beacon for the 'neighbouring Rajas and Chiegs' who 'will doubtless see the advantage of sending their sons to receive instruction at this place', but will also enable 'the riches' of eastern countries to be 'collected in exchange for the productions of European arts and manufactures'.[70] The culturalist rhetoric in Raffles' speech is subsumed here within a larger capitalist project to appropriate raw materials and 'confer the benefits of civilization' upon subject nations, a project propelled by both the ethnographic hierarchies of 'improvability' Raffles and his co-founders attach to various local populations and the scale of the 'native population' that they envisage as 'civilizing', including at least 'ten to fifteen millions' in the Malay Archipelago, which if extended to 'Siam, Camboja, Chochin-China and Tonkin' as well as China and Japan, will be the most important field of influence 'that ever offered itself to the contemplation of the philanthropic and enlightened mind'.[71]

Quoting Raffles' vision of the 'intellectual' and 'moral influence that can alone rule where physical power is weak', the same idealising rhetoric is used by the Singapore Free School over fifteen years later to represent itself as a 'light' within a wider British Empire, tending to the 'general amelioration and enlightening of the dark and uncivilized portions of the globe'.[72] If the closure of its Malay branch in 1842 fell short of its original goal to provide a college for 'native instruction', the school nonetheless continued to see itself as an ongoing 'source of information and enlightenment to the neighbouring states, and stations' from Siam to Penang.[73] Similarly, in the 1840s and 1850s, Logan conceived of his journal as 'systematically' bringing

---

[68] Raffles, *Minute*, p. 24.   [69] Raffles, *Minute*, p. 24.
[70] *Singapore Institution Free School Fourth Annual Report, 1837–38* (Singapore: Free Press Office, 1838), p. 55.
[71] Raffles, *Minute*, p. 4.   [72] *First Report of the Singapore Schools*, pp. 5, 10.
[73] *Singapore Institution Free School Eighth Annual Report, 1842–43* (Singapore: Mission Press, 1843), p. 4.

the 'light of European observation and science' to bear on a region whose 'plains, mountain and hill ranges' will soon 'be occupied and explored by British enterprize', while the Singapore and Raffles libraries positioned themselves regionally as well as globally, making allowance for outstation borrowers of books in Malacca, Penang, Sarawak, Sabah, and Johor, and extending 'library services to the borderlands where the influences of "civilization" were most diluted'.[74]

While British cultural institutions in Southeast Asia understood themselves as part of a global network of knowledge societies working to 'spread ... instruction, moral and intellectual' across the British Empire, the changing rhetoric they employed in the 1840s and 1850s suggests that they increasingly self-identified with a more regional interest group that linked the islands of the Malay Archipelago into an 'identifiable commercial unit'.[75] This conception of the British Straits Settlements involved a movement away from earlier institutional, administrative, and conceptual identifications of Southeast Asia as part of a 'Greater India' towards an insular or maritime consciousness focussed primarily on the Straits of Malacca – one that saw the region's entrepôt port economies as 'geographically as well as conceptually situated between land and sea', and as occupying a 'centrical' position within a network of British trading towns that formed the gateway to the Asia Pacific.[76]

At the same time, pre-existing and diasporic trading networks also connected British Southeast Asia to a complex transregional cultural geography that included not just the Malay and Indian Ocean worlds but also China, southern Africa, Australasia, and the Arabian Peninsula.[77] Writing from within a wider diasporic and Sinocentric public sphere in 1897, the *Straits Chinese Magazine* notably sees Raffles' legacy as a failure rather than a success, arguing that the British government had abrogated its responsibility to transmit elementary and secondary instruction in English to non-European populations in the Straits Settlements. Queen Victoria's 1897 Diamond Jubilee celebration provided a particular *point d'appui* for Lim Boon Keng, who urged the British Government to avoid 'act[s] of aggrandizement' and instead 'show to the whole world the high motives

---

[74] Logan, p. iii; Brendan Luyt, 'Imagining the User in the Raffles Library and Museum, Singapore: 1874 to 1900', Session 119: Library History, International Federation of Library Associations World Library and Information Congress (2006), 1–9 (p. 4) <http://origin-archive.ifla.org/IV/ifla72/papers/119-Luyt-en.pdf>.
[75] Webster, p. 926.   [76] Muller, pp. 184, 177.
[77] Sumit K. Mandal, 'Cultural Geographies of the Malay World: Textual Trajectories in the Indian Ocean', *Philological Encounters*, 1 (2016), 370–95.

which have actuated its interference with the *status quo* of the Malay States' by 'laying down the nucleus of a future University which will be to Malaya what Oxford and Cambridge have been to England'.[78]

R. W. Hullett, principal of the Raffles Institution, agreed with this proposal, noting that there were government-sponsored colleges of higher education in Ceylon and Hong Kong, and that the commercial need to import men from Europe was increasing because of a lack of suitable candidates in the Straits.[79] Using the same economic justification and depicting each educated Chinese person as themselves a centre for the diffusion of knowledge, Lim Boon Keng not only represents (British) institutional effects as vested in (Chinese) individuals, but also inverts British metaphors of enlightenment by applying a diffusionist rhetoric of his own: '[a]nother fifty years may see China one vast, teeming workshop. Every highly educated Chinese from a British colony will be a centre for the diffusion of British influence in this new Chinese world'.[80] When the idea of a Malayan university failed to find favour, Keng regrets that 'a short-sighted policy has prevented the establishment of a literary centre which will not only live but grow with time'.[81]

A longer two-part article on the history of the Raffles Institution in the *Straits Chinese Magazine* for September 1900 similarly depicts its history as a diversion of funds away from its original aim of 'native education' and towards 'the establishment of a Town Hall and Reading Room', which 'however excellent in itself is quite different from the *education of the natives*, the object Sir Stamford Raffles had proposed to himself in founding the Institution'. Once again characterising the Raffles Institution as an example of 'transmission failure', the *Straits Chinese Magazine* proposes that wealthy Chinese merchants inaugurate a Malayan college and technical school so that there is 'greater inter-provincial association for the spread of useful knowledge among the Chinese'. This college is conceived both as means of evading British proselytisation and as a way to thicken ties with China and other Chinese diasporas: 'The College is to prepare pupils who may be sent to China to open schools and spread the light of civilization without the awkward necessity of making science and art subservient to the requirements of religion'.[82] British metaphors of enlightenment and diffusion are thus appropriated by the Straits Chinese not for the purpose of replicating European discourses and institutions but rather

---

[78] *SCM*, 1.1 (1897), p. 27.   [79] *SCM*, 1.3 (1897), pp. 92, 93.   [80] *SCM*, 1.4 (1897), p. 94.
[81] *SCM*, 1.2 (1897), p. 71.
[82] *SCM*, 4.15 (1900), pp. 89, 91; Jon Klancher, 'Transmission Failure', in *Theoretical Issues in Literary History*, ed. by David Perkins (Cambridge, MA: Harvard University Press, 1991), pp. 173–95.

to provide a counterforce to racialised and proselytising British cultural institutions in Southeast Asia.

Conclusion

The creation of British cultural institutions in the Straits Settlements primarily emerged via self-organising social networks comprised of missionaries and middle-class trading communities. As a tight-knit community of cultural entrepreneurs, Scottish Presbyterian merchants helped to forge a civic culture in Southeast Asia that was made up of specific-purpose voluntary associations, where economic rationalisation and cultural improvement went hand-in-hand, pointing to what Karl Marx identified as the 'socialising' power of capital.[83] Dedicated to civic and cultural as well as economic improvement, and relying on obligations of reciprocity with Chinese, Malay, and South Indian trading communities, these merchants and other middle-class professionals increasingly positioned cultural institutions such as the Singapore Institution and the Singapore Free School regionally as well as globally, drawing on their commercial bonds with non-European elites for donations and support, and thickening local and regional ties by pulling people, goods, and print within the Malay Archipelago into ever closer proximity.

As the failure of the Singapore Institution to fully materialise as a centralised college of research and higher learning suggests, the public sphere they created was not always 'powerfully institutionalised', but it nonetheless promoted sociability, civic responsibility, and acculturation via the establishment of multi-ethnic associations such as the Straits Philosophic Society.[84] The rise of more formal cultural institutional structures and frameworks such as learned societies and public libraries in the second half of the century enabled not just the collection and classification of data but also its codification, systemisation, and dissemination, allowing densely networked flows of information to reproduce standardised knowledge and cultural goods across interconnected sites such as Singapore, Malacca, Penang, and occasionally Calcutta. Formal institutional frameworks thus provided enhanced opportunities for the global diffusion of knowledge via exchanges with European learned societies while at the same time promoting notions of British Southeast Asia as

---

[83] Karl Marx, *Capital*, vol. 3, trans. by David Fernbach (London: Penguin, 1981), p. 182.
[84] Harper, p. 273.

a discrete geographical region and area of study, with its own distinctive political, ethnic, and cultural identity.

Yet if colonial cultural institutions were at the forefront of the nineteenth century's expansion of knowledge in extra-European settings – opening their curricular to non-European languages and literatures, investing in local libraries and schools, encouraging sociability and mobility through the mixing of races and classes, and gradually expanding their franchise to admit women – they also contributed to the formation of a racialised and gendered colonial public sphere that shaped exclusionary and hierarchical understandings of cultural practice and value: in particular, via their promotion of English-language literacy, their standardisation of vernacular languages through Romanised scripts, their institutionalisation of modern (i.e. European-oriented) authors, genres, and canons, and their promotion of newly emerging disciplines such as ethnography. As this work of codification and standardisation suggests, by the end of the nineteenth century 'Malayness' was a contested and constructed category 'born out of confrontation with modernity and "invented" by a colonial historiography'.[85]

Colonial institutions in nineteenth-century Southeast Asia thereby mobilised culturalist discourses for the consolidation and the management of non-European peoples, nesting the 'positive freedom' or autonomy at the core of the culture concept within a 'liberal conception of negative freedom'.[86] At the same time, the Southeast Asian public sphere was not solely defined by 'gentlemanly capitalism'; nor were British cultural institutions the only or even the dominant engines of change in the region. Vernacular and even British-sponsored institutions reflect a robust sense of Malay and Chinese identity that increasingly resulted in the emergence of oppositional counter-publics. If the British hoped that the proliferation of European-style cultural associations, clubs, and institutions would naturalise the existing order, elite Chinese and Malay communities instead used the culturalist category of autonomous agency to critique colonial domination, alien legal codes and bureaucracies, western expansionism, and the 'anomic tendencies' of commercial society.[87] Non-European cultural institutions in Southeast Asia are therefore better seen as agents of conceptual innovation and assertive culturalist politics rather than as reproductions of British sociability or signs of civic maturation in non-European sites.

---

[85] Christina Skott, 'Europe and the Malay World', *Indonesia and the Malay World*, 42.123 (2014), 129–40 (p. 137).
[86] Sartori, pp. 678, 682.   [87] Harper, pp. 284–85; Sartori, p. 677.

CHAPTER 14

The Book as Medium

Sarah Crofton

Institutions have always shaped literature, providing organising principles, sources of funding, stamps of legitimacy, and means of dissemination. Over time, the institutions themselves may become less visible as the works, genres, and legacies they shaped persist beyond their original context. With luck and scholarly industry we can reconstruct their history from papers kept in archives, or the architecture of buildings that once housed them, from the correspondences of members, the trails of money across ledgers, or traces left in the works they supported. There will always be gaps – not just where papers that have been lost, but also where things were obscured from the start. Some institutions keep careless records. Some we may suspect of deliberate obfuscation in the records they do leave. And some present us with earnest testimonies of their activities so outlandish that they challenge us even now to decide how we are to categorise their work. Such is the case for the established societies of nineteenth-century Spiritualism. Though we have a great deal of self-reflexive literature produced by societies that banded together under a professed belief in their ability to communicate with the dead, there are confounding silences to confront when trying to piece together the real activities of groups so often accused of deliberate misdirection. To read their records is to ask again and again what truth hides behind assertions of posthumously composed poetry, mediumistic secretaries, and spirits setting print. The dead institutions of Spiritualism speak to us at great length through the texts they left behind; the question is whether we can trust that they are who and what they claim to be.

Nineteenth-century British Spiritualism was a self-consciously literary movement. Though the physical phenomena of séance manifestations and the dancing furniture parodied in the 'sympathetic sideboards' of Robert Browning's Mr Sludge were part of daily practice, by the end of the century the movement had already left a dizzying paper trail.¹ As the movement grew, pamphlets and books were an obvious medium through which ideas could be shared beyond immediate 'circles'.² Newspapers and journals created a sense of community, establishing networks between separate societies and individuals around the country. Papers with titles like *The Medium and Daybreak*, *The Two Worlds*, and *Borderland* shared news and offered a point of entry for new converts, directing them to spaces where they could meet others and learn more. As Mark Morrisson notes in his study of Occultist journals, '[e]sotericism simply could not have enjoyed the popularity it sustained for decades without the periodicals to perpetuate and disseminate not only occult knowledge but also a growing sense of an occult movement.'³ These periodicals assembled information and provided the movement with a structuring principle that was both temporal and ideological – their main pages assembled reports of events that gave the Spiritualist movement a sense of a recent past, while calendars of upcoming events sustained momentum into an immediate future. Beyond simply reflecting upon an existing movement, its periodical press was an intrinsic part of the infrastructure that allowed Spiritualism to form an institutional identity.

Spiritualist periodicals' advertisement pages were also filled with lists of books and publications that promised further validation of a countercultural belief in communication with the dead. Books were important. The autobiographies of mediums offered models for those looking to awaken their own powers, while publications of channelled writings provided proof of communication with the world beyond death. More than that, books, as we shall see, were a means by which the Spiritualist movement could borrow authenticity from elsewhere. At the death of Robert Louis Stevenson in 1894, W. T. Stead's occult monthly, *Borderland*, ran a long biography insisting upon the Spiritualist truths encoded in *Strange Case of Dr Jekyll and Mr Hyde*.⁴ An 1893 issue of *Medium and Daybreak* advertised a new edition of the complete works of

---

[1] Robert Browning, 'Mr. Sludge, "The Medium"', in *Dramatis Personae* (London: Chapman & Hall, 1864), pp. 171–239 (p. 175).

[2] Estimating the size of the Spiritualist community in Britain at any time is difficult due to the fragmented nature of the movement. An 1870 survey received 3,000 replies, but this was based on voluntary reports through local organisations, and at least one quarter of known regional groups did not respond. See K. G. Valente, '"Who Will Explain the Explanation?" The Ambivalent Reception of Higher Dimensional Space in the British Spiritualist Press, 1875–1900', *Victorian Periodicals Review*, 41.2 (2008), 124–49 (p. 145, n. 14).

[3] Mark S. Morrisson, 'The Periodical Culture of the Occult Revival: Esoteric Wisdom, Modernity and Counter-Public Spheres', *Journal of Modern Literature*, 31.2 (2007), 1–22 (p. 4).

[4] 'Our Gallery of Borderlanders: Robert Louis Stevenson', *Borderland*, 2 January 1895, pp. 14–24 (p. 14).

Shakespeare purporting to have been edited by the spirit of the Bard himself, altering the text 'to aid in removing the stubborn doubt that dims the eye of the Soul and makes man reckless'.[5] Anyone who had commanded respect in life could be grandfathered in as a true believer after death, and those who were known for their writings in life were particularly accessible to such paratexts and ventriloquism. When it came to asserting Spiritualism's own institutional clout, organisers who were already open to counting the dead among their active membership saw the value in recruiting spirits with legacies within the British cultural establishment.

By the 1870s, Spiritualists in Britain were beginning to consider in earnest the question of *how* they should be organised. The movement, which began in 1848 with the knocking spirits (or, for non-believers, the popping toe-joints) of the Fox sisters in New York, had crossed the Atlantic via touring mediums and seeded a generation of home-grown practitioners in Britain. Mediums established their reputation by word of mouth and led circles in private parlours. However, as the movement grew, so did the need to find a way of meeting new believers outside of the domestic space, and to move beyond personal introductions to attract and vet newcomers. Spiritualists needed official spaces where they might pool their resources, learn from each other, and 'turn their private explorations into a public and collective act that would spread the impact of their communication with the spirit world'.[6] That this was needed was more easily agreed to than the form it should take. G. K. Nelson's *Spiritualism and Society* chronicles the constant disagreements within the movement that sprang up around any attempts to form a centralised structure, and notes the particular fears that any centralising schemes would enforce one Spiritualist creed over another or devolve into minority rule.[7] This chapter looks at two particular institutions set up in answer to such questions: James Burns's 'Progressive Library and Spiritual Institution' (1863–94) and W. T. Stead's 'Julia's Bureau' (1909–12). Burns's project was responsible for a large portion of the most important literature published by Spiritualists during the 'golden age' of Spiritualism in the 1870s and 1880s.[8] Stead's sought to establish a public service for corresponding with

---

[5] 'Shakespeare's Plays', *Medium and Daybreak*, 3 March 1893, pp. 129–31 (p. 129).
[6] Simone Natale, *Supernatural Entertainments: Victorian Spiritualism and the Rise of Modern Media Culture* (University Park: Penn State University Press, 2016), p. 49.
[7] Geoffrey K. Nelson, *Spiritualism and Society* (London: Routledge, 2013), pp. 100–10.
[8] For a detailed account of British Spiritualism in the 1870s, see Alex Owen, *The Darkened Room* (London: University of Chicago Press, 2004).

the afterlife, and drew on the legacy of the Spiritual Institution's publications to do so. What both had in common, I argue, was a firm belief that the best form for a public institution of Spiritualism was that of a hybrid library and séance space. Each, in its own way, saw private reading from a shared collection as the basic activity around which membership should be organised. Importantly, this model allowed for an inner sanctum for a select few whose workings could be closely protected while presenting a public face that seemed to share the modern egalitarian ethos of open access to knowledge marked by initiatives like the Public Libraries Act of 1850.

The Progressive Library and Spiritual Institution

The Progressive Library and Spiritual Institution was established in 1863 and operated from 15 Southampton Row in Holborn until 1894. Its founder James Burns was one of the most active Spiritualists in nineteenth-century England. 'Progressive', to Burns, was an umbrella term for moral campaigns ranging from vegetarianism to phrenology to anti-vaccination. Principally, however, it named a social imperative to better the living through communication with the dead. Burns was also the publisher whose mark is to be found on the first editions of many important texts in British esotericism. He began his publishing career within the temperance movement and was converted to Spiritualism by some pamphlets he was asked to prepare for the press.[9] Becoming convinced of the imperative to spread the truth of Spiritualism, he brought his experience in the book trade to the task of propagandising for the movement. Burns began importing Spiritualist texts from America and set up a small lending library. Later he acquired two newspapers, of which one, *Medium and Daybreak*, became, in time, the most widely circulated periodical of British Spiritualism.[10] He found premises to house the library and his publishing business on Southampton Row, dubbed it the 'Spiritual Institution', and began commissioning new works and printing pamphlets and primers for a British market.

The Spiritual Institution quickly became a hub for other projects. Rooms above the library were used (at least at first) as a public séance space. They were also used for other Spiritualist activities like

[9] James Burns, 'A Short History of the Spiritual Institute', *Medium and Daybreak*, 4 May 1894, pp. 273–76 (p. 273).
[10] Frank Podmore, *Modern Spiritualism: A History and a Criticism*, 2 vols (London: Methuen, 1902), II, 165.

demonstrations, talks, concerts, and 'developing circles' (where hopeful believers sought to train their own mediumistic powers).[11] Burns was also instrumental in setting up Sunday services for Spiritualists and pushed for a children's lyceum. The breadth of his aims for the Spiritual Institution earned him some mockery even from fellow Spiritualists, among them Charles Maurice Davies, whose 1876 novel *Maud Blount, Medium* surely has Burns in mind when describing its 'Supernatural Lyceum':

> The Supernatural Lyceum was a somewhat ambitious undertaking, scarcely proportioned to the not very Atlantean shoulders of Mr. Blathersby, who was its presiding genius. It was intended to be a kind of Universal Provider for Spiritualists from the cradle to the grave, catching them at the former extremity of life in the hope of making Infant Phenomenons of them, and retaining their hold upon them until the last, on the chance of converting them into Rapping Spirits when *in articulo mortis*. It was a kind of school, clubhouse, and chapel rolled into one, and all comprised in the not very spacious accommodation of a first-floor over a barber's shop, in a back street of the W.C. district.[12]

If Burns's earnest multiplication of endeavours opened his project up to such parody, the Spiritual Institution nevertheless succeeded in becoming the de facto hub of the movement. American mediums stopped there on their tours, British mediums had a new space in which to collaborate, and at the centre of it there was the library and Burns's printing press.

By providing both a public stage and the support of this small publishing empire, the Institution helped to launch the careers of famous mediums like J. J. Morse and Emma Hardinge Britten. *Medium and Daybreak* advertised upcoming events and followed up with detailed reports of their proceedings, frequently referencing big names or famous Spiritualist events to embed each new success within a narrative of ongoing discovery. Books written by mediums could be bought on the premises or borrowed from or perused in the library. Works printed or reprinted by the Spiritual Institution's own publishing house came bound, of course, with advertisements for similar titles. The Institution also provided a modest income stream for up-and-coming practitioners through workshops and programmes of events. In 1871, the Institution's 'College of Mediums' offered a six-week course for five shillings, while regular weekly séances were two shillings a ticket.[13] Public events offered another venue for selling

---

[11] These were routinely publicised in *Medium and Daybreak*.
[12] [Charles Maurice Davies], *Maud Blount, Medium* (London: Tinsley, 1876), pp. 292–93.
[13] 'The College of Mediums', *Medium and Daybreak*, 9 December 1870, p. 285.

books, pamphlets, and copies of *Medium and Daybreak*. (Burns allegedly jealously guarded such opportunities to monopolise a potential readership and refused to allow other publishers to sell their wares at meetings associated with his Institution.[14]) There was a logistical challenge in establishing Spiritualism as an open movement and a financially sustainable enterprise.

It was the Spiritual Institution's library space that perhaps best lived up to the promise to be 'the only free and open place of meeting' for Spiritualists. This offered the most frictionless opportunity for the curious to browse Spiritualist ideas and fall into conversation with whomever might currently be onsite.[15] We can see evidence of the value of these more accidental encounters in the writings of A. E. Waite, now most famous as the creator of the modern Tarot deck. Waite attributes his early education in esotericism to the opportunities offered by the Spiritual Institution. Having been first enthralled by some copies of *Medium and Daybreak* found at a butcher's shop, he sought out 'the offices of the Spiritistic paper in question':

> [And] thither I fared to accordingly, namely, to Southampton Row, where I made a speaking acquaintance with James Burns, proprietor, printer and editor of the *Medium and Daybreak*. It proved among other things that he had begun to reprint *Anacalypsis*. ... My visit was repeated on several occasions, and I was like one beginning to awaken, while many hands beckoned me, as if from doors ajar.[16]

Whether true or not, this narrative of a young man's first revelatory encounter with the newspaper, which leads him to the front door of Southampton Row, where he is further enthralled by the other volumes to be found there, seems exactly the kind of story the Spiritual Institution was designed to facilitate. Spiritualist writing is, unsurprisingly, rife with clichés of thresholds, borders, lintels, portals, and entranceways. In Waite's account it is striking how simply the figurative doorway to secret knowledge is elided with the front door of 15 Southampton Row, an institution as important and welcoming in its real physical presence as in its abstract power. The movement as it is represented here is both an open book and an open door ready to show a newcomer all its workings.

It is helpful when considering the ethos of the Spiritual Institution to compare it to alternative models for organisation proposed by others in the movement, because it was not the only institution of spiritualism that had

---

[14] Nelson, p. 99.   [15] Burns, p. 275.
[16] Arthur Edward Waite, *Shadows of Life and Thought* (London: Selwyn & Blount, 1938), p. 58.

its own premises or that circulated literature. The British National Association of Spiritualists (BNAS), for example, was established in 1873 and headquartered around the corner in a house on Great Russell Street, where it maintained meeting rooms and a small library. There was undoubtedly a certain professional jealousy in the viciousness with which Burns opposed this 'farce of a mock Spiritualist Society' on his doorstep; however, there was also a genuine conflict in the philosophies of the two projects.[17] Importantly, they disagreed about the tenets under which members should assemble and about the products they should present to the outside world as best representing their cause. The BNAS had a written constitution, rules, and a formal declaration of its 'Principles and Purposes' – fundamentals of institutional bureaucracy.[18] It took upon itself the role of validating mediums, and its committees produced reports on test séances to present to the world as scientific evidence of the validity of mediumistic powers.[19] It is not surprising that the Society for Psychical Research (SPR) – the organisation most determined to establish Spiritualism's place among the emerging discipline of the sciences – was a direct outgrowth of the BNAS.[20] In contrast, the Spiritual Institution was firmly resistant to anything that might be construed as a binding charter or creed and for the majority of its existence was absolutely opposed to hosting or advertising test séances. Its alternative was always, simply, to begin with literature. Through 'tracts and papers' ten times more could be done than by 'patronising leaders, creeds, and expensive organisations'. As a library, the Spiritual Institution could comfortably hold a collection of disparate opinions bound together by a flexible catalogue without the need to impose any dogmatic unity. Daniel Cottom has observed of the Spiritualist movement that it included such diversity of opinion that it 'could not possibly recognise any heterodoxy except a total disbelief in the possibility of an afterlife'.[21] Beyond that, the limits of Spiritualism were the limits of a medium's experiences or imagination, both of which could be enhanced by access to literature. A library could contain lengthy disagreements, disquisitions, debates, and alternative routes to the same truth between its shelves and covers in a way that the constitution of an association could not. For Burns, revelation did not come from a set

---

[17] Burns, p. 274.   [18] *The Spiritual Magazine*, May 1874, p. 193.
[19] For a detailed account of test séances, see Owen.
[20] Richard Noakes, *Physics and Psychics: The Occult and the Sciences in Modern Britain* (Cambridge: Cambridge University Press, 2019), p. 248.
[21] Daniel Cottom, *Abyss of Reason: Cultural Movements, Revelations and Betrayals* (Oxford: Oxford University Press, 1991), p. 3.

text, but reading was the practice by which the spirit world could gain entrance and guide one to truth:

> The great source of knowledge on the subject of Spiritualism is the spirit-world.... A minor source of knowledge is the printing press, by which the revelations obtained direct from spirit-life are recorded, multiplied, and made available for wide circulation. This is often an indispensable accessory and forerunner of the direct form of spiritual teaching.[22]

Séances were 'not at all times so constituted that the most profitable form of teaching can be obtained through them', while a network of 'Associative Progressive Libraries' in every town 'might be made the basis of all that can be desired in the way of organisation'.[23] A literature-first model allowed the Institution to pick and choose the most convincing instances of mediumship and then, within that, allow readers to select for themselves the works that seemed most convincing in the order that made sense to them. Understood in this way, the purpose of the Spiritual Institution was to facilitate opportunities for enlightenment without the 'reiterated insistence upon the necessity of defining what Spiritualism is to stand for' argued for by those proposing nationalisation.[24] Spiritualism was not defined by any one text, but the whole collection was its tangible evidence.

The Next World Interviewed

What kinds of validation and sense of unified purpose were to be found inside the pages of the works commissioned by the Spiritual Institution? A closer look at some of the works published there captures a sense of a movement where readership and authorship were stages in a shared journey of enlightenment. James Burns encouraged mediums who worked with him to write down their experiences, which he then published. He filled the pages of *Medium and Daybreak* with their writings and advertisements for their books. Some of the most important texts of modern occultism were first published by the Spiritual Institution, including Emma Hardinge Britten's *Nineteenth-Century Miracles* (1871), Gerald Massey's *Concerning Spiritualism* (1871), William Crookes's *Researches in the Phenomena of Spiritualism* (1871), and Alfred Russel Wallace's *Miracles and Modern Spiritualism* (1875). These names, though famous within Spiritualist circles, were perhaps less well known outside them. Fortunately, the

---

[22] 'Spiritualists, Organise!', *Medium and Daybreak*, 9 December 1870, p. 284.
[23] 'Spiritualists, Organise!', p. 284.
[24] J. J. Morse, 'The Nationalisation of Spiritualism', *The Two Worlds*, 8 June 1894, p. 265.

Spiritual Institution had a second stable of authors from which to commission works: the dead. Key to the project of Spiritualism was the adamant insistence that ongoing communication with the deceased was possible and happening with increasing frequency. If visitors to Southampton Row came to learn from experts, they also hoped to encounter those who had preceded them into the 'Summerland' and could provide witness testimony of the truths of spirit life. Just as mediumistic experiences were shared beyond the immediate circle in books, the messages sent by the dead were collected and bound in volumes. In their pages, believers could learn directly from luminaries whose authority was borrowed from other institutions of which they had been members in their former lives. Judges, scientists, politicians, and authors were adopted as identities by spirit mediums hoping to spark recognition – and with it belief – from their readers. For example, the American medium Susan G. Horn stayed at the Spiritual Institution during some of the writing of her book *The Next World: Fifty-Six Communications from Eminent Historians, Authors, Legislators, Etc., Now in Spirit Life*. The unspoken selection criterion for the majority of the spirits whom Horn imitates in this collection is that they were already known to the public through their published writings.

Books such as these created the illusion of cooperative publishing work between the living and the dead in the service of Spiritualist education. The spirits were cast as students too, and happy to do their part in the work of the Institution. (The publisher's preface to *The Next World* tells us the medium's stay at Southampton Row 'seemed essential to the production of several articles'.[25]) In a typical example from Horn's collection, 'George Eliot' renounces the 'bare and flowerless belief' of materialism and testifies to her re-education and the loss of her 'doubts and uncertainties' in the spirit world. She presents her conversion as preordained:

> From the days of Aspasia, to those of Mary Wollstonecraft, Frances Wright, and down to my own times, certain women have been chosen as mouthpieces for heretical thoughts; have stood as strange erratic stars in the firmament, shedding forth a disturbing, independent light, and, at the moment when they had arrived at the height of their glory ... they have suddenly diverged from the path apparently marked out for them, and left those would-be followers ... to bemoan their loss with despair and mortification.[26]

Posthumous conversion narratives are a common theme, with the medium-writer interspersing commentary to encourage readers to

---

[25] Susan G. Horn, *The Next World Interviewed* (London: J. Burns, 1890), p. iii. [26] Horn, p. 154.

recognise the author as both a known authority and a fellow investigator. Horn argues, for example, that George Eliot 'analyses her own contradictory conduct as clearly as in her Novels she depicts the motives of her Heroines'.[27] The autobiography of a living medium segues into autothanatography from the channelled spirit, presenting it as the testimony of one more advanced in their learning. The rules of the genre are quite clear. The famous spirits must be recognisable as themselves from their writing, but now also recognisable as part of a community of investigators into Spiritualism.

These books tend, too, to be firm on the importance of such a community. Horn's 'Harriet Martineau' describes the spirit world as an intellectual meeting ground where 'thinkers of Europe and America' live together in Arcadia 'each adding his quota of work and knowledge to the whole'.[28] She credits her new understanding to the work of a community of right thinkers – a literary cadre of spirits ('among those I will name Miss Brontë, Dickens, Mrs. Gaskill [sic], Robert Chambers, and Wordsworth') who have drawn her away from the likes of 'Darwin, Huxley, Arnold, Comte, and Herbert Spencer'.[29] Whether living or dead, the influence of those with whom one surrounded oneself was a topic of concern for Spiritualists. The books in both their content and their form claim endorsement from representatives of legitimate organisations. And these known names are also an enticement, challenging readers to dip into the pages and seek out a sense of recognition.

There were, of course, always those who would never accept the legitimacy of these claims and some who actively sought to expose them as fraud. In his *Modern Spiritualism: A History and a Criticism*, Frank Podmore charges Burns directly with complicity in deceit:

> Whilst his enthusiasm for the social reforms which he advocated was genuine and fervent, it was impossible to doubt the sincerity of his belief in Spiritualism; but equally impossible to believe him as ignorant as he professed himself of the manifold wiles and trickeries practised by physical mediums within his doors and under his direct patronage and protection.[30]

However, we have no records from the Institute of the kinds of ruinous exposures of mediums that happened elsewhere. Books like Horn's – and the other channelled texts Burns stocked and published – took the place occupied by the test séance for the BNAS and SPR. In many respects they throw down the same gauntlet: do you believe that this work is, and can

---

[27] Horn, p. 154.   [28] Horn, p. 11.   [29] Horn, pp. 12, 9.   [30] Podmore, p. 165.

only be, the result of direct communication from the dead? However, the arena for debate has been relocated from physical tests to literary criticism. Unlike the ectoplasm that is revealed to be muslin, books are by their nature available to interpretation. The argument for or against their veracity becomes a sort of shadow form of attribution studies: Do you recognise the author's voice? Do these extended biographical details offer a convincing hermeneutic for interpreting this work and, perhaps, reinterpreting the author's earlier works? The borrowed authority of the spirit writer takes centre stage to be accepted or rejected, while the actual activities of the medium can recede back into the privacy of the inner sanctum.

Julia's Bureau

The chasm between what has been claimed and what can be known of the inner workings of an institution of Spiritualism is even wider when it comes to the library and séance bureau established by the famous journalist, and convinced believer in the value of trans-sepulchral cooperation, W. T. Stead. Mowbray House on Norfolk Road stood on the far side of the Strand from Southampton Row where the Spiritual Institution had held its own for three decades. But now it was 1909, and the Institution had been gone for fifteen years. Mowbray House's elaborate Gothic façade made it a fitting home for 'Julia's Bureau'. This was the culmination of Stead's Spiritualist ambitions: a free public service where the communications gap between the living and the dead could be bridged 'to help those who love to find each other again after the change called death'.[31] He had first announced his intention to open such an office in 1893.[32] The Bureau, though its street address would be in the mortal realm, would serve the needs of its posthumous clients just as much as those living. Stead's spirit guide assured him that they would be 'overwhelmed with application from both sides'.[33] In the three years the Bureau ran before Stead's untimely death on the Titanic, it reported that it had completed some 1,300 sittings for over 600 applicants – an impressive rate given the labour-intensive vetting process, which involved consultation with the living, the dead,

---

[31] W. T. Stead, 'The Exploration of the Other World', *Fortnightly Review*, May 1909, pp. 850–61 (p. 850).
[32] Edith K. Harper, *Stead: The Man: Personal Reminiscences* (London: William Rider, 1918), p. 46.
[33] [W. T. Stead], *Letters from Julia; or, Light from the Borderland* (London: Grant Richards, 1898), p. 102.

a secretary, a psychometrist, two separate mediums, and the Bureau's director.[34]

Again, as in any Spiritualist enterprise, signing up spirits of the highest calibre was the easy part. Stead's daughter, Estelle, would later brag about the illustrious nature of their clients from that side of the divide: 'Many were the religious discussions with, and communications from, those who had filled high places in the Churches of the world, as well as exciting political discussions with those who had held prominent office in Parliament and State'.[35] Perhaps the most high-profile activity of the Bureau was Stead's alleged interview with the spirit of William Gladstone on the subject of the 1909 Budget. *The Review of Reviews* reported on the event and assured readers of 'the extraordinary resemblance between the way in which Mr Gladstone talked then and the way in which he is reported as talking now'.[36] For anyone who was convinced, this was offered as evidence that the Bureau had a role to play in the most important matters of public policy. Newspapers *not* edited by W. T. Stead took a very different tone, however:

> That an office should be opened to carry on as a regular business communication with the dead, not secretly or doubtingly but openly with a view to obtaining answers which shall be good 'copy' on the questions of the day is little short of revolting. *Manchester Guardian*, 2 November 1909
>
> A sickening rigmarole of cant, imposture, and banality ... an impudent and blasphemous concoction devised to play upon the most contemptible phases of feeble-mindedness. *Pall Mall Gazette*, 2 November 1909

Stead's own fame was a boost for spreading word of the Bureau, but positive engagement with the project from the public was evidently less assured. Infiltration by sceptics was a perennial risk for any public Spiritualistic performance, where those with a quick eye and a quick hand could expose the trickery of the show. (Or, to put it in the parlance of Spiritualists themselves, could suppress the spirits, and psychically harm mediums through negative energies and slander.) An institution like Julia's Bureau was sure to attract those determined to expose its workings as fraudulent. Some vetting procedure was needed to keep out troublemakers while still offering a free public service. Though their approaches differ dramatically, Stead's solution was fundamentally the same as Burns's before him: the Bureau would present the world with a welcoming open

---

[34] Estelle Stead, *My Father* (London: Nelson, 1918), p. 303.   [35] Stead, *My Father*, p. 313.
[36] *The Review of Reviews*, November 1909, p. 411.

door, and redirect any intrusions into those aspects of the work that relied on secrecy towards discussions of a shared literary experience. Even for the Gladstone interview, Stead allowed the editor of the *Daily Chronicle* to set the questions but not to attend the séance.[37] Spiritualists's claims always stood a better chance of withstanding scrutiny if the focus was on the analysis of a text rather than the mechanics of its production.

Like Burns, Stead saw shared literature and 'preliminary study' as the solution to the problem, and Julia's Bureau included on its premises a 'Borderland Library'.[38] Where the Progressive Library had been the heart of the project of the Spiritual Institution, the Borderland Library (which included a number of the same titles) was explicitly invoked as a means to an end for testing the sincerity of those who wished to use the Bureau's services.[39] Would-be applicants filled in a number of application forms and then signed the following declaration:

> I ____, having done my best to study the subject of communications with the other world, hereby make application for the use of the Bureau ... I have read the pamphlet entitled 'Julia's Bureau and Borderland Library', and also the first series of 'Letters from Julia'. With a full understanding of conditions, limitations, and dangers therein defined, I make this application, and I am willing to submit in all things to the decision of the Director of the Bureau conveyed to me by one or other of her amanuenses.[40]

Stead's reasoning for this test was simple: anyone who was genuine in their application would welcome the opportunity to first read more about the topic and 'must be anxious to hear something of the testimony of those who claim to have succeeded in establishing such communications'.[41] The principal set text was his own work of spirit correspondence, *Letters from Julia, or, Light from the Borderland* (1898).[42] Applicants were expected to demonstrate interest in 'the best works that have been written by those who have made the question a subject of earnest study and patient investigation' and to have sought out at least some of the writings of important Spiritualists like Stainton Moses, William Crookes, or Alfred Russel Wallace.[43] The works of these men had all initially been published by James Burns. This curriculum

---

[37] 'Spirits and Budget', *Manchester Evening News*, 1 November 1909, p. 5.
[38] *Medium and Daybreak*, 8 April 1870, p. 1.
[39] A catalogue of books then held by the Borderland Library was published in *Borderland*, 4 October 1897, pp. 454–58.
[40] Stead, *My Father*, pp. 302–03.   [41] Stead, *My Father*, p. 293.
[42] For more on the character of Julia and the generic origins of her letters, see Sarah Crofton, 'The Spirit-Writing and Editorial Mediumship of W. T. Stead', *19: Interdisciplinary Studies in the Long Nineteenth Century*, 16 (2013) <https://doi.org/10.16995/ntn.659>.
[43] Stead, *My Father*, p. 294.

was a clever touch. It either weeded out those unwilling to take time to read those works from propagandists that had, for years, proved most successful at persuading the convertible or it laid blame for any later misunderstandings on their own ignorance. Combined with the insistence that all applicants prove a close relationship with the deceased (the Bureau was for the bereaved, not the curious) and the information gathered in the application forms, conditions were primed for any medium worth their salt to prepare a reading without need for any supernatural powers.

Julia's Bureau took the established trick of presenting the medium as a passive vehicle for spirit agency and extended it to possess an entire institutional apparatus. When announcing the project to the public, Stead explained that it would be run by a committee split evenly between the living and the dead with his spirit guide 'Julia' as chairperson.[44] Stead presented himself as the junior partner in their joint endeavour with Julia undertaking 'its direct operations from day to day'.[45] Therefore, as well as hiring mediums who would be the conduit between visitors and their dead relatives, another level of bureaucratic mediumships was required for managing the business of the bureau and channelling the directions of its chairwoman. Mowbray House would be the office space for all such activities and for meeting directly with clients. This allowed Stead the illusion of physically distancing himself from the project:

> I would not assume the responsibility of making the attempt if Julia had not assured me that she will personally decide which cases the Bureau shall take in hand.
> Those who believe that Julia is only a phase of my subconsciousness will be puzzled to explain how it is that she communicates with equal ease through me or through two or three other Sensitives. For the proper functioning of the Bureau my personal attendance will not be necessary.[46]

Even by the account of the Bureau's secretary, this distance was illusory. In fact, the central circle of mediums that made up the 'Inner Sanctuary' of the project met and made their plans in Stead's own home. Mowbray House was the premises of the library and the 'ministering agency' of the project.[47] Once again the public face of the project was a building open to all, full of books and visiting spirits with secrets waiting to be learned by anyone who chose to investigate.

---

[44] Stead claimed 'Julia' was the spirit of Julia A. Ames, an American journalist whom he had met briefly in 1890 and who died in 1891.
[45] Stead, 'Exploration of the Other World', p. 858.
[46] Stead, 'Exploration of the Other World', p. 861.   [47] Harper, p. 134.

Here we hit another lacuna in the record where the truth remains tantalisingly inaccessible because it was unrecorded. It is impossible now to know how many of those involved in Julia's Bureau believed in the actual existence of their spirit 'director' and who simply paid lip service. We also cannot know what impact this had on the day-to-day running of the bureau. Spiritualists like Stainton Moses and Etta Wriedt, who were among the Bureau's house mediums, maintained an unwavering professional persona of belief. Secretaries and administrators like Stead himself, his daughter Estelle, and his secretary Edith Harper write of Julia's factual participation in the work with no trace of irony or circumspection. On the one hand, Julia simply anthropomorphises the conceit that any institution has inherent continuous agency, obscuring the actual disorder and disagreement that may occur between its mere mortal constituent members. On the other hand, the existence or non-existence of Julia was the difference between seeing the Bureau as 'obvious and proper' or a 'sickening rigmarole of cant'.[48]

The Death and Life-After-Death of an Institution

Despite their ambitions to serve as the organisational foundation upon which could be built an ever-expanding network of collaborative work, neither the Spiritual Institution nor Julia's Bureau long survived the relocation of its founder to the other side of the great divide. Though the Spiritual Institution had been instrumental to many, it always rested on the labour of a single man. In a poignant editorial in May 1894, James Burns revealed the extent of his financial troubles and pleaded with readers of *Medium and Daybreak* to come together to save the Institution:

> The lease of this place expires in a few weeks. I have got to turn out and take my spiritual work with me.
>
> ...
>
> This is an earnest appeal. I ask you all to rally round this work. Put your hands in your pockets and find the means of lifting the burden. It is worthy of you to do so. You need not be ashamed of the work or of the worker. Perhaps the Spiritual Institution is the one thing in the Cause that does not stand in need of an apology.[49]

Neither support nor saving spirits manifested and the Spiritual Institution was closed. Burns died a disappointed man seven months later.[50] Shortly

---

[48] Stead, 'Exploration of the Other World', p. 850; *Pall Mall Gazette*, 2 November 1909, p. 9.
[49] Burns, pp. 275–76.   [50] 'Decease of Mr. James Burns', *Light*, 5 January 1895, p. 2.

after, his sons ended the twenty-five-year run of *Medium and Daybreak,* and the Progressive Library ceased its activities. Julia's Bureau, too, operated at a loss from the beginning, closing its office in the city after only a year. After Stead's sudden death aboard *RMS Titanic,* the 'inner sanctum' changed the focus of its work to seeking contact with Stead himself and never recovered its grand ambitions. Neither project can truly be said to have lived up to the task it set itself and crucially neither ever achieved the approbation of the greater public sphere.

The Spiritual Institution and Julia's Bureau were set up with at least the stated intention of doing institutional work on terms akin to many other literary organisations of their time. They took disparate elements of the Spiritualist movement – its literature, its mediums, its myths, its networks – and organised them into public-facing entities to transmit their beliefs and their literature. They sought to validate (and protect) the experiences of their members on a larger stage and were vocal in representing themselves as the route to acceptance and understanding of their cause at last. They failed because they could not establish their legitimacy in a broader cultural context and because the death of their founders left them without the capital, labour, or incentive to continue. Or, let us read the evidence another way. The Spiritual Institution and Julia's Bureau were organisations designed to defraud the public and brazenly mimicked the trappings of institutionality in order to do so. They built the careers and reputations of the mediums who wrote the literature they circulated, and who were insulated from direct attack by the organisational infrastructure. So long as the frontmen, whether themselves dupes or grifters, kept up the output of earnest propaganda, the pretence was enough to lure in the credulous and the bereaved. They were not earnest institutions formed to support a movement most deemed dishonest, but ersatz institutions engaged in a dishonest performance of sincerity down at an organisational level.

Whether 'wiles and trickeries' were practised under the roofs of Mowbray House and 15 Southampton Row and what those tricks might have been are questions of concrete historical fact. However, what we believe about them is likely to be based on our pre-existing willingness to accept that the dead can return to correct an edition of their work or to serve on a committee; it will not come from studying the surviving records. Today we can recreate much of the collection of the Progressive Library and the Borderland Library from their catalogues. Every edition of *Medium and Daybreak* is available for us to study, as are the *Letters from Julia.* Autobiographical accounts of daily work by those most involved were published and so survive in libraries around the world. Yet one cannot but notice that the traces that remain of these institutions are exactly those publications that each presented to the public as proof of their metaphysical claims. Perhaps the loudest silence is the irretrievable physical infrastructure of the buildings, now both demolished, that were each once the 'open door and metropolitan *locus standi*' of Spiritualism in London.[51] While the physical space in which people meet can help to shape the work of any organisation, there are some particular questions that arise around the physical spaces of Spiritualism that are not, perhaps, so pressing elsewhere. Many mediumistic phenomena are aided by careful control over furniture and fixtures. The Slade trial in 1876 focussed public attention, for example, on how much could be done to trick the credulous with a well-designed table.[52] One cannot help but wonder how much the legerdemain of the Spiritual Institution's 'College of Mediums' was aided by its opportunity to control a séance room of its own, or whether the sympathetic communication between Julia's secretaries was facilitated, in some way, by sideboards.

[51] 'Organisation', *Medium and Daybreak*, 2 March 1877, p. 136.
[52] Arthur Conan Doyle, *The History of Spiritualism*, 2 vols (London: Cassell, 1926), I, 289–98.

Index

Abdullah bin Kadir Abdul, 268
Académie Française, 13
Addison, Joseph, 69, 73, 78
Akenside, Mark, 75
Albertus University, 88, 93
Alexander I, 97
Altman, Rick, 125
Amalia, Anna, 83, 84–88, 90, 91, 94, 96, 100
Anacreontic poetry and song, 101–2, 105–19
Anacreontic Society, 11, 15, 101–19
anatomy, 55, 166–72, 174
Anderson, John, 143, 149, 196, 198–99, 202
Anderson's Institution, 136, 143, 144, 146, 148, 149, 152, 196, 198–204, 213
Antoinette, Marie, 110
Appiah, Kwame Anthony, 100
Arabic, 258
Arden, John, 141
Arnold, Matthew, 13, 250, 284
Asiatic Society of Bengal, 255
Askesian Society, 144, 148
assemblage, 8, 11, 65, 66, 70–71, 77, 78, 80–81, 104, 135, 242
assembly rooms, 141, 183
Aston, Francis, 32
Atterbury, Francis, 7
Auerswald, Sophie Charlotte Albertine von, 89, 91
Austen, Jane, 125
authors and authorship, 1, 3, 4, 9, 10, 13, 15, 18–22, 46, 49, 67–82, 94, 121, 122, 133, 160, 173–74, 186–91, 237, 238, 242, 244, 256, 269, 274, 282–85
autobiography, 268, 269, 284

Bacon, Francis, 30, 31, 186
Baczko, Ludwig von, 88
Baines, Edward, 209
Ballaarat Mechanics' Institute, 215–33
Ballard, George, 60
Ballard, J. H., 230

Banks, Joseph, 146, 147–48, 149, 150, 151, 152, 178
Baran, Paul, 138
Barckley, Henriette Elisabeth, 89
Barnard, Toby, 37
Barnstaple Literary and Scientific Institute, 246
Barton, Bernard, 192, 193
Batavian Society of Arts and Sciences, 264
Bath, 131, 138, 140, 141
Bayfield, Mrs. E. G., 131
beacons, 12, 257, 269–73
Beattie, James, 15
Becker, Howard, 123
Beddoes, Thomas, 138, 146, 149
Beecher, Phane, 37
Beechworth Athenaeum, 215–33
Beechworth Public Library, 220, 221–22, 228, 229, 232
Beechworth Public Library Museum, 220
Behn, Aphra, 71
Beighton, Thomas, 261
Bell, Beaupré, 51
Bell, William, 165, 169, 170, 172
belles lettres, 21, 210, 248
Benbow, William, 213
Bence Jones, Henry, 145, 146, 152
Benger, Elizabeth, 181
Benson, Charles, 54
Bentley, Richard, 24, 48
Berg, Maxine, 214
Berger, Joachim, 85
Berman, Morris, 145, 147, 155
Bernard, Thomas, 146, 147, 152–53
Besant, Walter, 18
Best, Graham, 51
Betham, Matilda, 181
Betham-Edwards, Matilda, 212
Birkbeck, George, 196, 198, 199–201, 204, 208, 212, 213
Birmingham, 138, 140, 141, 143, 146, 150, 156, 199
Black, Charles, 150
Blackmore, Richard, 70, 73

Index

Blair, Hugh, 21
Blänker, Reinhard, 94
Boate, Arnold, 36, 37
Boate, Gerard, 36, 37, 42
Bodleian Library, 41, 106, 112
Bodley, John, 41
Bodley, Josias, 41
Bodley, Thomas, 41
Bogost, Ian, 162, 169
Boltanski, Luc, 155
Bolton, 140
Böning, Holger, 94
booksellers, 77–78, 131–34, 141, 182, 237, 240, 261
Bose, Sugata, 261
Böttiger, Karl August, 97
Boulton, Matthew, 146, 148, 150, 151
Bourdieu, Pierre, 4, 11–12, 77, 186
Boyle, Robert, 32, 33, 36, 38, 42, 186
Braddon, Mary Elizabeth, 209
Brewer, David A., 20
Bristol, 133, 140, 146, 150, 156
Bristol Pneumatic Institution, 136, 138, 146, 149
British Association for the Advancement of Science, 156, 265
British Board of Agriculture, 146, 147
British Institution, 7, 153, 184
British Library, 106, 194, *see* British Museum
British Museum, 17, 20, 33, 178–95
    Cottonian library, 180
British National Association of Spiritualists, 281, 284
Britten, Emma Hardinge, 279, 282
Brougham, Henry, 184, 205
Brouncker, William, 33
Brown, Thomas, 188
Browning, Robert, 275
Bruce, Alexander, 34
Bruton, James, 249, 252
Buck, George, 26, 27–29
Burke, Edmund, 13, 112, 208
Burns, James, 277, 278–82, 284, 286, 287, 289
Burns, Robert, 3, 232
Butler, Samuel, 58, 73
Byron, George Gordon, Lord, 9, 136, 201, 205

Cain, Peter, 260
Calcutta, 255, 261, 264, 273
Calcutta General Committee of Public Instruction, 261
Calcutta Hindoo College, 259
Calcutta School Society, 261
Calcutta School-Book Society, 261
Callon, Michel, 153
Cambridge, 140, 156
Cambridge University, 26, 29, 42, 106, 272

Campbell, Thomas, 19, 136, 153
Canny, Nicholas, 37
canons, 21, 78, 102, 115, 125, 172, 243, *see* national canon
Capern, Edward, 246, 247, 249
Carver, Raymond, 126
Cary, Henry Francis, 191, 192
Cascardi, Anthony J., 5
catalogues, 9, 27, 45, 46, 48, 50, 51, 52, 54, 55, 128, 134, 157–77, 180, 189, 265, 290
Cavendish, Georgiana, Duchess of Devonshire, 101, 115, 130
Cavendish, Margaret, 42
Ceylon, 264
Chambers, Robert, 284
charities, 7, 46, 47, 48, 57, 64, 146, 229
Chaucer, Geoffrey, 73, 188
Chiapello, Eve, 155
Child, Robert, 36, 37
China, 261, 270, 271
Chinese
    languages, 258, 259, 268
    people, 257, 261, 262, 263
Chinese Christian Association, 262
Chinese Philomathic Society, 262, *see* Straits Settlements
Church of England, 7, 18, 19, 39, 196, 198, 210, 211, 213
Cibber, Colley, 69, 73, 193
cinema, 122, 125–26, 128, 129–30
Civil List, 10
Clark, Peter, 15
Clarkson, Catherine, 182
Clarkson, Thomas, 182
Clementi, Muzio, 102, 103
Clift, William, 165, 166, 169–72, 177
Clydesdale, Matthew, 201
Cobbett, William, 207
coffee house, 35, 47, 50, 103, 183
Coke, Edward, 27
Colclough, Stephen, 237, 241
Cole, Henry, 240
Coleridge, John Taylor, 185
Coleridge, Samuel Taylor, 19, 21, 136, 153, 185, 187, 238, 248
Collier, Jeremy, 188
colonialism, 5, 14, 25, 26, 29, 32, 36–43, 145, 158, 164, 216, 219, 255–74
Columbus, Christopher, 232
Comenius, Johannes Amos, 34
Comte, Auguste, 284
Comyn, Sarah, 5, 16, 22
concerts, 86, 103, 106, 109, 117, 118, 119, 130, 228, 231, 279
conversazioni, 218, 234

Cooper, Thomas, 142
Corfield, Penelope, 18
Cottom, Daniel, 281
Coughlan, Patricia, 37
Couper, William, 175
Crabb Robinson, Henry, 136, 184, 188, 194
Crawford, John, 265
Crofton, Sarah, 18
Cromwell, Oliver, 34, 42
Crookes, William, 282, 287
Cross, G. F., 229
Cross, Nigel, 3
Cull, Richard, 265
curators, 159, 161, 215, 229, 230

Daly, Ann, 158
Darnton, Robert, 239
Darwin, Charles, 284
Davies, Charles Maurice, 279
Davy, Humphry, 137, 145, 146, 147, 148, 149–50, 151, 153–54, 155
Davy, John, 149
de La Roche, Michel, 58
De Quincey, Thomas, 11, 136
de Saussure, Ferdinand, 122
de Tournefort, Joseph Pitton, 58
Defoe, Daniel, 31, 40, 41–42
Delbourgo, James, 161
Derby, 138, 140
Derrida, Jacques, 23, 67
Desaguliers, J. T., 139
Detroisier, Rowland, 204
Dibdin, Charles, 112
Dibdin, Thomas Frognall, 153
Dickens, Charles, 13, 20, 209, 232, 240, 247, 284
Dignum, Charles, 108, 112
dissenters, 16, 21, 142, 145, 198
    dissenting academies. *See* Kendal Dissenting Academy, Warrington Academy
Dohna-Schlobitten-Leistenau, Friederike Amelie von, 89
Dolven, Jeff, 74
Domhardt, Johann Friedrich, 91
Doncaster, 140
Draper, Don, 120
Dryden, John, 69, 72, 78, 188
Dublin, 77, *see* Royal Dublin Society
Dublin Philosophical Society, 26
Duchess of Devonshire. *See* Cavendish, Georgiana
Duffy, Kathrinne, 158
Dunn, Kevin, 31
Dupin, Charles, 201
Durie, John, 36, 37

Dury, Dorothy Moore, 36
Dyer, Rev. Samuel, 261

Earle, William, 128, 129
East India Company, 181, 182, 191, 192, 193, 257, 258
    Charter Act (1833), 257
Ecole des Arts et Métiers (Paris), 201
Ecton, John, 61
Edinburgh, 77, 133, 142, 145, 150, 255
Edinburgh School of Art, 204
Edinburgh University, 200
Education Act (1870), 18, 203
Edwards, Christopher, 52
Ekhof, Conrad, 96
Eliot, George, 250, 283, 284
Ellis, Henry, 189
Ellys, Richard, 62
Enlightenment, 31, 44, 64, 83, 90, 94, 96, 100, 262, 272
    popular, 22
    Scottish, 143, 260
    Transpennine, 138

Fadiman, Anne, 238
Farington, Joseph, 152
Favret, Mary, 249, 250
Fellowes, Robert, 210
Female Employment Regulation Act (1873), 231
Fentum, J., 107, 112, 116, 117, 119
Fermanis, Porscha, 5, 22, 23
Ferris, Ina, 186
Feuerbach, Paul Johann Anselm, 97
Flexner, Helen, 205
Flinders, Matthew, 232
Flint, Kate, 220, 221
Fontane, Theodor, 95
Foucault, Michel, 4, 9, 67
Fowler, Alastair, 122
France, 13, 41, 67, 149
Franklin, Benjamin, 140, 198
Franklin, Robert, 212
Frederick II, 96
Freiesleben, Christian Gottfried von, 96
French. *See* Académie Française
    language, 29, 93
    law, 189
    periodicals, 91
    salons, 88
French Revolution, 106, 112, 143, 149, 199, 245
Friedländer, David, 97
Friedrich Wilhelm II, 90, 93
Froude, J. A., 247
Furnivall, Frederick James, 247

Index

Gale, Roger, 52
Galloway, Alexander, 140, 145
Gamlyn, John, 48
Gardner, John, 16, 22, 143
Garnett, Thomas, 141, 144, 146, 149, 151–52, 198, 199
Garrick, David, 192
Gaskell, Elizabeth, 203, 284
Gay, John, 58, 69, 78
Gell, Alfred, 74
genre, 4, 12, 16, 22, 38, 40, 72–73, 78–81, 101–2, 117, 118, 120–34, 161–62, 167, 172, 176, 177, 185, 245, 269, 274, 275, 284
Geological Society, 144, 148
George III, 189
Gerbier, Balthazar, 37
German
    classicism, 84
    clocks, 209
    language, 83, 86, 89
Giddy, Davies, 150
Gigante, Denise, 187
Gildon, Charles, 129
Gill, Stephen, 250
Gissing, George, 191
Gladstone, John, 14
Gladstone, William Ewart, 286, 287
Glasgow, 77, 137, 143, 149, 150, 164, 200, 212, *see* Anderson's Institution, Hunterian Museum (Glasgow)
Glasgow Literary Society, 198, 201
Glasgow Mechanics' Institute, 201, 204, 205, 206–7, 209
Glasgow University, 143, 164, 198, 199, 200
Gloucester, 140
Goddard, Jonathan, 34
Godwin, William, 136, 179, 184, 185, 186, 188, 189, 191, 208
Goethe, Johann Wolfgang von, 85, 86, 87, 96, 97
Golden, Catherine, 240
Goldstein, Vida, 232
Golinski, Jan, 142
Googe, Barnabe, 37
Gordon, George, 110–12, 116
Gough, Richard, 45
Granovetter, Mark, 147
Grant, James, 190–91, 193
Gray, Thomas, 73, 81
Green, Edward, 52
Gresham College, 28–29, 30, 33, 34
Gresham, Thomas, 29
Griffin, Dustin, 80
Grimm, Friedrich Melchior, 96
Guild of Literature and Art, 20

Guthrie Davidson, James, 260
Guthrie, Alexander, 260

Hakluyt Society, 266
Hall, J. C., 206
Hamann, Johann Georg, 88, 90, 91
Harley, Robert, Earl of Oxford, 13
Harper, Edith, 289
Harris, John, 58
Harris, P. R., 181, 189
Hart, Helen, 230, 231
Hartlib, Samuel, 26, 30, 31, 32, 33, 34, 35, 36, 37, 39
Hauksbee, Francis, 139
Haydn, Joseph, 102, 103, 117
Hays, J. N., 144, 155
Hazelwood, Jennifer, 218
Hazlitt, William, 19, 136, 213
Henderson, L. J., 196
Henshaw, Nathaniel, 37
Herder, Johann Gottfried, 87, 88, 256
Hewerdine, William, 110–12, 116
Heywood, Thomas, 29, 39–40
Hill, Christopher, 33
Hill, Frederic, 235
Hill, Rowland, 238, 240, 241, 246, 247, 248, 250, 251, 252
Hippel, Theodor Gottlieb von, 88, 91
Hippisley, John Coxe, 152
Hodgskin, Thomas, 208, 212
Hollis, Patricia, 207
Holmes, Thomas, 210
Home, Everard, 165
Hone, William, 192, 193
Honeybone, Diana, 45
Honeybone, Michael, 45
Hong Kong, 264
Hope, Thomas Charles, 150
Hopkins, Tony, 260
Hoppen, Keith, 37
Horace, 62, 92, 98, 116
Horn, Susan G., 283–84
Hose, Archdeacon George, 267
Hose, George Archdeacon, 255
Howard, Henry, 52, 56–58, 61
Hudson, J. W., 210
Hughes, J. F., 131–33
Hughes, Josiah, 261
Hunt, Leigh, 188, 191
Hunter, John, 164, 165, 166, 171
Hunter, Michael, 33
Hunter, William, 158, 164, 165, 172, 175, 176
Hunterian Museum (Glasgow), 9, 163–77
Hunterian Museum (London), 9, 163–77
Huskisson, William, 211
Hutcheson, Francis, 143

Hutchings, Rev. E. S., 270
Huxley, Thomas Henry, 284

India, 22, 259, 261, 263, 271
  Bombay, 264
  languages, 258
  Madras, 264
  people, 261, 273
Inkster, Ian, 155
Innerpeffray Library, 15
International Council on Museums, 158
internationalism, 6, 34, 256, 263
Ipswich Mechanics' Institute, 211, 212
Italian, 13, 130, 213

Jacob, Margaret, 148
Jacobs, Edward, 128
James I, 24
Jameson, Fredric, 122
Japan, 270
Jerdan, William, 236, 237, 238
Johnson, Francis, 30
Johnson, John, 58
Johnson, Maurice, 44, 46–50, 51, 53–54, 55, 56, 57, 59, 60, 62, 63–64
Johnson, Samuel, 68, 70, 71, 72, 73, 78, 81
Johnson, Walter, 58
Johnston, Alexander Laurie, 260
Jones, Joseph, 231
Jones, Katherine (Lady Ranelagh), 36
Jonson, Ben, 39, 179
Julia's Bureau, 277, 285–89, 290
  Borderland Library, 287, 290

Kamuf, Peggy, 67–68
Kant, Immanuel, 88–89, 90, 93–94
Kaufman, Paul, 54
Kay, Carol, 81
Keats, John, 3, 101, 136, 232
Keir, James, 150
Kendal Dissenting Academy, 141
Keppie, Laurence, 164
Keyserling(k), Charlotte Caroline Amalie von, 83, 88–94, 95, 100
Keyserling, Heinrich Christian von, 90, 92–93
Keyserlingk, Gebhardt Johann von, 90
King's College London, 21
Kingsley, Charles, 247
Kittler, Friedrich, 1
Klancher, Jon, 8, 11, 13, 17, 23, 66, 183, 187, 198, 237, 244–45, 264
Klopstock, Friedrich Gottlieb, 96
Knebel, Karl Ludwig von, 86, 87
Knight, Arnold, 205
Knox, Vicesimus, 186, 189

Koehler, Karin, 20, 22, 23
Königlich-Preußische Akademie der Künste und Mechanischen Wissenschaften, 94
Königsberg, 83, 88–94
Korff, Friedrich Alexander von, 91
Körner, Christian Gottfried, 97
Körner, Minna, 97
Krishnan, Sanjay, 268
Kurland, Dorothea von, 83, 91, 94–100
Kynaston, Francis, 29–30

Lamb, Charles, 19, 136, 178–95
Lamb, Mary, 180, 181, 182, 184, 192, 193
Landon, Letitia Elizabeth, 237, 238
Lane, William, 124, 128, 129
Lang, Joseph, 46
Laskey, John, 173
Latour, Bruno, 136, 146, 153
law, 4, 10, 27, 55, 65–66, 157, 179, 189, 199, 248
lectures and lecturers, 19, 20, 36, 56, 65, 93, 136, 137–49, 151, 218, 230–33, 246, 247
Leech, John, 227
Leeds, 140
Leeds Mechanics' Institute, 202, 209
Leeds Philosophical and Literary Society, 16
Leicester, 57
Leicester Mechanics' Institute, 211
Leiden University, 36
Levine, Caroline, 242
Lewins, William, 245, 250
libraries, 16, 17, 21, 24–25, 35, 44–64, 85, 96, 120–34, 144, 157, 178, 181, 183, 184, 185, 186, 201, 204, 211, 212, 214, 215, 219, 221, 234, 246, 255, 258, 259, 263, 266, 267, 271, 278, 279, 280, 281, 285, 288, *see* Beechworth Public Library, Bodleian Library, British Library, Innerpeffray Library, New York Apprentices' Library, Raffles Library and Museum, Sheffield Mechanics' Library, Spalding Gentleman's Society, United Chinese Library, Wisbech Town Library
  circulating libraries, 15, 22, 120–34, 141, 183, 241
  Parochial Libraries Act (1708), 46, 63
  public libraries, 220
  Public Libraries Act (1850), 18, 278
  Schliebensche Palais in Königsberg, 89, 91
  subscription libraries, 4, 15, 51–52, 60, 64, 65, 260
Library of Useful Knowledge, 184
Lim Boon Keng, 262, 263, 271, 272
Linnaean classification, 173
Linnaean Society, 148
literary and philosophical societies, 18, 197, 206, 262, *see* Leeds Philosophical and Literary Society, Manchester Literary and

Philosophical Society, Newcastle upon Tyne Literary and Philosophical Society, Sheffield Literary and Philosophical Society
Liverpool, 14, 138, 140, 141, 142, 205
Liverpool Royal Institution, 7, 14
Löbichau, 83, 94–100
Locke, John, 186
Logan, James Richardson, 264, 265, 266, 267
London, 7, 14, 17, 21, 27–30, 33, 37, 47, 77, 103, 124, 127, 130, 136, 137, 139, 140, 141, 144–45, 149, 151, 153, 164, 170, 178, 187, 234, 246, 247, 255, 264, 278, 285, 291, *see* British Institution, British Museum, Hunterian Museum (London), Royal Institution, Russell Institution, Spitalfields Mathematical Society, Surrey Institution, University of London
London Corresponding Society, 249
London Ethnological Society, 264
London Institution, 144, 145, 178, 183
London Mechanics' Institute, 205, 208, 209, 210
London Society of Arts, 246
London Working Men's College, 247
Louis XVI, 199
Lubar, Steven, 158
Lukács, Georg, 124
Lyncker, Karl Wilhelm Heinrich, 87
Lyon, Stephen, 56

Macaulay, Catharine, 181
Macerone, Francis, 213, 214
magazines, 6, 13, 207, 212, 213, 214, 219, 223
Malacca, *see* Straits Settlements
  Anglo-Chinese College, 259
Malay
  language, 258, 259, 265, 268, 270
  literature, 268
  Malay culture, 268
  people, 257, 258, 261, 262, 263, 268, 269
  societies and clubs, 262
Malay Archipelago, 265, 266, 270
Malcolm, James Peller, 180
Maley, Willy, 5, 12
Manchester, 140, 141, 142, 143, 156
Manchester College of Arts and Sciences, 197
Manchester Literary and Philosophical Society, 15, 16, 142, 197, 198
Manchester Mechanics' Institute, 203, 204, 212
Manning, Thomas, 178, 184
manuscripts, 24, 45, 46, 54, 55, 59, 63, 87, 96, 119, 128, 162, 163, 165, 170–72, 173, 175, 176, 177, 178, 180, 182, 238, 239, 243
Marsden, William, 265, 267
Marsh, John, 105
Martin, Benjamin, 139, 140, 148

Martineau, Harriet, 203, 211, 247, 248, 284
Martineau, John, 209
Marx, Karl, 201, 208
Massey, Gerald, 282
Massey, Richard Middleton, 51, 57
Maurice, F. D., 22
McArdle, Mary Lillian, 230
McCalman, Iain, 110, 112
McGurl, Mark, 126
McKie, Douglas, 196
McLane, Maureen N., 2
McVeigh, Simon, 102, 106, 115, 116
mechanics' institutes, 16, 17, 20, 22, 196–214, 215–33, *see* Ballaarat Mechanics' Institute, Glasgow Mechanics' Institute, Leeds Mechanics' Institute, Leicester Mechanics' Institute, London Mechanics' Institute, Manchester Mechanics' Institute, Van Diemen's Land Mechanics' Institute
Medem, Johann Friedrich von, 95
medicine, 37, 38, 138, 142, 164, 199, 211, 248, *see* anatomy
Mee, Jon, 105, 138
Mee, Jon and Matthew Sangster, 65, 66, 68, 72, 82, 104
Mendyk, Stan, 37
Menke, Richard, 240
Merck, Johann Heinrich, 85
Merry, Robert, 101
Mill, John Stuart, 232, 250
Millar, John, 143
Miller, Thomas P., 21
Milton, John, 13, 20, 25–26, 30, 38–39, 73–81
Minerva Press, 124, 128, 129
minutes and minute books, 9, 45, 46, 50, 54, 59, 65, 104, 161, 200–5, 216–19
missionaries, 258
  London Missionary Society, 261
Mittell, Jason, 125, 126
Molyneux, William, 26
Montaigne, Michel de, 188
Moor, James, 199
Moore, Thomas, 101, 184, 185, 194
Moray, Robert, 34
Moretti, Franco, 128
Morgan, Edwin, 202
Morris, Charles, 107–9, 112
Morris, R. J., 5
Morrison, Mark, 276
Morrison, Robert, 259
Morse, J. J., 279
Moses, Stainton, 287, 289
Motherby, Johanna, 89
Motherby, Robert, 89
Moyes, Henry, 141

Mozart, Wolfgang Amadeus, 102, 117
Mühlpfordt, Herbert Meinhard, 91
Mullen, Mary, 242
Müller-Wille, Staffan, 161
Multigraph Collective, 161
Murdoch, William, 206
Musäus, Johann Karl August, 86
Musenhof, 22, 83–100
museums, 18, 30, 44, 55, 144, 157–77, 178–95, 215, *see* British Museum, Hunterian Museum (Glasgow), Hunterian Museum (London), Raffles Library and Museum, Spalding Gentlemen's Society
Museums Act (1845), 18
writer's house museums, 3, 4, 9
Musson, A. E., 144

Napoleon, 100, 184, 213
national academies, 13
National Trust, 252
nationalism, 22, 25, 94, 250, 256, 263
national canon, 21, 78, 268, 274
national character, 6, 12, 22, 85
Nelson, G.K., 277
networks, 2, 8, 10, 12, 23, 27, 30, 35, 36, 44, 83, 84, 99, 112, 120–56, 179, 205, 221, 225, 233, 242, 243, 244, 245, 246, 247, 254, 255–74, 276, 290
Neve, Timothy, 56, 57
New York, 277
New York Apprentices' Library, 205
Newcastle upon Tyne, 138, 140, 141
Newcastle upon Tyne Literary and Philosophical Society, 16
newspapers, 54, 101, 103, 104–7, 110, 112, 116–17, 119, 141, 149, 179, 183, 189, 200, 207, 211, 212, 215, 216, 217, 221, 225, 230, 237, 240, 249, 251, 276, 278, 286
Newton, Isaac, 32, 186
Nichols, John, 44, 45
Nicolson, William, 49
nodes, 44, 135, 140, 145, 156, 256, 264–69
Norwich, 140, 248

Oberg, Achim, 135, 147
O'Donnell, Molly C., 72
Office of Address, 32, 34–35
Opie, John, 153
orientalism, 268
Owen, Dorothy, 45
Owen, Richard, 170, 171, 172, 177
Oxford, 140, 150, 156
Oxford University, 26, 41, 42, 272

Paine, Thomas, 151
Palmer, James, 171–72
Palmerston, Viscount, Henry John Temple, 247
Pancaldi, Giuliano, 149
Panizzi, Anthony, 194
Parke, William, 110, 115
Parthey, Daniel Friedrich, 97
Paul, Jean, 97
Payne, Robert, 37
PEN, 6
Penang, 261, 270, 273, *see* Straits Settlements
Penang Free School, 270
periodicals, 13, 15, 25, 50, 78, 86, 91, 140, 179, 183, 185, 187, 189, 213, 218, 219, 234, 235, 237, 238, 240, 241, 245, 248, 251, 253, 257, 264–68, 270, 276, 278
manuscript periodicals, 87
Peterborough Gentlemen's Society, 45
Petty, William, 31–32, 33, 36, 37
Pfalz-Zweibrücken, Karoline Henriette Christine Philippine Luise von, 90
Philips, John, 73, 74, 75, 76
Philips, Richard, 204
Piatolli, Scipione, 97
Picart, Bernard, 62
Pine, John, 62
Playfair, John, 199
Pleyel, Ignace Joseph, 102, 103
Podmore, Frank, 284
Poe, Edgar Allan, 121
Polletta, Francesca, 160
Poor Laws, 146, 147
poor houses, 99
Poovey, Mary, 4
Pope, Alexander, 58, 69, 72, 73, 74, 78
Post Office, 22, 234–54
Post Office Library and Literary Association, 234–35, 249, 251
Powell, Walter, 135, 147
Priestley, Joseph, 142
Prior, Matthew, 73, 78
Pritchard, James, 265
Professional Classes Aid Council, 10
Progressive Library and Spiritual Institution, 277, 278–85, 287, 289, 290, 291
publishers, 41, 86, 97, 122, 123, 124, 237, 238, 239, 242, 278, 280, *see* Minerva Press, Fentum, J.

Radcliffe, Ann, 124
Radcliffe, Mary Anne, 127
Raffles Library and Museum, 255, 256, 266, 269, 271
Raffles, Stamford, 258, 259, 264, 267, 269, 270
Rainey, Lawrence, 6
Ram, Robert, 48

Index

Ramsay, Nigel, 45
Rawnsley, Hardwicke, 252–54
Read, William H. M., 260
readers and reading, 1, 2, 127, 128, 130, 132, 134, 151, 173, 178–95, 197, 211, 212, 218, 219–24, 234–54, 261, 264, 280, 282–84, 287–88, 289
Reading, 138, 140
Recke, Elisa von der, 97
Reeve, Clara, 124
Rehbein, Angela, 242
Religious Tract Society, 260
republic of letters, 15, 25, 88
Richardson, Jonathan, 78
Rieder, John, 124, 126
Rieppel, Lukas, 158
Robins, Brian, 102, 104, 106
Robinson, Eric, 144, 196
Robinson, Mary, 101
Robson, Mark, 23
Roche, Regina Maria, 129
Rock, William Frederick, 246, 247
Roscoe, William, 14
Rotch, Benjamin, 209
Rotheram, Caleb, 141
Rotunno, Laura, 234
Royal Academy of Arts, 15
Royal Asiatic Society, 255
  Straits Branch of the Royal Asiatic Society, 255, 256, 266, 267, 268, 269
Royal Asiatic Society of Bengal, 264
Royal Bounty Fund, 10
Royal College of Surgeons, 164
Royal Dublin Society, 261
Royal Exchange, 29
Royal Geographical Society, 264
Royal Institution, 7, 136, 137, 141, 142, 144, 145–56, 178, 198, 201
Royal Literary Fund, 3, 9–10, 13, 18, 19, 20, 22
Royal Society, 3, 26, 30, 33–35, 42, 44, 58, 146–48, 156, 178
Royal Society of Literature, 18, 19
Rumford, Count (Benjamin Thompson), 145–53, 155
Russell Institution, 136, 144, 145, 178
Russell, Gillian, 17, 19
Ryves, Eliza, 181

salons, 88, 89, 96, 97
Sartori, Andrew, 256
Saxony-Gotha-Altenburg, Emil Leopold August, Duke of, 96
Saxony-Gotha-Altenburg, Ernst II, Duke of, 96, 99
Saxony-Gotha-Altenburg, Luise Dorothea, Duchess of, 95

Schatz, Thomas, 125, 126
Schiller, Friedrich, 87
schools, 20, 28, 29, 48, 53, 62, 67, 86, 96, 98, 141, 199, 203, 224, 238, 255, 258, 261, 263, 268, 272, 274, *see* Penang Free School, Singapore Institution Free School, Spalding Grammar School
  missionary schools, 259
Schurman, Anna Maria van, 36
Scott, Honoria, 132–33
Scott, W. Richard, 159, 160, 163, 174
Scott, Walter, 121, 124, 183, 211
Secord, James, 154
Seed, John, 211
Selznick, Philip, 159
Shakespeare, William, 13, 20, 73, 78, 180, 212, 277
Shapin, Steven, 25
Sheffield, 140, 205
Sheffield Literary and Philosophical Society, 205
Sheffield Mechanics' Library, 205, 211, 212
Shelley, Mary, 136, 202
Shelley, Percy, 136, 238
Sher, Richard, 143
Siegel, Carl August, 95
Singapore, 255, 258, 260, 261, *see* Raffles Library and Museum
Singapore Institution, 256, 258, 259, 260, 261, 264, 265, 266, 269
Singapore Institution Free School, 256, 258, 259, 260, 261, 270, 273
Singapore Library, 256, 260, 269, 271
Sinha, Mrinalini, 257
Siskin, Clifford, 245
Six Acts (1819), 196, 207, 212, 213
Skelton-Foorde, Christopher, 127
Skinnell, Ryan, 163
Sloane, Hans, 33, 180
Smart, Alexander, 252
Smirke, Robert, 189
Smith, Adam, 143
Smith, Sydney, 153
Smyth, James Moore, 69
Society for Bettering the Condition of the Poor, 146, 147
Society for Psychical Research, 281, 284
Society for the Diffusion of Useful Knowledge, 240, 246
Society of Antiquaries, 14–15, 44, 65, 71
Society of Authors, 10, 18
Socrates, 232
Song Ong Siang, 262, 263
South Sea Bubble, 39
South, Robert, 42
Southey, Robert, 13, 185, 188

Spalding Gentlemen's Society, 15, 22, 44–64, 65, 66
Spalding Grammar School, 46, 48, 50, 51–56, 59, 61, 62, 63
Sparke, Joseph, 52
Spence, Catherine Helen, 232
Spence, Joseph, 62
Spencer, Herbet, 284
Spenser, Edmund, 73, 78
spiritualist societies, 11, 275–91
Spitalfields Mathematical Society, 197
Sprat, Thomas, 3, 33
St Clair, William, 127
Stägemann, Johanna Elisabeth von, 89
Stagg, William, 57
Stanislaw August I, 90
Stationers' Company, 12
Stead, Estelle, 286, 289
Stead, W. T., 276, 277, 285–89, 290
Stein, Charlotte von, 87
Stevens, Anne H., 22, 72, 121
Stevens, R. J. S., 115
Stevenson, Robert Louis, 276
Stewart, Dugald, 199
Stewart, Larry, 148
Stock, Dora, 97
Straits Chinese Literary Association and Reading Club, 262
Straits Philosophical Society, 262
Straits Settlements. See Malay Archipelago, Singapore
Strong, Charles Rev., 231
Stukeley, William, 60, 63
suggestion books, 216, 222
Surr, Thomas Skinner, 130–32, 133
Surrey Institution, 7, 136, 144, 145, 178, 184
Swift, Jonathan, 13, 32, 39, 40, 58, 69, 73, 78
Swinney, Geoffrey, 161
Symner, Myles, 36

Talfourd, Thomas Noon, 187
Tan Teck Soon, 262
tavern, 9, 102, 183, 199
  Crown and Anchor, 103, 209
Taylor, John, 40
Teacher, John, 176
Tennyson, Alfred, 247
Thacker, Eugene, 140, 145
theatres, 12, 85, 86, 90, 96, 108, 141, 182, 192
  Covent Garden, 184
  Drury Lane, 180
Thelwall, John, 101
Thomas, Kate, 244, 247, 248
Thompson, E. P., 210
Thümmel, Hans Wilhelm von, 98–100

Tiedge, Christoph August, 97
Tischgesellschaft (Table Society), 89, 90, 93
Todorov, Tzvetan, 121
Tomlinson, Ralph, 105
Tomlinson, Samuel, 263
tourism, 2, 279
Trumpener, Katie, 128
Turner, Martha, 232
Twells, Alison, 206
Tylecote, Mabel, 210

Ulbricht, Justus, 85
UNESCO, 6
Unitarians, 232
United Chinese Library, 263
universities, 3, 4, 20, 21, 26, 27–30, 33, 36, 45, 59, 67, 143, 175, 194, 199, 202, 203, 210, 272, *see* Albertus University, Cambridge University, Glasgow University, Leiden University, Oxford University
University College London, 21
University of London, 21, 27, 37
Ure, Andrew, 196, 198, 201–4, 213

Van Diemen's Land Mechanics' Institute, 216
Ventzke, Marcus, 88
Virgil, 98, 190
Viswanathan, Gauri, 22, 269
Vogel, Brant, 38
Volta, Alessandro, 149, 151
Voltaire, 96
voluntary associations, 5–6, 258, 263, 273

Waite, A. E., 280
Walker, Adam, 138, 141, 142
Walker, Herbert, 211
Walker, Thomas, 141
Wallace, Alfred Russel, 282, 287
Wallis, John, 42
Walpole, Horace, 121, 124
Waring, John, 48, 52
Warrington Academy, 21
Watt, Gregory, 150
Watt, James, 141, 146, 148, 196, 199
Weber, Max, 5, 159
Weber, William, 118
Webster, Charles, 37
Webster, Thomas, 151
Weimar, 84–88
Wieland, Christoph Martin, 85, 86, 87, 96
Wilberforce, William, 147, 152
Wilkinson, R. J., 268
Willesby, Thomas, 48
William of Orange, 37

Williams, David, 19
Williams, Raymond, 7, 12, 257
Wilmot, John, Earl of Rochester, 70
Wilson, John, 40
Winckles, Andrew, 242
Winstedt, R. O., 268
Wisbech Town Library, 51, 57, 61
Wolf, Ernst Wilhelm, 86
Wood, Dustin Frazier, 15, 22
Wood, Robert, 36
Wooler, Thomas, 207
Wordsworth Trust, 9
Wordsworth, William, 2, 21–22, 101, 136, 179, 187, 250–51, 252–54, 284
Worsley, Benjamin, 36
Wriedt, Etta, 289

Yamamoto, Koji, 38
Yeo, Eileen, 204
York, 138, 140, 156
Young, Edward, 73
Young, John, 177

For EU product safety concerns, contact us at Calle de José Abascal, 56–1°, 28003 Madrid, Spain or eugpsr@cambridge.org.

www.ingramcontent.com/pod-product-compliance
Ingram Content Group UK Ltd.
Pitfield, Milton Keynes, MK11 3LW, UK
UKHW021503220625
459949UK00018B/548